Empire of Pleasu

D1188274

Empire of Pleasures

Luxury and indulgence in the
Roman world

Andrew Dalby

London and New York

First published 2000
by Routledge
11 New Fetter Lane, London EC4P 4EE

Simultaneously published in the USA and Canada
by Routledge
29 West 35th Street, New York, NY 10001

First published in paperback 2002

Routledge is an imprint of the Taylor & Francis Group

© 2000 Andrew Dalby

The right of Andrew Dalby to be identified as the Author of this
Work has been asserted by him in accordance
with the Copyright, Designs and Patents Act 1988.

Typeset in Garamond by Taylor & Francis Books Ltd
Printed and bound in Great Britain by Biddles Ltd, Guildford and
King's Lynn

British Library Cataloguing in Publication Data
A catalogue record for this book is available from the British Library

Library of Congress Cataloging in Publication Data
Dalby, Andrew, 1947–
Empire of pleasures : luxury and indulgence in the Roman world /
Andrew Dalby.
Includes bibliographical references and index.
1. Latin poetry–History and criticism. 2. Luxury in literature. 3.
Rome–History–Empire, 30 BC–AD 476. 4. Senses and sensation in
literature. 5. Dinners and dining in literature. 6. Drinking customs
in literature. 7. Food habits in literature. 8. Pleasure in literature. I.
Title.

PA6029.L87 .D35 2000
871´.0109355–dc21
00-035317

ISBN 0–415–18624–2 (hbk)
ISBN 0–415–28073–7 (pbk)

Contents

Illustrations

Figures

Maps

Preface

The inspiration for this book came from reading Edward Schafer's *The Golden Peaches of Samarkand* and *The Vermilion Bird*, explorations of the exotica of ancient China as they are reflected in Chinese poetry. Although one can read all about the Roman Empire and its products in several extremely well-informed texts – in Strabo's *Geography*, in Pliny's *Natural History*, and (among many other modern scholarly works) in Tenney Frank's *Economic survey of ancient Rome* – one does not quite know from these how the Roman Empire seemed and felt to the averagely informed reader of Roman literature. This is the information that I have tried to gather.

The method is obvious enough. Details are drawn from the geographical and historical sources and from archaeology only to the minimum extent needed to tell a coherent story. It is the literature that is privileged: what it has to say, whether in extended descriptions or in brief epithets, is (I hope) reported faithfully and sensitively. In this way, the poetry and literary prose of the Empire is made to paint in something of its own background.

Xenophon (I once claimed) 'wrote books that he intended to be useful'. So do I. If it achieves its purpose this book will help those who read Roman literature to understand how writers and contemporary readers sensed the Empire in which they read and wrote; it will help historians and archaeologists to imagine the world of the senses that belongs with the world of monuments and inscriptions, dates and deposits. Since we do actually have, from such source materials, a mass of information on the 'real' geography of the Roman Empire, this literary geography may also help those who work in a similar way on other literatures from cloudier historical contexts – the Homeric poems, for example – to assess the historical picture that they draw from their literary texts.

I want to thank Richard Stoneman and his colleagues at Routledge for their confidence, fully matching mine, that there was useful work to be done here. The Runciman Award for *Siren Feasts* and the Sophie Coe Prize, both in 1997, gave me time to read and write. Maureen made sure I used it fruitfully. John Wilkins made salutary comments on the text. Anne Flavell checked some facts and references that I could not. John Arnold helped me wrestle with Sulpicia.

Le Bourg, 79120 Saint-Coutant
3 July 1999

1 Introduction

A geography of luxury runs through the literature of Imperial Rome. *Persica*, the golden peaches whose name pinpointed Persia as the source of their worldwide migration; *Caecubum*, a fine, rare wine from Latin vineyards once prized, afterwards neglected: these flavours were identified and tasted in a single word. Spices and perfumes were respected for their distant origins and high price. From an occupational noun and an ethnic adjective – *servus Aethiops*, black African slave; *copa Surisca*, young Syrian bar-girl – the reader had already drawn an impressionistic image, an image that would be sharpened as the author added detail: the shimmering thighs of a dancer, the brand and shaven head of a recaptured runaway.[1]

Twenty words evoked the sounds and smells of a city street, 'a patissier's varied cries, and a sausage-vendor and a confectioner and all the proprietors of cookshops selling their wares, each in his distinctive accent', one of the same streets into which young Nero used to disappear, dressed in the rags and the hood of slavery, to drink and brawl.

A poem listed, with a satirical edge, the fashionably homely produce of a country estate:

> A fine plump kid, tenderest of the herd, will come from the Tiburtine farm, with more milk in its veins than blood; and mountain asparagus gathered by the farmer's wife after her spinning; then big warm eggs wrapped in straw; and their mothers; and grapes preserved half a year but as good as when they were fresh; and apples fresh-scented from their harvest baskets, cured by the cold of autumn of the dangerous roughness of their juice.

A mythical wedding scene was at the same time a sketch of the supernatural fertility, the wild wealth of meadows and mountains that characterised Thessaly among the regions of the Empire:

> All the flowers that the fields bear, that Thessaly creates in her high mountains, that the warm breeze of Favonius engenders beside a rippling river – all these Chiron brought, plaited together in garlands.

Permeated with the joyful aroma, the house itself laughed. Now the river god Peneus is here, leaving the green vale of Tempe and her overhanging forests to the songs of the dancing wood-nymphs, and he is not empty-handed: he has pulled lofty beeches up by the roots, and tall straight-stemmed bay trees, with a swaying plane and a slow-growing poplar, and a wind-tossed cypress ...

In texts like these the Roman Empire may be recaptured as it was sensed and imagined by those who lived in it.[2]

Nowadays we need help if we are to see these pictures. We no longer have, present to our minds, the mass of poetry and prose that a lettered Roman absorbed month by month. Nearly all of it is lost. Few of us now, when we read, feel the words on our tongues. Romans did: they read aloud and therefore at a measured pace. In our rapid reading we are tempted to gloss over the adjectives. They have been called clichés, or stock epithets, or tired formulas, as excuses for discounting them. The undertones that once were sensed by every intelligent reader have to be reconstructed with the help of dictionaries and commentaries: another step that we often skip.

Yet we can go some way towards rebuilding a mental geography of the Roman world, a composite of sense-impressions. This rebuilding is as necessary for the understanding of Roman history as for the reliving of Roman literature. Ancient historians, for whom the written word is a principal source of information, cannot neglect the thoughts that lie behind it. The Empire pictured by its inhabitants is no less real than the Empire of the archaeologist's spade, and the aim of this book is that we may be better able to survey how the provinces and their products were present in the minds of Roman writers and readers. Those who work on ancient literature need to know how any one text or author relates to the general picture; for these, too, the aim here is to recreate a fuller image of the world that literate Romans saw around them, and in doing so to clarify the words and intentions of individual ancient writers. And I hope that this book will show readers who are new to classics that Roman literature and history are worth exploring.

This book describes not how things were but how they seemed – and how they tasted, too: there are recipes here, from contemporary sources, for some luxurious and exotic flavours and aromas of Roman literature.

Quotations and references

All the texts that are used here are listed and dated in the index of ancient sources (p. 310). Unless otherwise stated, the translations from Latin and Greek are mine, but I have often drawn on the phraseology of earlier translations. What I have tried to do – I have not always succeeded – is to milk these texts for their immediacy and precision, not for their poetry. Readers are urged to look at the originals if they can, or to compare what I give here with other translations.

So as not to tire the eye, references are given in the text only to those sources that are quoted at length. There are additional references in the endnotes. These point to selected texts that support the quotation given or reinforce the argument.[3] I often need to cite the same text more than once. In that case I have generally quoted it once in full, and there I always give the precise reference; elsewhere I have quoted as briefly as possible, with a cross-reference to the page where the full quotation will be found.

Source material

The poetry and literary prose of the Empire are the sources for this book.[4] They are in several languages. Latin was the language of the ruling class, the language of all who aspired to join it, and the lingua franca of the West. Originally the spoken language of Rome and its neighbourhood, Latin was a medium of written literature by 200 BC. Greek has a much longer literary history, traceable to 700 BC. By the time Roman power spread to the eastern Mediterranean, in the second and first centuries BC, Greek was the lingua franca of this region, from Sicily eastwards to the Levant. It retained this status and was also in Roman times the first language of science, technology, medicine and philosophy. A Roman higher education consisted of study in Greece or Asia Minor, in the Greek language. Aramaic, the administrative language of the old Persian Empire, remained important from Palestine and Syria eastwards, far across the Roman eastern frontier. Aramaic was the current language of Jewish literature. These were the three supra-regional languages of the Empire.

Most texts quoted here are in Latin. Greek and Aramaic appear from time to time; but these literatures less frequently adopted the imperial perspective and the wide geographical reference typical of contemporary Latin poetry.

The spotlight is on the literature of two centuries, from about 50 BC to AD 150. To give a perspective I have sometimes quoted, with due warning, texts from later times, even as late as 600. Views of the world were changing all this time, and a fundamental change is marked, towards 400, by that intelligent historian Ammianus. While reasserting that Rome is 'destined to rule as long as men exist' and had 'won laurels from every shore of the wide world', Ammianus knows that Roman literature will one day be read by foreigners, *peregrini*, to whom the city's destiny and present condition will be unfamiliar (p. 13). Latin, Greek and Aramaic were indeed losing the power to divide the whole Roman world among themselves.[5] By 600, they were no more than the most venerable of the languages of literature in the world that the Romans knew.

Sometimes the later texts particularise the classical Roman view of the Empire and its borders, like Agathias's view over the garden of his lodging in Pera, mother hens clucking to their chicks under the cypresses, linnets chirping, frogs croaking in the brambles (p. 161) and like Imr al-Qais's image of the Arabian desert with 'dung of antelopes spattered like pepper-corns', in an ancient Arabic poem (p. 184). Sometimes they contradict it, as does Gildas, writing in Latin in praise of his native Britain, with its 'clear springs, constantly rippling over shingle as white as snow', (p. 101), and Lazar P'arpec'i, an early Armenian historian, describing the lost province of Ayrarat, 'its encircling mountains beautiful and rich in pasture' (p. 185). All four of these sixth-century authors knew well the lands that Rome ruled, but the venerable city was – as Ammianus foresaw – more fabulous than real to them.

Each Roman author's personal contribution stands out starkly. Vergil and no one else will sketch the disastrous flood of the Padus in 44 BC (p. 89). Martial alone will sing the beauties of Bilbilis (p. 106). Only Statius will admit to the fun he had at Domitian's celebration of the *Saturnalia* (p. 231). From no others but Martial and Rutilius will we know that, as one stood on the hill of the Janiculum and looked back at Rome, one heard the cries of the Tiber boatmen and the applause of the theatre audience (pp. 20,38).

Each author has his own sensuality. From Martial we know the aromas of the Empire – that of amber warmed in a virgin's palm (p. 264), that of a veteran's boot (p. 93), that of a 'fuller's jar of piss, just smashed' (p. 37); from him we know that a connoisseur judged Corinthian bronze by its smell (p. 241). From the poem *Aetna* we can sense the smoke of sacrifice rising verti-cally in the still air from the tiny altar at the summit of Etna (p. 117). With Martial and Juvenal we know the leaking arches of the aqueducts that over-leapt the crumbling Capena Gate (p. 42). Cicero and Horace both lay awake listening to the frogs of the Pomptine marshes (p. 44); only Horace tells of the quarrels of boatmen and slaves that added to the nocturnal ambience of Forum Appi (p. 44). Only from Dio do we hear the clamour of the literary festival that was a part of the Isthmian Games at Corinth: 'Writers were reading their nonsense aloud. Poets were reciting their verses to the applause of other poets' (p. 147).

Ancient authors, like modern ones, interact with readers. 'They say that my verses are recited even in Britain', says Martial (11.3). In the same book he gives a complimentary, slightly teasing, appraisal of the Roman culture of the British lady Claudia Rufina (p. 87). Clearly we owe this insight into the spread of Roman culture in Romano-British society to the fact that Martial had heard that Claudia Rufina was a reader of his poems. We can see this because Martial responds more openly to his readers than any other Roman author: but all authors respond.

The literature used in this book comes from individual experience and from literary tradition. We do not need to distinguish them here. These currents flow together: both make up the literary landscape that readers derived from reading, and these readers included future generations of authors.

Two distinct elements in Roman texts comprise the literary geography that is reconstructed in this book. There are descriptions of sights, scenes, travels (we shall return to these); there are also brief phrases and allusions in which a place-name is wedded to a defining detail of place, products or people.

Typically formed of noun and adjective, these phrases are characteristic of classical Latin style. Even more than the descriptions, they map the landscape in which literate Romans placed themselves. They continued to be made as long as classical style influenced current writing. Readers of recent classics will recall the pleasure with which they first encountered Milton's

> *... barren plains*
> *of Sericana, where Chineses drive*
> *with sails and wind their cany wagons light,*

Byron's *Seville ... famous for oranges and women* and Housman's *Strasburg, a city still famous for its geese*.[6] Such phrases have a long history. The line of transmission begins around 700 BC with the *Iliad* and *Odyssey*, the written monuments of archaic Greek oral narrative. Phrases, often consisting of noun and adjective, formed the building blocks of that poetry. Using them as briefer authors use words, the epic poets spoke of 'Agamemnon king of men', 'white-armed Hera', 'Crete of a hundred cities', 'rosy-fingered Dawn', 'life-giving Earth'.

In archaic epic such formulae did not vary with narrative context. 'Rosy-fingered' was a proper epithet for Dawn even if storms were brewing. The Earth was life-giving even if corpses had been laid in it: 'the life-giving Earth held them fast already, in Lacedaemon, in their native land'.[7] Yet the phrases did vary: poets commanded a range of them, shaped so that any space available in a hexameter line could be filled with a phrase in the required grammatical form. This was what they were for.

Classical poets drew much of their stylistic armoury from the archaic epics. In lyric, tragedy, comedy and later epic, phrases recur that are just like the epic formulae, neatly characterising people and places. But the later authors composed at leisure, in writing. They did not need a range of formulae, identical in import, to fill different metrical gaps, and had forgotten the crucial part that the formulae had played in the construction of traditional verse. The pure repetitions in the *Iliad* and *Odyssey* were admired less than other features of their style, and were imitated with discretion. The later poets had the time and the inclination to vary their descriptive phrases according to whim, and according to narrative context.

This is the lineage that gave birth to the geographical epithets and allusions of Roman literature, six hundred years after the archaic epics. Latin poets, seldom unconscious of Greek antecedents, are writing in a language with its own rhythms.

They have given new life to the old phrases.[8] The place-names map the known Roman world. The *Odyssey* already reached out beyond the Aegean, from 'middle Argos' all the way to the 'Ethiopians, most distant of men';

but Homeric geography blurred with distance. Roman authors, still at home among the commonplaces of their predecessors, add the 'red-haired Batavian' (p. 206), 'naughty Cadiz' (p. 107), the 'warlike Cantabrian' (p. 102), 'deceitful Parthians' (p. 187).

Rare in Homer,[9] a particular type of phrase linking a geographical adjective with a common noun is ubiquitous in classical Latin texts. In some, the adjective is to be given its literal meaning: when Martial, a Spaniard, spoke of 'Gallaecian gold' (p. 102) he knew what he meant and he meant it precisely. In others, poetic tradition contributes more than geographical truth to the image, as when Vergil supplies his Saharan nomad with a Laconian dog and a Cretan quiver (p. 87). In others again, the poet spends the wealth of the whole Roman world.

> *Gaudentem patrios findere sarculo*
> *agros Attalicis condicionibus*
> *numquam dimoveas ut trabe Cypria*
> *Myrtoum pavidus nauta secet mare,*

wrote Horace: 'the man who likes to plough his ancestral fields will never be stirred, even by the salary of an Attalus, to slice the Myrtoan sea with Cyprian keel as a fearful sailor' (Horace, *Odes* 1.1.11–14). There was no reason to offer a ship built in Cyprus rather than elsewhere to the Roman farmer turned sailor that Horace conjures up, or for that sailor to cross the Myrtoan Sea rather than another, or for the wealth of the province of Asia (bequeathed to Rome by Attalus), rather than another, to pay his remuneration; but Cypriot timbers were sound (p. 171), Asia was a source of Roman wealth and luxury (p. 161), and the Myrtoan was one of those seas best avoided.

We return to the fuller descriptions of cities and landscapes in Roman poetry. They appear, a novelty, in the late first century BC. We can hunt for Greek antecedents for them, for example in Odysseus's evocation of his native island in the *Odyssey*,

> I live in clear-seen Ithaca. There is a mountain on it, steep Neriton with tossing leaves. Around it islands, many of them, live very close to one another, Dulichion and Same and wooded Zacynthos. It lies land-bound, highest of all in the salt [sea], towards the dark, the others further off towards the dawn and the sun; rough, but a good parent.
>
> *Odyssey* 9.21–28

Few descriptions of this kind are found in classical and Hellenistic Greek literature.

The appearance of geographical descriptions in literature parallels their occurrence in visual media. Images of conquered provinces and cities were paraded, along with the spoils and the captives, in Roman triumphal processions. Livy writes of 'a depiction of the capture of Syracuse' in a triumph of 211 BC, and Tacitus of 'depictions of mountains, rivers and battles' illustrating Germanicus's victories in Germany, displayed in AD 17.[10] These were ephemeral. We do not know how they looked. Trajan's Column is one of a series of more permanent representations of conquered provinces. It portrays Trajan's two Dacian campaigns, with representations of places supposed to be recognisable by means of visual 'epithets'. Sometimes they still can be recognised; sometimes the clues are lost.[11]

The antecendents of Roman triumphal geography lie in the Near East, not in Greece. Analogues are found in Hellenistic royal display; earlier, too, in Assyrian and Persian reliefs, for example at Sennacherib's palace at Nineveh.[12] From the reliefs a guide could tell the story to a viewing audience, just as the poet or another performer, reading from a manuscript, narrated Latin literary texts to their audience.

2 Imperium sine fine

The link made at the end of the previous chapter between Assyrian and Roman triumphal art belongs with a more general observation. The Roman Empire was a successor to earlier empires and destined to be the last and greatest of them all.[1] By the second century BC Rome's empire was already foreseen. The future was evident to statesmen such as the Greek historian Polybius, who had plenty of time for observation during his seventeen years as a hostage in Rome. It was also clear to the less rationalistic author of the so-called *Sibylline Oracles*, Greek verses written in a Jewish milieu under a highly honoured 'seventh king of Egypt':[2]

> How many kingdoms of men will be raised up? The house of Solomon will rule first of all, and the Phoenicians, who disembark on Asia and other islands, and the Pamphylians, Persians and Phrygians, Carians and Mysians, and Lydians rich in gold. Then the overbearing and impious Greeks. Another diverse race, of Macedonia, will rule: they will come as a terrible cloud of war on mortals. Heavenly God will destroy them from the depth. Then will begin another kingdom, white and many-headed, from the western sea. It will rule over much land, and will shake many, and will thereafter cause fear to all kings.
>
> *Sibylline Oracles* 3.166–178[3]

A new and different empire was also foreseen in the Aramaic book of *Daniel* (7.23), 'the fourth beast: there will be a fourth kingdom upon Earth which will be different from all kingdoms: it will devour the Earth, tread it down, and crush it'. Like the passage quoted from the *Sibylline Oracles*, *Daniel* is dated to the mid-second century BC. Among Roman observers in that same century even the least triumphalist noted Rome's inexorable rise in power. The satirist Lucilius wrote: 'So it is: Romans have been beaten, they have lost battles, but never a war, and only wars matter!' (613). Two hundred years later these prophecies and forebodings had been fulfilled.

It had been said that Rome's would be the next great empire, greater than any before. Few doubted that that was now true. 'Already', Horace addresses Augustus, the hitherto unconquerable Cantabrian, Mede, Indian and fleeing Scythian, all marvel at you, guardian of Italy and of ruling Rome. Nile who hides the sources of his waters, and Hister, and swift-flowing Tigris, and monster-filled Ocean that roars around the far-off Britons, and the land of Gaul that does not fear death, and hard Iberia, all these obey you; the slaughter-loving Sygambri lay down their weapons and praise you.

Horace, *Odes* 4.14.41–52[4]

Ruling an Empire without predestined limit, or fated to be bounded only by Ocean,[5] 'the Roman victor possessed the whole world': these are the first words of the model epic supplied by the poet 'Eumolpus' in Petronius's *Satyricon* (p. 10).

It had been said that Rome's empire would be different from all its predecessors: that was now fact. The third-century Jewish scholar Johanan bar Nappaha was probably correct in identifying Rome as the subject of the prophecy in *Daniel*, already quoted, which foresaw the difference.[6] The Greek orator Aristides, lecturing to Romans in the second century, makes this difference a matter of praise:

Your predecessors established an arbitrary, tyrannical rule. They were masters and slaves of each other in rotation…. They succeeded each other as if taking turns in a ball game. Macedonians had a period of enslavement to Persians, Persians to Medes, Medes to Assyrians.

Aristides, *Roman Oration* 91[7]

Rome alone remained free throughout her preparation for world rule.

As a result, Rome's subjects now benefited from a different philosophy of empire, as Aristides went on to explain (p. 13). Previous empires had maintained local particularities. Rome eradicated them:

There is no need now to write a book of travels and to list each country's laws…. You prescribed common laws for all, putting an end to the previous state of affairs, amusing to describe but intolerable in practice; you made it possible to marry anywhere.

Aristides, *Roman Oration* 102

This was said sixty years before the emperor Caracalla extended Roman citizenship to all free inhabitants of the Empire; a logical development, given the approach to government that Aristides describes – an approach natural enough in an empire which, unlike its predecessors, had from the beginning been 'many-headed'. Rome, though now led by *principes* (we call them 'emperors'), retained its annual consulships, its Senate and its patronage, the symbols and manifestations of a collective practice of government.

The vices of empire

It was predicted, in the *Sibylline Oracles* for example, that Rome would swallow the wealth of the world.[8] From Biblical texts Jewish scholars of Roman times showed exactly how this had happened. Joseph had gathered the world's wealth in Egypt. The Jews, in their exodus, stripped the Egyptians, and held the treasure in Israel until, 'in the fifth year of King Rehoboam, King Shishak of Egypt ... carried off the treasures of the Temple and the Palace; everything, even the golden shields that Solomon had made'. Zerah, King of Cush, took it from Shishak; Asa, King of Israel, took it from Zerah and sent it to Damascus. Jehoshaphat took it back and it descended to Ahaz: Sennacherib the Assyrian took it from him. Hezekiah took it back again. Finally the Babylonians took it from Zedekiah, the Persians took it from the Babylonians, the Greeks took it from them, the Romans took it from the Greeks. In Rome the wealth of the world now remained; and Rome was known to be Esau's kingdom of *Edom*, the 'red' country, bloody in its conquests (*Talmud Babli, Pesahim* 119a), whose wealth would be dispersed across the world in the time of the Messiah.[9]

The Jews were not the only people who saw that riches formerly theirs had disappeared into the Roman economy. Gildas thus summarised the effect of the Roman conquest of Britain five centuries before his time: 'All of her bronze, silver and gold was to be stamped with the image of Caesar' (*Ruin of Britain* 7). Whether Gildas had this from local tradition or surmised it, he was right. Rome sucked in local wealth and, for the Empire's administrative purposes, recoined it.

Romans were ready to criticise themselves for greed. Consider two observers of the first century of Empire. Petronius, once governor of Bithynia and author of the most cynical and realistic of Roman fictions, the *Satyricon*, died, a luxurious suicide, after falling out of Nero's favour in AD 66. In his novel he inserted a little epic of the Roman Civil War, supposed to be turned out impromptu by one of the main characters, the aesthetic poet Eumolpus. The 'Roman victor' with which this *jeu d'esprit* begins

> possessed the whole world ... but was still unsated. The seas were swept by his heavily laden ships. If [beyond his frontiers] any coast or any land was still exporting yellow gold, it was his enemy: the Fates had already prepared the war by which its wealth would be acquired.
>
> Petronius, *Satyricon* 119.1–7

Petronius's close contemporary, the soldier Pliny, compiled an encyclopaedia of the world and its wealth, the immense *Natural History*. He continually reminds the reader that Nature is generous and that humans are greedy and wasteful, modern Romans more than any before them.[10] Pliny died in AD 79 because, having led a detachment of the Roman fleet at Misenum across the Bay of Naples to the rescue of the inhabitants of the doomed territory of Pompeii, he became too interested in the eruption of Vesuvius and its effects. Others escaped; Pliny stayed and was overcome by the fumes.

Both Pliny and Petronius were passionately concerned with the city at the centre of their lives, its Empire, its wealth and the uses that its wealth served. Each made a catalogue of Roman luxury, Pliny reflecting, Petronius transforming. Neither was sufficiently devoted to the luxury that Rome had offered to cling to it above all else. Pliny was obsessed by the trade in spices and perfumes, as is evident from his compulsive detailing of its profits and deceits, yet he himself lived simply, bathed and dined hastily and spent every available moment in research.[11] Petronius, 'unlike most people who spend all they have, was not regarded as a glutton and a wastrel but as a scholar of pleasure'. He became Nero's *arbiter elegantiae*, a kind of 'master of ceremonies' to that luxurious emperor (Tacitus, *Annals* 16.18–19). In this role Petronius effortlessly retained the upper hand. As he prepared to die, 'he smashed his fluorspar ladle, which had cost 300,000 *sestertii*, just so that Nero's table should not inherit it'.[12] The anecdote is in Pliny's *Natural History* (37.20).

Roman authors offer contradictory answers to a question that was of great interest to them: when was Rome infected by love of luxury? In the first century BC the historian Sallust dates the event to Rome's overseas victories a hundred years before, notably the final defeat and destruction of Carthage in 146. Until then, in his opinion, Romans were generous in divine worship, frugal at home, true to their friends; afterwards 'leisure and riches, thought so desirable, were a curse and a misery. Lust for money grew, then lust for power; these were the foundation of all evils' (*Catiline* 9–10). True, the events of that period brought copious wealth to Rome. The geographer Strabo attributes to this enrichment, when Rome destroyed Carthage, the sudden demand for slaves that led to the establishment of Roman traders on the Greek island of Delos, which now became a major slave market (p. 126).

At first, however – Sallust continues – the new vices grew slowly. Real avarice came after the dictator Sulla had seized power, and his political proscriptions became an excuse for his followers to enrich themselves: 'everyone robbed and thieved; one fancied a house, another a farm. The victors showed no restraint. They committed foul and cruel acts against Roman citizens' (*Catiline* 11.4). Sallust was not alone in identifying Sulla's expropriations as a watershed in Roman political morality, a disastrous model for the future.[13]

Sallust identifies another catalyst of Rome's moral decline. Sulla, on campaign in the province of Asia, had allowed his army to indulge in Asiatic luxuries, not only wine and sex but also the plundering of works of art (p. 162). This also was a landmark for others than Sallust. His older contemporary Cicero had made a similar catalogue of Asia's temptations, 'wives and children of our allies, works of art of temples and towns, gold and treasuries of kings' (p. 120), and thought it worth remarking that his client Murena had managed to serve on the Asiatic campaign without succumbing to immorality (*For Murena* 11).

In the generation after Sallust, Rome's historian Livy traced the seeds of luxury much further back – to an earlier campaign, this one also in Asia Minor, Gnaeus Manlius Vulso's defeat of the Galatians in 189 BC. The Galatian booty had corrupted Vulso's army.[14] The evidence was to be observed daily in the behaviour of his victorious soldiers as they loitered in Rome, waiting to celebrate their triumph. Their faults were linked with their 'cithara-girls, harp-girls and other festive amusements' and, once more, with antiquities and fine furniture. Cooks, too, first reached Rome in Vulso's baggage train, Livy asserts (p. 120).

The pleasures of empire

Perspectives changed. One reads less, in literature of later centuries, about how the provinces were stripped of wealth to supply the lusts of Rome. She had transformed herself from a conquering city into a world empire; as new provincials became Romans, and as settled legions had to give up plunder and to pay for their living, wealth spread outwards again.

The change was gradual. It had been foreshadowed in Rome's capacity to grant citizen rights to cities and towns in Italy. But the mid first century BC, when Cicero and Sallust observed Roman avarice and provincial impoverishment, was the very point at which this change gathered momentum, not least because of the extensive recruitment of armies. Legionaries, if not already citizens, gained citizenship and a grant of land after service. If Rome's transformation can be identified with any single figure, it is Julius Caesar. Most ambitious of the ambitious politicians of the period, he recruited many legions and conquered and governed vast new territories. As he defeated his rivals, their legions too were taken into his service. Eventually, great numbers of disbanded troops were beholden to him for their status and their land. At the moment of his assassination Caesar was patron to an impressive proportion of Rome's citizens and subjects.

The heir to this patronage was Caesar's adopted son Octavian, soon to achieve even more universal authority and to be titled *Augustus* and *princeps*. Augustus and his successors took their position seriously. Rome itself, centre of power, home of the Senate and a numerous and unpredictable proletariat, naturally benefited from the well-directed generosity of the *principes*. Seven wonders of the world had been identified without reference to Rome,[15] but all of them – Memphis and its pyramids, Babylon, the soft Ionians' temple of Diana, the Carians' mausoleum and the rest – would soon give way to the great *Amphitheatrum* (Martial, *Spectacula* 1), built by the twelfth of the Caesars, Domitian. In its half-ruined state the Colosseum, as it came to be called, still towers over modern Rome (see also p. 230), one example of the many public works with which the imperial city was embellished.

Eventually Rome lost its privileged status. By the mid fourth century, under mounting threat from the north and east, the Empire had been divided. Its eastern half was ruled from Constantinople, its western half from Milan. Like Vienna after 1918, Rome had become a big city without a big destiny. We return to Ammianus for a perspective on its past greatness.

> Foreigners who read this history, if any do, are likely to wonder why, when it turns to events at Rome, it is all about riots and drinking-shops and such unsavoury things. I shall explain the matter as plainly as I can.
>
> When Rome, destined to rule as long as men exist, first gave signs of worldwide brilliance, Honour and Fortune, usually at odds, agreed a permanent truce, and so the city's power continued to grow.... From their cradle to their later childhood, a period of about three hundred years, her people fought wars with nations just beyond her walls. In their prime, after many a struggle, they reached across the Alps and beyond the sea. Boy and man, they won laurels and triumphs from every shore of the wide world. Now, in old age, their mere name is sometimes enough for victory, and they live peacefully.... Our venerable city has at length given over to the Caesars the right to rule their patrimony, as a frugal, thoughtful and generous parent might do to her own children. Nations bask at leisure, lands are peaceful, there are no quarrels over elections, the tranquillity of Numa's time has returned. Over all the earth Rome is called mistress and queen; the authority of her grey senators is revered; the Roman people is named with honour and fear.
>
> Ammianus 14.6.2–6

This praise of the doyenne of Empire is given with scarcely any irony. Whatever went on in Rome, it had remained true, almost until Ammianus's time, that the provinces prospered and were embellished under Rome's authority and in her honour.

In 156, towards the end of the Empire's most peaceful period, Aristides had drawn a collective portrait of its urban landscape. 'Every locality is full of gymnasia, fountains, colonnades, temples, workshops, schools' (*Roman Oration* 97); a Roman would have added aqueducts and baths. Long after the Empire had crumbled away, when many of its cities were in ruins, Romans were still held in awe for their public works; as in an early Anglo-Saxon poem that depicts a ruined Roman city, its fallen towers, cracked walls, sagging roofs, and – still imaginable in the seventh century – its fine buildings, bath-houses with the noise of crowds, and particularly its hot streams channelled 'to give a warm bath at the heart of the house: that was pleasant!' (p. 101). The map of Europe is studded with the hot mineral baths that the Romans first developed and called *Aquae* 'waters', *Balnea* 'baths', *Fontes Calidi* 'hot springs', *Thermae* 'hot baths'.

Roads and travel

If some who lived in the Empire, like Aristides, were able to feel that it belonged to them, this was partly because of the spread of citizenship and the Roman life style; partly because of the possibility of engaging in a political or military career; and partly because of the new ease of travel throughout this vast and peaceful region. It is Aristides, again, who observes that this is crucial. As before, he speaks as a Greek (this time he says so) caught up in the empire-wide culture of Rome:

> Nowadays Greek or non-Greek may travel, light or loaded, wherever he wishes, as comfortably as if from home to home. Cilician Gates, narrow sandy approaches to Egypt through Arab country, inaccessible mountains, wide rivers, inhospitable tribes of barbarians: none is now a threat, whether one is a Roman citizen, or simply one of those united under Roman leadership.... You have measured and mapped the entire civilized world; you have spanned rivers with all kinds of bridges, cut highways through mountains, provided staging posts. You have accustomed every region to a settled and orderly life.
>
> Aristides, *Roman Oration* 100–101

In India of the second century BC, the meritorious Aśoka made clear the benefits that he brought to man and animal by improving the roads and by planting shady trees and digging wells along them.[16] Far to the west, Rome, too, was already in road-building mode: and there was plenty to do. In much of Europe, Romans eventually surveyed and built a network of all-weather metalled roads, *viae stratae*, such as had not existed at all up to that time, studded with officially listed and maintained *mansiones* 'staging-posts'. The network was Empire-wide, embracing difficult mountain routes along with the uncompromising straight stretches, from town gate to hill crest to river crossing to the next town gate, that are still easily identifiable on modern maps.

It was the banyan (*Ficus bengalensis*) that Aśoka planted to give roadside shade. Rome, like Aśoka's empire, planted shady trees: but these were planes (*Platanus orientalis*), 'swaying planes' of Catullus, 'barren planes' of Horace and Martial.[17] Their spread to market places and belvederes across Europe can be traced – both in palynology and in literature – largely to Roman times. 'Who would not be surprised', observes Pliny (12.6–8) sententiously, 'to hear that trees have been transplanted from one climate to another simply to give shade?' Rome's milestones were another innovation that has been helpful to many:

> *Intervalla viae fessis praestare videtur*
> *qui notat inscriptus milia crebra lapis,*

as we are reminded in a fifth-century poet's travel narrative. 'Each milestone is a respite to the tired traveller' (Rutilius 2.7–8).[18]

In preparation for the literary exploration ahead, it is necessary to know something of how it felt to travel in the Empire.[19]

Long journeys normally involved sea travel, quicker and more comfortable than a comparable road journey. Merchant ships criss-crossed the Mediterranean carrying cargo and passengers. A traveller or a party needed to find a ship sailing in a suitable direction, and to change to another when opportunity presented; it is appropriate, therefore, in this section that we skip from traveller to traveller in recreating the experience of Imperial roads and seaways.

Paul of Tarsus was one of a group at Caesarea under guard of a Roman centurion in 58. Bound for Rome, they first boarded 'a ship of Adramyttium bound for the eastern Aegean'. Three hundred and fifty years later the young Patrick, a runaway slave, reached an Irish harbour in about 410 hoping for a passage to his native Britain. He found only a ship bound for Gaul. He was refused by the captain but smuggled aboard by the crew, who were hoping for some sexual recompense.[20]

Ships generally coasted or island-hopped. It was comfortable to spend the night ashore; Paul's vessel, for example, put in first at Sidon, where Paul had friends and stayed with them on parole. Rutilius, a contemporary of Patrick, put in to shore almost every night on his journey northwards from Rome towards Gaul. Sometimes his party camped: 'We mark out our overnight camp on the sandy beach. A myrtle thicket provides for an evening camp-fire. We make little tents, with oars for props, a pole set crosswise forming the roof'. Sometimes they were close enough to a farm or village to look for accommodation. South of Populonia 'we landed, looked for habitation, and wandered through a park, admiring the fishponds…. A bad-tempered Jew ran the place. He charged us for damaged hedges and distressed water-weed, and put a price on the water we had used'. Whenever possible, one set sail early to take full advantage of daylight for navigation: 'We weigh anchor at that uncertain moment of dawn when the return of colour first allows the fields to be distinguished' (Rutilius 345–348, 377–386, 217–218).

Some open sea crossings were so much more direct than coastal routes that their use became standard practice. On putting out from Sidon, Paul's vessel took to the open sea, making east and north of Cyprus, 'the wind being against us. We crossed the open sea off Cilicia and Pamphylia and reached Myra in Lycia. There the centurion found an Alexandrian ship bound for Italy and put us aboard'. This second vessel, encountered by chance, might have taken them all the way. But the weather worsened.

> Making heavy weather for a good many days, and with difficulty gaining Cnidos, since the wind was still against us we sailed by Salmone and to leeward of Crete by Cape Salmone; rounding it with difficulty we came to a place called Fair Havens, near which was the city of Lasaea. A good deal of time had passed and the voyage was becoming risky because the Fast was now over.
>
> *Acts* 27.1–8

For Luke, this Day of Atonement at the end of September warned of the end of safe sailing.

The timetable of travel was uncertain. A day might easily be lost, or might have to be spent on other pursuits than travelling:

> We use the enforced delay in the neighbouring forest, glad to exercise our limbs in the pursuit of game. The innkeeper lends us hunting gear, along with dogs trained to scent out a lair. We surprise a boar, fearsomely tusked – trap him in our wide-meshed nets.... Our songs lighten the weight of the prey we carry back.
>
> Rutilius 621–630

Life at sea had its discomforts; and there were taboos. There must be no trimming of nails, no cutting of hair. This latter rule should have been easy to remember, given the bristling beard of a typical mariner, but the fictional Encolpius and his companions unwisely ignored it when they decided, while on the high seas, to disguise themselves as runaway slaves: another passenger, 'leaning over the side to vomit, happened to see in the moonlight that our barber was at work on us at dead of night'. Whatever might have come of such a foolish act in reality, in this story the offenders risked lynching, and were lucky to escape the full measure of the flogging that was eventually decided upon to propitiate the ship's guardian spirit.[21]

Those brave enough to take to the sea in winter would find the journey uncomfortable. The poet Ovid went dramatically into exile at Tomis, on the Black Sea, for reasons he managed to mystify and his readers have never quite disentangled, in AD 9. He determined to leave Rome in winter, and took ship for Corinth. 'I cross the Ionian Sea against my will', he avers, embarking on the near-shipwreck episode of his mournful *Tristia*. 'Fear forces me to be brave': he observes the rising wind, the ship's timbers creaking and groaning, mountainous waves crashing down on the vessel and on its *picti dei*, 'painted gods', the very sea bed stirred up by the storm. And he is rather proud to have gone on writing poetry *en voyage*.

Ovid disembarked at Corinth, crossed the isthmus, and found a ship to take him onwards. It continued stormy. Often, as he crossed the Aegean, 'some of the sea was in the ship',[22] and he had had enough of the sea in winter: while his baggage continued through the Bosporus into the Black Sea, Ovid struck north by land from the Thracian coast of the Aegean (p. 157). He never suffered shipwreck; from others there are stories of shipwreck followed by wanderings on inhospitable coasts.[23] Paul's party, blown westwards off course from the neighbourhood of eastern Crete, was cast ashore on Malta: 'the centurion ... ordered that those who could swim should jump off first and make for land, and then the others, clinging to planks or to various bits of the ship'. They had to winter there: islands in the high seas were altogether isolated at that time of year.

Three months later we set out in an Alexandrian ship, called the *Dioscuri*, which had wintered in the island. We landed at Syracuse and stayed there three days, then continued to Rhegium. Next day a south wind came up: we reached Puteoli in two days, where we found Brothers and were invited to stay for a week.

Acts 28.11–14

Travellers found plenty of interest on the road from Puteoli to Rome. Paul's party, like many others, took to the road. 'Brothers from Rome, hearing of us, came out to meet us as far as Forum Appii and Tres Tabernae' (*Acts* 27.43–28.15). We shall see something of this road in our exploration of Italy: it was the *via Appia* from Rome to Brundisium, the same road on which Horace had began a journey southwards a century before, in 38 or 37 BC, accompanying Maecenas on a crucial diplomatic mission.

Horace has little to say in his lively poetic diary of difficulties on the road, except when they crossed the main Appennine ridge, 'Apulia began to show us her famous mountains, scorched by the *Atabulus*, and we would never have got across them at all but for a farm near Trivicum which took us in'.[24] He exaggerates: but in spite of all Rome's road-building, difficult country remained, and traveller and mount might have hard work to do, as at the beginning of the magical narrative of Apuleius often known as *The Golden Ass*.

We had surmounted steep hill tracks, slippery stream beds, dewy mountain pastures and soft meadows, I and my white Thessalian horse. He was fairly exhausted. I was beginning to be saddle-sore, so I tore off some leaves, jumped down, carefully wiped the sweat from his brow, stroked his ears, unfastened his bit, and walked on slowly, allowing him a natural relief for his tiredness and hunger. He breakfasted as we walked, turning this way and that to the grass beside the track.

Apuleius, *Metamorphoses* 1.2

The difficulties need not be overdrawn. In another poem Horace remarked that, as a man of no pretensions, he was free to travel anywhere – and road travel came to his mind as the example. If he had to keep up appearances,

I'd have to take along a friend, and his friend ... I'd have lots of grooms, lots of horses to find hay for, a caravan of wagons for my slaves. As it is, I can just set out on a gelded mule and go as far as Tarentum if I fancy.

Horace, *Satires* 1.6.101–106[25]

As travel becomes easy and normal we can even observe the emergence of tourism.

'Let's go to Campania', people say. Then, tired of the fine living, 'Let's visit the wild places, let's make for the mountains of Bruttium and Lucania'. But something is missing in the desolation. 'We'll go to Tarentum with its wonderful seafront, its mild winter, its farmland that is rich enough for the great city that Tarentum once used to be'. But no, they have been away from the applause and the noise too long. They want human blood. 'Let's head back to the City'.

Seneca, *Dialogues* 9.2.13, abridged

Although Horace's party accompanying Maecenas gradually became a large one, they still put up at friends' houses when they could. At Formiae 'Murena lent us his house, Capito his kitchen'; later 'we stayed at Cocceius' well-supplied farm, overlooking the inns of Caudium'. If there was no help for it, the inns were there. Horace gives an amusing sketch of the inn at Forum Appii (p. 44). Further along the road he spent the night in an inn at Beneventum where

an attentive landlord almost burnt his place down while spit-roasting some lean thrushes: a stray flame from falling embers in his old kitchen climbed up to lick at the ceiling. You could see hungry guests rescuing their dinner and terrified slaves trying to put out the fire.

A manual of farming around this time advises its readers to buy a property not too close to a busy road, because 'thefts by passers-by and the continual putting-up of travellers are bad for prosperity' (Columella 1.5.7). In remoter districts well-placed farms did serve additionally as inns. 'The little farm nearest the Campanian Bridge put us up', says Horace; later, at the 'farm near Trivicum' already mentioned, 'the smoke made our eyes water: there were damp branches burning in the fireplace, leaves as well. Here I very stupidly waited up till midnight for a girl who didn't keep her promise' (Horace, *Satires* 1.5). A rosier view of the welcome available to the tired traveller and his mount comes from a playful poem traditionally attributed to Vergil and named from its first word *Copa*, 'bar-girl'. The reader is to imagine a wayside inn and farm, with its own cheese and wine, its own fresh and conserved fruit.

Surisca the bar-girl, her hair caught up in a Greek headband, trained to sway her quivering backside in time to the castanet, is dancing tipsily, wantonly, in the smoky tavern, smacking the noisy reed-pipes against her elbow. You're tired: why be out in the heat and dust? Better to recline on your drunken couch! There are mugs and cups, ladles, roses, pipes, lyres, and a summer-house cool under its awning of reeds, and Pan-pipes playing a shepherd's tune as if they were whispering in a Maenalian cave. And there is *vin ordinaire* just poured from a pitchy jar, and a watercourse running by with an insistent murmur. There are

Figure 1   Dancer with cymbals. Detail of a cartouche in the triclinium of the House
of the Vettii, Pompeii

Source   By permission of the Soprintendenza Archeologica di Pompei

violet wreaths, too, with a yellow flower, and melilot twined with
crimson rose, and the lilies picked from beside a virgin stream that
Achelois brings in willow baskets. There are little cheeses that she dries
on rush mats, and waxy autumn-ripe plums, and chestnuts and lovely
red apples: there is wholesome Ceres, there is Amor, there is Bacchus.
There are blood-red mulberries, grapes in slow-ripening bunches, and a
green cucumber hanging from its stem: there is the Guardian of the
orchard, armed with his willow sickle and his fearsome phallus.

Come on, tinker, your tired little donkey is sweating, give it a rest!
Vesta loves a little donkey. The cicadas are splitting the trees with their
noisy song, the lizard has found a cool lair in the hedgerow, and if you're
wise you'll recline and drink straight out of the midsummer jug, or send
for some new crystal cups if you fancy. When you're tired, lie down in
the shade of the vine, wind a wreath of roses around your nodding head,
and savour the lips of a fresh young girl. Damn that man with the old-
fashioned eyebrows – aromatic wreaths are no good to you when you're
dead and burnt! Do you want your garland on your tombstone, woman?

Give me the wine and the dice now, and damn anyone who cares about tomorrow. Death is twitching my ear: 'Get on and live,' he says, 'I'm coming.'

Copa[26]

The illusions of travel provide a series of examples in Lucretius's exploration of the senses in his philosophical poem *De Rerum Natura*. 'When we see the square towers of a city in the distance, they often appear round'; a puddle 'formed in a gap between the cobblestones of a highway' offers to the eye a downward view apparently as wide and open as the sky above; the ship on which one is departing seems stationary, while the one beside it, still moored, appears to move; when one's horse comes to a standstill in midstream, the current makes it appear to be moving upstream; islands, seen at sea, may appear as an unbroken range of mountains, though there may really be space between them for the passage of a fleet (Lucretius 4.353–425).

We now set out on our survey of the Empire, giving a last, hallucinatory glance at its capital city – to which we shall return last of all – as seen through the eyes of a reluctant departing traveller:

I like to look back every so often at the City, to trace the lines of the hills to the limit of vision, to be led on by my pleasure-seeking eyes to the favourite places that they think they can still see. It is not by its smoke that I know the city of the ruling *Arx*, the world capital.... On the contrary: a brighter zone of heaven, and a clear horizon, mark the brilliant contours of these seven hills. Here the sun is always shining, and the special daylight of Rome seems particularly limpid. Every so often my ears catch the echo of the Circus games: bursts of applause remind me that the theatre is full; familiar shouts are heard in the echoing air. Are they really carried to me across the miles, or do I fondly imagine them?

Rutilius 189–204

3 Ausonia

From the beginning of their literature, Romans were schooled to take a bird's eye view of their native Italy, specifically a view from the East. Two Greek names for Italy, *Ausonia* and *Hesperia*, the 'land of the evening sun', were almost as familiar as its Latin name *Italia*. The peninsula stretched a thousand miles, said Rutilius, from Liguria in the north to the straits of Messana, dividing the storms of the Tuscan Sea from those of the Adriatic. Its shape he compared to an oak leaf, the spine formed by the Appennine range, divinely placed, perhaps, to protect fertile Latium: only a few passes cross these mountains.[1]

The land and its people

Each of the further provinces of the Empire has its literary character, its typical landscape and products – and its typical poetic epithet. Italy is so familiar that it gets scarcely an epithet. It is the 'rich Ausonia' of Silius, a farm of unmatched fertility and quality: 'What emmer shall I compare to Campanian, what wheat to Apulian, what wine to Falernian, what oil to Venafran?' (Varro, *On Farming* 1.2.6). Vergil, in the *Georgics* (2.143–160), gives us a hymn of praise to the farmland of Italy: its bumper crops, its wine, its olive trees, its thriving flocks and horses and the 'white herds of Clitumnus'. In Italy it was always spring. Animals bore young twice a year, trees were double-fruiting. There were no tigers, no lions, no hemlock and scarcely a sufficiency of snakes (Vergil's attentive reader here recalls Cato's advice to keep a snakeskin, whenever you come across one, for use in medicine).[2] It was a land of fine cities and of strong hill-towns in local stone, rivers washing against their ancient walls; a land of lakes, Larius greatest of all, Benacus with a surge like the sea; a land wealthy in silver, copper and gold.

Italy was every Roman citizen's own farm, Rome's essential link with the gods that give food and fertility.[3] These thoughts are encapsulated in the first *Elegy* of Tibullus.

I shall be a smallholder, and plant tender vines and big apples at the proper season, with my own skilled hand. Be with me, Hope! and give me heaps of produce, and full vats of sweet must; for I honour every solitary tree-trunk in my fields, and every old stone where ways meet, with a garland of flowers; every year's fruit is offered in libation to the farmer's god. Blonde Ceres, you shall have a coronet of wheat from my land, to hang at your temple door; in the fruit garden shall be placed the red guardian, Priapus, to frighten the birds with his dreadful sickle. *Lares*, faithful guardians of a farm once rich and now poor, you too must accept my gifts: in the old days a slaughtered heifer was the purification for countless young bulls; a little lamb is now the offering for my shrunken fields, and this lamb shall fall for you, and the peasant young-sters shall shout, 'Io! Give us harvests, and good wine! ... Thieves and wolves, spare my small flock; look to the big herds elsewhere for your prey: I purify my shepherd every year; I sprinkle peaceful Pales with drops of milk.

Tibullus 1.1.6–36

The gods here honoured by Tibullus will reappear later in this chapter: Ceres, goddess of the wheat harvest; the Lares, protectors of the farm, its hearth and its household (including slaves); Priapus, armed with red-painted phallus and sickle, guardian of the orchard; Pales, the shepherd god. Cato, whose practical notes *On Farming* are the earliest surviving work of Latin prose, necessarily gives generous space to religious observance. He instructs that the Feast for the Oxen be held, with an offering to Jove and Vesta, when the pear blossoms and before the spring ploughing begins; that the Harvest Sow be sacrificed to Ceres; that when a new field is to be cleared an expiation be made, with the sacrifice of a piglet, lamb and calf (the *Suovetaurilia*, 'Pig and Sheep and Bull'), to the unknown and unnamed spirits who guard the place. In midwinter, when little happened in the fields, the festivals of *Compitalia* and *Saturnalia* were celebrated with abundant wine. Rome was hospitable to eastern gods, but we have listed gods that look after Italy.[4]

The Italian countryside was neither uniform nor unchanging. In classical times wealthy Romans multiplied their country estates and demonstrated their power over the landscape.

Our regal structures leave few acres to the plough. Everywhere orna-mental ponds can be seen bigger than Lake Lucrinus. Barren plane-trees are crowding out the elms; violet beds and myrtle bushes and all those cartloads of perfumery are stinking out the olive-groves that once produced fruit for the farmer; and the densely-branching bay trees close out the sun. This was not the commandment given us by Romulus and bristly Cato; this was not the ancient way.

Horace, *Odes* 2.15.1–12[5]

But this ancient landscape had the power to regenerate itself. 'Look about you. You will see the very stones mastered by age; tall towers in ruin and their masonry crumbling; temples and images of the gods defaced, their destined span not lengthened by any sanctity that avails against the laws of nature' (Lucretius 5.306–310).

> *Trepidant urbesque caducae*
> *inde, neque est aliud, si fas est credere, mundo*
> *venturam antiqui faciem veracius omen;*

'So cities tremble and are liable to fall', writes the unknown author of a scientific poem on Mount Etna. 'There can be no surer sign of the truth, if truth it is, that the world is destined to return to its primeval state' (*Aetna* 172–174). Rutilius, in the fifth century, meditates further on the ruins of the past as he contemplates the rock on which the fortress of Populonia had stood. 'Traces of walls remain; houses lie buried under an expanse of rubble. We must not complain of our own mortality, when we see by example that cities themselves can die' (p. 80).

Lucretius, reconstructing the far-off origins of agriculture, incidentally reconstructs the formation of the classical Italian landscape:

> Day by day they forced the woodland to creep further up the hillside, surrendering the lower reaches to tillage. Over hill and plain they extended meadowland and cornland, reservoirs, and water-courses and laughing vineyards, with the distinctive strip of blue-grey olives running between, rippling over hump and hollow and along the level ground. So the countryside assumed its present aspect of variegated beauty, gaily interspersed with luscious orchards and marked out by encircling hedges of luxuriant trees.
>
> Lucretius 5.1370–1378

Details of this image recur in other sources. Varro names estates whose boundaries had been defined by plantations of pines, cypresses or elms, the latter a most productive tree, he adds, because it provides wood for fencing and for burning and foliage for animals, and is the ideal support for tree-trained vines (*On Farming* 1.15).

The stone roads of the second and first centuries BC were well adapted to wheeled traffic, and many ox-carts groaned along them. 'Whole buildings by the roadside are shaken and jarred by the lesser weight of a wagon … they quake when a cobblestone jolts the iron-rimmed wheels' (Lucretius 6.548–551). Hedges, fences, stone walls and earth banks were all to be seen, in different terrains, as field boundaries. Along the drove roads, the long distance routes by which flocks of sheep made their annual journeys to and from summer pasture in the mountains, common land provided temporary pasture.

Snaking through cultivated land, streams and rivers were marked by poplars, willows and reed beds, planted for their utility to the farmer,[6] and by spring and autumn mists. 'If there is an excess of vapour, mists form, as happens in plains and fields irrigated by a stream: the air thickens into cloud as it rises from the valleys' (*Aetna* 312–314). The walker who followed these streams into the upper valleys could reward himself with the discovery of virgin springs and new flowers; he would find blackberries, strawberries and other such wild fruits as a nomadic shepherd can offer to his bride – such as Ovid imagined the Cyclops Polyphemus offering to his ungrateful Galatea. Here was wild country: torrents, swollen by a storm, could destroy all in their path. Forest fires were sparked by two trees rubbing together in the wind. In still weather, disturbing echoes in an deserted valley would remind the traveller that gods and spirits, known or unknown, were ever close at hand.[7]

On the peoples of Italy Roman and Greek perspectives differ. Greeks had not been specially interested in middle Italian ethnography. There were Greek settlements of long standing on the southern coasts: Naples and Tarentum the best known of them. To the north was Etruria, with its own strange language and culture, somewhat comparable to those of the East. Greeks had found it easy to classify all the country folk between these two, Romans included, as *barbaroi* 'barbarians' and *Opikoi* 'Oscans' – the second seemed to at least one Roman a dirtier word than the first – and to despise them all equally.[8] But one feels confident that the Greek littérateur Philodemus, the same whose philosophical library survived miraculously to modern times in the 'House of the Papyri' at Herculaneum, had been able to rely on the sense of humour of his Roman patron, L. Calpurnius Piso,[9] when he wrote:

> That foot, that leg, I'm dying for those thighs, that arse, that bush, that waist, those shoulders, those breasts, that slender neck, those hands, those maddening eyes, those utterly indecent gyrations, those most excellent kisses, and you can kill me now for those deep vowels – so what if she's Oscan and called Flora and can't sing Sappho? Didn't Perseus fall in love with Andromeda? And she was Indian.
>
> Philodemus 12 [*Anthologia Palatina* 5.132][10]

Romans did not need such reminders that they sprang from peasant roots. Originally 'forest dwellers, unskilled in war' (Naevius 11 Strzelecki [Macrobius 6.5.9]) their ancestors 'breathed garlic and onions, but their minds were noble' (Varro, *Menippean Satires* 63 Bücheler). Possibly things had been better in the old days.[11] But Romans, at all events those visible in literature, were now city dwellers. Those who were wealthy enough demonstrated the fact by their ownership of country farms, of summer pastures and possibly also of transhumant flocks. 'Why add Lucanian mountain pastures to your Calabrian ones?' Horace asks an imaginary tycoon (*Epistles* 2.2.177–178). Italy, under the Roman Empire, had become Rome's country farm.

Rome's Italy

Once a modest town on the northern edge of Latium, excellently sited at one of the peninsula's narrower points where the Tiber valley penetrates the mountains, Rome became dominant in Italy in the course of the third and second centuries BC. As the city accrued power, wealth and empire, Romans looked to their Italian farms for simple, old-fashioned, fresh, healthy produce to prove that they were still true-born farmers even while they competed to consume the luxuries of the world.

A philosopher could argue that one needed nothing of all the rest, certainly not the fine house with its gold images of youths holding flaming torches to illuminate banquets prolonged into the night, its halls gleaming with silver and gold, its 'carved and gilded rafters ringing to the music of the lute. Nature does not miss these luxuries when men recline in company on the soft grass by a running stream under the branches of a tall tree and refresh their bodies pleasurably at small expense', though the philosopher had to admit that this arrangement would work best in spring sunshine (Lucretius 2.23–33).[12] There were others prepared to say that a modest country farm was all they wanted: Tibullus often assures his 'Delia' that nothing will make him happier than to share his simple farm and its simple life with her if he can wrap her in his arms (which he promises will be *teneri* 'tender', an adjective more often used of girls and young boys: p. 262). His contemporary, the poetess Sulpicia, would not have fancied any of this. To judge from the generally frustrated tone of Tibullus's elegies, Delia did not fancy it either.[13]

The better plan is to have a house in Rome as well as a country farm. Thus equipped, all the time that he is in Rome a person of fashion can safely wish to be in the country, with all its 'baskets, hearths, pigs, and smoky offerings to Pales' (Persius 1.71–72). Horace explores the usual sentiments repeatedly, not without humour: 'Hercules, fatten my flock, but not my head' (*Satires* 2.6.14–15). He imagines addressing his *vilicus*, his slave farm manager, to take up the paradox that while those in the city long for the country, those at the farm long for the city and its excitements:

> Keeper of the woods and the farm that makes me what I am – the farm that you dislike although it feeds five hearths and sends five fine fathers to Varia market – my mind and my thoughts carry me to where you are; they love to race the distance that separates me from you. I say that the countryman is happy, you say the townsman. When you were a city boy you secretly prayed for the country: now you're a manager you want the city, the Games and the baths. The brothel and the greasy cookshop drive you to pine for the city, I know, along with the facts that that neighbourhood will grow pepper and incense sooner than grapes, and there's no inn nearby that can serve you wine, and no pipe-playing slut so that you can bounce up and down to her music.

Well, I used to sport flimsy togas and neat hair, I used to be able to talk that expensive Cinara into doing it free (as you know), I drank the flowing Falernian from midday on, and what I like best now is a light lunch and a doze in the grass on the river bank. You wish you were gnawing city rations with the boys, and you're praying to join them; my smart houseboy envies you your firewood and flock and garden.

Horace, Epistles 1.14, abridged

When the Roman landowner does go down to the country, he will surely be accompanied by a caravan of friends and clients.[14] For his own satisfaction and for theirs, his farmhouse will be equipped with a good fire in a hospitable hearth, as sketched with gusto by Martial in a poem on which we shall pause for a moment.

Our Faustinus's villa at Baiae is not set off with fancy myrtle groves. Its wide fields give no unnecessary space to barren plane tree or clipped box hedge. Its wealth is truly and barbarously rustic. Generous Ceres stuffs every corner. Many a wine-jar breathes ancient vintages, and the hairy vine-pruner brings in the late grapes after November, when midwinter is on its way. Fierce bulls roar in the deep valley; even the calves, not yet horned, itch for a fight. His dirty barnyard birds range free – noisy goose, jewelled peacocks, flame-winged flamingo, painted partridge, speckled Numidians, pheasant from impious Colchis. Proud cocks tread Rhodian hens. His towers resound with the beating wings of doves and the cries, here of wood-pigeons, there of turtle-doves. Greedy piglets run after the *vilica*'s skirt, and the tender lamb awaits its mother's full udder. Milky home-born slaves surround the peaceful hearth, where generous logs blaze for the festive *Lares*.... He stretches a tricky net for greedy thrushes, hauls in a captive fish with his vibrating line, or brings home a doe caught in his trap. The cheerful town slaves dig the easy garden; needing no *paedagogus*, the naughty long-haired boys are happy to obey the *vilicus*; even a delicate eunuch enjoys the work. No countryman visits empty-handed; one brings pale honey in its combs, and a *meta* of cheese from the forest of Sassina; another offers sleepy dormice, another a kid whimpering for the shaggy doe, another an unsuspecting brace of capons; the tenant farmers' strapping daughters are sent in by their mothers with baskets full of gifts. The neighbour is invited in when his day's work is done. Nothing on the table is meanly earmarked for tomorrow's dinner: all are well-fed; the servant gets his share and has no cause to be jealous of the tipsy guest.... As for *you*, you cart vegetables, eggs, chickens, apples, cheese and fresh grape juice out to your painted villa: it isn't the country at all, it's a town house out of town.

Martial 3.58

Wealthy 'Faustinus' is Martial's imagined example of putting one's Italian estate to its proper use. Wealthy he certainly is: his estate is – of all places – at Baiae (see Map 3), the most dissolute and expensive of Roman holiday resorts (p. 52); he keeps a fine range of exotic and luxury birds (the 'Numidians' are guinea-fowl, p. 109) alongside his dirty barnyard fowl, and even those are a fighting breed (p. 150); he leaves some of his grapes to dry partially on the vine, to make the costly sweet wine called *passum* (p. 137); and he is sufficiently indulgent to the long-haired boys he keeps in his city mansion to take them all along with him to the seaside. Like Horace's, Faustinus's estate is partly let to tenant farmers and partly run from his own farm, which is managed by slaves, including the *vilica* 'manageress', who looks after household matters and the hens and pigs; all are responsible to the *vilicus*. The slaves are pictured as forming a settled household, the home-born youngsters called 'milky' because reared on mother's milk, as a practical writer on agriculture recommended.[15]

There is no call for Faustinus to be modest. While nibbling the roasted dormice – glazed in honey and rolled in poppy seeds (Petronius 31) – any client and guest will have a fine view of the rampant fertility typified by his stuffed sacks of grain (*Ceres*), his combative bulls and his tenants' nubile daughters, and this is all just as it should be. At the end of the poem we see how 'you', unlike Faustinus, get it wrong. You, too, have invested in a country estate: it may well bring in money, but it does not bring you your own food, your own wine, your own rustic wealth and fertility that your slaves can share with the *Lar* (their guardian spirit) and that you can share with your clients. Varro, a century before, had made a similar point to Martial's. 'Some people even construct dining couches in their fruit store, to have dinners there. Since fashion allows people to do this in a picture gallery, where art sets the scene, why should they not enjoy a scene set by nature, in the form of a beautiful arrangement of fruit? – just as long as they do not buy the fruit in Rome, as some do, and take it out and arrange it in their fruit stores just for the dinner party!' (*On Farming* 1.59.2).[16]

Visits to the farm were all very well, but one could not be visiting the farm for very much of the year. The proper use for a country farm thus had to include a supply of fresh farm food for oneself and one's guests in Rome. This was the greatest commonplace of all: we shall see the result when we finally return to Rome, its luxuries and its menus (p. 247). For the present, let Martial remind us that farm food in Rome was not a pleasure confined to the wealthy and their guests.

> Cackling barnyard birds, eggs of the same, golden lightly-dried Chian figs, baby offspring of a bleating goat, olives too young to bear winter, parsnip just tinged with early frost – do you think they all came in from my farm? How sweet of you to make that mistake, Regulus! My bit of land sends nothing to Rome except me. Whatever you get from your farm manager and your tenant farmer in Umbria, and from your market

garden just out by the third milestone, and from the Tuscans and the Tusculans, I have the whole Suburra supplying me.

Martial 7.31

Rome's shops and markets (*Suburra* says it all: p. 215) were rich indeed: they drew their produce from the market gardens around Rome, from the farms of Italy, and from every province of the Empire; and they, as a matter of fact, supplied practically all the food the city ate.

Varro's speaker claims with easy confidence that the best Italian produce was better than any in the world (p. 21). Italy was so rich in fruit trees, he adds, that it seemed to be all one orchard. Fruit varieties were indeed developed enthusiastically by Italian growers. Among pears, Vergil names *Syria* (p. 65) and 'heavy *volaema*': the latter, big enough to fill the hand, were particularly good for conserving, in sweet wine, if they were picked slightly underripe. The *Matiana* apple, with a little wine, made the emperor Domitian's favourite supper when he had eaten heavily at midday.[17] The figs of Italy, milk-white sap still seeping from their freshly-picked stems, are evoked in a lovely line by Ennius:

Fici dulciferae lactantes ubere toto,

'sweetness-bearing figs, milky from full udders' (*Annals* 448 Skutsch). *Prima ficus* 'the first ripe fig' was a handy name for the moment at the end of August when the weather changed and the figs began to ripen. *Piro florente* 'when the pear blossoms' was, for Cato, a good date to fix for sheep to leave their winter pasture:[18] the lowland farmer, his meadows now vacated by the transhumant flocks, should celebrate the Feast for the Oxen and begin the spring ploughing (p. 22).

Vines and olives provide two of Varro's examples. Italy as a whole numbered tens or hundreds of varieties of both, as it does now, though only a few emerge in literature or otherwise make themselves known to us. For olives, there is the 'bitter *pausia* berry' of Vergil's *Georgics*, one of the kinds that was best for conserving; for vines, the *duracina* or 'firm-fleshed' kinds that came to market as table grapes. Suetonius quotes a private letter of Augustus, 'As I came home from the *Regia* in my litter I ate a bit of bread and a few *duracina* grapes' (*Augustus* 76).[19]

When it came to wine, Italy was better endowed than *ampeloessa Phrygia*, the 'Phrygia rich in grapes' of Homer's *Iliad*, so Varro asserts. Vergil dared to call its grape varieties and their names uncountable (others had said the same of those of Greece) though his list of them is both short and confused.[20] Italy's wine-growing districts, too, were numerous. Another agricultural author was able to list four famous Italian regions – 'there is no doubt that of all the vines on earth, those of Massic, Sorrentine, Alban and Caecuban vineyards are supreme in the nobility of their wine' (Columella 3.8.5) – without even mentioning the one that for many authors was identi-

Figure 2   Basket of fresh ripe figs (in the original some are green, some purple).
Detail of wall painting from Oplontis (Torre Annunziata, Italy)

Source   By permission of the Soprintendenza Archeologica di Pompei

fied with high quality wine: 'what wine shall I compare to Falernian?' had
been Varro's rhetorical question (p. 21).[21]

Italy was also the land where the concept of the vintage year or *millésime*
first flourished. Pliny, who likes to trace beginnings, seems to show the
beginning of this.

> As to the rest, no one variety, but one year, is famous: all varieties gave
> of their best when L. Opimius was consul, the year the tribune C.
> Gracchus stirred the people to rebellion and was killed. That year,
> Rome's 633rd, the weather was splendid ('ripe', as they say) thanks to
> the sun. Its wines have lasted about 200 years already, though now
> reduced to something like rough honey, the natural state of wine in its
> old age; they are no longer drinkable by themselves nor dilutable with
> water, their formidable maturity having developed into bitterness, but
> are medicines, used in tiny doses to improve other wines.
>
> Pliny 14.55

This last practice, adds the great second-century physician and gourmet
Galen, was calculated to deceive the unskilled buyer into thinking he was
getting a good vintage wine (*On Good and Bad Juices* [6.805]).

Pliny's benchmark, the Opimian vintage, was 121 BC. His details are persuasive: he is no doubt right that even the very best made wine of that very finest year could not still have been drinkable two hundred years later. Cicero, before him, had said something similar. Yet others of Pliny's time, and even later, imply that Opimian wines were actually still available for drinking; and that it was perfectly possible to relish wines a hundred years old, wines that would have diminished through evaporation from the jar and that would need to be strained through linen to clear them before drinking.

Also renowned as years of fine wine were the consulships of Anicius in 160 BC, of Torquatus in 65, and of Taurus in 26.[22] Horace calls once for a jar 'that remembers the Marsian conflict', the Social War of 91–89 BC (*Odes* 3.14.18); he vows an annual dinner with wine 'put up to smoke in Tullus's consulship', 66 BC (*Odes* 3.8.11–12). In a famous ode,

> *O nata mecum consule Manlio ...*

he addresses an amphora of Massic wine that had been laid down in the year of his own birth, 'born, with me, in the consulship of Manlius' (*Odes* 3.21.1).

Rome's neighbourhood

The growth in Rome's power and population had had a powerful effect on the neighbouring countryside. The city itself, like the smaller towns of Italy, had once been full of gardens and orchards. Pliny is right in identifying this as a contrast between past and present, for, as he put it, 'at Rome a garden was in itself a poor man's farm. The plebeians "went to market" to their own gardens' (19.51). By his time it was a mark of affluence if a Roman ate and entertained in his town house from the produce of his own land. We know of scarcely any fresh food produced within the walls of Rome in its great days, the exception being aviaries that farmed small birds. Not only the city but the whole region had lost its rural character. Near Rome, even in the second century BC, pasture had to be given over to alien flocks of sheep in the lambing season, to feed the luxury market for spring lamb and soft cheese.[23] Near Rome, the owner of a farm was well advised to maximise his returns by concentrating on produce for which people in the city would pay high prices: table grapes (as Columella put it, 'It is only worth planting vineyards for fruit if the farm is so close to a town that it can be sold fresh to market traders like tree fruit. In this case you must choose early and firm-fleshed [*duracina*] varieties': *On Farming* 3.2.1), apples, figs, pomegranates and pears to be sold fresh, quinces, apples, figs, pears and sorbs to be sold as conserves, nuts, the kinds of olives suited to light conserving for the luxury table (Cato specifies '*orchites* and *posia* olives, which are best preserved, young, in brine, or crushed with lentisk seed'), and fresh vegetables including *bulbi*, 'grape-hyacinth bulbs'. It was also lucrative to grow violets, roses and other flowers 'for wreaths', along with aromatics such as myrtle and bay. If close enough to a stream, one would grow willow to sell for firewood (Cato, *On Farming* 7–9;

Varro, *On Farming* 1.16). This was all wanted within easy reach of the city's markets.

There was a cost. The small towns that, according to history, had once thrived in the neighbourhood of Rome, thrived no longer. No Roman writer really discusses this. Most likely their land had been bought up by city people, their gardens and orchards were worked by slaves, and what used to be the houses and barns of local smallholders were now storage sheds for bulk produce and, beyond, 'weekend cottages' (as we might say) detached from their former fields. The results are clear. There were people, no doubt, but no community of respectable citizens such as would share in religious rites (Cicero, *For Plancius* 23). It is not so far to Lucan's vision of a nightmare future, the result of Rome's civil wars, when the buildings of Gabii, Veii, Cora, Alba and Lavinium would all be ruins, roofed by nothing but dust: derelict places 'where no one would live or sleep unless overtaken by night' (7.392–401).

Two main roads led south-east from Rome. Both crossed the Alban hills. Beyond the hills, the *via Appia* would be the low road, reaching the coast at Tarracina and eventually turning inland again to Capua. The *via Latina* was the high road, serving inland Latium and the Liris valley. Both, for some miles outside the gate, were lined with the tombs of Romans great and not so great. So was the *via Labicana*, a by-road that ran eastwards from the *Porta Esquilina*, passed the shrunken township of Labici about fifteen miles from Rome and rejoined the Latin Way a little further on at the inn called *ad Pictas*. The highlands here, watched over by the three hill-towns of Labici, Signia and Anagnia, marked the point where orchard and market garden gave way to fertile farmland: poets wrote of 'men of Labici, skilled with the plough', of the 'crumbling loam of rich Anagnia, productive in grain' and of 'foaming Signia with its sour must' – a sour must from which an astringent medicinal wine was made, 'good after six years, but much more effective when older' (*Epitome of Athenaeus* 27c). Signia was equally famous for its pears, called *testacea* 'tile-red' by some; and for its concrete, *calx Signina*, incorporating broken crocks.[24]

Two kinds of *lupae* might startle the traveller who found himself on one of these roads as the light began to fail. There were the wild grey wolves of Italy. They were a part of Roman mythology and ritual: Rome would not have been founded without them, the twins Romulus and Remus having been suckled by a wolf in infancy. A grey wolf, *rava lupa*, might still come down at night from the Alban hills around Lanuvium, so Horace reminds us. And then there were the cheap whores who worked in the crumbling tombs that lined the highways (p. 43).[25] These are also *lupae* in Latin, and typical of them was the *flava lupa* 'fair-haired slut' of Juvenal's satire (6 O.15 –16). 'Even a flaxen-haired slut out of a ruined tomb would refuse to drink out of that – even if the wine were Alban or Sorrentine!'. With a similar intonation Martial advises an imagined exhibitionist to 'learn modesty from Chione or Ias – even those filthy sluts conceal their trade in tombs' (1.34).

The Latin Way passed by Tusculum, perennially famous as the birthplace

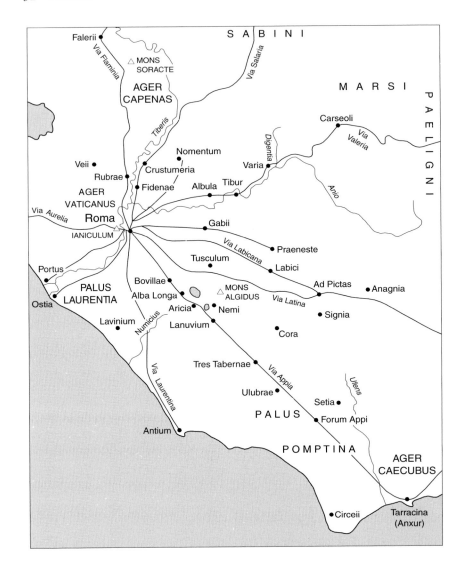

Map 1   From the Faliscan pastures to the white rock of Anxur: Rome's
neighbourhood

of Cato the Censor. Well-sited on a hill looking towards Rome, pleasantly
open to the morning sun, Tusculum was no doubt where Cato had developed
his 'property near the City', *fundum suburbanum*, as a fruit and flower garden
to profit from Roman markets. The market gardens here, guarded by stone
walls, are named to us for their roses and violets. In more expansive times
this would be a fashionable place for your luxurious marble villa, and

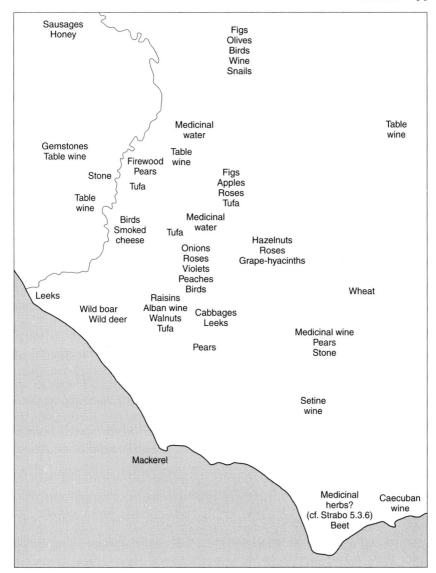

Map 2 From Faliscan sausages to Caecuban wine: local specialities of Rome's neighbourhood

Tusculana, Albana became shorthand for 'country estates conveniently close at hand'. The old town walls were poetically 'Circean', *Circaea moenia Tusculi*, because, when all of Italy laid claim to Homeric ancestry, it was realised that

Tusculum had been founded by Telegonus, son of Odysseus and Circe, who lived not far away (p. 41).[26]

As it passed Tusculum the Latin Way was already among the volcanic Alban hills, ruled by spirits known and unknown. On the right would appear *amoena Algida* 'the beauties of mount Algidus', better characterised as *gelidus Algidus* 'icy Algidus', for it is cold indeed to those who have just climbed from the Tiber banks.[27] At the southern end of the ridge were the sacred lake and woods of Nemi (p. 43). These mountains and lakes, these forests and hill pastures, 'these sacred groves of Alba, these lightning-blasted trees' (Lucilius 644) form the numinous landscape where Alba itself stood: a small hill town outstretched along a narrow ridge, *Alba Longa* in full, revered as the antique city founded by Aeneas. This tiny place had been the new Troy, *Dardania Alba*. This was the resting-place, *Palladia Alba*, of the mystic Palladium, sacred to Minerva. From here, centuries later, Rome itself had been founded. The emperor Domitian, very conscious of Rome's legendary and religious history, built himself a magnificent villa in the Alban hills (nicknamed the *Albana Arx*, the 'Alban fortress': from its high vantage point it seemed to command Rome). It broke into the old walls of Alba and it faced the Alban Lake, on which Domitian, a lover of silence, used to glide in a boat that made no sound at all, for it was towed at a distance by another (Pliny, *Panegyric on Trajan* 82). The emperor honoured Minerva here and instituted five-year games, 'Alban Games' at which little presents, 'Alban olives', 'Alban gifts' were exchanged.[28]

The southern slopes of these Alban hills, with their 'cold, moist soil and climate', were planted with the *eugenia* grape (p. 115), and they produced the best wines of the neighbourhood of Rome. There was a rare dry type; sweet. *Albanum* was reckoned high among wines, worth several years in cellar, very heady when mature. At least one poetic gastronome recommended smoking Alban grapes to make raisins (Horace, *Satires* 2.4.72), and he might have had in mind an instruction on this subject handed down by the venerable Cato.[29]

A little further out was 'Setia on its vine-growing slope', *pendula Setia* 'hanging Setia' (is it the hill-town that 'hangs', or its bunches of grapes?) whose villas and vineyards looked down from their stronghold on Forum Appi and the Pomptine marshes. This was a good place to want to have an estate.[30] Setian wine had rapidly become a rich man's fancy (*Setia cara*, 'expensive Setian') once it had been dignified by Augustus's favour, or, as Silius puts it with mild exaggeration, 'reserved for the table of Lyaeus [Bacchus] himself' (8.376–377). Little sips of Setian were worth the considerable cost of cooling with snow, using the very best equipment for the job, a *colum nivarium* or snow colander. A cheaper snow-bag could be used instead; the result of that might be to spoil the flavour.[31]

Among all the dying townships Gabii, twelve miles due east of Rome, is the name that comes up most often. Horace teasingly imagines a Greek village 'more deserted than Gabii or Fidenae' (p. 118). Gabii had long ago been an important place, a city with which Rome had hammered out a treaty. Now it was empty but for the mineral springs and the roadside stalls, both of them of passing interest to Romans who paused briefly here for a lunch or a cold but health-giving dip, half way to Praeneste.[32] *Altum Praeneste, frigidum Praeneste*, 'High Praeneste, cold Praeneste' was a pleasant hill town and (because of its legendary past) a good place to sit and read about the Trojan War. Praeneste lived on Roman holidaymakers and on Roman markets. It was close enough to send down supplies not only of hazelnuts, evidently typical of the town and named after it *nuces Praenestinae*, but also a variety of rose celebrated for its fine aroma, an ingredient in *rhodinum* perfume.[33]

Just to the north of Gabii, across the River Anio 'where the road goes to the cold citadel of Herculean Tibur, where frosted Albula's sulphurous waters smoke, milestone four from the City marks a country estate, a sacred grove, acres loved by the Muses. Here a rough portico gave summer shade' to Regulus, till it fell and nearly killed him, so Martial's little poem assures us (1.12). The waters of Albula, *crudae Albulae* 'raw Albula', *cana Albula* 'frosted Albula' are actually nine miles further on. The three small lakes, *frigidi fontes*, are sulphurous: their water, specially reheated, was prescribed for Augustus's arthritis.[34]

This road, almost parallel with the one to Praeneste, led on to Tibur, sited above picturesque falls, 'with twin white crags, each topped by towers, and between them the river-nymph of Anio forever plunging into her deep pool' (Propertius 3.16.3–4). Tibur had been a strong fortress once, *superbum Tibur, Tibur supinum*, 'proud, high-lying Tibur', protected by walls attributed to its legendary founder Catilus. Now it was a healthy mountain resort: *mite solum Tiburis*, 'the mild land of Tibur'. The weather was typically cool, like the best evenings in Naples, said Marcus Aurelius (p. 55). Romans, accustomed to heat, sensed it as 'icy', *Tibur glaciale*. It was cold because it was humid, *umidum Tibur*, with spray rising continuously from the river (*gelidus Anio*, 'cold Anio') in the dramatic landscape at and below the waterfall, 'the house of echoing Albunea, the cascading Anio, the grove of Tiburnus and the orchards irrigated by variable channels' (Horace, *Odes* 1.7.12–14). Here was the 'deep shade of Tibur', *densa Tiburis umbra* – the great forest of the local goddess Albunea, echoing to the continuous roar of the falls, foggy with the poisonous exhalation of a sulphur spring. Here her oracle could be consulted. The river Anio kept the apple orchards along his banks well watered, and the river himself is described as *pomifer*, 'apple-laden', by two bold poets.[35] The *pomifera arva Anienicolae Catilli*, 'apple-laden meadows of Catilus who lives beside the Anio' produced apples that were good, but to at least one uncompromising gastronome not as good as Picene:[36] no doubt, coming from so close to Rome, they were rather too cheap to be prized. Statius admires a patron's *chateau* that commanded both banks of the river.

Full of boulders below and above, Anio here silences his swollen rage
and his foaming noise, as if he dare not disturb the poetic days and
music-filled nights of tranquil Vopiscus; home is on either bank. Am I
to admire the gilded beams, the Moorish lintels on every side, the
patterned veins of glittering marbles, the nymphs scurrying through
every bedroom? The courtyard that watches the lower river, or the other
that looks back towards the silent woodland, and enjoys unbroken peace
and those soft murmurings that induce a languid sleep? Am I to watch
the stream that flows from the sulphur springs and laughs at the
nymphs gasping in the [cold] river alongside? Need I tell of the feasts
held now on this bank, now on that; the gleaming white pools; the
springs that well up deep beneath the water's surface; and *Marcia* who
soars across the gorge, boldly bridging the river with her lead-lined
channel? In this shade Tiburnus reclines; here Albula likes to dip her
sulphurous tresses.

Statius, Silvae 1.3.17–75, abridged[37]

The 'Salt Road', *via Salaria*, ran north from Rome along the left bank of
the Tiber towards the Sabine country: in places the country was so low-lying
that dykes were needed to protect the road from flooding. It passed 'old
Fidenae', classed by the poets with Gabii among the almost deserted townships; then another dying town, Crustumeria – noted only for the stone
walls with which its orchards were guarded and for the *Crustumium* or
Crustuminum, a delicate kind of pear, the very best in Pliny's view, the kind
that would have to be grown very close to Rome if it were to find a market.

This road skirted the costly territory of *siccum Nomentum* 'dry Nomentum',
where the grammarian Remmius Palaemon was said to have bought an
estate and, having improved it, sold it to Seneca for four times the price. 'At
that time the reputation of the Nomentan region was at its height, and
Seneca's estate was second to none. There is good evidence that on his property each *iugerum* of vineyard produced eight *cullei* of wine' (Columella
3.3.3). This fits very well with what we hear elsewhere of Nomentum and
its wine – mostly from Martial, who lived in Rome but had a house at
Nomentum.

Martial generally claimed, with truth or inverted snobbery, to get
nothing at all from his own country garden. He is, even compared with
other supposedly autobiographical poets, remarkably inconsistent; but this
detail is probably not far from true, because if he had really acquired a large
estate at Nomentum, poetry had been a more profitable business for him
than seems likely. He did have some land, one poem seems to say: a laurel
grove; room for a couple of rustic altars at which his manager made offerings. Still, he had little need to mount guard over his orchard. His
Nomentan wine and Nomentan apples were the produce of local, very profitable, vineyards and market gardens which supplied the shops and markets
of the Suburra, and that is where he bought them.[38] No one supposed that

Nomentan wine was good. Quite the contrary: its growers went for high yield, and achieved it, as we see from the story of Seneca's estate. Nomentan wine was very plentiful, it was cheap to transport to the consumers of Rome, and it had one most apposite and saleable quality:

> The wine that is born in Nomentan fields, Ovidius, throws off its own character and name as it adds each year to its age. A really old jar can be given whatever name you please!
>
> Martial 1.105

In the first two centuries of Empire the walled city of Rome was entirely on the left, southern, bank of the Tiber. This, the greatest river of Roman Italy, was *flavus Tiberis* 'yellow Tiber', yellow with sand; it was *Tuscus Tiberis, amnis Tuscus* and even *Lydium flumen* 'the Tuscan stream, Lydian river' because it divided Rome from Etruria.[39] The river flowed close under the walls; the less-polluted stretch just above the city, curving around the *Campus Martius*, offered summer bathing (p. 240).

Pons Sublicius, the oldest and for many centuries the only bridge at Rome, had been built entirely of wood, without metal nails or clamps, in accordance with an oracle, and whenever necessary it was repaired in the same way. It is the *roboreus pons*, 'oak bridge' of Ovid (*Fasti* 5.621–632) and the *hiera gephyra*, 'sacred bridge' of Dionysius of Halicarnassus, upon which, every year, old men made of rushes were offered to the River in an ancient ritual.

> In my time the Romans still did this annually on the Ides of May.... They make the appropriate sacrifices, and then the *Pontifices* (the high priests), the Virgins who guard the undying fire, the Generals, and other citizens who may properly attend sacred rites, bring effigies made to resemble men, thirty in total, and throw them from the Sacred Bridge into the waters of the Tiber. They call the effigies *Argei*.
>
> Dionysius of Halicarnassus, *Roman Antiquities* 1.37.3[40]

The unwalled districts on the other side are called *litus Etruscum* or *Lydia ripa* 'the Etruscan bank, Lydian bank'.[41]

This was the smoky and smelly side of the river. The law and custom of ancient cities tended to exclude some industries from sites within the walls because they produced noxious fumes or risked causing fires, and Rome was no exception. Workshops on the right bank engaged in chemical trades – hence, in a poem by Martial (1.41: p. 222), the hawker (*ambulator*) from across the Tiber whose trade is to exchange matches for broken glass. The glass was wanted for remelting; both match-making and glass-blowing were carried on across the river. So were leather trades: 'Thais smells worse than a miserly fuller's jar of piss, just smashed in the middle of the road ... worse than a Transtiberine hide snatched back from a dog', says Martial picturesquely of an imaginary lady (6.93).[42]

Also across the river was the main area of Jewish settlement in Rome.

> The majority were Roman freedmen, originally brought to Rome as prisoners of war and manumitted by their owners. They had not been made to alter their national customs. [Augustus] was aware that they had places for prayer and came together in them, especially on the weekly holy day, for education in their traditional system of belief.
>
> Philo, *Embassy* 155–156

There were several synagogues in Rome, including those 'of the Freedmen, of the Cyrenaeans, of the Alexandrians, of people from Cilicia and Asia' (*Acts* 6.9).[43] There were also several Jewish catacombs, and the largest of them was along the road to Portus on this right bank of the Tiber.

Beyond Rome's trans-Tiber suburbs was a growing belt of pleasure gardens: Caesar's gardens downriver, Agrippina's gardens opposite the *Campus*, Domitia's gardens to the north; here too was the *Stagnum navale*, Augustus's artificial lake for naval displays.[44] The hill called *Ianiculum* gave an unrivalled view across the City. Martial describes a garden there.

> From here you can see the Seven ruling Hills and get a view of all of Rome, and the hills of Alba and Tusculum, and the cool places around the City, old Fidenae, little Rubrae, and the fruity grove of Anna Perenna that delights in virgin blood. You can see the market trader on the *via Flaminia* or the *Salaria*, but his cart is silent! His wheels won't disturb your sleep; nor will the sailors' shouts nor the dockers' curses, yet the *Mulvius* is close by and barges are gliding down the sacred Tiber.
>
> Martial 4.64

There was an area of vineyards across the Tiber, in the *ager Vaticanus* north from the City. It was poor land – 'the Capuans will not think the *ager Vaticanus* ... worth comparing with their own rich and fertile fields' (Cicero, *On the Agrarian Law* 2.96) – but it was surely profitable: as at Nomentum, growers were excellently placed to sell to Roman markets, and clearly they aimed at quantity. Their wine was famous, at least to Martial. 'Your wine-cup has a snake painted on it by Myron's hand, Annianus – and you drink Vatican. You drink poison!' (6.92); 'You'll drink Vatican, if you fancy vinegar' (10.45); 'If the God himself gave me nectar, it would turn to vinegar and the treacherous plonk [*vappa*] from a Vatican jar' (12.48). He warns that 'must put up in Vatican jars' is not worth mixing with well-aged Falernian wine (1.18): it is a commonplace that Falernian demands the best (p. 49).

By Imperial times there were several bridges across the river: furthest north was the *pons Mulvius* which carried the *via Flaminia* on its way from

Rome towards Ariminum and Gaul. It was at this Mulvian bridge that Cicero's agents surprised and arrested Catiline's agents, accompanying the ambassadors from the Allobroges, in one of the dramatic moments of the struggle against Catiline; and it was along this road that Martial imagined the variegated population of imperial Rome, from Knights to visiting Moors, assembled to watch and applaud the longed-for arrival of the new emperor Trajan.[45]

The *Flaminia* was straight enough to show off your charioteering skills, if you had your mistress standing beside you in a *lacerna* (Juvenal 1.58–62). For some miles there were tombs on each side of the road, including that of Paris the *pantomimus* who had been crucified by Domitian. The first stage on this road was *Rubrae*, just outside Rome: this was a red tufa quarry, the City's nearest source of stone, and beside it was a *cauponula* 'low tavern' well named *ad Saxa Rubra* 'The Red Rocks',[46] where Mark Antony once spent a heavy day. He drank far on into the evening, claimed Cicero accusingly, just so that he would arrive in Rome unnoticed after dark (*Philippics* 2.77).

Making due north, the Flaminian Way cut off a wide curve of the Tiber to the east. The territory between the road and the river, the *ager Capenas*,[47] was notable for the shrine of a local goddess, 'where rich Feronia is honoured before all others, and holy Capenas irrigates the river meadows' (Silius 13.84–85). These meadows and groves, *luci Capeni*, were dominated by 'white Soracte', *candidum Soracte*,[48] the snow-clad mountain that opens a famous ode of Horace.

> You see how the snow stands deep on white Soracte, and the groaning woods can no longer carry the burden, and rivers are frozen into hard ice. Dispel the cold! pile wood generously on the fire, Thaliarchus, and bring out a *bouteille* of my more distinguished four-year-old Sabine. Leave the rest to the gods: let them calm the winds that fight over the seething sea, and at once the cypresses and the old ash trees will be still
>
> Horace, *Odes* 1.9; see also p. 258

These swaying *orni* (manna ash, *Fraxinus ornus*) and the whole mountain with its poisonous exhalations were sacred to the *Di Manes* and to *Dis Pater*, gods of the underworld in whose honour priests walked barefoot over burning coals. People came a long way to see the annual ceremony.[49]

Beyond was Falerii, whose little sausages, *breves Falisci*, were almost as famous as the grassy meadows, *herba Falisca*, that nourished a splendid herd of cattle. The *niveae iuvencae*, 'snowy calves' of these meadows were suitable for procession and sacrifice in Rome. Their whiteness was said to be due to the water they drank.[50] Veii, in the hills to the west, was an old Etruscan town, an old enemy of Rome and an early conquest. Veii now sent nothing to Rome but its wine, another of the cheap suburban wines of Rome, the 'thick lees of brown Veientan' which you had better drink, if at all, from a Campanian earthenware mug.[51]

Along the coast of Latium there was a line of towns equally dependent, for their economic character or their very existence, on Rome.

To the left of the Tiber mouth was Rome's traditional port of Ostia, founded, it was said, by Ancus Martius, one of the seven ancient kings. Ostia boasted a lighthouse, visible far out to sea but glowing, like other ancient beacons, with a steady light and thus potentially deceptive, for it might be confused with a star. The Tiber became a 'two-horned' river when a new channel, to the right of the other, was opened up and a new port, Portus, developed at its mouth. The left branch silted up and became unnavigable: river traffic thus concentrated on Portus, but Ostia, easily accessible by road from Rome, remained a major port.[52] Ostia's literary name was made by its sailings, its landings and the capacious and cosmopolitan taverns pictured by Juvenal: 'send to Ostia for him, Caesar, look in the big cookshop there: you'll find him lying alongside some brawler, in among sailors and thieves and runaways, with hangmen and coffin-makers and the silent cymbals of a supine priest of Cybele' (p. 220).

A few miles south-east was Lavinium, honoured as Aeneas's landfall and the true and historic home of Rome's guardian *Penates*. Lavinium was now simply the little town to which one came by way of the *via Laurentina* and from which one approached the Laurentian marshes. Midnight at Naples, said Marcus Aurelius, was warm, like the *Laurentia palus* (p. 55). Why did a Roman know what midnight was like in such an inhospitable-sounding, frog-infested country? Because those Romans fortunate enough to own a property here had not only a seaside residence in the country within seventeen miles of Rome, but also the income from letting excellent winter pasture for sheep and the opportunity to hunt the famous wild boar of the Laurentian woods and marshes. One would go to some trouble in the business of hunting a boar, even if a supercilious gastronome were afterwards to dismiss the result with 'the Laurentian boar is bad, fattened as it is on sedge and reed' (Horace, *Satires* 2.4.42).[53]

The younger Pliny had a house here, on the sea front and closer to Lavinium than to Ostia.

> There is more than one way of getting there. You can either take the *Ostiensis*, with a turning at milestone eleven, or the *Laurentina*, turning off at milestone fourteen. Both of the side-roads are sandy part of the way, so rather heavy and slow going for carriages, but quick and smooth on horseback. The view on either side is varied; sometimes the roads are closed in by belts of woodland, sometimes they look across wide meadows with flocks of sheep and herds of cows and horses, driven down from the mountains in winter to thrive in these grasslands in the spring-like climate.
>
> Pliny, *Letters* 2.17.1–3

The same letter tells us a little of how Roman landscape gardeners handled a villa garden along this exposed coast.

> The ride is marked off with a box hedge, with rosemary filling the gaps. Box thrives where it is protected by buildings, but dies when exposed to the wind and to spray, even if the sea is relatively distant. Inside the circuit of the ride there is a leafy, shady footpath: the soil here is soft and yielding even to bare feet! The kitchen garden has plenty of mulberries and figs: the soil suits these two trees very well but is not so good for others.
>
> 2.17.14–15[54]

The Laurentian coast was a pleasant holiday resort:

> the sea front is pretty, from sea or shore: the line of houses, continuous in places, occasional in others, looks like a succession of towns.... The sea offers excellent sole and crayfish, and all farm produce is supplied by my own lands, milk in particular.
>
> 2.17.27–28

South-east again, beyond the river Numicius and the venerable grove of Anna Perenna,[55] was *spissi litoris Antium*, 'Antium with its sandy shore', a fishing town whose harbour was continually in danger of being choked by sand. Holidaymakers could imagine going fishing here for *lacertus* (chub mackerel, *Scomber colias*), if the weather was calm enough to do more than stroll and count the waves, because this was also *gratum Antium*, 'pleasant Antium', thirty-five miles from Rome, a favoured but sometimes foggy villégiature. Cicero, in 59 BC, found it refreshingly out of the touch with city politics, and that was just what he liked about it. But fashion crept up on it: Nero was born here; Domitian had a villa here. Antium honoured the goddess Fortuna, or rather the two *Fortunae Antiates*, Fortuna Victrix and Fortuna Felix. Their temple housed an oracle whose reputation was improved by the rumour that it had warned Caligula to watch out for a Cassius, the actual name of his assassin.[56]

A few miles further on from Antium was a rocky promontory, *Circaeum iugum*, the 'Circean hill', and the old hill town Circeii. It was supposed to be named after Circe, daughter of the Sun, the witch of Homer's *Odyssey*. On these hills her magical herbs had been picked; here Nereids and nymphs worked in her palace, sorting herbs and flowers into baskets under her direction. If Circeii did not fit their metre, poets felt free to call the place *Circe* instead. *Blanda Circe* 'sweet Circe' was a fine source for oysters (*Ostrea edulis*), in Horace's parodic gastronomy.[57] Not far east of Circeii was Tarracina, where the Appian Way reached the coast. It is to that highway that we now return.

Figure 3   Fishing scene. Detail of a mosaic in the Bardo Museum, Tunis
Source   Photograph: R. Stoneman

From Rome to Rhegium

The *via Appia* was begun by Appius Claudius Caecus in the year of his consulship, 312 BC. His aim was a new road from Rome to Cumae, the old Greek colony on the northern Campanian coast. That was completed by 308. Later, still called *Appia*, the road was extended by way of Capua and Beneventum to Brundisium, the starting point of the shortest sea crossing to Dalmatia and Greece. But its literary traffic, at any rate, was chiefly taking the fashionable route to Rome's most fashionable seaside resorts.

The traveller left Rome by the *Porta Capena*, a loading point for carts (Martial 2.6). *This* traveller is the Umbricius imagined by Juvenal as departing from Rome in disgust for a new life in quiet Cumae (p. 51):

> While his whole house was being loaded on a single wagon he paused at the old arches, the dripping *Capena*. Here Numa had his midnight meetings with his girl friend; but now the sacred spring, its grove and shrine, are farmed out to Jews, whose furniture is a bundle of straw and a basket: each tree must pay its way, the People now insist, and so the *Camenae* are turned out and the woods go begging. We went down into 'Egeria's Valley', towards the artificial grottoes. These waters would surely possess a truer holiness if the pool had grassy banks, and the free-born tufa had not been raped by [foreign] marble.
>
> Juvenal 3.10–20[58]

Two of Rome's great aqueducts passed directly above the Capena Gate. Juvenal suggests the monumental, leaking arches; a sacred spring nearby; and, in the valley beyond, some modern marble encrustation that had spoilt the sanctity of one of Rome's holiest places, where King Numa's picnics with the sweet-voiced goddess Egeria, *suavis sonus Egeriai*, had inspired him to codify the city's laws. In the stream Almo that flowed in the valley the priests of Cybele washed their sacrificial knives.[59] A spring just outside the gate was sacred to Mercury, god of thieves. Salesmen prayed here for indulgence of past and future perjuries, bringing with them the stock they aimed to sell. They themselves, and their stock, had to be sprinkled with holy water, scattered by sprays of bay leaves (Ovid, *Fasti* 5.673–692) which, in the political conditions of Juvenal's time, had to be paid for. The Appian Way, like other roads from Rome, was lined by tombs. Statius lets us sense the feelings that centred on these family memorials – and the aromas too, the cassia, myrrh, incense, cinnamon and other exotics that belonged to death.[60]

> There is a spot just in front of the city where the mighty Appian Way begins, where Cybele washes away her grief in Italian Almo, and ceases to remember the streams of Ida. Here your peerless consort ... laid you, delicately arrayed in Sidonian purple, blissfully to rest. The passage of years shall not harm you; time shall not labour to wither and spoil your beauty, such is the perfumed richness breathed by this noble marble. Why, you are changed into multiple forms, you are reborn! you are this Ceres in bronze, this bright Cretan girl, this Maia under the canopy, that innocent Venus in the middle: the gods are pleased to take on your own lovely features. There is a crowd of servants to attend you, raised to obedience; incessantly couches and tables are ready to your desire. This is your home! It is your home! Who ever would give it the sad name of tomb?
>
> Statius, *Silvae* 5.1.222–238

'I left the great City and put up in a little inn at Aricia. Heliodorus, most scholarly of all Greek teachers of rhetoric, was with me' is the opening of Horace's poetic itinerary (*Satires* 1.5.1–2). Having set out on the Appian Way he had passed Bovillae and Alba, as other travellers did, without remark; he had climbed the hill of Virbius and descended the *clivus Aricinus* 'hill of Aricia' without taking notice of the beggars who clustered at these two places where carriages slowed and riders dismounted.[61] Aricia, his stopping place, was a town 'most ancient in years, our ally under law, our neighbour in territory, most honourable in the nobility of its citizens', as Cicero insisted in the course of scoring a point off Antony (*Philippics* 3.15). It had a greater claim to fame: this was *nemoralis Aricia*, 'Aricia with its grove'. Here, at the southern extremity of Mount Algidus, were dark woods of oak and holm-oak surrounding the mysterious lake of Nemi with a rich and amenable grove and temple of *suburbana Diana*. 'The long boundary fences are draped with hanging threads, and the Goddess has merited the placing of many a votive tablet. A woman whose prayer has been answered is often seen, her brow wreathed, bearing a burning torch from the City to this shrine'. The shrine was tended by a runaway slave who had gained the position of *rex nemorensis* 'King of the Grove' by breaking off a bough from a tree in the grove and then killing his predecessor in single combat (Ovid, *Fasti* 3.263–272). Incidentally a young man who wanted to pick up a girl was well advised to stroll in Diana's grove. The virgin goddess, in her disapproval of Cupid's arrows, would ensure that the wound he received was serious.[62]

Although the inns of Aricia were the first regular day stage on the Appian Way, you might press straight on and try to reach Forum Appi by evening. Lanuvium, a few miles along the road, sent pears to market in Rome; cockcrow at Naples was coldish, like Lanuvium, said Marcus Aurelius (p. 55). *Tres Tabernae* 'Three Inns' came next, and Christians from Rome had come out this far to meet the party among whom were Paul and Luke. The road was now downhill to a village, Ulubrae, famous only for its insignificance – it was the *vacuae Ulubrae*, 'empty Ulubrae' of Juvenal. This was where the Pomptine Marshes began,[63] 'the Pomptine marshes that breed disease, where the misty swamp of Satura covers the land, and the dark Ufens drives his black and muddy current through unsightly fields and dyes the sea with slime' (Silius 8.379–382). 'I write from the Pomptine country', said Cicero to Trebatius. 'I stopped for the night at M. Aemilius Philemo's, and I can hear my clients now outside the window: I mean ... a vast army of frogs that has descended on Ulubrae to have an all night party in my honour' (*Letters to Friends* 7.18).

Luke tells us that some of the Roman Christians had come on from Tres Tabernae to the market town of Forum Appi (*Acts* 28.15: p. 17), overlooked by the vine-growing slopes of Setia. It would have been unwise of them to go beyond Forum Appi: thereafter the two parties could have missed one another. The road continued, but the traveller had the option of changing to a potentially more comfortable canal barge, on which the journey could continue overnight while one slept peacefully.[64] Horace sketches what could go wrong at this point.

> Then to Forum Appi, full of boatmen, barmen and other miscreants. Lazily we had made two stages of this: the smart-paced do it in one, but the Appia is pleasanter if you take it slowly. This was where I declared war on my stomach (it was the dreadful water) and sat there in a bad temper while my chums had their dinner. Night cast its shadows over the earth, the sky was painted with constellations, and the slaves and the boatmen began to exchange insults. 'Get her over here!' 'That's three hundred aboard already! No more room!' Fares paid, mule harnessed: it took an hour. The gnats and the marsh frogs kept me awake; then the

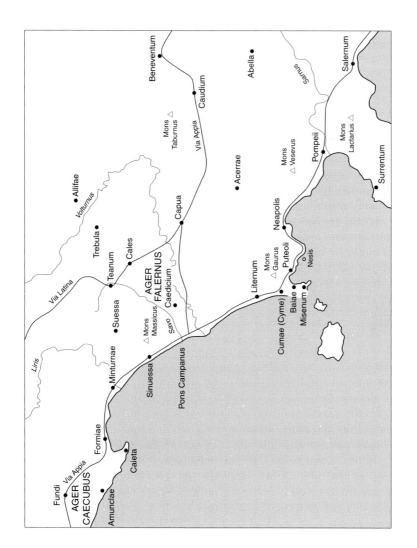

Map 3   From the ager Caecubus to Surrentum: fertile Campania and its hinterland

boatman, soused in cheap wine, sang about his long-lost lover and one of the passengers piped up in competition. The passenger got sleepy at last; the lazy boatman let the mule graze, tying its harness to a rock, and lay on his back snoring. When day came and we realised the boat was not going anywhere, a hot-headed traveller jumped out and set about the mule's hindquarters and the boatman's head with a willow switch. At the fourth hour we landed at last, and rinsed our faces and hands in Feronia's waters. We lunched and trailed up the three miles to Anxur on its gleaming rock, visible from afar.

Horace, *Satires* 1.5

Thus Horace and Heliodorus had taken three days over a journey that 'the smart-paced', with a more active boatman and mule, could have managed in twenty-four hours – but necessarily concluding with an exhausting uphill walk from the waters and 'green grove' of Feronia's shrine, at which travellers by barge must alight, to 'Anxur' on its cliffs overlooking the sea.

Anxur had been the Volscian name for this stronghold. 'The Volscian lost Anxur', and only the hexameter poets kept the name going, because its ordinary Roman name, Tarracina, will not fit into hexameters. Now a quiet seaside retreat, to the poets this was still *superbus Anxur* 'proud Anxur', *impositum saxis late candentibus Anxur* 'Anxur high on its white cliff, shining in the distance', *candidus Anxur salutiferis aquis* 'white Anxur with its healing waters'.[65]

This was where the Appian Way became a coastal road. The traveller followed the shore of the Bay of Amunclae, named after a deserted city (often the spelling is *Amyclae*, with an attractively classical echo of the name of a town near Sparta; the epithet *tacitae Amyclae* 'quiet Amyclae' truly belongs to its namesake).[66] Its place was taken by Fundi, scarcely noisier, its only economic role having been to ship the local wine of the *ager Caecubus*. This vineyard 'in the poplar marshes in the bay of Amyclae was once the most celebrated of all for full flavour. It has been killed by the grower's neglect, by the smallness of the ground, and more still by Nero's project for a ship canal from the lake of Baiae to Ostia' (Pliny 14.61).

Caecuban, traditionally made from vines grown 'married' to trees, had been a great wine, one to be kept for many years.[67] Galen had the privilege of tasting it; but by his time its production had long ceased. After such lengthy maturing, he said, you could not tell whether its tawny colour had been originally red or white – but at that age it was really too bitter to be good drinking (*On Good and Bad Juices* [6.805]). It was one of those wines to be valued rather than drunk. Certainly it was to be kept under lock and key, though for all your precautions you cannot take it with you beyond the grave: 'Your Caecuban, though you keep it behind a hundred locks, will be finished up by your deserving heir: it is he who will stain your mosaic floors with wine in feasts more opulent than those of high priests' (Horace, *Odes* 2.14.25–28).

Horace, on his poetic journey, passed through the Caecuban vineyards without remark, though he knew and loved their wine. He spent the next night at Formiae, a little walled town twelve miles on from Tarracina[68] and a pleasant holiday resort, *temperatae Formiae*, 'mild Formiae ... here just the tips of the waves are brushed by the light wind', writes Martial; in fact the 'tips of Thetis' is his expression, allowing us to imagine the undulant curves of the goddess of the waves lightly goose-pimpled in the breeze:

> The waters are not quite still. Brightly painted boats ride on the lively calm of the sea, driven by a breeze that is like the pleasant freshness that comes to a girl when she wafts her fan to keep the horrid summer away. At Formiae your fishing rod has no need to go to sea for its prey: you can watch the fish from your dining-couch or your bedroom and toss out a line for it. If it is windy out there, Formiae's well-guarded table can laugh at the storms. Its fishing lake stocks turbot and home-bred pike; a pampered lamprey swims in to order; the usher announces a respectable grey mullet; old red mullets are sent for and up they come.
>
> Martial 10.30

Next came the harbour of Caieta, supposed to be named after Aeneas's nurse, and so itself called *Dardanis Caieta* 'Trojan Caieta' and *nutrix Aeneae* 'nurse of Aeneas' by Martial. To Cicero it was *portus Caietae celeberrimus* 'the very well known port of Caieta', but then Cicero was rather free with such expressions.[69]

A few miles on, the road crossed the clear waters of shady Liris, 'a placid stream that pretends to be motionless, never affected by rain' (Silius 4.348–350). 'I have tried the waters of many rivers', wrote Cicero in a dialogue, 'but never one colder than Liris' (*On Laws* 2.6). They meandered through the realm of the goddess Marica, *silva Maricae* 'the wood of Marica', *palus Maricae* 'the marsh of Marica' among whose rushes Marius, after seventy years of adventurous life and six consulships, sank to his neck in mud in a vain attempt to escape Sulla's emissaries.[70]

Just here was the market town of Minturnae, *palustres Minturnae* 'marshy Minturnae', *graves Minturnae* 'oppressive Minturnae', where Marius, having been pulled out of the mud, was taken for execution (but he escaped).[71] And we are in wine country again. Horace speaks of wine bottled 'between marshy Minturnae and Petrinum-under-Sinuessa' (p. 256), and he means the wine of *mons Massicus*, of *Massicus uvifer* 'the grape-laden Massic hill', another high-class name among Italian wines: 'This vintage never flowed from a Paelignian press; this grape did not grow on Tuscan props. No, a happy jar of old Opimian is being drained, a Massic store-room yields us its blackened amphoras' (Martial 1.26). Massic wine would keep for years, and would become a heavy and heady vintage as it grew old, *obliviosum Massicum* 'forgetful Massic'.[72] A wine buff would remind you that after opening it should stand in the fresh air for a while before drinking (Horace, *Satires* 2.4.51–54).

The market town of Sinuessa, *niveis frequens Sinuessa columbis* 'Sinuessa with its many snow-white doves' was next along the coast from Minturnae. It was the centre of the trade in Massic wine. It had something more to offer: it was *mollis Sinuessa* 'soft Sinuessa', *Sinuessa tepens* 'warm Sinuessa'. Its mineral spring produced *Sinuessanae undae*, 'the waves of Sinuessa', creating a warm water pool that would cure sterility in women – a convenient excuse, one poet observed, for a woman to travel away from home and meet her lover – and senility in men. Narcissus, Claudius's faithful minister, had retired to the baths of Sinuessa, to recover his failing health in its soft climate and healing waters, at the moment when the empress Agrippina struck at the old emperor with her poisoned mushrooms. Narcissus himself returned to Rome, to prison and suicide.[73]

For whatever reason, Horace's party avoided the inns of Sinuessa. 'The little farm nearest the Campanian Bridge put us up' (Horace, *Satires* 1.5). That bridge over the little river Savo marked the border between Latium and Campania. 'This is where *felix illa Campania* begins', Pliny tells us, applying a Latin adjective equally appropriate to cheerful people and to fertile farmland; and he steps back mentally to survey the landscape. 'From this curve of coast rise the vine-laden hills' which he will lay out in order. To his left, as he gazes inshore, are the Setine and Caecuban districts that we have already passed through. Directly before him, the Falernian slopes, and the Calene hills behind. Flanking these on each side and rising boldly, the mons Massicus to the left, the volcanic Gaurus to the right. Far off beyond Gaurus is the high promontory of Surrentum, also covered in vines.

> These shores are watered by hot springs, and they are renowned above all other seas for their fine fish and shellfish. Nowhere does the olive yield a richer oil. This prize of the pleasures of mankind has been held by Oscans, Greeks, Umbrians, Etruscans, Campanians.
>
> Pliny 3.60–61

This, then, was the beginning of the most famous, if not in all eyes the finest, of the wine regions of Italy. 'The *ager Falernus* begins at the Campanian bridge: you turn left, taking the road to Colonia Urbana (founded by Sulla in Capuan territory). You enter the *Faustianus* about four miles after passing the village of Caedicium (which is six miles out of Sinuessa)' which also supplied cheese for the Roman market. 'It is sometimes said that *Caucinum* is the wine from the hill tops, *Faustianum* from the middle slopes, *Falernum* from the low'. Of these three Falernian *terroirs*, *Faustianum* had the highest reputation, but 'this wine, too, is now past its best because the producers have aimed for quantity rather than quality'.

For all that, 'no wine of today commands greater respect' (Pliny 14.62–63). Falernian was *ardens* 'fiery', so that you might need to cool it down with spring water (p. 246) or – paradoxically – with hot water. It was *forte* 'strong'. In Horace's mind it was *severum*. The word means something more than 'dry': wines are generally dry unless doctored, but only Falernian is said to be 'severe', and we might taste something of the *aglianico* of modern Campania in this uncompromising adjective.

When Silius decides to explain the invention of wine (7.162–211), it is at the humble but hospitable cottage of Falernus, on mount Massicus, that Bacchus produces the magical liquid. 'Take my gift,' says Bacchus, 'strange to you as yet, but fated to spread the name of the vine-dresser Falernus across the world,' and Falernus renders slurred thanks to the God before falling into drunken sleep. Falernian is ubiquitous in Roman poetry. Sometimes the name is attached to details that persuade the reader to take it literally. Sometimes *Falernum* is there because it is the single word that proves it was a good wine and a good party. Elms are 'Falernian elms' because this is the tree to which vines are best 'married';[74] why, even the distant aroma of a broken jar of Falernian was evocative (p. 264). And not only in poetry. In precisely the same way, Falernian was actually ubiquitous in Roman festivity. The whole Empire seemed to be drinking it: could all that Falernian really be genuine?[75]

Falernian was one of those wines that was more valuable the more years you had it in storage. We read often enough of 'old Falernian', or of the *vetulus Falernus* 'Falernian that's getting on a bit' of Catullus and Martial. The value increased, especially of the best-reputed vintages: drinkability, however, reached a peak and then declined, a fact that Cicero used to make a moral point:

> 'Just as if one liked Falernian wine, but did not want it so new as to carry the name of last year's consuls, and did not look for it so old as the consulship of Opimius or Anicius....'
> 'But those are the best vintages!'
> 'So they are, but excessive age does not give us the smoothness that we look for, it is not truly drinkable.'
>
> Cicero, *Brutus* 287

The speaker goes on to compare the Anician vintage of Falernian, over a hundred years old when Cicero was writing *Brutus*, to the literary style of Thucydides, a comparison which many a student of classical Greek will easily grasp.[76]

Falernian wine was not all of the same style. Pliny talks of 'three styles, *austerum, dulce, tenue*', meaning roughly 'dry, soft, light'; it is the first of these, one supposes, that could be further characterised as *severum*. Some Falernian was *niger* 'black' (as deep red wine really is when not seen through glass). Some was amber-coloured, for the best quality of amber on the Roman market was named 'Falernian' after the wine; this colour, *xanthos* in Greek, belonged especially to the produce of the *Faustianum* terroir. Galen describes this kind of Falernian as 'moderately sweet'.[77]

The severity of Falernian could be modified, by the fastidious or health-conscious gourmet, but at the risk of wasting the considerable expenditure that had been laid out on high quality wine. You could sweeten it by adding fresh sweet must, but it would be stupid to add 'must put up in Vatican jars' – from the poor vineyards on the right bank of the Tiber – to well-aged Falernian (Martial 1.18). You could make a fine *mulsum* 'sweet aperitif' with Falernian (p. 141); you could argue that it was unwise to drink Falernian at all unless 'diluted' with honey, and then it must be the best honey, from Mount Hymettus.[78] Horace's budding gastronome, the fictional Catius, was taught that this was quite unwise because Falernian is strong, you drink *mulsum* on an empty stomach, and you should fill empty 'veins' with mild foods only (*Satires* 2.4.24–27), but there was certainly an opinion that new Hymettian and well-aged Falernian were an appropriate match (p. 142).

The Campanian Bridge and the *ager Falernus* have taken us briefly from the coast: this is where the extended Appian Way turned inland for Capua and eventually Brundisium. We now return to the busy and noisy coast road, built by Hercules himself (it was said) but long in need of Domitian's repairs:

> What fearful sound of hard flint and heavy iron fills the stony *Appia* where it elbows the sea? Certainly no Libyan hordes are thundering, no foreign chieftain scours restlessly the Campanian fields in treacherous warfare, nor is Nero cutting a canal, and making a way for squalid swamps by slicing up the mountains.

None of the above, Statius assures us. Not for the first time, he is commemorating the public spirit of the ruling emperor Domitian

> who, impatient with the slow journeys of his people and the soil that clogs every journey, is straightening tedious diversions and paving a new road upon the heavy sands, happy to bring the Euboean Sibyl's home and the curves of Gaurus and sweltering Baiae nearer to the Seven Hills.

'Here, in times past, the slow traveller rode a wet axle, swaying as if crucified, while the unfriendly earth sucked at his wheels…. But now a journey that once took a solid day is over in just two hours', adds Statius, scarcely exaggerating at all the best possible time from the Volturnus bridge to Cumae. He describes the road-building in progress – the only such description in Roman literature. It was noisy work, Statius makes clear:

> the shores and the waving woods are on the move; the sounds can be heard all through the cities between, and vine-bearing Massicus sends back the broken echoes to Gaurus. Quiet Cyme and the Liternian marsh and sluggish Savo marvel at the noise.

At last the road is built:

> Its auspicious threshold is an arch as vast as the rainbow, shining with
> the Emperor's trophies and with all the marble of Liguria. This is where
> poor *Appia* is abandoned: the traveller turns off and increases his pace.
> One who leaves Tiber at dawn may be sailing the Lucrine lake as
> evening falls.
>
> Statius, *Silvae* 4.3, abridged

Yes, this was just about possible for a dispatch rider able to change horses
regularly, the total distance from Rome to Baiae being 140 miles.

On, then, to the seaside towns of Campania, crossing the wide Volturnus
near its mouth, *vadosus Vulturnus* 'Vulturnus with its shallows', *fluctu sonorus
Volturnus* 'Volturnus with its noisy waters' and its rushy banks,[79] and passing
through the wetlands of Liternum, called by Ovid *lentisciferum Liternum*
'lentisk-bearing Liternum', an adjective one might have expected to belong
to the Greek island of Chios (p. 151).[80]

Cumae was a very ancient Greek foundation, a colony of Chalcis in
Euboea but afterwards an Oscan township, *veteres Cumae* 'old Cumae', *Euboica
urbs* 'the Euboean city'. It was now a shrunken place, *quieta Cyme* 'quiet
Cumae', *vacuae Cumae* 'empty Cumae',[81] a picturesquely old-fashioned
municipality where a woman caught in adultery would be driven through
the streets on a donkey and given the ambiguous epithet *onobatis* 'donkey-
mounted' (Plutarch, *Greek Questions* 2).

Cumae still had economic assets under the Roman Empire. Its supply of
clay made it a centre for the manufacture of Campanian red earthenware,
which belonged to the general class known as 'Samian', the cheap tableware
and kitchenware that Rome used every day – including *patellae* and *patinae*,
typically Italian baking-dishes unknown in Greek usage. 'Samian pots can
keep my party going, and slippery clay turned on a Cumaean wheel', said
Tibullus (2.3.47–48) sounding the same slightly defiant note with which
Horace insists that Campanian ware garnishes his own sideboard (p. 223).
There was certainly an opinion that such cheap crockery as a *Campana trulla*
'ladle', for example, ought to be confined to the kitchen, and would be seen
doing duty as a wine-ladle only if the person giving the party were practically incapable of spending money.[82]

Once the Greek gateway to Capua, 'empty Cumae' now served rather as
the Roman 'gateway to Baiae, a charming coast and pleasantly secluded (I'd
rather choose Prochyta itself than the Suburra!)' Juvenal's parenthesis
(3.2–5) points up his ironic understatement. Cumae was indeed almost as
deserted as the rocky offshore islet of Prochyta.

At this point the traveller entered the actively volcanic region of
Campania, extending as far as Vesuvius and most often given a new-fangled
mythological name, *campi Phlegraei* 'Phlegraean fields' after Phlegra in
Greece, the place where Zeus struck the Giants with lightning. The name

could stretch as far as the peak of Vesuvius itself, *vertex Phlegraeus*, but it applied especially to the strange country defined by the triangle of roads between Capua, Cumae and Puteoli, *sulphure pingues Phlegraei sinus* 'the Phlegraean shores, rich in sulphur', well known as the site of violent eruptions in past times: 'now cold for many years, yet forever excreting sulphur in rich supply. It is collected as merchandise' (*Aetna* 432–434). The real local name of these Phlegraean fields was *Leboriae*, and as Campania had the most fertile soil of Italy, so Leboriae excelled in Campania.

Here was the fabled Avernus, *stagna Averni* 'the pool of Avernus', *nebulosum litus Averni* 'the foggy banks of Avernus' over which no birds flew, and any that did were asphyxiated by the sulphurous fumes continually renewed from hot springs feeding the lake. Its poisoned and ominous waters, *Avernales aquae*, were needed in witchcraft, for here too was the entrance to the underworld: the name *Avernus* could easily be transferred by poets from the lake in Campania to the world below. Here was the Sibyl's cave, where oracles were sought and given: every Cumaean was the chaste old hag's fellow-citizen. She was seven hundred years old, in Ovid's time, and still had three hundred years to live.[83] The backbone of the district was the crater-formed ridge of Gaurus, *sulphureus Gaurus, Gaurus inanis* 'gaping Gaurus' with its volcanic vents, *frondentia Nysaea cacumina Gauri*. Its crests were 'Nysaean' because these apparently barren volcanic slopes were leafy with the vine beloved of Nysaean Bacchus. Its wine was the 'Cumaean wine' of Athenaeus.[84]

There are few more startling contrasts, in Roman geography, than the contrast between Cumae and its close neighbour 'Baiae, golden shore of happy Venus, pleasant gift of proud Nature' (Martial 11.80), the holiday playground of the rich and leisured aristocracy of Rome.

As you crossed the narrow promontory of Misenum you passed from the sulphurous miasma of the Phlegraean fields to the shore of the Bay of Naples. This bay was 'the mixing-bowl', *Krater*, in Greek. The shores between the two capes of Misenum and Surrentum were 'entirely laid out with towns and villas and gardens in an unbroken line, giving the appearance of a single city' (Strabo 5.4.8). And first you came to Baiae.

'No bay in the whole world is brighter than pretty Baiae', says a rich man about to build his villa there (Horace, *Epistles* 1.1.83). Facing the brightest of morning sunshine, this 'pleasantest of beaches', *blandissima litora*, earned Baiae the names of *liquidae Baiae, aestuantes Baiae, vaporiferae Baiae*, 'cloudless, sweltering, steamy Baiae'.[85] Only the most circumspect of poets paid attention to its claimed Homeric ancestry and its threateningly volcanic neighbourhood (the founder was Baius, one of Odysseus's sailors, so it was said, and Silius called this 'the Ithacan seat of Baius, burning with the Giants' breath': 8.538–539). Others allowed themselves to be seduced by its scenery. The hillsides were green with myrtle groves, admittedly not the most useful of garden plants except for one quality much in demand at Baiae: they provided aromatic wreaths for banquets. Luxury villas were scattered across the seaward-facing slopes and, in some cases, boldly invaded the realm of the sea.

Convalescents took sulphur baths in the naturally hot springs, the clear warm air performing the usual function of a Roman hot bath by stimulating the perspiration. So, in Martial's logic, 'a white nymph swims the sulphureous waters' of Baiae – she is frosted white with crystallised sulphur. The more active could enjoy the pleasures, with none of the usual frustrations, of sea-fishing, by walking out along the harbour moles: these were lined with fish farms.[86] And visitors probably spent a good deal of time on the beach and at the table.

Baiae was a resort where fine seafood and money came together in a perfect marriage. *Apicius* tells us of a local seafood dish, *Embractum Baianum*, a lavish way to use sea urchins.

> BAIAN CASSEROLE: minced oysters, mussels, sea urchins. Put in the saucepan chopped toasted pine kernels, rue, celery, pepper, coriander, cumin, raisin wine, fish sauce, *caryota* dates, oil.
>
> *Apicius* 9.11 [9.14 Flower and Rosenbaum; 433 André]

The Lucrine lake, seaward from Avernus, was renowned for its shellfish, *Lucrina conchylia, concha*. These are Greek words: there are Latin equivalents, but Greek was evidently traditional, among consumers as well as fishermen, for this luxury local product. Some species may have been brought from Greece to be farmed in the controlled environment of the lake. There were excellent oysters, but the great speciality of the Lucrine lake was *peloris* (probably carpet-shell, French *palourde*, *Venerupis decussata*). In a poem by Martial an ordinary *aquosa peloris*, from open sea (probably *Venerupis aurea*, French *clovisse*, half the size), is served to the client while the patron is getting a famous *Lucrina peloris* from the lake itself (p. 99); and the fineness of this fictional patron's discernment is confirmed for us by the specialist dietary writer Xenocrates.[87] Horace allows us additional local detail. We can now see that he is ridiculing the gastronomic precepts, not inventing them: 'New moons swell the slippery shellfish; yet not every sea is fertile in the succulent shell. A Lucrine *peloris* is better than a Baian purple-shell. Oysters are born at Circeii, urchins at Misenum, but soft Tarentum boasts its saucer-like coquilles' (*Satires* 2.4.30–34).[88]

A stay at Baiae was bound to be expensive. One went there to enjoy oneself, and one did so in society – a society that spent freely on its pleasures, gastronomic and otherwise. Baiae was also sufficiently far from Rome for Rome's own moral rules to be relaxed.[89] A Roman tourist expected sexual fun at Baiae. That is why, when planning to swap Baiae for a Lucanian seaside resort, Horace fantasises about a *Lucana amica* 'Lucanian girl-friend' (p. 57). Baiae was a good place to find a lover, but was not as healthy as its reputation, Ovid joked: he knew a man who had come back to Rome with a wound in the heart. Baiae was 'where unmarried girls become public women, where old men turn into boys again – and a good many boys are turned into girls' (Varro, *Menippean Satires* 44 Bücheler). As he set about destroying anything that was left of Clodia's reputation, Cicero had no doubt of persuading his Roman audience that passers-by could have observed her engaging in 'the most degrading acts' under that sunniest of skies in the course of her well-attended beach parties at Baiae (*For Caelius* 47–49).[90]

To either side of Baiae were seaports: each of them, not surprisingly in Baiae's neighbourhood, had a gastronomic speciality. Noble Misenum, *nobiles Miseni*, was out along the promontory beneath a beetling rock. This was a naval base, and a source of sea urchins in Horace's parodic gastronomy.[91]

In the opposite direction one passed the Lucrine lake, divided from the sea by a spit of sand which Agrippa reinforced to make a safe road. Then, around the bay, one came to Puteoli, an important place. The afternoons were hot, said Marcus Aurelius (p. 55): it faces south-west. It produced the earth known as *Puteolanus pulvis*, pozzolana, used in making cement and concrete; and a red pigment used in painting and cosmetics, *purpurissum*, made of chalk coloured with shellfish purple. Puteoli had once been a Greek city. It was so no longer, but its old Greek name, *Dicarchis, Dikaiarkheia*, is found in poetry both Latin and Greek. In its artificial harbours – protected by long moles built from its own native concrete, as Strabo observes – Puteoli received the fleets of the whole world, notably the fleet that brought Rome's grain from Egypt. Seneca describes 'all the mob of Puteoli' gathering at the harbour as the flagships lead the way across the bay. Puteoli had as much claim as Ostia to be considered Rome's seaport, though this role was threatened by Claudius's developments at the Tiber mouth. Most of the luxuries and rarities of the Roman Empire were to be seen from time to time at Puteoli: Mucianus (says Pliny) had seen elephants disembark, rear end first, off a ship in Puteoli harbour.[92]

The dirty, muddy coast road ran on from Puteoli to Naples, passing through a long, wide tunnel. If you sailed, you passed close enough to wooded *Nesis*, the 'little island', to note that it was overrun with rabbits, a gastronomic delicacy unfamiliar in most of Italy.[93]

Naples had once been the *nea polis*, the 'new city' among the Greek colonies hereabouts. Now it was an ancient place and still a centre of Greek culture, the culture of words and books and pleasure for which Romans reserved their leisure hours. It was *docta, facunda, otiosa Neapolis* 'learned, amusing, leisured Naples' and, since it had a Homeric by-name as well (Parthenope was supposed to have been one of the Sirens) it was *dulcis Parthenope* 'sweet Parthenope', *in otia nata Parthenope* 'Parthenope born to leisure'. 'They are Romans now, but numerous features of the Greek way of life survive there', wrote Strabo (5.4.7); any Greek city had its witty and learned courtesans, as Romans knew well, so a typical *meretrix Neapolitis* 'Neapolitan courtesan' was no surprise (Afranius 136). To the gastronome Naples offered wine, roast chestnuts (says Martial) and, much more important, the Lucullan fish ponds, *Neapolitanae piscinae*. Not the least of the

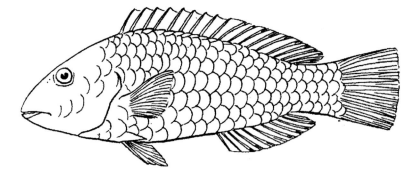

Figure 4   *Euscarus cretensis*, that stunning little fish the 'parrot wrasse'
Source   From D'Arcy Thompson, *A Glossary of Greek Fishes* (London, 1947)

delicacies bred here was the *scarus* (*Scarus cretensis*, parrot-wrasse). This stunning little fish, with its purple back, pink sides and violet tail with an edge of white, is not especially good to eat. What Romans liked was its beauty – to display this it was brought to table still alive – and its rarity: it had been unknown in Italian waters until an ambitious gastronome had taken the trouble to catch a large number of them in the Aegean and transport them to the fishponds of Campania.[94]

> Naples has become even more of a Greek city because of the number from Rome who have retired there, looking for health, rest and relaxation, teachers in particular. There are plenty of Romans who happen to like the Greek way of life ... and have fallen in love with Naples and come to live there too.
>
> Strabo 5.4.7

The emperor Marcus Aurelius weighed up the attractions of the city in a private letter to his tutor Fronto.

> The climate of Naples is quite nice, but terribly changeable. Every five minutes it turns colder or warmer or wetter. To begin with, the middle of the night is warm and Laurentan; cockcrow is coldish and Lanuvian; the still of night and first light and dawn are icy, just like Algidus; then morning is sunny and Tusculan; afternoon is hot and Puteolan; when the sun takes his bath in the sea it gets milder, Tiburtine fashion; and that is how it stays through the evening, till bedtime.
>
> Marcus Aurelius [Fronto, *Letters* vol. 1, p. 142 Haines]

The land south-east of Naples was under the shadow of Mount Vesuvius, *vaporiferus Vesevus* 'smoking Vesuvius', whose summit was burnt and barren but whose lower slopes were of wonderful fertility, equally suitable for crops and herds. The *murgentina* vine, 'the same as *pompeiana*', had been transplanted here from Sicily and gave high yields in the rich volcanic soil, vying with *gemina minor*. Already Cato had advised on what aspect would suit each of these two varieties. The river Sarnus, *Pompeianus Sarnus*, flowing gently through these meadows, reached the sea at Pompeii.[95]

From here the Bay of Naples curves westwards to a mountainous peninsula. The hill pastures of *mons Lactarius* were later renowned for the rich milk of their cows, recommended to invalids and attributed to the lush pasture of that volcanic soil (Cassiodorus, *Variae* 11.10).

On the northern coast was *Surrentum molle Zephyro salubri* 'Surrentum, gentle with its healthy west wind' – ideal ground, because of its climate, for the *gemina minor* grape variety, which liked a western breeze, but not a south wind. These generous north-west-facing slopes produced one of the noblest wines of Italy, said to have been highest of all in reputation in the early period before Falernian came into its own – but we are told this only by much later sources. In the early Empire it was fashionable to be slightly supercilious about *lenia Surrentina*, 'light Surrentine wines'.[96] Tiberius, who no doubt served it to his guests on Capreae, called the stuff *generosum acetum* 'full-bodied vinegar'. Caligula, not to be outdone by his predecessor, labelled it *nobilis vappa* 'noble plonk'. It was appropriate, said Martial (14.102), not to drink Surrentine wine out of *murrina picta* (p. 188) or gold, but to use earthenware – Surrentine ware, with modelled decoration in low relief.[97] Martial makes history here: this is the first time in the history of gastronomy that anyone suggested serving a local product with appropriate local tableware.

Just off the promontory of Surrentum was Capri, *Capreae*, poetically noted as the rocky lair of mythological Telon but also of a historical figure. 'Who has not heard of Nero's nasty executions, or of the rocks of Capri, obscene domain of a perverted old man?' asked Claudian rhetorically (*Panegyric on Honorius' Fourth Consulship* 313–315). This was the sour emperor Tiberius: it was indeed on Capri that he enjoyed his legendary indecencies and sent the occasional oracular and deadly letter to Rome.[98]

Surrentum was on a side road. The main road south from Naples crossed the ridge and made directly for Salernum, whose attractions were humorously explored by Horace as he thrashed about for a possible replacement for Baiae, with which he claimed to be in dispute:

> How's the winter at Velia, and what's the weather like at Salernum? What kind of people round there? What's the road like? You see, Antonius Musa said 'Not Baiae!' So Baiae is cross with me: I take a cold bath in winter, it complains; I have absconded from its myrtle groves; I spurn its famous sulphur baths that drive any lingering ailment from the muscles. Baiae dislikes invalids who dip their heads and their stomachs under the waters of Clusium or make for Gabii and the cold country. I must go elsewhere, and steer my horse away from the familiar inns.... Which town has better supplies of wheat? Do they drink rain-

Map 4   Southern Italy and Sicily

water from tanks, or do they have perennial wells? because I've no time for their wine. On my own farm I can put up with anything; when I go to the seaside I want a full, mellow wine to soothe my cares ... and make a Lucanian girl-friend think I'm young. Which has more hares in its hunting grounds? Which has more wild boars? Which bay provides more fish and sea-urchins? I want to come home as fat as a Phaeacian.

Horace, *Epistles* 1.15.1–25[99]

From this point southwards, crossing from Campania into Lucania, the coast road led to 'warm Paestum', 'twice-bearing Paestum', a pretty place best known for its rose-gardens, *rosaria tepidi Paesti, biferi Paesti*. These roses came to Roman markets by sea, and were claimed by Martial to be better than Egypt's finest, which happened to have been sent as a present to Domitian.[100]

The road from Rome to Rhegium ran through inland Lucania, missing Paestum. Instead it followed the valley of 'dry Tanager' and the 'groves of Silarus', under mount Alburnus 'leafy with holm-oaks' through a country known to Vergil for its gadflies (*Georgics* 3.146–151) to reach Cosilinum, notable for the annual fair which – in the sixth century – had been held since time immemorial in the Marcilianum meadows outside the town at a sacred spring, sacred once to the nymph Leucothea and after her to St Cyprian, miraculously pure under both religions.

> Everything exported by industrious Campania, by the wealthy Bruttii, by the Calabrians rich in herds and by the versatile Apulians, and everything that Lucania herself has to offer, is displayed among the stock of this excellent market. You may see the broad meadows there forested with beautiful arbours, and temporary houses woven from fresh fronds, and a crowd of people singing and laughing. There are no walls visible, yet you may see the splendour of a proud city.
>
> Cassiodorus, *Variae* 8.33

The *opulenti Brutii* 'wealthy Bruttii' occupied the toe of Italy. Theirs was a mountainous region, productive of reddish *Brutia dura* 'hard Bruttian pitch', useful medicinally and in construction, product of the *taeda* (stone pine, *Pinus cembra*). The landscape was dominated by the forested mount Sila, *magna Sila*. The lowland pastures were rich in oxen (here lived the *formosa iuvenca* 'pretty calf' around whom Vergil weaves a bovine love story: Vergil, *Georgics* 3.219). The hill slopes were purple with vines, yielding a sweet white wine as aromatic as incense, a wine that Cassiodorus, Bruttian by birth, knew as *Palmatiana*. Bruttium was especially productive, at least at the end of the Empire, in horses, for the dense shade of its forests protected them from flies and provided green fodder even in the heat of summer. Here even the peasant could enjoy the fine food that townsmen expect. The round cheeses of Mount Sila, *casei Silani*, were of wonderful whiteness and smoothness. The cities of the region, such as the Bruttian capital Consentia and the neighbouring harbour town of Clampetia, were regarded by Livy, an earlier and less sympathetic observer, as *ignobiles civitates* that did not deserve the title – for all their warm climate that persuaded apple trees to fruit twice a year.[101] The road from Rome passed through Consentia and returned to the coast near Tempsa, a little town that was celebrated poetically for copper, *Temesaea aera*, on the chance that the abandoned mines near here were the *Temese* mentioned as a source of copper in the *Odyssey*.[102]

Rhegium is the end of this road, busy with crossings to Sicily and with more distant voyages. Cicero, leaving Italy in troubled times in the summer of 44 BC, was coasting from Pompeii to Rhegium and outlined, to his confidant Atticus, the possible onward routes from which he would have to choose. Leucopetra, the southern tip of Italy, appears on the evidence of this letter to have been the terminal for fast Tarentine passenger boats that followed the old Greek coasting route from Sicily along the 'instep' of Italy and thence to Corcyra and Ambracia.

> So far (I have now reached Sicca's place at Vibo) my voyage has been comfortable rather than strenuous, by oar in large part: no northerlies. We were in luck to cross both the two bays we had to cross (of Paestum and of Vibo) with sheets level. So I arrived at Sicca's a week after leaving Pompeii, having stopped for one day at Velia.... But when I reach Rhegium I suppose I shall there have to consider, *pondering a lengthy voyage*, whether to make for Patrae by a cargo boat, or by the little Tarentine ferry to Leucopetra and from there to Corcyra; and if I choose the freighter, whether direct from the Straits or from Syracuse.
>
> Cicero, *Letters to Atticus* 16.6[103]

The territory of Rhegium was mountainous, said Cassiodorus, too dry for pasture and for grain though adequate for vines and deep-rooted olives. Endives, however, grew especially sweet at Rhegium. The moray eels taken in its waters had a milky delicacy of flavour, and had been renowned at least since the earliest known gastronomic author instructed the readers of his *Life of Luxury* to 'buy the moray, called floater, at the narrow straits of Italy – if you can'.[104] Under the early Empire 'morays used to be brought to the fish ponds of Rome from the Sicilian Strait: that is where the best are found, gluttons tell us ... they are called *plotai* 'floaters' in Greek, *flutae* in Latin, because they sometimes float on the water's surface in the heat of the sun' (Macrobius, *Saturnalia* 3.15.7).

The southern hinterland

The road to Rhegium has taken us through a series of famous coastal cities, great wine districts and what would certainly now be called holiday resorts. Traditional Italy lay in the background.

From Rome to the Campanian Bridge we skirted Latium, the first home-land of the Latin language. We saw nothing to explain why the region is characterised as *Latium ferox* 'savage Latium' in the poetry of the Empire. 'Mars is to be honoured in Latium, because he presides in warfare', Ovid insists.[105] Though the peace of Latium had scarcely been disturbed since the early first century BC, historically it was where Rome had first established her power in the course of long and bitter warfare. Even before that, Latium was where Aeneas had fought his battles to build the new Troy on Italian soil. Many a quiet, insignificant, dying or lost township comes equipped with a poetic epithet asserting its ancient prowess (Vergil, *Aeneid* 7.601–802).

Via Latina, the Latin Way, was the route from Rome through inland Latium to Capua: through a country that was once warlike and still somewhat flinty. You passed Ferentinum, so quiet a country town that Horace selected it as the one place to go if you can't stand travel and noise and inns (perhaps he once looked for an inn there and did not find one: *Epistles* 1.17.8). You passed below Arpinum, its typical citizen the *Arpinas hispidus* 'rough Arpinian', most famous among them the rough and heroic Marius, born to *Arpinas paupertas* 'Arpinian poverty', and the more complex and sensitive Cicero.[106] You passed through Aquinum in the Liris valley, known for a cheap red or purple dye, *Aquinas fucus*, cheap or poor enough that one had better not be foolish enough to confuse it with Tyrian.[107] And 95 miles out of Rome was the market town of *nebulosum Casinum* 'foggy Casinum'. The local speciality here was green oil, properly made by picking olives before they ripened,[108] an expensive procedure: the potential of the berries, in quantity terms, is being wasted, and it is interesting that the practical Cato, who farmed at nearby Venafrum, suggests economising by using only windfalls, thus leaving the whole remaining crop to mature.

> Make green oil as follows: Collect windfall olives as quickly as possible. If dirty, wash them, clear them of leaves and manure. Make oil one day or two days after picking.
>
> Cato, *On Farming* 65

Teanum and Cales were the nearest towns to Suessa on the road to Capua (Map 3). The flourishing town of Teanum, capital of the Sidicini, produced table olives that were among the best in Italy, just as its neighbour Venafrum produced the best oil. Cales, lying just above the *ager Falernus*, was a producer of wine. *Molle Calenum* 'soft Calene' was once rated very high. Some said it was healthier than Falernian. Maecenas, every Augustan poet's patron, liked it, says Horace.[109]

But Teanum and Cales were already in Campania, *pinguis Campania* 'fat Campania' to Propertius, *felix Campania* 'fertile Campania' in Pliny's prose, with its black soil that could be stirred into dust clouds by a north wind but grew the best emmer in Italy – or in the world – and also grew the aromatic and medicinal plant melilot, known to Romans from its use in wreaths as *serta Campanica, sertula Campana* 'Campanian garlands' (*Melilotus officinalis*). Ethnically, Campania was a melting pot: Greeks had long occupied the coast; Oscan was the language of the country, and *Osci* was the name for people who spoke it. But *dives Capua*, 'wealthy' and multilingual Capua, once Etruscan-ruled, then independent, now Roman, governed the fertile farmland where many Romans now had large slave-run estates.[110]

To Romans, in fact, *Campani* meant both the people of the city, and the people of the whole region of which it was the capital.

'The Campanians are proud. Of course they are! Proud of the excellence of their soil and the abundance of their crops; proud of their healthy, well-planned, beautiful city', said Cicero, stirring prejudices in ill-planned Rome (*On the Agrarian Law* 2.95: see p. 209). To early Romans Capua's senate had been *senatus Campanus* and its walls had been *moenia Campana*. Later Romans took a long time to forget that the *aemula virtus Capuae* 'presumptuous bravery of Capua' had led the city into an alliance with Hannibal. Had that alliance triumphed, Capua would have taken the place of Rome as first city of Italy.

It was confidently said that the luxury of Capua had softened up Hannibal and his army for their eventual defeat. This luxury was displayed in bright-coloured drapery, *peristromata Campanica*, and in many other imported goods: Capua had for centuries been the great trading centre in this part of Italy, one main reason for the establishment of Cumae and other Greek colonies along the coast.[111] Central, then, to its wealth were the two markets, *Albana* and *Seplasia*. The latter was a perfume and spice market, and a kind of capital of this trade as far as Italy was concerned, so that a new singular form *Seplasium* came to be used as a general term for such aromatic merchandise (Petronius 76). We might have thought this simply an illiteracy on the part of Petronius's speaker, but similar formations are not unusual linguistically and this one was certainly adopted by other Roman businessmen as well as by the fictional Trimalchio.[112] 'I beg and pray you, as you hope to have plenty of *sirpe* and *laserpicium* this year and to get it all exported to Capua safe and sound' – exclaims a character in Plautus's play *The Rope* (629–630). The setting is Cyrene, sole exporter of that particular product (p. 110) and it is evident that to a Roman audience of the second century BC Capua was the one most obvious landfall for a valuable cargo of spices. It was also, at least in Cato's time, the centre for buying all kinds of products made from that useful Spanish plant *spartum*, 'esparto' or Spanish broom, *Lygeum spartum* (p. 104).[113]

Among the most fertile districts of Campania were the territories of Acerrae – the flood plain of the river Clanius was fertile and versatile farmland for crops and herds[114] – and Abella (see Map 3). This town was 'poor in cereal fields', *pauper sulci cerealis Abella*, but cereals are not everything: it was linked with two other foods. *Nuces Abellanae* were actually named after it: they were a cultivated hazelnut or filbert (*Corylus avellana, C. colurna*), hence French *aveline* 'filbert'. And in poetry we hear of *moenia maliferae Abellae*, the 'walls of apple-bearing Abella'.[115] It has been suggested, because of this association, that the name *Abella* is an Italic descendant of the prehistoric word from which English *apple*, Welsh *afal* and Russian *jabloko* also derive.

Campania shared its local language, Oscan, with the much more mountainous region of Samnium that bordered it to the north-east. This in fact is the Italic language of central southern Italy, a close relative of Latin but with a very different fate. Gradually *Osci* would come to mean little more than 'Italian peasants' in Latin usage, and Romans knew that the Greek equivalent name *Opikoi* had an even stronger pejorative force, 'barbarous, unlettered Italians': Latin *Opici* took the same meaning. The emperor Marcus Aurelius asks Fronto to 'correct my Greek before you pass this letter on to your mother. I don't want her to think me an *Opicus*' (Fronto, *Letters* vol. 1, p. 124 Haines).

The once formidable military might of Samnium eventually came to be remembered only in the name of the *Samnis*, a style of gladiator who fought in military armour. *Osci ludi* 'Oscan plays' was just another way of saying 'Atellan farces', one of the coarser of the kinds of entertainment that could be seen in Rome, originally typical of Atella in Campania.[116] The country girls of central Italy were coarse too, in men's writing, and their Oscan accents were funny; but they were healthy, vigorous, sunburnt, attractive and possibly available.[117]

Only three Samnite towns are noted in Roman literature for their fine produce, all three close to the border of Campania. Venafrum was where Cato grew up: 'I spent all my boyhood in frugality, privation and hard work – reclaiming the Sabine rocks, digging and planting those flinty fields' (*Speeches* 128 Malcovati); and Cato tells us the ritual that he himself had had to follow to placate the spirits of newly cleared land (p. 22). In literature this town is *Campane Venafrum* 'Campanian Venafrum' because the border wavered, *unctum Venafrum* 'oily Venafrum', *viride Venafrum* 'green Venafrum', green with leaves and with green oil. It was famed for its berry (*baca*) – that is, for its olive groves, some of which Cato himself had surely planted, and most of all for its oil, *Venafranum*, best for flavour, best also as a vehicle for perfumes. Can any other oil be compared with it? asked Varro. Horace thought that of his beloved Tarentum just as good, but he knew that Venafran was what gourmets chose. Sure enough, both Horace and Juvenal select *Venafranum* as the epicurean oil with which to souse an epicurean fish.[118]

Southwards down the valley of the Volturnus – 'the very well known country of Venafrum and Allifae' in Cicero's customary superlatives (*For Plancius* 22) – was Allifae, whose lands are described elaborately by Silius as 'not unloved by Iacchus', *Allifanus ager Iaccho haud inamatus* (Silius 12.526–527), perhaps because of its wine, perhaps because of its Allifanian cups (Horace, *Satires* 2.8.39) from which, after all, the wine god may drink as well as his votaries. Not far away to the south was the hill town of Trebula, damp Trebula with its deep valleys and its cool green fields; an ideal place for a summer and autumn villa, thought Martial, even cooler than Tibur: why, Tibur might become one's winter resort! (5.71). Trebula produced wine and Cato bought wine-jars here, but the town was known in Rome for its cheese.[119]

The Appian Way, which we followed to the Campanian Bridge, continued via Capua and from there crossed southern Samnium. It skirted mount Taburnus, good olive country, *magnus Taburnus* 'big Taburnus', also in poetry *Caudinus Taburnus* because the route by which it was skirted was even better known. It passed through Caudium and *furculae Caudinae, fauces Caudinae* 'the Caudine forks, Caudine defile', where a disastrous ambush destroyed a Roman army.[120] All that was long ago, and Caudium was now simply a stage on the road, provided with inns which Maecenas and Horace and their party avoided by staying at 'Cocceius' well-supplied farm, overlooking the inns of Caudium. From there we made straight for Beneventum', where the inn caught fire (*Satires* 1.5: p. 18). An important place in medieval times, Beneventum appears in Roman literature most frequently for its citizen Vatinius, a cobbler and buffoon of Nero's time who was immortalised in cups (Toby jugs, we might call them) that were modelled in imitation of his long-nosed profile.[121]

From Beneventum two roads ran towards Apulia and the port of Brundisium. The Appian Way, 'a whole day's journey longer than the other, but more of a carriage road', made for Venusia, Horace's birthplace, then Tarentum, then north-east. The shorter route started north-east from Beneventum, and this section was a mule track in Horace's time; then, entering Apulia, it turned south-east towards Canusium, Barium and along the coast to Brundisium. Horace's route, on the journey we have followed from time to time, took the Appian Way at first, an exhausting up-and-down road (see quotation on p. 18); but they were on home ground. 'We took the next twenty-four miles on wheels, and stopped at a little town that won't fit into these hexameters, but here are your easy clues: they sell the vilest water and the very best of bread and the clever traveller loads up with some of both' (*Satires* 1.5). They had reached the poet's own home town, Venusia.[122] 'Am I a Lucanian or an Apulian? The Venusian settler ploughs the frontier on which these meet. He was sent there (and the Sabellians expelled, the story goes) to leave no territory unguarded by Romans over which an enemy might invade, whether the Apulians or the Lucanians threatened war' (*Satires* 2.1.34–39).

Horace is a poet of all of Italy, but he traces his inspiration to the countryside around his beloved Venusia.

> Once, as a child on mount Voltur in Apulia, tired with play and sleeping outside my wet-nurse Pullia's cottage door, fairytale wood-pigeons covered me with fresh-fallen leaves. It was a marvel to all who live in the nest of lofty Acherontia, the Bantine pastures and the rich grounds of low Forentum that I could sleep there uninjured by black vipers and bears, that I had been covered with gathered leaves of sacred bay and myrtle, a brave baby and divinely favoured. Thus I am yours, Camenae, yours when I make the ascent to hilly Sabines or when I am pleasured by cool Praeneste or high-lying Tibur or liquid Baiae.
>
> Horace, *Odes* 3.4.9–24

The river Aufidus, fierce, impetuous and far-resounding according to its faithful poet, slowed in its bed as it entered the northern Apulian plain, this land of *Daunia* with its *lata aesculeta*, 'wide forests of durmast oak' (*aesculum, Quercus petraea*), a land whose young men's bodies stained the Mediterranean with blood as a result of the carnage of the Civil War.[123] In this country lay Luceria, 'noble Luceria' according to Horace, a wool town (*Odes* 3.15.14). Beyond, projecting far into the Adriatic, was the forested mount Garganus, *Garganum nemus* 'the grove of Garganus'. We read of *querqueta Gargani* 'the oak woods of Garganus' (*quercus, Quercus robur*), and of the *orni*, manna ash trees, bare in winter; we hear the noise of the North Wind as it stirs the boughs and the rumble of landslides that foretold the battle of Cannae;[124] we see 'the many fires that the shepherd sees from his seat on Garganus, when the uplands of Calabria are burnt and blackened to improve the grazing' (Silius 7.364–366).

From Venusia Horace's party took a cross country route to Canusium, a town well known for its wool and for the capes that were made from it, *Canusinae fuscae* and *rufae*, 'brown and red Canusians'.[125] They had loaded up with bread and water 'because at Canusium the bread's gritty and the water-jug's still empty ... the road worsened till we reached the walls of fishy Barium; then Gnatia, a settlement not favoured by the water-nymphs, amused us with its claim that incense melts without fire on the steps of its temple. Brundisium is the end of a long story' (*Satires* 1.5). Apulia was the driest region of Italy, *siticulosa Apulia*, 'Apulia panting with thirst' (*Epodes* 3.16); why, Seneca was even to write of the deserts of Apulia.

Those who lived in this *vacuum*, this 'empty country' were the *Apuli idonei* 'clever Apulians' of Cassiodorus and Horace's *perusta solibus pernicis uxor Apuli*, 'sunburnt spouse of an agile Apulian' (*Epodes* 2.41–42). Their agriculture was adapted to a hot and dry environment. Caravans of asses carried oil, wine and grain to Brundisium for export. Apulia's excellent wheat was stored in well-ventilated granaries out in the fields.[126] It was good country for horse-breeding. Most important of all, its wide, level plains were winter pasture, as they still are, for numerous flocks of sheep that spent their summer high in the Appennines. The biannual journey might be a long one – two hundred miles, for example, from the winter pastures that belonged to Varro's farm near Reate. The wide drove roads can still be seen on modern maps. Apulian and Calabrian breeds of sheep were traditionally counted among the finest in the world. Tarentum was the centre of the trade in their wool, as we shall see.[127]

The two seaports at the southern end of the Apulian coast were Horace's *piscosum Barium* 'fishy Bari' and Brundisium – 'where Italy ends' at least in the minds of those who hoped to sail from Brundisium to Greece. 'We were waiting for a passage' (Cicero, *Letters to Atticus* 5.8) will have been the story of more than one traveller with nothing to do but browse among the second-hand book stalls.[128]

Calabria was the region of the heel of Italy. Its people, like those of Apulia, were stockbreeders, the *peculiosi Calabri* 'Calabrian herders' of Cassiodorus. There were snakes. Sheep from the winter pastures of Calabria migrated, before the big heat came, to spend the summer in the Lucanian uplands – these, whether Vergil knew it or not, were the 'far-off hill pastures of well-fed Tarentum' in Vergil's *Georgics*. The region differed linguistically from the rest of Italy: resemblances have been seen between the language of the *Messapi* of Calabria and that of Dalmatia across the Adriatic. It also had a considerable Greek population. There were many small Greek towns around the coast, but Greek culture centred on the one major city of Calabria, Tarentum, dominated by the 'towers of the Oebalian citadel', *turres Oebaliae arcis*.[129]

Satur, molle, imbelle Tarentum 'well-fed, soft, unwarlike Tarentum' was soft because it met in full the Roman stereotype of a luxury-loving Greek city, a city whose luxury neither the persuasive speech nor the pregnant silence of her famous philosopher Pythagoras had ever been able to cure (Claudian, *Manlius' Consulship* 157–158).

Horace has often at the front of his mind the journey from Rome to Tarentum and Brundisium, two cities that could very well stand for 'Greece' to him and to other Romans. He was himself balanced between Latinism and Hellenism, his own birthplace lay on one of the roads between the two, and his literary mission had been to bring the lyric genres of archaic Greece to Rome. However this may be, he writes the journey up at length (several quotations above). It is the journey that comes first to mind when he ruminates on his own freedom to travel where he likes (p. 17). He even makes a proverb out of it, 'Does Appius' road or Minucius' get you to Brundisium sooner?' (*Epistles* 1.18.20).[130]

'Soft Tarentum boasts its saucer-like coquilles' in Horace's gastronomic extravaganza (p. 53). This big shellfish, Latin *pecten* (pilgrim scallop, coquille Saint-Jacques, *Pecten Jacobaeus*) was well worth tasting: 'Wholesome, easily digested and good for the bowels. Take with cumin and pepper', advised Diphilus of Siphnos (Athenaeus 90f), the oldest positive evidence in the whole Mediterranean of the use of pepper as a condiment. Earlier gastronomes had already described the 'great big scallops' to be found at Ambracia, just across the straits from Tarentum; Horace's satire is, as usual, far from fantasy. Those who would like to savour his edict in more detail may learn how these flavours were combined in Imperial cuisine:

CUMIN SAUCE FOR OYSTERS AND SHELLFISH. Pepper, lovage, parsley, dried mint, tejpat leaf, fairly generous cumin, honey, vinegar and fish sauce.

> *Apicius* 1.29.1 [1.15 Flower and Rosenbaum; 31 André]

Tarentum's good name in luxury came also from the 'milky' pears called *Syria*.[131] Salt from the *Tarentinus lacus*, never deeper than knee height and dried out every summer, was 'sweeter and whiter than any other' and useful medicinally. More important were the cosseted sheep of Tarentum, marshalled in sheepfolds and wrapped in leather coats to protect their fleeces – they are the *pellitae oves* 'jacketed sheep' of Horace. Their significance in Mediterranean trade is signalled by the fact that Tarentine fleeces and Tarentine wool were known outside Italy simply as 'Italian'.[132] Bales of this wool were tied with reeds for transport.

It seems likely that Tarentum was the trading centre for the wool of Calabria and Apulia generally. Martial's geography, in his address to his new tunic, is inaccurate otherwise:

> Tell me, toga, welcome gift from eloquent Parthenius, as pride of which flock do you wish to be praised? Did the Apulian grass of Ledaean Phalantus spring up for you, where Galesus irrigates the meadows with Calabrian waters? Did Tartessian Baetis, nurse of the Iberian fold, wash you while you were still a sheep? Did your wool survey the many mouths of Timavus, which the good [horse] Cyllarus drank, whose riders were stars? You had no need to be stained with the poison of Amyclae; Miletus did not earn the glory of your fleece. You are whiter than lilies, whiter than privet flowers before they fall.
>
> Martial 8.28[133]

Elsewhere he gives first prize among fleeces to those of Apulia, surely including rather than excluding the Tarentine ones. The whiteness of Tarentine wool is widely praised – but 'God omitted to create purple and red sheep', observed Tertullian, and to this fine white wool was sometimes applied a dye, of the colour of violets, that was extracted locally from the shellfish *Murex brandaris*. Tarentine dye, *Tarentina rubra*, in the first century BC had fetched nearly 100 *denarii* a pound on the Roman market. Here too were woven *tarantinidia*, seductive golden-tinted veils made of the 'wool' of the *pinna*, the shellfish *Pinna nobilis*.[134]

Somewhere near Tarentum were Lucan's 'warm cow-pastures of mount Matinus', *calidi buceta Matini*; Horace compares himself as poet to a Matine bee gathering the lovely thyme of the hillsides.[135] But when they are being as specific as they know how, poets consistently return to the bank of the little river Galaesus, *niger Galaesus* 'black Galaesus', five miles from the city, as the softest and most beautiful locality in all the neighbourhood of Tarentum. This was evidently one of Horace's own favourite places. From these yellow fields, *flaventia culta*, the honey was as good as that of Mount Hymettus; the green olives rivalled those of Venafrum. The wool was of the very best – a really confident poet could equally call the river *Galaesus albus* 'white Galaesus' because of the wool! This same poet could call a beloved boy slave *niveus Galaesus* 'snow-white Galaesus', and, in mourning the death of a little girl slave, Erotion, could describe her as 'softer than a lamb of Phalantine Galaesus' (Martial 5.37).[136]

West of Tarentum Lucania begins. We have already crossed the western edge of this varied region. The forested hills of its mountainous centre had

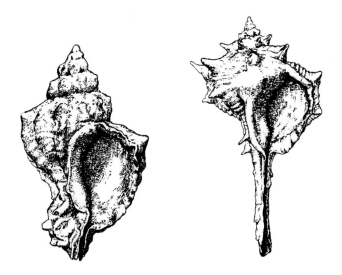

Figure 5   The two Mediterranean sources of purple dye. Left: *Murex trunculus*;
           Right: *Murex brandaris*

Source   From D'Arcy Thompson, *A Glossary of Greek Fishes* (London, 1947)

plentiful game. Here assiduous hunters, benighted far from home, could be imagined sleeping out in the snow (wearing their leggings, *ocrea*, a local word apparently) all so that Rome should be supplied with wild boar. Bears, too, came from the caves of Lucania to Roman amphitheatres.[137] The most unexpected animal for which Lucania was known was the elephant, whose early name in Latin was *Luca bos* literally 'Lucanian ox', because elephants were first encountered by Roman soldiers when they fought the invasion of southern Italy by Pyrrhus of Epirus in 280 BC.[138]

Lucania has the distinction of launching into world cuisine the oldest of all surviving named recipes, the spicy smoked sausage *lucanica*, an idea brought back to Rome by soldiers returning from southern warfare. Already in Martial's time the original link between the recipe and its homeland was no longer felt, and he could write 'My name is *Lucanica*, daughter of a Picene pig' (13.35).[139] A recipe is given in *Apicius*:

> Crush pepper, cumin, savory, rue, parsley, mixed herbs, bay berry, fish sauce, and mix in well-beaten meat, rubbing it well into the mixture. Then, adding fish sauce, whole peppercorns, plenty of fat, and pine kernels, stuff into an intestine (pulled as thin as possible) and hang in the smoke.

> *Apicius* 2.4 [61 André]

Lucanica, under various modern descendants of the Latin name, is still well known in several Mediterranean countries and even in Brazil. It usually takes the form of a single long sausage not twisted into sections.

The Greek city of Thurii was on Lucania's southern coast. It farmed the land that formerly enriched Sybaris, land whose regular yield was said to be a hundred to one. The territory was irrigated by two rivers, the Sybaris and the 'fishy waters of pebbly Crathis' (Ovid, *Fasti* 3.581). Their water had a remarkable property: 'Crathis and Sybaris ... give to hair the colour of amber or of gold' (*Metamorphoses* 15.315–316). There were no ruins of Sybaris. Its enemies had diverted the rivers to wash away its site. But they could not destroy its name, synonymous with luxury: a name that was given, for example, to an erotic book, *Sybaritica* by Hemitheon. And Sybaris had proclaimed the first known patent law in the world, giving cooks who invented a new recipe sole rights in it for a year.[140]

Further south, on the eastern shore of Bruttium, were three more Greek cities. First was *Magnus Croton* 'Croton the great',[141] long ago the successful rival of Sybaris. It was 'a town built on a high rock. We were lost and did not know what town it was, but a farmer told us it was Croton, a very ancient city, once the greatest in Italy ... since ruined by continual warfare' (Petronius 116).

Beyond Croton was *Navifragum Scylaceum* 'Scylaceum where ships are wrecked', notable according to its late Roman citizen, Cassiodorus, for its cheese, its wine and its beauty.[142] And the virgin pine forests of *Narycia*, whose prosaic name was Locri Epizephyrii, were a joy to see (Vergil, *Georgics* 2.437–438). Here we have reached the southern tip of Italy's southern peninsula, and we are close to Rhegium.

The northern hinterland

The *via Valeria* (see Map 1), a continuation of the road from Rome to Tibur, penetrated the central Appennines, making for the tribal territories of the Marsi, Paeligni, Marrucini and Vestini – now economically dependent on the markets of Rome. The first town on the road, however, belonged to the Sabini: it was Varia, the nearest market town to Horace's Sabine farm (p. 25). Catullus's cottage had been somewhere near, if it could be labelled either Tiburtine or Sabine (p. 269).

North of Varia was the side-valley of the river Digentia in which Horace's property lay. The bushes there were laden with red cornels and plums; oak and holm-oak provided the animals with acorns and their master with shade. You would think the greenery of Tarentum had come nearer to Rome (*Epistles* 1.16.8–11). Above it rose *amoenus Lucretilis*:

> pleasant mount Lucretilis ... where my stinking billygoat's wandering wives meander safely through the woods, looking for hidden arbutus and thyme, and the kids do not fear green snakes or fighting wolves –

Figure 6   *O fons Bandusiae splendidior vitro* ... The 'Bandusian spring more brilliant than glass', near Horace's Sabine farm, is addressed in *Odes* 3.13, and is correctly promised fame through Horace's poetry

Source   Photograph: R. Stoneman

whenever the valleys and the smooth rocks of sleeping Ustica re-echo the sweet flute [of the god Faunus].

Horace, *Odes* 1.17.5–12[143]

There had once been a threat to Rome from the *finitimi Marsi* 'neighbouring Marsi' but now the threat was past. In any case the Marsi were already best known in Rome as snake-charmers and sorcerers. Their power was exerted partly in words – Marsian words, Marsian chants (*Marsa nenia*), the sounds of magic. It was demonstrated partly in side-shows in the streets of Italian towns. Audiences came away with the impression that Marsi were immune to snake-bites, which would not be in the least surprising if, as was said, they were descended from the son of Ulysses and Circe and if one of their goddesses, Angitia, was a sister of Medea.[144]

The Marsi could fight and they could also send snakes to sleep by charms, and rob a serpent's tooth of its venom by simples and spells.

> They say that Angitia, daughter of Aeetes, first revealed magic herbs to them, and taught them to tame vipers by handling, to drive the moon from the sky, to stop the flow of rivers by their incantations, and to bare the hills by calling the forests down.
>
> Silius 8.495–501[145]

If the country around Rome, from Alba Longa to Nomentum, was Rome's market garden, then mountainous central Italy was its farm. Passing through the high valley of Carseoli, 'the cold land of Carseoli, unsuited to olives but good for grain' (Ovid, *Fasti* 4.683–684) the road reaches another Alba, 'the inland Alba set among its watery fields, compensating by its orchards for its lack of corn' (Silius 8.506–507). In the forested mountains that were visible all around were Marsian boars, hunted with nets to provide a delicacy for Roman banquets (Horace, *Odes* 1.1.28).

The 'wine from Marsian cellars', if Martial has it right, came from grapes grown and pressed on Paelignian hillsides: 'Paelignian farmers send down this cloudy Marsian. Don't drink it: give it to your freedman to drink' (Martial 13.121). Ovid (below) and Galen thought there was something to be said for sweet Marsian.[146] Honey, too, came to Rome from here, 'the nectar gathered by Pelignian swarms'. Horace, who was fascinated by witches, talks once of a Paelignian sorceress, but whether her skill would be different from that of a Marsian we have no idea.[147]

Nasone Paeligni sonant, said Martial (1.61), the Paelignians keep talking about Naso – that is, the poet Ovid, Q. Ovidius Naso, whose birthplace was Sulmo. Silius agrees with Ovid as to one of the excellences of this town: they both call it *gelidus Sulmo* 'cold Sulmo', which is praise, of course.

> I am at home in Sulmo (one of the three Paelignian districts), a narrow land, but watered by wholesome streams: the summer sun may crack the ground and the star of the Dog of Icarius may burn, but clear waters still run through the Paelignian meadows, and rich grass grows green in the gentle soil. This country is good for grain and better still for grapes; an occasional field grows olives, and along the slow river banks, in the springy grass, green leaves shade the moist earth.
>
> Ovid, *Amores* 2.16.1–10

The Vestini, to the north-east, sold cheese at Rome, presumably goats' or sheeps' milk cheese from the mountains.[148] Vergil describes its making and marketing.

> The milk they get at dawn and through the day they press at night. The milk they get at evening and sunset they carry out in wicker-covered jars at daybreak, if the shepherd is going to town, or else they season it with not too much salt and store until winter.
>
> Vergil, *Georgics* 3.400–403

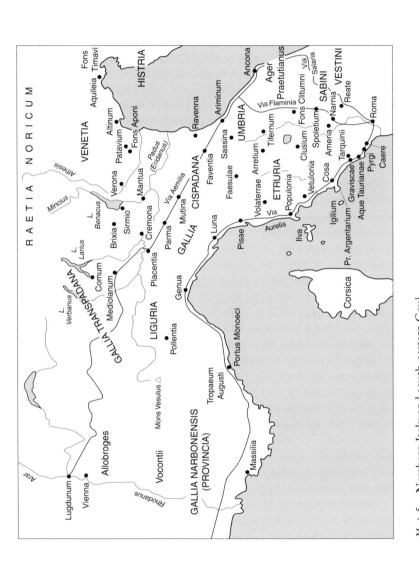

Map 5 Northern Italy and south-eastern Gaul

In our survey of the neighbourhood of Rome we followed the *via Salaria* 'Salt Way' as far as the skirts of Nomentum. The hill-country of the Sabini began at this point. This Italic people had a very close historic relationship with Rome. In the early days there had even been a Sabine village among the Seven Hills of Rome.

Sabinae occur rather often in Roman poetry. Their typical epithets possibly constitute an unfair slur on contemporary Sabine women: they are reminders of the utterly memorable involvement of Sabine women in the origins of Rome, when the men who had founded the new village hosted a festival for their rustic neighbours and seized wives for themselves, making do (as classical poets saw it) with *horribiles, immundae, rigidae, tetricae*, 'dreadful, unwashed, graceless, ugly' countrywomen. Sabine women, in the poetic stereotype, were possibly given to magical practices, and the rest of their time was taken up in cultivating their farms rather than their bodies.[149] Whatever truth may lie in the story of the 'rape of the Sabines', the Sabine dialect contributed a good many loanwords to its relative Latin, a sign of close interaction over a long period in the past. Sometimes they are doublets: from Sabine, *popina* 'cookshop' – the purely Latin doublet is *coquina* 'kitchen'; from Sabine, *olla* 'cooking pot' – the doublet is *aula*. Several of the loanwords, including these, are very closely concerned with the everyday life of rural Italy, *lupus* 'wolf', *bos* 'ox, cow', *robus* 'red-brown' (used of oxen and of wheat), *scrofa* 'sow', perhaps *caseus* 'cheese'.

The Sabine country, in one of Cicero's superlatives, was *flos Italiae ac robur rei publicae* 'the flower of Italy and the oak-tree of our State' (*For Ligarius* 32).[150] By his time its economy was shaped by the demands of the big city. It sent fresh figs to Rome, the *Sabina* fig, which had to be marketed quickly because it lost its colour in a few days (Varro, *On Farming* 1.67). These were *olivifera arva* 'the olive-bearing fields', too. Juvenal thought of *baca Sabina* 'the Sabine berry' as a typical product familiar from childhood (3.85) but no one suggests that Sabine olives were especially good.[151] Small birds were caught and bred for the Roman table in aviaries, most of them leased in Sabine country by wholesale butchers working the city markets. Sabine country was ideal for this purpose because of the large number of wild thrushes (*turdi*) that gathered there and were caught in nets.[152]

Sabine wine was well known in Rome, though none of the wines from Rome's northern hinterland counted among the best names, not Sabine or Paelignian or Marsian or Nomentan or Tuscan. To Galen, Sabine wines were generally *leptos* 'light' (*On Good and Bad Juices* [6.806]). To Martial, Sabine was *plumbeum* 'leaden':

> You can afford amethyst cups, Cotta, and you can afford to dip them in black Opimian. You're only toasting me in Sabine *conditum*, and you ask me if I want it in gold! Why put leaden wines in a golden goblet?
>
> Martial 10.49: on *conditum* see p. 247

Horace talks of *vile Sabinum* 'cheap Sabine', but he is laughing at himself. His own farm was in Sabine country (p. 68) so the wine that he made was Sabine. He bottled it himself *Graeca testa* 'in used Greek amphoras', which looked no worse when served at a meal – sweet Greek wine was an expensive luxury at Rome – and might well contribute something to flavour and bouquet, as sherry casks do to whisky. Naturally he often speaks of drinking Sabine, even his four-year reserve, *quadrimum Sabinum merum* (Horace, *Odes* 1.9; p. 39); and, yes, you could really keep Sabine seven to fifteen years, we are told.[153]

Given these various associations of the Sabine country, best summarised as 'homely', it is no surprise that, according to Catullus, people who did not want to hurt him said that his country cottage was not Sabine at all but Tiburtine (p. 269)! But if you were less concerned with cutting a dash in Roman society, 'Sabine' might do very well. The polymath Varro, one of Horace's *ardui Sabini* 'hilly Sabines', was born in Reate in the Sabine country and retained a farm there. Sheep from the summer pastures in these mountains spent the winter in far-off Apulia. In the foothills, vines were typically not trained on trellises or trees but simply raised on temporary props when they were laden with fruit.[154]

Passing between the typical field walls of Reate's territory, the *Salaria* continues north-east towards Picenum. We are still in Rome's country farm. Picene apples and Picene olives – fine, large table olives – were the local produce that came to market in Rome; these olives, said Martial, fattened Picene thrushes for the Roman table.[155] Two really good wines of the Empire, Hadrianum and Praetutianum, came from the southern Picene hills: Hadrianum was already ancient in fame.[156] A type of bread (no one knows what type) was named Picentine: Picentine loaves were served at fine dinners (Macrobius, *Saturnalia* 3.13.10: p. 248) and formed an ingredient in elaborate and costly dishes:

> ANOTHER, APICIAN *SALA CATTABIA*. Put in a mortar celery seed, dried pennyroyal, dried mint, ginger, coriander leaf, seeded raisins, honey, vinegar, oil and wine. Crush. Put in a pan bits of Picentine bread and mix with chicken meat, kid's sweetbreads, Vestine cheese, pine kernels, cucumbers, dried onions chopped fine. Pour the liquid over. At the last moment scatter snow on top and serve.
>
> *Apicius* 4.1.2 [126 André]

The *Salaria* was the shortest route to one of the best known cities on Italy's Adriatic coast, the seaport of Ancona at the northern extremity of Picenum. On this road, most probably, the emperor Trajan travelled on his way to fight the Second Dacian War in 105. His nocturnal departure from Ancona is depicted on Trajan's Column (casts 207–212).

The city was intended to be identified at sight. It has naval dockyards and two temples, one of which is a Temple of Venus on a hilltop, reached by a zig-zag path: a tiny statue of Venus Anadyomene appears at its entrance.

And there is an arch on the seaward end of a projecting mole, crowned by three nude male statues. This is Trajan's Arch: it still stands, but its depiction on the Column is artistic licence, since it had not been begun when Trajan set out and it had not yet been completed even when the Column itself was dedicated. In fact the Arch was finally topped by statues of Trajan himself, his wife Plotina and his sister Marciana. Its newsworthiness would immediately help any contemporary viewer of the scene to identify Ancona.

Ancona's coinage often depicted Venus; the city was under her special protection. Her hilltop temple is suggested by Juvenal's expression, 'the House of Venus that surmounts Doric Ancon' (4.40).[157] This rock was imagined by Lucan as one of the two bulwarks of Italy, breaking the force of the Dalmatian Sea (2.399–402).

On the opposite bank of the Tiber from the *Salaria*, the *via Flaminia* makes northwards from Rome towards the Po valley. It was one of the busiest highways of Roman Italy. Its importance increased in later centuries, when the Western Empire came to be ruled from Milan: but the invasions and settlements of Goths were bad for the rural economy and had left behind them damaged roads and broken bridges, if Rutilius is correct in attributing blame: 'violated by Getic sword and fire ... the Aurelian Way no longer fetters the rivers with bridges' (p. 75). It is ironic to find Cassiodorus in due course complaining on behalf of a Gothic king that the Flaminian Way needs repair. He also criticises overcharging at inns along the route: a standard scale of charges was imposed. But the poor state of the *Flaminia* had been proverbial as far back as Martial's time.

After crossing a corner of Etruria the Flaminian Way entered Umbria, *montana Umbria*, the mountainous region that produced the very best wild boar according to Horace's parodic gastronomy, though Statius, also playful, ranks Tuscan boars even higher (p. 267). The road parts from the Tiber valley, passing below Narnia on its precipitous rock, a small hill town encircled by 'white Nar with its sulphureous water'.[158]

Ameria, in the hills to the left of the road, was identified with a species or variety of willow, one of the three recognised by Roman farmers: 'The Greek is yellow-coloured, the Gallic is dull purple with very thin canes, the Amerine has slender brown canes' (Columella 4.30.4). The canes of this Amerine or Sabine willow were especially suited to a most important task: *Amerina retinacula* 'Amerine ties' fastened vines to their stakes. They were used in basketry too: Cato specifies 'Amerine carrying-baskets' as part of the equipment of his typical vineyard.[159]

Spoletium, further north, produced a sweet, golden wine, not of the top class; yet, as Martial said, better old Spoletine wine than Falernian must.[160] To the north again lay the famous source of the Clitumnus (*fons Clitumni*), one of the beauties of Italy. The main spring was at the foot of a hill clothed with ancient cypresses; its banks were green with ash and poplar, its waters cold as snow. The old temple of the god Clitumnus was surrounded by other smaller shrines each with their own springs. 'The people of Hispellum, to whom the deified Augustus presented the place, maintain a public bathing pool and an inn' (Pliny, *Letters* 8.8).[161]

Far off in the hills of northern Umbria lay the sacred lake and forest of Sassina, *Sassinas silva*, gastronomically the star of the whole region: it was from here that a well-known mountain cheese came to Roman markets, formed into a typical pyramid shape, *meta*.[162] The fertility of the *ager Gallicus*, the Adriatic coastal strip of Umbria, had been legendary in the second century BC, when Rome seized this land to settle retired legionaries on it.[163] But no gourmet foods came from this district in later Roman times. From Ariminum, chief town of the *ager Gallicus*, the Aemilian Way continued north-west into Cisalpine Gaul: we pause at the bridge over the *puniceus Rubicon* 'brown Rubicon' that marked the frontier of Italy and Caesar's step into civil war (Lucan 1.183–227).

The last of the great roads radiating from Rome is the *via Aurelia*, which crossed Etruria on its way to Genoa and southern Gaul. Like the Flaminian Way, in later Roman times the Aurelian Way too had fallen into disrepair. 'I have chosen the sea', wrote Rutilius, 'because lowland roads are flooded by rivers and mountain roads are rough with rocks. Violated by Getic sword and fire, Tuscan country no longer mixes forests with homesteads, and the Aurelian Way no longer fetters the rivers with bridges' (37–41).

From the Etruscans, as from the Greeks, Romans had once learnt many of the arts of luxury that they afterwards made their own; the Roman attitude to sex and its pleasures owed something to the Etruscan example (p. 265). They called the country *Etruria* and its people *Tusci*: poetically they might be *Tyrrheni*, the Greek name, or even *Lydi* in bold assertion of the persistent rumour that Etruscans had originally been migrants from Lydia in Asia Minor.[164] Etruscan culture had once dominated central Italy, and Romans had once studied the Etruscan language and literature 'as we now study Greek' (Livy 9.36).

By the time of the Roman Empire the old civilisation was on the way to oblivion; but it persisted through Roman religion. *Etruscae coronae*, golden 'Etruscan crowns', decorated triumphant generals; *Etruscum aurum*, an 'Etruscan gold' amulet was worn by Roman boys of equestrian family. *Tyrrhena sigilla* or *signa Tuscanica*, bronze figurines of Etruscan make, were known all over the empire.[165]

Etruscan priests were still required in Rome on ominous occasions. After the Capitol was struck by lightning in the consulship of Cotta and Torquatus, soothsayers from all Etruria gathered in Rome to predict the approach of death and fire, the overthrow of the laws, civil war throughout Italy, and the downfall of Rome and its dominion unless the gods were placated (Cicero, *Against Catiline* 3.19). Etruscans were easily pictured as *colorati Etrusci*, their skins darker than the typical Italian, their bodies more rotund, their religion and its rituals (*Etrusca disciplina*) utterly distinct.[166]

Figure 7   Etruscan haruspex or seer. Etruscan bronze of the fourth century BC, now in the Museo Gregoriano, Vatican

Source   By permission of Monumenti Musei e Gallerie Pontificie, Archivio Fotografico, Vatican City

Vergil imagines the *pinguis Tyrrhenus* 'plump Etruscan' blowing on his ivory pipe at sacrifice (*Georgics* 2.193).

Tuscan dogs were a useful, working breed, shaggy, not especially fleet-footed, but good at finding and following a scent: they were 'pointers', showing the huntsman where the hare was lying concealed. On the other side, Tuscan boars were typical of those brought to the Roman arena for a wild beast hunt; and when they came to the table, Statius, for one, ranked Tuscan boars *generosior* 'fuller flavoured' than Umbrian (p. 267). A Tuscan boar was to be treated properly: an epigram of Martial agonises lightly over whether to accept one as a present, considering the volume of Falernian wine and special *garum* that must be blended in its sauce, and the weight of costly pepper demanded as seasoning (7.27).

Tuscan wine was well known in Rome. Possibly it was the best of the light vintages of central Italy, but this was its level and no higher: it did not rival the great wine districts of Campania.[167] Under the early Empire Arretium was one of the centres that produced the kind of crockery known, to Pliny and ourselves, as 'Samian'. It was made from local red clay. Arretine ware was generally matt in finish, contrasting with the glossy red of later Gaulish ware; it was delicate in fabric and finely decorated. 'We urge you not to spurn Arretine ware: Porsena was happy with Tuscan crockery', says one of Martial's gift verses (14.98), but, in spite of the pretended example of this famous old Etruscan warrior, Arretine ware was not prized by those who could afford to spend more.[168]

There was a great contrast between mountainous inland Etruria and the relatively low-lying coastal strip. When the dastardly Catiline was plotting revolution in 63 BC his headquarters were near Faesulae *in Etruriae faucibus* 'within the passes of Etruria', at a place dangerous in Roman memory (through these passes Hannibal had brought his invading army to slaughter the Romans at Lake Trasimene) and at an elevation where – Cicero teased – the winter frosts and snows of the Appennines might well turn out to be too much for the fashionable young bankrupts Catiline had gathered to his cause, though of course they had been training themselves to endure cold by dancing naked at their all night parties.[169]

By contrast with the big and productive estates farmed by chain gangs in the unhealthy Tuscan lowlands,[170] in the highlands there were smaller estates. The younger Pliny, in the scholarly retirement that preceded his last posting to Bithynia, had two country retreats, both of which offered good hunting: he could winter in the Laurentan marshes (p. 40) and he could while away a cool summer at Tifernum, in the high valley of the Tiber. It was not very far from Arretium (beside whose 'cold river' Sulpicia managed to avoid spending her birthday: p. 216) but not very close to anywhere. It was a part of Italy that was unfamiliar to many.

I loved your care and concern [Pliny writes to Domitius Apollinaris] urging me not to spend the summer at my Tuscan place because you were sure it would be unhealthy. True, Etruria is really oppressive and really malarial along the coastal strip: but I am a very long way from the sea, in fact I am in among the Appennines, and they are thoroughly bracing! So that you won't be afraid for me any more, here is the climate, the geography, the scenery: you will enjoy listening and I shall enjoy telling you.

The climate in winter is cold and frosty, hopeless for myrtles and olives and any other trees that need a mild temperature all year, but bay trees grow and they do very well: they are sometimes killed off by the cold, but not oftener than in the neighbourhood of Rome. The summer is wonderfully temperate.

The countryside is very beautiful. Picture to yourself a vast amphitheatre such as could only be a work of nature; the great spreading plain is ringed round by mountains, their summits crowned by ancient woods of tall trees, where there is a good deal of mixed hunting to be had. Below them the vineyards spreading down every slope weave their uniform pattern far and wide, their lower limit bordered by a belt of trees. Then come the meadows and cornfields, where the land can be broken up only by heavy oxen and the strongest ploughs. The meadows are bright with flowers, covered with clover and other delicate plants which always seem soft and fresh, for everything is fed by streams which never run dry. There is abundant water but no marshes, because of the downward slope: any water that the land does not absorb runs off into the Tiber, which flows through these fields. You would be in ecstasy at the view of this countryside from the mountains. It seems to be a painted scene of great beauty rather than a real landscape.

Pliny, Letters 5.6.1–13, abridged[171]

His own house, Pliny adds, is on the lower slopes, and he describes it in loving detail. Behind it is the main ridge of the Appennines, and even on a still and cloudless day there is a breeze from the mountains. 'Now you know why I am glad to have my Tuscan villa and not one in Tusculum or Tibur or Praeneste', he concludes. 'My slaves, too, keep healthier here (forgive me for adding): of all the ones I have ever brought with me I have not lost one' (*Letters* 5.6.45–46).

Etruria offered not only mountain climate but also mineral springs to Roman health-seekers: Strabo thought that, being relatively close to the city, the waters of Etruria attracted more Roman visitors, in total, than did fashionable Baiae. Among them were the tepid waters near Clusium, *fontes Clusinae*, for invalids to dip their aching heads or stomachs in. One of the lesser spas was Aquae Taurianae, in coastal Etruria a few miles from Centumcellae. Rutilius visited these baths in the course of his poetic journey from Rome. 'Its waters are not spoilt by a sour taste', he writes, 'nor are they hot and coloured with smoking sulphur: their clean smell and pleasant taste confuse the visitor, who wonders whether they are better for drinking or for bathing!... A pretty poem by Messalla, affixed to the gateway of the sacred place, encourages the visitor to linger' (251–270).[172]

We set out on the Appian Way accompanied by Horace, who travelled to Brundisium with Maecenas about 38 BC. More than four centuries after Horace – separated by the whole extent of the *pax Romana*, the Imperial peace which had at last crumbled and would never return – Rutilius returned home from Rome to Gaul and narrated his journey along the Tuscan coast in fresh and vivid verse, a lament for what was already lost and a quiet celebration of the beauty that remained. He chose to sail, since the roads were bad: if he had ridden, his stopping places might have been just the same.

There was first the old Etruscan foundation of Caere on a hillside facing the sea, 'once called Agylla, a name lost in time' (226), once active enough in Mediterranean religious politics to build a treasury at Delphi. Then came Caere's harbour town, Pyrgi, whose name means 'the towers' in Greek: this coast was studded with towers for sighting shoals of tunny. A unique Phoenician-Etruscan bilingual inscription has been found here in modern times. *Veteres Pyrgi* 'old Pyrgi' would long ago have been busy with Greek and Phoenician visitors. It had been a rich place, until Dionysius of Syracuse sacked it on his Corsican expedition; the satirist Lucilius still found *scorta Purgensia* 'whores of Pyrgi' not hard to imagine.[173] All that Rutilius can say, six hundred years after him, is that Pyrgi 'was once a little town and is now just a large farm' (223–224).

Castrum Novum, too, was broken 'by the waves and by time. An ancient gate marks the half-ruined place, over which, modelled as a small statue in stone, rules the god with horns upon his shepherd's brow' (227–230). Centumcellae was not in ruins. There was an inner harbour right inside the town and another beyond (237–246). Pliny the Younger had seen this in embryo: a natural bay was being converted into the vast new harbour. The northern side had already been strengthened with a mole, and a southern mole was under construction. At the entrance an island was rising from the water: already it acted as a breakwater, tossing the waves high into the air. 'As time goes on it will look like a natural island' (*Letters* 6.31). Castrum Novum has been identified with S. Marinella, four miles south of Aquae Taurianae (Map 5). Centumcellae was modern Civitavecchia, three miles west of Aquae Taurianae.

The harbour town of Tarquinii, Vergil's *intempestae Graviscae* 'oppressive Graviscae',[174] is to Rutilius 'the few towers of Graviscae, oppressed by marshy odours in summer. Still, the forested neighbourhood is green with dense woods, and the shadows of its pines play upon the inshore waters' (281–284). Cosa, which had once been a port of some economic importance, he describes as 'the old untenanted ruins and overgrown walls of abandoned Cosa ... they say it was a plague of mice that forced the people to leave their hearths and move away' (285–290).

At this point in Rutilius's journey the road would have been shorter than his sea voyage. Half way along the Tuscan coast he had to make a long detour, where '*mons Argentarius* stretches out among the waves, confining the blue curves between its two peaks. Across the hills it is six miles at the narrowest, but the circuit by sea is twenty-four'. Out at sea, beyond this 'succession of scattered crags' (315–321) lay the 'wooded peaks of Igilium', *Igilii silvosa cacumina*. They had served many as a refuge when Alaric invaded Italy in AD 410 (315–336). North again and further off shore was the larger island of Elba, *Chalybum memorabilis Ilva metallis*, 'Ilva, famous for its Chalybian mines, than which the soil of Noricum has produced no richer yield' (351–352). The islanders, 'few in number, but cheerfully armed in their native iron' in the romantic vision of Silius (8.615–616) used to melt down the iron into lumps and sell them to traders, who took them across to the markets on the mainland for sale. For the Chalybes, typical Anatolian iron miners transplanted by Rutilius to Elba, see p. 167.

Elba faces the mainland promontory of Populonia, with a harbour at its foot and an old Etruscan city – the only one actually on the Mediterranean coast – on the cliff; but it was in ruins long before Rutilius's time.[175]

> Where a steep peak rules the waves beneath, some ancient epoch selected a strong rock as lookout point and established a fortress there which would be of double use to mankind, as a protection for the country and as a mark for navigation. There is now no monument of that earlier period: hungry time has consumed the great buildings. Only traces of lost walls remain, and the houses lie buried under an expanse of rubble. We have no right to complain of our own mortality, when we see by example that cities themselves can die.
>
> Rutilius 405–414

North from here, navigation was tricky. The town of Volaterrae lay well inland, but offshore were the dangerous reefs of Volaterrae and of Pisae, pictured by an earlier poet as a bulwark of Italy, breaking the waves of the Tyrrhenian sea (Lucan 2.399–402). The salt pans of Volaterrae were well known, and Rutilius pauses to describe them (455–484). He was now at last in a more prosperous country, arriving at *Portus Pisanus*, Pisae's harbour town, where he 'admired the nearby harbour, a fine-looking place, famed as the market for Pisan produce and for the wealth of the sea' (531–533) and took the opportunity of a holiday.

> I moored my boats in the safe harbour and drove to Pisae along the public road. A friend, a tribune with whom I once served, lent me horses and offered a carriage as well.... I explored the old city, the child of Alpheus, circled by the twin waters Arnus and Ausur, which form the cone of a pyramid at their confluence.
>
> 559–567

Strabo had already observed that the two rivers 'lift one another up so high as they clash that two people standing on opposite banks cannot see one another'. Pisan produce included stone and timber, the latter used for ship-building but also for building work at Rome.[176]

Along this coast the harbour and city of Luna marked the extremity of old Italy: beyond lay Liguria, part of the province of Cisalpine Gaul. *Lunai portus* Persius (6.9) calls the place, evoking the archaic Latin of Ennius; 'there is no larger harbour anywhere to house innumerable boats and shut out the sea' (Silius 8.480–482). Luna was a striking landmark with its *candentia moenia* 'dazzling white walls': this was 'a land rich in marble that revels in its bright colour so much as to challenge the virgin snows' (Rutilius 2.63–68). Luna white marble had been one of the three stones used in the tomb of the emperor Nero; it was the 'Ligurian marble' that we saw gracing Domitian's arch to commemorate his new road from Sinuessa to

Cumae. This most distant town of Etruria had a second distinction: its cheese was known in Rome, stamped, naturally, with the emblem of a crescent moon, *luna*.[177]

4 Vesper

> From Gadeira to the city of the seven hills, a sixth of the journey is to the banks of the Baetis where the cattle low; then a fifth to the Phocian soil of Pylades, land of Taure, so named from the abundance of cattle; then to craggy Pyrene an eighth, plus the twelfth of a tenth. Between Pyrene and high Alp is a quarter. As Ausonia begins, a twelfth brings you in sight of the amber of Eridanus; and I am blessed, for I have gone another two thousand and five hundred from there. The Palace on the Tarpeia was my destination.
>
> Metrodorus, *Palatine Anthology* 14.121

This little mathematical puzzle in Greek verse accompanies a traveller from the furthest west – the city that was Gadeira to Greeks, Gades to Romans, Cadiz to us – to the very heart of Empire, the Palatium on the Tarpeian Rock, Rome's imperial landmark. It was a journey of many weeks.

The road was good and evidently busy, with regular stages and inns: already in Polybius's time, around 150 BC, some inns were to be found in this region, and they had their own set pattern of trade.

> When travellers in that country make overnight stops at inns they do not bother with the price of individual items, but ask how much it costs for a man to stay. The innkeepers generally take guests at the rate of half an as (that is, a quarter of an obol) to cover everything that will be needed; they seldom charge more than this.
>
> Polybius, *Histories* 2.15.5

Soon the idea occurred of advertising services and perhaps prices in Gallic inns on a placard just inside the entrance: 'Traveller, please step inside. There is a bronze tablet which will answer all your questions'.[1] We may enlarge our appreciation of these hostelries with the fourth-century lament of the native of Gaul Sidonius:

Figure 8   Kitchen work. Drawing from a relief on a tomb at Frascati
Source   By permission of British Museum Press

I might still tearfully take refuge in a dingy tavern, my eyes watering, my nostrils stopped against the smoke from the kitchen, where from aromatic saucepans the scent of sausage and thyme and juniper berries rises, and the steam of cooking pots mingles with the smoke from spitting frying pans. Here, when a feast-day begins to grind out its raucous ballads, and to stir up the genial quarrels of the soldiery, I, roused by the Muse of my drunken host, shall croon a worthier song ...

Sidonius, *Letters* 8.11.3, verses 41–54

Metrodorus has calculated his armchair journey at 15,000 Greek *stadia* (1,875 Roman miles). Following his itinerary in reverse, 2,500 Greek *stadia* (312 Roman miles) is the precise distance from Rome to Genoa along the *via Aurelia*; Genoa, though certainly not in sight of the Padus or Eridanus (the river Po) (see Map 5) is the nearest one gets on this road to a view of it. From Genoa to the Trophy of Augustus *in Alpe summa*, the highest point on what is now the Grande Corniche, is precisely 1,250 *stadia*, one-twelfth of the total journey. From here across southern Gaul *in summo Pyreneo* 'to the pass over the Pyrenees' Metrodorus makes it 3,750 stadia: in fact it is somewhat less, 3,425 *stadia*, if following the coast road to the Col de Pertus, but a great deal more if making for the inland pass at Roncesvalles. From the Pyrenean crossing, Pallantia, in the country of the Vaccaei (*Taure*), should be 2,000 *stadia* away according to Metrodorus: from *summo Pyreneo* near Roncesvalles to Pallantia the distance is precisely 2,040. From Pallantia south to Gades Metrodorus calculates 5,500 *stadia*: and the distance by way of Castulo in the upper valley of the Baetis – an odd but not impossible route to follow – is very close to that.[2]

Peoples of the West

The population of Rome's western provinces was varied, but in literary cliché not too hard to characterise.

The typical Gaul or Celt, *Rhodani potor* 'drinker of Rhone water' was big and fleshy, at least in the view of the Spaniard Martial. We read in his epigrams of *pinguis Gallia* 'greasy Gaul' (p. 99), of an *ingens Lingonus* 'huge Lingonian' (member of a Belgic people) and of *crassa Burdigala* 'fat Bordeaux' (p. 261). The Gaul was also white-skinned: Giton, in Petronius's fiction, drily suggests a disguise as Gaulish slaves, 'chalking our faces so that Gaul will recognise us as one of her own' (102; p. 178). Some were fair-haired, like the *flavus Carnutis* remembered by Tibullus. *Galla credulitas* 'Gallic credulity' became a commonplace, ever since Caesar asserted that the Gauls believed anything they heard from travellers and were ready to base important decisions on rumour. Caesar further typified his redoubtable opponents as 'inclined to revolution'. And Horace came down hard on the Allobroges, a Rhone valley people, for this trait. His formula *novis rebus infidelis Allobrox* expresses, far more persuasively than a longer sentence could have done, the undoubted fact that the Allobroges had once been 'unreliable when *we* were having a revolution'. They had taken up arms against Rome at the time when the state was in turmoil because of the attempted reforms of the Gracchi.[3]

Catiline attempted to capitalise on this supposed tendency, and on the Allobroges' indebtedness to Roman financiers, to win their support for his conspiracy in 64 BC, but the Allobroges' envoys wisely played a double game and Catiline lost.[4] They had colluded with Cicero's people – the right side – and this was possibly in Cicero's mind when he later grandly emphasised

> the bravery, firmness and importance of the province of Gaul.... It is the flower of Italy, the pillar of the Roman state, the glory of our dominion. And the municipalities and colonies of the province of Gaul are quite united, it seems, in the intention of maintaining the authority of this Order and the rule of the Roman people.
>
> *Philippics* 3.13

The Gauls were warlike if given the chance; the *Belgae* of the north-east more warlike than the rest, as Caesar explained.[5] Typical Gallic military costume was a cloak, *sagum* (p. 98), and striped trousers in red or other bright colours. Romans were dingy by comparison. Typical Gallic warrior ornament included a torque, a collar of twisted gold. 'Their hair was golden, golden were their beards; bright were their striped capes, and their milk-white necks were encircled with gold', wrote Vergil (*Aeneid* 8.659–661), imagining a picture of those early Gauls who had captured Rome.[6]

Gauls were athletes, horsemen and charioteers. Some significant terms in this subject area entered Latin as Celtic loanwords: *draucus* 'professional athlete', *mirmillo* 'a type of gladiator' who wore Gallic armour, *caballus* 'horse' (this became the usual term for horse in the Romance languages), *veredus* 'horse', *ploxenum* 'cart', *esseda* 'chariot' – and we notice the *mulier essedaria* 'woman charioteer' on the Games programme in Petronius (p. 233). Under the Empire these Gallic skills were guided into new channels; they were evidently demonstrated in the amphitheatre but also, far more important, in the auxiliary regiments of the Roman army. The best of Roman cavalry came from Gaul, said Strabo.

Many Gauls were scattered across the Empire as slaves. As late as AD 69 the whole citizen body of Cremona was enslaved, and such slaves did not sell well near home.[7] To the east, Liburnia and Illyria recur in literature as sources of slaves, the *horridus Liburnus* 'bristling Liburnian' being named more than once as the typical slave porter or usher seen in the streets of Rome. He bristled because he wore a rough woollen hooded cloak, *cucullus Liburnicus* (a garment also connected with Gaul) made from a Liburnian fleece that was closer to hair than wool.[8]

The *intima regna Liburnorum*, 'hidden kingdom of the Liburni' before it came under Roman rule had been a nest of pirates, as had the whole fractured northern and eastern coastline of the Adriatic. Livy classed Illyri, Liburni and Histri together as savage peoples, infamous for piracy. These pirates had long been known and feared in Greece. They descended on merchant ships and harbour towns in their swift ships, *saeva Liburna* 'wild Liburnians', the highly manoevrable vessels that were taken up by the Roman navy and that helped Augustus to win at Actium, though fearsomely overshadowed by the high towers of Antony's big warships.[9] Illyria and neighbouring Epirus were important sources of slaves under the early Empire, and one of the reasons is made clear by Varro in discussing the selection of slaves for farm work. Overseers should be given 'their own mates from among their fellow-slaves to bear them children. This makes them more reliable and more attached to the property. Because of such relationships as these, slave families from Epirus are preferred and fetch a fairly high price' (*On Farming* 1.17.5).

Britain was well known to have a Celtic population related to that of Gaul, of looser build, not so fair-haired. Under Augustus, British slaves were already familiar. 'I saw some myself in Rome: they were mere boys, yet half a foot taller than the tallest Roman – but gangling and not at all well-proportioned' (Strabo 4.5.2). Poets already foresaw 'the unviolated Briton' paraded in chains on the Sacred Way in a Roman triumph, alongside floats bearing embroidered displays of Britain and its people.[10]

The best known facts about Britons were that they were fierce and blue, *caerulei Britanni*, *picti Britanni*, using blue woad as warpaint; and that they wore baggy trousers. In a list of places best left unvisited, Horace includes *Britanni hospitibus feri* 'Britons, fierce to their guests'.[11] They continued to be 'fierce' in Roman poetry for many generations after the Roman conquest. 'Ocean knew his merits, Thule knew them, and the lands that the fierce Briton ploughs', wrote Rutilius in the fifth century, in praise of a provincial administrator (499–500), at the moment when Roman troops were finally saying goodbye to a province that had been at peace internally for three hundred and fifty years. It was more reasonable to allude to the savagery of the extremities of Britain. Claudian reminds the emperor Honorius that his father Theodosius had camped in Caledonian frosts: as a result of his border skirmishes the Orkneys were red with Saxon slaughter; Thule was warmed by Pictish blood; icy Ireland mourned the heaps of dead *Scotti*.[12]

Spaniards were as fierce as Britons, in earlier Roman poetry: we find *truces Hiberi, impacati Hiberi* 'cruel, unpacified Iberians'. The typical Spaniard, however, looked very different from Gauls or Britons. Martial was a Celtiberian; and whatever the ethnic mixture that created this people, in looks he describes himself as an Iberian and not a Celt.

> You walk about with your wavy locks shining, I am unruly with my Spanish hair. You are smooth from your daily resin, I have hairy legs and hairy jowls. You have lisping lips and a feeble tongue: why, my little girl has a stronger voice than you.... Stop calling me 'brother', Charmenio, or I may start calling you 'sister'.
>
> Martial 10.65[13]

Martial, least reticent of poets, is reticent on one topic that has fascinated observers of Spain. Catullus, by contrast, gladly assures his readers that Egnatius, his Iberian rival in Lesbia's bed, brushed his teeth with urine like all his countrymen:

> If you were a City man or a Sabine or a Tiburtine or a fat Umbrian or an obese Etruscan or a dark and toothy Lanuvian or a Transpadane (we reach my own people at last) or anyone else who cleans his teeth with pure water, I still shouldn't want you to flash them everywhere, because nothing's sillier than a silly grin. But you're a Celtiberian. Now in Celtiberia people brush their teeth and gums each morning with the product of their bladders – so the shinier that tooth of yours, the more piss you've swallowed.
>
> Catullus 39.10–21[14]

The population of the Roman provinces of north Africa is characterised in literature in a more nuanced way than that of western Europe. The former dominion of Carthage had become the Roman province of *Africa*, so named because it was at first Rome's only African possession. It was rich farmland, destined to be Rome's granary (p. 108). Beyond its borders newer Roman possessions would eventually form a continuous strip, a kind of buffer zone. In this region there had been a partial change from nomadic to sedentary life, so Sallust, for example, considered. He identifies the two modes of life with two ethnic names: nearer the coast were the Libyes, inland the less civilised Gaetuli. Both of these 'peoples' had once been classical nomadic barbarians, in Sallust's reconstruction, living on grass and the flesh of wild animals, without recognised customs or laws; and the Gaetuli had changed little (*Jugurtha* 18–19). Sallust is no doubt right about the gradual shift. Vergil pictures the traditional nomadic life more fully:

> Libyan shepherds, their flocks, the scattered roofed huts in which they live: what of them? Often their sheep browse onward all day, all night, through a whole month, far out into the desert, and come to no inhabited place, so wide are those plains. The African farmer carries everything with him, house, god, weapons, Amyclaean dog and Cretan quiver – like a brave Roman of the legions making his long march with his heavy pack on his back.
>
> Vergil, *Georgics* 3.339–347[15]

The typical dwellings of north Africans, mentioned here by Vergil, are *tuguria* or more precisely *mapalia* 'nomads' huts', long and narrow, constructed with curved ribs like a ship. The adventurous Marius, having fled Italy, is pictured as living in one of these in the ruins of Carthage, before returning to wreak havoc in Rome; but *mapalia* gradually become nothing more than a Latin metaphor for disorderly houses.[16]

When north Africans settled elsewhere in the Empire the distinction between nomads and sedentary farmers lost its relevance, and the names of Libyan and Gaetulian are not used. 'African' was a useful general term, and *Afra* is the name of a fictional old whore and of a real brothel-keeper at Augusta Vindelicorum, who was converted to Christianity, along with three of her staff, when St Narcissus, Bishop of Gerona from 304 to 307, put up by mistake at her establishment and, undaunted, set to work.[17] Moors were the people of the far west, the province of Mauritania: Santra, a fictional slave cook in a scurrilous epigram of Martial, fathers on his master's wife a Moorish-looking boy with crinkly hair (p. 213). Numidia and Mauritania, formerly independent states in north Africa, were both eventually engulfed in the Empire. Their peoples are characterised as horsemen and javelin-throwers – and, in common with practically every ethnic group outside Italy, changeable and unpredictable.[18]

The peoples of the West are from the beginning given traits that placed them lower on the scale of humanity than Romans of Italy. If opponents in war, they are fierce and warlike, but changeable, unreliable, and in the event unsuccessful. Within the Empire they are auxiliary soldiers or slaves or engaged in less than respectable trades. Their physical appearance is in some way extreme: Gauls are big and white, Spaniards are hairy, Africans are black.

These stereotypes are never forgotten, but they are gradually overlaid. Horace looks forward with irony to the *peritus Hiber*, the 'educated Spaniard'. The western provinces were soon to be the source of Roman citizens, senators, emperors; of advocates, of authors. Martial's appraisal of Claudia Rufina is slightly ahead of the trend ('Claudia Rufina is a daughter of the blue Britons, but how Latin is her mind! And what beauty of form! Italian mothers could take her to be Roman, Greek mothers to be one of their own': 11.53). By the time of Claudian there is no irony at all in a characterisation of 'Gaul with her learned citizens', and the Western peoples in general are given a characteristic that is at first sight unexpected: their eloquence. Had not Augustus, always a fashion-setter, found little *Mauri* boys amusing companions and good talkers?[19]

Cisalpine Gaul and the mountain provinces

Metrodorus's calculations (p. 82) bring to light a recurring contradiction in the mental geography of the Empire. Did he enter Italy (*Ausonia* in his vocabulary) when he crossed the Alps, or when he reached Luna?

Liguria and the Po valley are northern Italy to us, and they were northern Italy to Metrodorus. But to most earlier Romans this was part of Gaul. The valley of the Po or *Padus* was in fact the first Celtic-speaking region to come under Roman rule. To some, as probably to Cicero in the fulsome tribute to Gaul already quoted (p. 84), this region north of the Apennines and within the circuit of the Alps *was* Gaul. More specifically it was *Gallia Cisalpina* 'Gaul on this side of the Alps'.

The region was subdivided by the river Padus (hence the *Transpadani* of Catullus on p. 86, 'people of the far side of the Padus') and in a broader sense was defined in Roman poetry by its rivers and mountains. 'Ligurian plains and Venetian mountains shall bless them. Alpine peak and glacier shall be clothed in blushing roses. Athesis shall echo choral songs, winding Mincius shall whisper through his reeds, Padus shall make harmony with his amber-bearing alder trees', writes Claudian at an imperial wedding (*Fescennine Verses* 2.6–15). Among lesser rivers Vergil alludes to the winding Mella that flowed by Brescia. In its neat valleys shepherds gathered *amello*, a bitter herb useful to beekeepers (Vergil, *Georgics* 4.271–280). Catullus, who like Vergil was a native of Cisalpine Gaul, pictures for us a torrent high in the hills. He compares a friend's timely assistance to

> a crystal brook high on a mountain top that gushes forth from a mossy rock and after tumbling headlong down the steep valley sweeps straight across the highway thronged with people – welcome refreshment to the traveller in his weary sweat, when the sultry heat cracks the parched soil.
>
> Catullus 68.57–62

In Claudian's verses, quoted above, the alder trees of the Padus banks are familiar (black alder, *Alnus glutinosa*) but the assertion that they are amber-bearing may come as a surprise. The amber trade route began on the Baltic coast and traditionally reached the Mediterranean near the mouth of the Padus. As *Eridanus* the river was for ever identified, in Greek poetic geography, as the source of amber; the legendary trees on its banks were to Greek poets *aigeiroi* (black poplar, *Populus nigra*). But it was not true, Lucian had to conclude after enquiry, that poplars on the banks of the Eridanus shed tears of amber because of the death of their brother Phaethon. He had hoped (he asserts) to be able to hold out his cloak under a poplar tree and get a life-time's supply of amber. The boatmen disabused him of this idea. 'I was as cross as if I had let the amber slip through my fingers: I was already thinking of all the uses I would make of it.' He had also heard (he insists) that the swans of Eridanus were singers, colleagues of the god Apollo, who had turned into swans hereabouts. 'Man, will you never stop lying about our region and our river?' replied the boatmen in chorus. 'We have worked the river almost since we were children. We sometimes see a few swans in the riverside marshes. They croak, and tunelessly at that: your crows and jack-daws are Sirens by comparison' (*On Amber* 3–5).

The truth about the Padus was that, normally calm, it was potentially more violent than any other river that flows through rich farmlands to the purple sea. *Fluviorum rex Eridanus* 'the Padus, king of rivers' might rise to a dizzy crest, flooding its valley, washing away whole alder forests, sweeping away herds of cattle along with their sheds. This was one of the natural disasters that coincided with Caesar's assassination; Vergil, who grew up at Mantua, was no doubt an eye-witness.[20]

Several of Rome's western provinces were noted for their wool and wool-lens. Whether they ever rivalled those of Tarentum and Apulia was a matter for contention: 'WHITE WOOLS. Apulia has the name for the best sheepskins, Parma for the next best. The sheep that comes third acknowledges Altinum' according to a gift poem by Martial (14.155), while Columella (7.2.3) gives the order differently: Altinum best of all, along with Parma and Mutina; then Apulia and Calabria, with Tarentum the best among these. *Gallica Parma* and Mutina both belong to Cisalpine Gaul south of the Padus. Mutina produced a *bathytera* 'deeper, thicker' grade of fleece that fetched a special price.[21] North of the river, Verona, Catullus's birthplace, produced *lodices* (a regional word), blankets or ponchos. Augustus wore one when exer-cising;[22] in preparation for a different exercise Quartilla's maid spread one on the floor before getting to work on Encolpius's libido (Petronius 20.2). The territory of Mantua was sheep pasture too: 'But if you prefer to keep flocks and herds, and whether lambs or goats (damaging to crops), then look for the far-off hill pastures of well-fed Tarentum, and the fields that Mantua has lost, grassy meadows beside the river, home to swans', wrote Vergil (*Georgics* 2.195–199), reminding his Imperial reader not for the first time of the land confiscations at Mantua and Cremona that had impoverished Vergil's family with many others: *squalent abductis arva colonis*, 'the aban-doned fields are going to ruin'.

Among the cities of *Gallia Transpadana* Mantua shines out in literature as the home of Vergil.[23] We have read his sketch of the Padus in flood, and will in due course see Mantua's own river Mincius through his eyes (p. 229). North of Mantua, at the point where the river Athesis emerges from its long

Alpine valley, lies Verona, *terra docti Catulli* 'homeland of learned Catullus' and no doubt equally proud of its native poet[24] even if his dry wit had made it out to be a typically provincial city: 'Now when you say that it's a shame for Catullus to be at Verona, where everyone of the upper class has to warm his limbs in an empty bed: no, Manlius, it's not a shame but a sorrow', wrote Catullus (68.27–30) in a poetic letter, conscious of his distance from Rome and from his beloved Lesbia.

Under the early Empire Verona had two local products of note. One was the 'Raetian' wine that came from vineyards in the Athesis valley, upriver from Verona: these vines also produced smoked raisins, a favourite in Rome until the emperor Tiberius began a fashion for African raisins. The second was *panaca*, a kind of earthenware: 'PANACA. If you have visited the homeland of learned Catullus, you will have drunk Raetian wine from my fabric' (Martial 14.100).

As the local wine Raetian was naturally drunk around Verona. Further afield, Augustus liked it and sometimes drank a lot of it, which is surely why Vergil works it into his desultory list of vines and wines in the *Georgics*:

> *et quo te carmine dicam*
> *Raetica? nec cellis ideo contende Falernis!*

'Where shall I place you in my poem, O Raetian? Just don't claim equality with Falernian cellars!' (2.95–96).[25] It will indeed have been an 'acquired taste': all praise to Cato and Augustus if they saw the oenological future more clearly than their countrymen. Raetian wine was unique in its effect on the Roman palate. No other wine then known in the Graeco-Roman world was matured in wooden barrels: all other wines of Italy, Greece and the eastern Mediterranean grew old in earthenware vats. And these wooden barrels were waterproofed with the aid of good Cisalpine pitch, which made its own special contribution to the bouquet of Raetian wine.

Along the northern edge of *Gallia Cisalpina*, west from Verona, lie the great Italian lakes. Sirmio looked out on lake Benacus that surged like the sea: 'Sirmio, gem of all peninsulas and islands ... hail, lovely Sirmio! Rejoice with your master! And you, waves of lake Larius, ripple with all your laughter!' (Catullus 31). Comum overlooked the great and beautiful lake Larius.[26] 'Are you studying, fishing, hunting, or all at once?' wrote Pliny the Younger to Caninius Rufus. 'You can do all three beside our native lake Larius. The lake offers you fish, the woods all around offer game, and the glorious seclusion is your opportunity to study'. Pliny had several houses here, one rising high on cliffs with a view over the lake, a second beside the shore: 'you can fish from your bedroom window, practically from your bed, just as if you were in a boat'. Caninius's house boasted a cloistered garden where it was always springtime, a dense grove of plane trees, a green and sparkling brook, and baths that caught the sun all day.[27]

On the Adriatic coast of Cisalpine Gaul the old city of Ravenna, famous

Figure 9   Treading the grapes. Relief now in the Archaeological Museum, Venice
Source   Photo Scala, Florence

for its pelicans,[28] grew in importance through Roman times. Augustus built a naval base here. At first surrounded by lagoons, later protected by walls, Ravenna continued to control the navigation of a string of shallow waters, protected from Adriatic storms by sandbanks, that could be navigated far northwards, beyond the site where Venice was one day to be founded, towards Aquileia. Silius, in an epic catalogue, lists warriors 'from Verona, round which the Athesis flows; from Faventia that so carefully cultivates her ubiquitous pine-trees; from Pollentia rich in dusky fleeces; and then the men of Ravenna, who row slowly with heavy oars over muddy waters as they part the stagnant waters of their lagoon' (8.595–601, abridged).

Liguria lies at the south-west edge of Cisalpine Gaul, a mountainous province; its people were stony too. They were *Ligures duri atque agrestes*, 'hard-working peasant people: their land has taught them that nothing grows without assiduous cultivation and a lot of work' (Cicero, *On the Agrarian Law* 2.95). The Vagienni, whose territory lay inland, built shelters over their threshing-floors, because it so often rained at harvest time. *Coebanum*, a Ligurian cheese, was available at Rome; *lingurium*, a red amber, was found on the Ligurian coast; the herb called *ligusticum* (*Levisticum officinale*, lovage) was said to have originated here. 'The local people use it instead of pepper, as an ingredient in sauces', said the pharmacist Dioscorides (3.51).

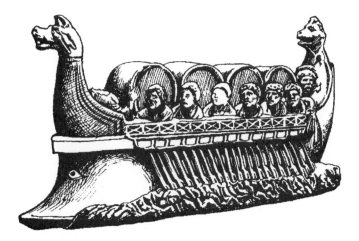

Figure 10   Wine ship carrying wooden barrels. Drawing of a sarcophagus at Neumagen, Roman Germany; now in the Rheinisches Landesmuseum, Trier

Source   By permission of British Museum Press

Classical Roman cuisine used lovage alongside pepper in practically every savoury dish.[29] Liguria's most valuable product was 'POLLENTINE WOOL. Not only wools, mournful in their dark grey colours, but also cups come from Pollentia... It is suited to shaven slaves summoned to wait at table, and not those of the first rank' (Martial 14.157–158). The wool was used in Ligurian tunics and *saga* 'cloaks'. Genua, modern Genoa, the province's main port, was the trading centre for Ligurian woollen goods, 'in which' (Strabo neatly confirms Martial's observation here) 'the majority of the households of Italy are dressed'.[30]

North-east of Cisalpine Gaul, at the head of the Adriatic, was Venetia. Aquileia, in eastern Venetia, comes into literature later; in earlier Roman times the only well-known city of Venetia was Patavium, a proud if provincial place, birthplace of the historian Livy.[31] Altinum, a smaller place to the south, produced wool; Patavium was known for woollen goods. There were *tunicae Patavinae*, made with *trilix* 'triple weave' and intended for winter wear. 'PATAVIAN TUNICS. Patavian triple weave requires many fleeces: it takes a saw to cut these thick tunics!' (Martial 14.143). Then there was *gausape, gausapum*, 'frieze', cloth which had a nap on one side and would make a good winter cloak, *paenula gausapina* (you would hardly fancy putting it on in August) or alternatively 'A SQUARE FRIEZE RUG. The Catullus country will send you blankets; we [the rugs themselves are addressing their lucky recipient] are from the region of Helicaon' (Martial 14.152).[32]

Six miles from Patavium were the pellucid, clean-tasting mineral springs called *aquae Patavinae* or *fontes Aponi*, described in full by the untiring pen of Claudian. In Martial's phrase these springs were *fontes Aponi rudes puellis* 'the springs of Aponus, unkind to girls' (p. 239). Four hundred years later Cassiodorus explained what Martial meant. If a woman entered the bath while men were there, it boiled, as if in outrage that the two sexes should bathe together naked. According to Cassiodorus's description there were three chambers, in the first of which the water was too hot to swim in, while in the third it was cold. But there were weeds and brambles growing beside the pools, the surrounding gardens were a wilderness, the buildings were ancient and crumbling.[33]

Far off at the eastern extremity of Venetia is the Timavus, a remarkable river half of whose long course is underground. It emerges through several mouths at the Adriatic shore, partly below sea level: 'through its nine mouths the sea breaks in with a mountainous roar, and threatens the land with noisy waves' (Vergil, *Aeneid* 1.242–249).[34] The hilly promontory of Histria was a producer of olive oil – unlike Cisalpine Gaul and Venetia; its coastline was gradually becoming studded with seaside villas and pleasure resorts. The bays and hills of Histria would one day be to Ravenna what Campania and Baiae had been to Rome.[35]

To the reader of Roman literature Dalmatia, also known as Illyricum, is among the most obscure provinces of the Empire – as mysterious as the *Illyrici sinus*, the 'fjords of Illyricum' that punctuate its Adriatic coastline (see Map 8). Salona, administrative capital of Dalmatia, is probably the city at which Trajan disembarks and sacrifices, on Trajan's Column (casts 224–228), in the course of his journey from Italy to fight the Second Dacian War. Behind the scene of sacrifice are shown a theatre, a round-arched gateway and a cloistered garden; a merchant ship rides in the harbour.[36] In *aurifera Dalmatia* 'gold-bearing Dalmatia' the miner came home pale-faced from study of the underworld, as yellow as the gold that he had unearthed! The province exported not only gold but also pitch. And the Vardaici of southern Dalmatia gave their name to a most important item of army equipment, the soldier's boot:[37]

> The stench of the dried-out bed of a marsh, the fumes of raw *Albulae*, the stale reek of a salt-water fishpond, a sluggish billy-goat on top of his nanny, a Veteran's *vardaicus*, a fleece twice stained with purple, a Jewess's Sabbath fart, a defendant's dreary sigh, filthy Leda's smoking lamp, wrestlers' mud made with Sabine lees, a fox in flight, a viper's lair – yes, I would rather smell of any of these than what you smell of, Bassa.
>
> Martial 4.4

The remaining smaller provinces that form a semicircle around Cisalpine Gaul are best known for their mountains and their savage inhabitants. We hear of the Pannonians 'scattered to their high mountains' by Germanicus, of the 'fortresses of Noricum' and of the successes of Drusus and Tiberius in

Raetia: 'Keen Drusus ... hurled down the Genauni, an implacable people, and the swift Breuni, and their citadels that stood upon the fearsome Alps. His elder brother joined the bitter fight, and, with good omens, scattered the vast Raeti' (Horace, *Odes* 4.14.10–16). The region offered little of value: Pannonian dogs, Norican iron and weaponry, good hunting of wild boar.[38] The Alps, trending west and then south, reach what Romans considered their highest peak in *Vesulus mons*, source of the Padus. There was wild boar to be hunted here as there was in Pannonia.[39] The great mountain range ends precipitously at the Mediterranean coast at Portus Monoeci (modern Monaco):

> In the airy Alps there is a place where a Greek deity broke down the mountains to the shoreline and it is possible to land. It is a holy place, with altars to Hercules. Winter covers it in hard snow; it raises a frosty summit to the stars. It is as if the sky itself has fallen: the place does not warm to the rays of the noonday sun or the breezes of springtime. Its rocks are solid with ice and winter frost.
>
> Petronius 122.144–150

The high Alps, once cleared of Rome's enemies, became Rome's perimeter wall, pierced by few practicable passes. The Alps were Italy's insurance against invasion. But they were never poetic favourites. They are not only *tremendae Alpes* 'fearsome Alps' but also *latebrosae Alpes* 'seclusive Alps', offering so many places of concealment; *aeriae Alpes* 'airy Alps', and this adjective is not intended as praise;[40] *hibernae Alpes* 'wintry Alps'.[41]

Transalpine Gaul

Roman contact with Gaul beyond the Alps, *Gallia Transalpina*, began with her long-standing and powerful ally, Massilia, and with the *Provincia* 'the Roman province' acquired in the second century BC to the west and the north of Massilia. *Provincia* remained the common nickname (hence its survival as modern *Provence*) for the territory that was afterwards officially known as *Gallia Narbonensis* after its administrative capital, Narbo. In his remarkable campaigns of the fifties BC Caesar conquered wide new lands that were destined to be the last refuge of the western Roman Empire in the 470s AD, when Italy was lost. They were initially distinguished from the *Provincia* under the name of *Gallia Comata* 'long-haired Gaul', a name soon obsolete.

Massilia itself (Greek *Massalia*) was settled by Greeks in the sixth century BC and became the intermediary between Gaul and the wider Mediterranean world.

> From the Greeks the Gauls learned a more civilized way of life and abandoned their barbarian ways. They took to tilling their fields and

walling their towns. They even became used to living by law rather than force of arms, to cultivating the vine and the olive.

Justin 43.4.1–2

Law and arable farming were better established in Gaul than Justin realised, but it is certainly true that Greek culture spread to Gaul by way of Massilia. Strabo completes the picture:

> There are still traces in Massalia of the old manufactures of instruments and naval equipment.... But nowadays all citizens who have the aptitude for it pursue oratory and philosophy. For some little time the city has been a college for the Gauls, and has trained this barbarian people to be so thoroughly Greek as even to write contracts in Greek. Nowadays even noble Romans go there for their education, as an alternative to study in Athens. The Gauls, now at peace, have been ready to adjust their way of life to the Massaliot example, not just individually but at the municipal level. They welcome *sophistai*: some are employed by individuals, others by city governments, like doctors.
>
> Strabo 4.1.4–5[42]

Justin is generally thought to be right about the vine and the olive, both of which have remained staples of the agriculture of Provence ever since their introduction. Pliny gives a rapid, dismissive survey of the wines of Roman Provence:

> Between Pyrenees and Alps is Massilia, with wine of two flavours. One, called 'sappy', is especially fat in flavour: this is for mixing with other wines. The reputation of Baeterrae is confined to Gaul. On the other wines of *Narbonensis* nothing need be said: they have set up a factory to produce them, altering them with smoke, and even (I wish I did not have to say this) with herbs and toxic drugs. One dealer even falsifies the flavour and colour with aloes.
>
> Pliny 14.68

Massaliot wine was nice, but the production was small. It was thick and fleshy, said Galen.[43] Baeterrae is modern Béziers, nowadays a centre for the wines of Saint-Chinian and Faugères. The smoked wines of Massilia, of which Pliny disapproved, are mentioned several times by Martial, *fumea vina Massiliae*, 'musts cooked in Massilian smoke', 'barbaric poisons ... produced by the wicked smokeries of Massilia', to place the citations in increasing order of disgust.[44] Someone must have liked them, and it requires no leap of imagination to liken them to the modern cooked wines of Rivesaltes, Banyuls and Maury, though these receive their special *rancio* quality through slow baking in the sun, not in smoke-rooms. The wines doctored with herbs have also their modern counterparts, vermouth and pastis from the south of

Figure 11 Nîmes: sixteenth-century topographical view. The shrunken medieval city
displays many signs of its past as Roman Nemausus, including the *Arènes*
or amphitheatre (left), the *Maison Carrée*, originally a temple to the
grandsons of Augustus (centre), the great aqueduct known as *Pont du Gard*
(top right), and the circuit of the abandoned walls. The *Tour Romaine* (top
centre) is really Roman, though the traditional form of the name is *Tourre-
Maigne* 'Big Tower'.

Source   From Braun and Hogenberg, *Civitates Urbis Terrarum*, vol. 1 (Cologne, 1572)

France being as popular still as the outlawed absinthe used to be. Although
not included in Pliny's list here, wines of the Rhône valley were already
known in Rome. In its sheltered microclimates the Allobrogian grape
produced the *picatum* wine marketed at Vienne (*pulchra Vienna, vitifera Vienna*
'beautiful, vine-growing Vienne', Martial called it), said to have the natural
taste of pitch although it was not matured in pitched barrels, as Raetian
wine was.[45] South of there, the territory of the Vocontii produced a version
of *passum*, raisin wine, 'locally called *dulce*'.

> They keep the grape hanging on the vine for an especially long time,
> with the stalk twisted; or some make an incision in the vine shoot, into
> the pith; others dry the grapes in the sun on tiled roofs. It is always the
> *helvennaca* grape that is used.

Pliny 14.83–84[46]

It was the Romans who first developed gardens and orchards in Gaul: archaeological evidence for this is as clear as negative evidence can be. Literary evidence comes later, in the poems of Venantius Fortunatus in the sixth century. He tells of the private garden of his patroness Ultrogotho at modern St Germain-des-Prés near Paris, lush with the green grass of spring, with roses, with shady vines heavy with grapes, with red and yellow apples ready to fall at the first breeze, as fine in aroma as they are sweet in savour (*Poems* 6.6). Elsewhere Venantius writes to Gregory, historian and Bishop of

Map 6   Western half of the Roman Empire

Tours, thanking him for a present of apples and grafted apple saplings, *graf-fiola*, and hoping that Gregory will one day feast on the apples of Paradise (*Poems* 5.16).

A local species of maple, *acer Gallicanus* (*Acer pseudoplatanus*, sycamore) was used for making tables (*mensa acerna*) and beds.[47] Two breeds of dogs originating in Gaul were well known in the Empire. One was simply called-*catulus Gallicanus* 'Gallic dog'. When full grown (its friends were unable to deny) it was shaggy and ugly: it whined and had a vicious look, but was good for tracking. As a puppy it was something else: 'If you want to hear all the charm of this little puppy, this page would not be enough for my story', asserts Martial's gift poem (14.198).[48] The second breed was the 'keen *vertragus*, hunting for his master, not for himself: he will bring you a hare in his teeth without a mark' (Martial 14.200). Its name was said to mean 'swift runner' in Celtic.

The three provinces formed from Caesar's conquests were *Gallia Belgica, Aquitania* and *Gallia Lugdunensis*, the last and largest named after Lugdunum. This city was regarded in some ways as the Gallic metropolis, site of the altar of Roma and Augustus erected by all the peoples of Gaul. Here, 'at the sixteenth milestone from Vienne', the emperor Claudius was born. 'I saw a mountain looming over two rivers', said Hercules, addressing the dead Claudius in Seneca's satire, 'exactly facing Phoebus as he rises; there great Rhodanus flows with his rushing stream, and Arar quietly laps the shore with still waters, wondering which way to steer his course. Was this the land that nourished your Spirit?' (*Apocolocyntosis* 6–7). Seneca knew the place well. The great granite spur of Fourvière looks down on Lyon from the west, facing the rising sun. The flowing together of swift Rhône and slow Saône (*Rhodanus, Arar*) would become a commonplace of the Latin poetry of Gaul.[49]

More of the rivers of Gaul emerge in later literature. First the *Mosella*, modern Moselle, in a pretty fifth-century poem, Ausonius's *Mosella*. Then *Sequana*, the Seine, with its fishy waters, and *Liger*, the Loire (already *caerula lympha* 'blue stream' to Tibullus) whose 'glassy waters' bordered the farm of Bishop Felix of Nantes: 'the river refreshes it with its waters, the vines shade it with their leaves, and the whistling north wind whips the long grass in the meadows'. The north-west extremity of Gaul was Armorica, modern Brittany, which could with pardonable exaggeration be described as 'the furthest region of the world', *ultima regio in orbe*.[50] Among Gallic cities we read in poetry of fat Bordeaux, *crassa Burdigala*, with its numerous profes-sors; of Toulouse, sacred to Pallas, *Palladia Tolosa*, producer of square cheeses, eventually lost to the Visigoths, *capta Tolosa*; and of the citadel of Poitiers, *Pictavae arces*.[51]

The Bituriges, whose name survives in modern Bourges, became known for their ironwork (Rutilius 353) but the best known product of the three provinces of Gaul was wool and woollens. *Sagum*, to begin with this word of Celtic origin, was a coarse woollen cloak. Celtic soldiers had dressed for battle in cloaks and trousers. Romans never took to trousers, but Roman soldiers and others became habitual wearers of Celtic cloaks.[52] They were soon well known in Italian cities, though far below Tyrian city 'suits' in respectability. 'You eat Lucrine *peloris*, I get the one from the sea – but my throat is no less free-born than yours. You are dressed by Cadmean Tyre, I by fat Gaul: do I have to love you in purple, Marcus?' (Martial 6.11). Why *pinguis Gallia*, 'fat Gaul'? Gauls were big and fleshy, but Martial really means 'greasy Gaul' because of the greasy Gallic wool from which *saga* were made. The wool and the cloaks came from the country of the Leuci between Moselle and Marne, *Leuconica saga*, and also from the Lingones and the Santones; from the last two there also came a typical hooded cloak, *cucullus, bardocucullus*. This Latin word, a Celtic or Germanic loan, is the origin of the modern 'cowl' and 'cagoule'. We know what these ancient grey cagoules looked like from the statuettes of hooded figures that are found at the sanctuary of Dea Sequana at the source of the river Seine. Martial also talks of *Gallica palla*, a short Gaulish tunic or coat.[53] Gallic wool could naturally be used for stuffing pillows and cushions as well. 'LEUCONIAN STUFFING. Are your bedstraps too close to your feather mattress for comfort? Take these fleeces, shorn for Leuconian cloaks. – CIRCENSIAN STUFFING. Marsh reed chopped up is called Circensian stuffing. The poor man buys this straw instead of Leuconian wool' (Martial 14.159–160).[54]

Britain

> Three unfortunate counsels of the Island of Britain: to give place for
> their horses' fore-feet on the land to Julius Caesar [*Ulkessar*] and the
> men of Rome, in requital for Meinlas; and the second, to allow Horsa
> and Hengist and Rhonwen into this island; and the third, the three-fold
> dividing by Arthur of his men with Medrawd at Camlan.
>
> *Triads of the Island of Britain* 59[55]

With hindsight it was an unfortunate decision. Caesar established a Roman presence. From his time there were more Roman traders in Britain and more British princes in Rome; it no longer mattered to strategists that Britain belonged to a different world, that it lay beyond the shores of the known sea, that the signs of the zodiac were seen in an alien configuration in British skies.[56] Augustus's much talked-of expedition *in ultimos orbis Britannos* 'to the Britons, furthest people of the world' never happened, but Claudius would invade in AD 43; and not long afterwards even the blue-shielded Brigantes of the north were to be seen wearing Roman chains.

Britain was cold, inhospitable, *ferox provincia* 'a savage province',[57] scene of bravery and bloodshed. 'I don't want to be Caesar, to walk among the Britons, to suffer Scythian frosts', Florus hummed (p. 201); he might as well have located the frosts in Britain as in Scythia. Statius addresses Crispinus, son of Vettius Bolanus who had completed the Brigantian campaign, a bold young Roman soon perhaps to take part in Agricola's northern adventure in Caledonia in the 80s:

> To which countries, to which of Caesar's worlds are you posted? Will you breast the Northern rivers and the choppy Rhine waters, or sweat in the hot acres of Libya? Will you set Pannonian mountains trembling, and the shifty Sauromatae? Will sevenfold Danube be your lodging?... Or will you tread the sand of Solyma, and the captured palm-groves of Idume, who planted her fruitful orchards for a [Roman] conqueror?
>
> Are you to revisit the scene of your own brave father's victories? How wild Araxes will thrill with joy! What pride will swell the Caledonian moors! I foresee some ancient native of that bloodthirsty country telling you, 'This was your father's judgment seat! This was the very mound where he stood to address his cavalry! Along this line – do you see – he built guard posts and forts; this is his wall and moat. These weapons were his offerings to the god of war: read the dedications. This was his own cuirass that he would put on at the call to battle, and *this* is the one that he stripped from the British king.'
>
> Statius, *Silvae* 5.2.132–149[58]

The Romans remembered Britain for the bitter campaigns that they had fought there, 'veterans butchered, cities burnt, armies cut off: they fought for their lives, never mind victory' (Tacitus, *Agricola* 5). Britain remembered the Romans for the cities that they had built and the luxuries that they had brought with them. Cities in Britain scarcely appear in Roman poetry – though we can read of the British usurper, Magnus Maximus, as *Rutupinus latro* 'the bandit of Rutupiae'; his home city (modern Richborough in Kent) had been celebrated already in the first century, for oysters.[59] But they are remembered later. A city lost to the Saxons in the seventh century is mourned as

> the white town in the breast of the wood; this is its symbol ever: blood on the surface of its grass. The white town in the land; its symbol is green graves, and blood under the feet of its men. The white town in the valley; glad is the kite at the bloodshed of battle. Its people have perished.
>
> *Elegy on Cynddylan*[60]

Most admired later were the hot baths that the Romans had developed.

> The third wonder of Britain is the Hot Pool in Huich country, surrounded by a wall made of brick and stone. Men may go there to bathe at any time, and every man can have the kind of bath he likes. If he wants, it will be a cold bath; if he wants a hot bath, it will be hot.
>
> Nennius 67

While most other monuments of Roman Britain were crumbling, these confident structures remained for the people of later centuries, both British and Saxon, to explore and to take pleasure in. Nennius surely means to describe *Aquae Sulis*, modern Bath, lost to the Saxons in 577. An early Anglo-Saxon poem seems to be a meditation on Aquae Sulis too, though nothing specific confirms the identification:

> This wall was well-built, but fate broke it. The fortress has crumbled, and the giants' work is rotting. Roof timbers have snapped, towers have fallen, gatehouses are cracked by frost; tiles that kept out storms are cracked, sagging, undermined by age. The makers and builders are in the earth's grip, dead and gone, in the grave's grasp, and a hundred generations have passed.... There were fine buildings, bath-houses, tall gables and the noise of crowds, many mead-halls full of revelry: fate changed it all.... There were men once, cheerful, flashing their rich gold, heady with wine, gleaming with armour, who gazed on gold, on silver, on carved gems, on the wealth of their stores, on glowing amber, and on this fine town and its wide realm; and on the stone-built courts where hot streams flow copiously and are caught up by this wall in its lap, to give a warm bath at the heart of the house, and that was pleasant! and then they let the warm water run across the grey stone into this round pool ...
>
> *The Ruin*

We can read of Britain as the Romans saw it in the pages of Caesar and of Tacitus. But if we want a more sympathetic view of the cold and foggy province, we must look to an author who writes from the standpoint of Britain.

> Its shores are varied by the mouths of many rivers, notably Thames and Severn, arms of the sea along which luxuries from overseas used to be brought by ship. It was embellished by twenty-eight cities, numerous towns, and well-planned fortifications – walls, embattled towers, gates and castles, whose sturdily built roofs reared menacingly skyward. Like a chosen bride in varied finery, it is arrayed with wide plains and pleasant hills ideal for a flourishing agriculture, and with mountains that offer convenient pasture to transhumant flocks; flowers of different colours regale the walker's eye. It is watered by clear springs, constantly rippling over shingle as white as snow; sparkling rivers, gliding with a soft murmur and ensuring sweet sleep to any who lie on their banks; and lakes brimming over with a cool swell of living water.
>
> Gildas, *Ruin of Britain* 3[61]

Beside their cities, roads and baths, Romans introduced new plants to Britain, notably garden vegetables and fruits; one piece of literary evidence is Pliny's history of the spread of the *cerasus* (sour cherry, *Prunus cerasus*) from Anatolia to Italy (p. 166) and westwards: 'There were no sour cherries in Italy before L. Lucullus's defeat of Mithridates, 680 years from Rome's foundation. He brought them here from Pontus; 120 years later they crossed the ocean to Britain' (Pliny 15.102). Pliny's dating is in the AD 40s, coinciding with Claudius's invasion of Britain. But the Romans failed to establish the grape vine in Britain. Roman soldiers stationed here, unless of high enough rank to command supplies from abroad, had to learn to like British ale, brewed from *braces* 'malted barley'.[62] However, thanks to the Roman appreciation of stronger beverages, those who eventually defended Britain against the Saxon hordes had a wider range of intoxicating drinks to fortify them for battle. In addition to ale and the luxurious import wine, mead had joined the repertoire. It is the only local product that could have attained an alcoholic strength similar to that of Italian wine by straight fermentation. *Gwin a med o eur vu eu gwirawt*, a poet sang of the Britons who fought at Catterick, 'wine and mead from gold vessels was their drink'; *med evynt melyn melys maglawr*, 'they drank mead, yellow, sweet, ensnaring'; *gwin a med a mall a amucsant*, 'they enjoyed wine and mead and malt'; and, with a further refinement of half-forgotten luxury, *ervessit gwin gwydyrlestri llavn*, 'he drank the wine of brimming glass vessels' (*Gododdin*). Glassware had been imported into Britain even in Strabo's time.[63]

In return for the luxury that Rome brought to Britain, Britain sent little back to Rome: its gold; its tin, known in the ancient world long before the name of Britain was heard; its dogs, 'a swift breed, ideal for hunting in our world' (Nemesianus, *Cynegetica* 225–226) and used locally in warfare;[64] and, of all things, its washing-tubs: 'BASCAUDA. Here I am, a barbarian tub from the painted Britons: nowadays Rome gladly calls me her own' (Martial 14.99).[65]

Spain

Romans fought for two centuries for the mastery of Spain, a period far longer than was required for the subjugation of Gaul. Numantia, metropolis of the Celtiberi and symbol of their resistance to Roman conquest,[66] fell at last in 133 BC. With Carthage, it had been one of the 'two great threats to our dominion', *duos terrores huius imperi*, that were destroyed by Scipio Africanus (Cicero, *For Murena* 58).

In brief, Spain was *aurifera terra* 'gold-bearing country'.[67] North-western Spain, homeland of the *bellicosus Cantaber*, 'warlike Cantabrian',[68] subdued only under Augustus, repaid its conqueror in gold, *Gallaicum aurum* (editors spell it *Callaicum*), the reddish gold of north-western Spain that 'the Asturian digs in Gallaican fields'. The district was rich also in copper, lead and red lead, *minium*, after which the river Minius was said to be named.[69]

Spanish rivers were rich in gold dust. We find in poetry *aureus Tagus* 'golden Tagus', 'the yellow gravel of Tartessian Tagus'; *dives Hiberus* 'the rich

Hiberus'; 'Baetis, whose sparkling waters tinge the fleeces gold'.[70] The river Salo, *Salo Celtiber* with gold-bearing banks, flowing beside 'Bilbilis, proud of her gold and her iron' was particularly well known for metal-working – hence it was *rigidus Salo* 'rigid Salo'.[71] Martial offered 'a dagger, engraved with the mark of a narrow circle: Salo dipped this hissing blade in his icy waters' as a relatively cheap Saturnalia gift, contrasted with a *parazonium*, a far more costly present of officer's dagger and swordbelt (14.33–34).

Spain lies at the same latitude as Italy. A certain similarity in climate predisposed Romans towards a favourable view of what the country offered. 'Spain is fit for cereal crops and friendly to the vine, and there is no land in which the tree of Pallas rises higher' (Silius 1.237–238).[72] In a fuller evaluation, therefore, Spain was a land of varied wealth.

> Spain does not suffer extreme heat like Africa, nor continual wind like Gaul. It lies between them; its temperate climate and healthy seasonal rains make it fertile in all kinds of crops, to the extent that its abundant production of all kinds of foodstuffs meets not only local needs but also those of Italy and Rome. From Spain come large quantities of wheat, and also of wine, honey and oil. The country has excellent deposits of iron and herds of swift horses... There is plenty of flax and esparto; no land is richer in red lead. The rivers ... flow gently, irrigating vineyards and plains ... and most of them are rich in gold, deposited as gold dust.
>
> Justin 44.1.4–7[73]

There is high praise for Spanish olive oil and honey. Spanish fish sauce, 'made from the juices of a Hiberian fish', was possibly the best in the Roman world. This *garum* or *liquamen* was a considerable item of Mediterranean trade, packed in amphoras like oil and wine. The product of the fermentation of fish, or of the discarded parts of fish, *garum* was indispensable in the Roman kitchen. This dark-coloured, strong-tasting and strong-smelling liquid was the way in which salt was normally added to the diet: in the recipes in *Apicius liquamen* is called for in nearly every dish, salt in only three out of 478. Its manufacture was a lengthy process.

> LIKOUAMEN is made thus. Fish entrails are put in a pot and salted (little fish, especially sand-smelt, small red mullet, picarel or anchovy, or any small enough, are used whole) and left to cook in the sun, stirring frequently. When the heat has cooked them, the sauce is extracted thus: a deep close-woven basket is inserted into the centre of the jar containing these fish, and the sauce seeps into the basket: so *likouamen* is obtained, filtered through the basket. The solid residue makes *alix*.
>
> *Geoponica* 20.46.1[74]

Spanish fish sauce breaks into literature inauspiciously at Nasidienus's disastrous gastronomic dinner, but other sources confirm its quality. It was produced in very large quantities, as is evident from archaeological exploration of Spanish salteries.[75]

Spanish wine was already beginning to be famous, competing with Italian vintages at a level that Roman connoisseurs are careful to judge precisely. As a wine producer, *Tarraco vitifera* 'vine-growing Tarraco'[76] was second only to Latium, in a phrase of Silius (3.369–370): he means that its wine was nearly as good as Alban and Setian, the best wines of Latium in the late first century AD. Martial, not one to undervalue the produce of Spain, judges similarly: 'So far from rivalling the Campanian vintage, Tarraco produced this wine to compete against Tuscan jars', he says in a gift poem (13.118), placing it well below Falernian but in competition with other wines of central Italy. There was bad wine in Spain too, *faex Laietana*, 'Laietan dregs' from the neighbourhood of modern Barcelona, no doubt a sharp memory of Martial's homeland (1.26).

Already in the second century BC Spain was exporting that useful product *spartum* (esparto, *Lygeum spartum*) and Capua in Italy was importing it. It was used in shoes, in pressing bags for olives and grapes, and in ropes[77] – hence a supposed former galley slave is said to have flanks scarred by 'Iberian ropes', *Hibericis funibus* (Horace, *Epodes* 4.3).

There were Spanish breeds of dogs and of horses: in fact two Gallaican breeds of horses, the larger *Theldo* and the smaller *Asturco* 'Asturian'. Nero had a favourite Asturco. They were good enough to promise to a pretty boy, and more costly than the amorous pedagogue of Petronius's tale could really afford; and they could be trained to perform to music.[78] Famous too were Spanish rabbits: this was definitely a localised species in early times, not very well known in Italy and apparently quite unknown in Greece. Catullus marks down the origin of the hated rival Egnatius, 'son of rabbity Celtiberia', distinguished by his thick beard and his teeth brushed with urine.[79]

To the reader of Latin literature the central place of central Spain is unavoidably Bilbilis in Celtiberia, Martial's birthplace,[80] to which he eventually returned after his years of relative fame in the great city. 'While you wander restlessly in the noisy Subura, Juvenal', he gloats, 'my old Bilbilis, proud of her gold and her iron, has taken me back and made me a peasant. I get up to a fire heaped with logs from the neighbouring holm-oak wood, a fire that the housekeeper crowns with many a cooking-pot' (12.18, abridged). He adds some details on the attractive young huntsmen of Celtiberia, an enthusiasm that he considered Juvenal to share. Another addressee is asked whether it can be better to hunt for frogs in the Laurentan marshes than to be throwing red mullets back into the river because they weigh less than three pounds; to make your meal off stale *peloris* rather than off Spanish oysters just as good as those of Baiae and so plentiful that a master will let his slave boys eat them; to go hunting and catch nothing but foxes or badgers, when Martial in Spain is pestered by hares that come and trip over his fishing-nets! Any orders from Bilbilis? (10.37).

Figure 12   Hare feasting on grapes. Central panel from a mosaic floor in late
Roman Antioch

Source   By permission of The J. Paul Getty Museum, Malibu, California

But the place-names of Spain grated on the Italian ear. Mindful of
Horace's poems on the neighbourhood of Venusia, Martial meets the challenge.

> Offspring of Celts and Iberians, with pride and pleasure we shall versify
> the rough place-names of our country. Bilbilis, best of all sources of
> savage metal, defeating the Chalybes and the Noricans. Platea, noisy
> with iron: Salo, temperer of weapons, encircles her with his narrow but
> violent stream. The sanctuary and the choruses of Rixamae; the festive
> dinners of Carduae; Peteris, blushing with twined roses; Rigae, the
> ancient theatre of our fathers; the Silai, experts with the light javelin;
> the lakes of Turgontum and Turasia and the clear shallows of little
> Tvetonissa; the sacred holm-oak wood of Burado, through which even
> the laziest traveller goes on foot.
>
> > Martial 4.55

Martial's enthusiasm for the Spanish countryside, its forests, its cold
rivers, its mountains (these latter admired at a safe distance) appears
nowhere more clearly than in the poem in book I of his *Epigrams* that is
addressed to a fellow Spaniard, Licinianus.

You will never be forgotten by the Celtiberi. Our dear Spain sings your praise. Now, Licinianus, you are to visit lofty Bilbilis, proud in its armour and its horses. You shall see old snow-capped Caius, holy Vadavero's rugged peaks, and the sweet grove of tender Boterdus, blessed by generous Pomona. You shall swim the easy currents of warm Congedus and the gentle lakes of the nymphs; thus relaxed, you shall temper your body in the narrow Salo, colder than steel; as you picnic there, Voberca herself shall offer game to your arrows. Shaded by sheltering trees, you shall weaken the force of a cloudless summer beside the golden Tagus. Freezing Dercenna, and Nutha colder than snow, shall quench your burning thirst. But when frosty December and lifeless midwinter roar with the hoarse North Wind, you will return to the sunny shores of Tarraco and your own Laietania, and sacrifice home-bred boars and hinds trapped in nets, and run down a wily hare upon your fine horse – and leave the stags for your bailiff to deal with. The very forest will approach your fireside, dirty-faced children will ring the hearth, as you shout to the huntsman to join your meal.

Martial 1.49[81]

The lushest region of Spain was Baetica, named after the river Baetis (modern Guadalquivir). Poets might call it *Tartessus*, the name of the legendary kingdom that had flourished here, centuries ago, when the Greeks were exploring the Mediterranean; ethnographers could call it *Turdetania*. 'Baetis, whose hair is bound with a wreath of olives, whose sparkling waters tinge the fleeces gold, who is loved by Bromius and by Pallas' (Martial 12.98), 'Tartessian Baetis, nurse of the Iberian fold' (8.28: p. 66) was renowned for its sheep, whose fleece had an attractive naturally grey-brown colour. Martial can talk of a little girl's 'hair nicer than the wool of a Baetic flock' (p. 263). He can weigh 'a bale of Spanish fleeces' against ten whole *aurei* and various other estimable gifts in deciding what to give an older girl who has been particularly accommodating (p. 260). Admittedly Martial is a native of Spain; but his is not the only praise to be found for the sheep and the wool of Baetica.[82] From these fleeces were made *Baeticatus*, *lacernae Baeticae*, clothes and especially capes of Baetic wool. Other wool had to be dyed; Baetic wool imparted a natural (though dull) colour, or so Martial's gift poem proudly asserts: 'My wool tells no lies ... my own sheep dyed me' (14.133). The old port of Gades was the centre of trade in Spanish sheepskins and fleeces. The agricultural writer Columella tells how his own grandfather, a farmer at Gades, had cross-bred African and Tarentine sheep to improve the native stock.[83]

The great inland city on the Baetis was 'rich Corduba', 'Corduba, glory of the gold-bearing country', and most fulsomely 'Corduba, more fertile than oily Venafrum, as free-flowing as the oil-jars of Histria, whose sheep are finer than those of white Galaesus and falsified neither by murex nor by madder' (Martial 12.63). Corduba was the home of the two Senecas, the teacher father and the philosopher son; home also of the one and only Lucan, epic poet of the Civil War. Here was a plane tree, dense with foliage, planted by Julius Caesar's own hand. Down river, as the Baetis swelled, was Hispalis 'washed by a stream as wide as the sea'.[84]

Gades (modern Cadiz) was a very ancient place, capital of legendary Tartessus. We have met several places 'at the end of the world', and this was another, *remotae Gades, hominum finis Gades* 'distant Gades, Gades the edge of humankind'. Lying outside the Pillars of Hercules (the twin rocks at the Straits of Gibraltar) the city itself was naturally sacred to Hercules, with a venerable temple and a unique ritual: the divine adventurer was worshipped by male priests only, with a perpetual flame and with no images.[85]

But 'the associations of the place were not entirely wholesome,' to quote Leary's commentary on Martial. *Improbae Gades, iocosae Gades* 'naughty, sexy Gades' was famous for the slave dancers it sent to Rome. Telethusa (whether she is a real person we cannot know) is celebrated in epigrams by Martial and the poet of the *Priapeia* (19.1: p. 230): 'Skilled in sexy movements to the rhythm of the Baetic beat, and in dancing in the modes of Gades ... Telethusa has driven her former master mad: he sold her as a slave – now he's buying her back as his mistress' (Martial 6.71).

Whether the dancing girls of Gades had any historic link with the *ambubaiae* of Syria is, I think, unknown. The first historical sign of their existence is in the narrative of Eudoxus, who attempted a circumnavigation of Africa in the late second century BC. Eudoxus loaded a ship at Gades with *mousika paidiskaria* 'girl artistes' along with physicians and 'other artisans', intending to sell them all profitably in India. Familiar with the Indian Ocean trade, he was evidently confident of finding a market for European girls in India, as there certainly was later.[86] In a typical act the performers, solo or in a group, were dancers, singers and instrumentalists, setting up an insistent rhythm with cymbals (*Tartesiaca aera* 'Tartessan bronze') and bells (hence Statius's *cymbala tinnulaeque Gades*: p. 231); Martial could imagine a young Roman dandy humming *cantica Gaditana* 'Gaditan songs' to himself. But the most enthralling feature was the dance: the shimmering of the thighs, the sinuous motions of the girl's arms and her whole body that repeatedly brought her buttocks almost to the ground. 'With such tremulous vibrations, such languid caresses, she would make old Hippolytus masturbate', writes Martial in a poem designed to accompany the expensive gift of a dancing girl (14.203). The whole performance was so erotic that Martial on one occasion manages to extend the epithet *improbus* 'naughty' from the dancers themselves to an owner and trainer, producing an *improbus magister* 'improper impresario from Gades'.[87]

Africa

Africa terribilis 'fearsome Africa' was the scene of many a Roman battle including some of the bitterest fighting of the Civil War,[88] and it was a place where rich Romans eventually had huge estates, piling wealth into their barns from Libyan threshing-floors. Pliny said that half the province of Africa was owned by six landowners; it was conceivable in Horace's poetry that some one plutocrat would join Libya with distant Gades under his sole ownership.[89]

The province of Africa, as originally constituted in what is now northern Tunisia, belonged to a continent of Africa: the homonyms encompass a world of contrasts. The original province was eminently suitable for grain (there were districts where the normal yield was said to be a hundred to one): Horace talks of 'all the wheat in Africa'; Cicero lists Sicily, Africa and Sardinia as Rome's 'three granaries', *tria frumentaria*; Aristides, 150 years later, alters the list to Sicily, Africa and Egypt.[90] Africa was also good for cattle and sheep; it was not suitable for all tree fruits but Carthaginian gardening skill made the most of the opportunities. Pomegranates, figs and olives did well. The approach by sea was violent and treacherous; poets often recalled the Syrtes with their dangerous reefs, *barbarae Syrtes* 'barbarous Syrtes where the Moorish sea is always stormy'.[91] Beyond the Roman provinces, the desert was utterly inhospitable.

> Where Africa spreads her untilled plains, the burnt land bears nothing but the poison of snakes in plenty; yet where a temperate strip blesses the fields, her fertility is not surpassed by Henna's crops nor by the Egyptian husbandman. Here the Numidians rove, a people ignorant of the bridle: the light switch they ply between the horse's ears steers it no less effectively than the bit.
>
> Silius 1.211–217[92]

Two breeds of north African horses were recognised in the Empire, Mauritanian and Mazacian. Both were long-maned, with ugly heads and badly-shaped bellies. They were hard-working, though unused to the bridle. The emperor Nero had a favourite Mazacian horse. There was also a breed of Libyan dogs.[93] The huntsmen, horses and dogs had serious work to do. Africa was *nutrix ferarum* 'nurse of wild animals' (Vitruvius 8.2.24) – and this is surely the cliché that lies behind Juvenal's dry *nutricula causidicorum Africa* 'Africa, nurse of lawyers' (7.147). The Numides, the Libyes, the Gaetuli and the Marmarici were the peoples who hunted lions, *Marmarici leones, Libycae leaenae*. At least one poet thought that the Gaetuli could charm lions,[94] and one other poet could think of no prouder death for 'a lion at whose rule lions themselves would tremble, one to whom the marble-painted Nomad country would offer the crown' than to fall a prey to the Roman populace in the amphitheatre. 'How well his broad chest became the hunting spears! What joy he took in his fine death!' (Martial 8.53).

The most valuable products of Africa that were available for display in wealthy Roman households were citronwood and marble. 'Happy forests, the gift of Atlas' were the forests on the slopes of mount Atlas where the *Libyssa citrus* flourished. This was a species of cypress (*Thuja articulata*, citronwood), 'child of a Moorish forest', especially valued for tabletops made from a single cross-section of the trunk, obliquely named by Martial *Libycae trabes* 'Libyan plinths'. They were, perforce, small: Roman dining did not demand the large oblong tables of modern usage, and citronwood tables were of the correct size, of demonstrable value, of wondrous mottled beauty – and with an aroma of citrus or lemon, whence the tree's Latin name. They are among the favourite purchases of many a Roman fictional connoisseur. The table's base will ideally be made of Indian, or perhaps more appropriately African ivory.[95] Its attractive aroma rendered citronwood suitable for more romantic uses, such as writing-tablets (an expensive present in a poem by Martial) and, in Propertius's imagination, panelling or ornaments in a 'citronwood bedroom', *thyius thalamus*.[96]

The marble was *Nomadum lapis* 'Numidian stone', Libyan yellow marble or giallo antico from the quarries at Simitthus, near modern Ghardimaou in Tunisia. These 'columns from furthest Africa', 'from the deserts of Africa' (slightly inexact) were incorporated in the first controversial memorial for Julius Caesar, erected in the Forum Romanum and eventually destroyed. Numidian marble had a firm place in the Roman Imperial repertoire, in which the construction of baths, of public buildings and of tombs required the use of several coloured stones, from different regions, side by side (p. 240): 'His fine warm baths were built of every kind of marble, whether found at Carystus or exported by Phrygian Synnas or the African Nomad country or washed by Eurotas with his verdant stream' (Martial 9.75). *Libyci lapilli* 'African gravel' was the same marble used for a footpath.[97]

Africa supplied several delicacies to the Roman table. Highly prized was the guinea-fowl, *Afra avis, Numidica* 'African bird, Numidian' (*Numida meleagris*).[98] The *Afra coclea* 'African snail' was said by gastronomes to be of high quality and good for the delicate digestion of an epicure:[99]

> Simmer, whole, in water, then, without flavouring, roast on hot coals. Take with wine and fish sauce.
>
> Pliny 30.44

Punici mali 'Punic apples' (*Punica granatum*, pomegranate) demonstrated by their Latin name that they had come to Italy from Carthage: they were eventually widely grown.[100] 'The authority of the emperor Tiberius gave an especially good name for smoked grapes to the smokeries of Africa', Pliny tells us (14.16). Statius knew of 'Libyan olives', conserved in oil that gradually soaked through their papyrus wrapping as they were carried home from market (p. 215). Even while Carthage flourished, fresh figs from Africa had been available in Rome.

'Cato once brought into the Chamber an early fresh fig from Africa, and held it up for senators to see. "I wonder," he said, "how long ago you think this fig was picked?" Not long, they agreed. "Quite right," said Cato, "it was picked at Carthage, three days ago. That is how close our enemy is to our walls." The Third Punic War was at once begun' (Pliny 15.74 – 5).

The origin and location of Carthage were known to every Roman: an ancient city founded by colonists from Tyre, directly facing Italy and the far-off Tiber mouth, rich in resources (Vergil, *Aeneid* 1.12–13). One more thing that everyone knew about Carthage was that this city was *aemula imperii Romani* 'a rival to the dominion of Rome'. The 'proud heights of hated Carthage' were a focus for enmity, and the name of Carthage's great general, Hannibal, served as a metaphor for a devastator.[101] But the old Carthaginians had been fraudulent not by nature – Cicero generously insisted – but because of geography. They had had plenty of training in the arts of deception, in negotiating with merchants of many nationalities who visited their busy harbours (*On the Agrarian Law* 2.95). By his time it was safe enough to be generous on the subject. In accordance with the famous injunction of Cato, *Carthago delenda est*, Carthage had been razed at the end of the Third Punic War, and its rich farms and orchards had become Roman. Its purple-dyed cloth – a luxury whose manufacture had been learnt from Tyre and Sidon – was still produced.[102]

The wealth of Lepcis Magna, *Lepcis in remotis Syrtibus avia* 'unapproachable Lepcis beyond the distant Syrtes', was in goathair. Here the river Cinyps (now Wadi Kaam) reached the sea. Its valley, arid now, was then green enough to support flourishing herds of goats. The beards, greying chins and shaggy coats of Cinyphian he-goats were sheared to make sails, tents, hunting nets apparently (*lina Cinyphia*) and felt slippers (*udones Cilicii*).[103]

Further east, the old Greek colony of Cyrene (Map 8) remained an exporter of wheat. Its special wealth, the wonderful spice called *silphium* (also in Latin *laser, laserpicium*) had been well known under the Roman republic, 'excellent in kitchen use and in medicines; worth its weight in silver *denarii*' according to Pliny. It was exported to Capua like other aromatics.[104] 'Bordering on Cyrenaea', wrote Strabo, 'is the country that produces *silphion* and this plant's eventual product, the Cyrenaic resin. It came close to dying out when the natives, in the course of some dispute, erupted and destroyed the roots of the plant. They are nomads' (17.3.22). It soon became clear that the supply had not recovered after all. *Silphium* had never been successfully cultivated: the trade always depended on controlled tapping of the wild plants. Pliny tells us how things were a hundred years after Strabo. 'For many years now it has not been seen in that region; the agents who lease grazing land, scenting higher profits, overgrazed it for sheep pasture. The single stem found within living memory was sent to the emperor Nero'. He adds that a substitute was imported from Iran (known to us as asafoetida: p. 189). The silphium of Cyrenaica occurs twice more in the historical record, in the very literary correspondence of Bishop Synesius in the early fifth century. Either Nero or Synesius ate the last of it, and it is now extinct.[105]

Figure 13   Arcesilas, King of Cyrene, supervising his city's trade, possibly in
silphium; he is attended by the royal cat and a stray lizard. Spartan black-
figure cup of the sixth century BC

Source   By permission of the Bibliothèque nationale de France, Paris

The islands

It was unwise to embark on open sea voyages in winter. Thus the islands of
the western Mediterranean were inaccessible for several months each year.
There was a scale of inaccessibility: travel to Sicily was only interrupted in
stormy weather; Malta and the Balearic islands would expect few visitors
between October and April.

The ships that sailed from Ebuso (modern Ibiza) to Rome brought the
excellent figs of the island, carefully packed in wooden boxes for sale to
gourmets.[106] The Balearic islands were most famous, however, for the
Balearis funda 'Balearic sling', a specialised weapon made of coarse hemp
(*stuppa*) and loaded with lead balls to lethal effect.[107]

'Corsica with its blind rocks' – the unseen reefs around its shores[108] – was a
dangerous and threatening place. It loomed in the distance as one sailed
northwards along the Tuscan coast of Italy. 'Corsica begins to show her dark

mountains: the shadowy cloud cap, equally dark, makes the ridge seem higher than it is' (Rutilius 431–432), and the island had little to offer. There was bad wine, 'black poison from a Corsican jar' (Martial 9.2). There was real poison too. The *cicuta* (*Conium maculatum*, hemlock) of Corsica was a useful plant to the compounder of drugs, and brought with it memories of murder and execution. Socrates had been condemned to death by drinking hemlock, and Plato's dialogue *Crito* describes the gradual effect of the poison on him. Well aware of this Corsican export, poets are inclined to ask why exactly Corsican honey was so bitter. Did it taste of hemlock, as Ovid hints; or of box, as the historian Diodorus thought; or is it simply that Corsican thyme had a dreadful flavour as well? Even the wax produced by Corsican bees had a hint of 'the flower of the tall hemlock' about it: writing-tablets bringing a bitter message must clearly have been coated with Corsican wax, sent as tribute to Rome as it had once been sent to Etruria (Ovid, *Amores* 1.12.8–10).[109]

Due south of Corsica lies the largest island of the Mediterranean.

> There is a big island shaped like a human foot: its old settlers called it Sardinia. It is a land rich in grain, and convenient for those voyaging towards the Poeni or the Italians. The district that is nearer to the Africans is a flat landscape and offers good harbours; the north-facing parts are inhospitable, rocky, stormy and noisy with sudden gales, so that a sailor curses these dangerous mountains. On this island there is sickness for men and cattle, so malarial is the air, so secure is the reign of the South Wind, the North being shut out.
>
> Claudian, *War Against Gildo* 507–515

Sardinia was one of the 'three granaries' of Rome, and it had iron mines.[110] Like Corsica, it was known as a source of medicines and poisons, *Sardorum gramina* 'poisonous herbs from Sardinia', and – no coincidence, this – of bad honey.[111] But the island gave its name to an excellent small Mediterranean fish, *sardina* (pilchard, sardine, *Sardina pilchardus*), good when eaten fresh, popular in preserves. The *sardes* of Gades were the very best pickled fish that he had tasted, wrote Galen.[112]

North of Sicily in stormy seas (Map 4) lay the Aeolian islands, realm of the mythical Aeolus, son of Hippotas, *Hippotadae regnum terraeque calenti sulphure fumantes* 'the kingdom of Hippotas's son, the islands smoking with hot sulphur' (Ovid, *Metamorphoses* 14.86–87). There were seven: 'all have suffered big volcanic eruptions. The resulting craters and fissures are visible today' (Diodorus 5.7). Three islands are well known in literature. Aeolia or Lipara was the palace of Aeolus, master of the winds.[113] Strongyle was 'rich, and not only in sulphur and bitumen. There is also a stone capable of generating fire' (*Aetna* 436–437).[114] Hiera, with its sheltered harbour, was 'once called Therasia. It is now Hiera ['holy'], because there is a hill on it that belches out flames at night: it is sacred to Vulcan' (Pliny 3.93) and sometimes identified as Vulcan's workshop and the caves of the Cyclopes. But these were more often located on the slopes of mount Aetna. The definite alternation between the volcanic activity of Aetna and of the Aeolian islands proved that there were underground passages between the two.[115]

'There is a fertile island Melite, and near it a sterile one, Cossyra, beaten by the waves of the Libyan strait' (Ovid, *Fasti* 3.567).[116] Malta had been a Carthaginian colony. It was wholly burned, massacred, devastated and stripped of its valuables by a Roman army in 254 BC, when a triumph was celebrated for a naval victory over the 'Cosyraeans and Carthaginians',[117] and it remained obscure from this time onwards, known only for one luxury item, the Maltese lapdog. These little pets were familiar as early as the fourth century BC – earlier still, if it was really true that the people of Sybaris had fancied them. Under the Empire you could insult an enemy by calling him a 'Maltese lapdog', *Melitaion kynidion* (Lucian, *Symposium* 19). A Greek epigram by Tymnes [*Palatine Anthology* 7.211] is an epitaph for a Maltese lapdog with the grand name of *Tauros* 'bull'.[118]

We come at last to Sicily. 'There is a land projecting into the open sea at three promontories, called from its shape *Trinacria*. It is a favourite home of Ceres. She has many cities there; among them is fertile Henna with its culti-vated lands' (Ovid, *Fasti* 4.419–422). This triangular island had many names. It might be *Trinacria, terra Trinacris*. It might be *Sicilia* – that was the name in ordinary prose: it might be *Sicania*. The two indigenous peoples who had eventually been submerged among the Greek and Punic settlers were known as *Sicani* and *Siculi*.

Figure 14   'Fertile Henna with its cultivated lands.' The plain of Enna

Source   Photograph: R. Stoneman

The three promontories of Sicily were Pachynum, facing the rainy south winds, Lilybaeum, open to the gentle west, and Pelorus, facing the Bears and the north.[119] Pelorus looked across the *navifragus fretus* 'straits where ships are wrecked' between Italy and Sicily, and was a landmark on the Mediterranean seaways. 'Sailor, from the Ram's Head of Crete to Peloris of Sicily is six thousand stadia', wrote the mathematical poet Metrodorus [*Palatine Anthology* 14.129]. It was also *piscosus Pelorus* 'fishy Pelorus'; a good place for *xiphias* (*Xiphias gladius*, swordfish) as the Sicilian gastronome Archestratus had advised (40 [Athenaeus 314e]); a good place both for hunting and for fishing.[120]

The old Greek city now resettled as Messana stood on the straits, just across from Rhegium. It was the 'place that takes its name from a curving sickle' because its earlier Greek name, *Zankle*, was borrowed from the local Sicel language in which this word meant 'sickle'; as if to confirm the point, the old coins of Zankle had shown a bird's eye view of the city's sickle-shaped harbour. The straits were guarded by the savage, though mythical, Scylla and Charybdis.[121]

Excepting a few coastal cities, northern and western Sicily was believed to have declined sadly from its former prosperity. 'The rest of the once-settled lands are now given over to shepherds, like most of the interior', wrote Strabo – but Sicily had been famous for its sheep for hundreds of years; it was the *Sikelia polymalos* 'Sicily of many sheep' of the fifth-century BC Greek poet Pindar. Later 'pastoral' poets, both Greek and Latin, would find it a natural location for their tales of shepherds and shepherdesses.[122] Poetry aside, the number of slave shepherds and cowherds in Sicily had been great enough to fuel the terrible 'Servile War' of about 135 BC, whose story is told by the native historian Diodorus (34/35.2).

In spite of the excessive spread of sheep farming, Sicily had a name for agricultural fertility. In particular Henna was renowned, *fertilis Henna*, a city sacred to Ceres; so was Leontini, near the east coast, though no longer important in Roman times.[123] Strabo insisted on the variety of Sicily's rich produce: its grain, its honey and its saffron could be counted superior to those of Italy. Sicily was one of Rome's three great granaries.[124] The best Sicilian honeys – and these were among the best in the whole Roman world – were *mella Hyblaea*, gathered by 'Sicanian bees' from the sunny slopes of Hybla.[125] The big landowners of Sicily had kept large herds of cattle as well as sheep, and this would remain the case in Roman times. The cows' milk cheese and the pork of Sicily had been well known in fifth-century BC Athens. Even in the sixth century Sicilian pigs were a recognised fine breed: the discerning Polycrates, King of Samos, had stocked his royal farm with them.[126]

The earliest developments in Sicilian gastronomy certainly go back to the fifth century. King Gelon's great victory over the Carthaginians, in 480 BC, resulted in the enslavement of great numbers of captured soldiers, who were employed on public works. With its allocation the city of Agrigentum

(Greek *Akragas*) built not only the magnificent temples whose ruins can still be seen but also an elaborate pool, nearly a mile in circumference, thirty feet deep, and fed by natural springs. It was soon a fishpond, 'offering food that was both plentiful and luxurious. A great number of swans came to live on the lake, making it a beautiful sight. The pool was afterwards neglected and became choked, eventually drying up; but the land around it was very fertile, and they planted it out in vines and fruit trees' (Diodorus 11.25.4–5). By the end of the fifth century Greece knew all about 'Syracusan tables and Sybaritic festivity', all about Sicily and 'the life there described as happy, filled with Syracusan and Italiot tables ... a life of being filled up twice a day and never sleeping alone at night'.[127] Mithaecus, the first individually famous Sicilian cook, had made his name and written his cookery book. Archestratus 'of Syracuse or Gela', the earliest true food writer, had codified the local gastronomic knowledge of the coastal cities of the Greek world about 350 BC.[128]

We know all too little of the Roman gastronomy of Sicily. We do at least know that olive relish, *epityrum*, was a speciality of Sicilian origin,[129] and thanks to Cato we even have a recipe for it.

> Green, black or mixed olive relish to be made thus. Remove stones from green, black or mixed olives, then prepare as follows: chop them and add oil, vinegar, coriander, cumin, fennel, rue, mint. Put in a preserving-jar: the oil should cover them. Ready to use.
>
> Cato, *On Farming* 119

It is not known what grape varieties were preferred by the Greeks or the Carthaginians of Sicily, but no fewer than three varieties important in the Roman world traced their origin to the island. *Aminnia* was a group of varieties, ranked high for the body and vigour of their wine, improving as it did with age. Pliny lists five sub-varieties: Pliny, Cato and Columella all give somewhat different names and classifiactions. There were kinds that produced smaller grapes, better for wine, and those that were larger, better for eating fresh and for conserving.[130] The *eugenia* grape originated at Tauromenium in Sicily: it was transplanted to Alba, near Rome (p. 34), and the Alban slopes turned out to suit it well, though 'elsewhere it practically loses its nature' (Columella 3.2.16). It is supposed to be the modern *ugni blanc*, now popular again in Mediterranean lands though not one of the noblest varieties. The *murgentina*, also Sicilian and evidently from the territory of Morgantina, was found to grow well in the volcanic soil near Vesuvius and from its popularity in that district was also called *pompeiana*. As to the wines produced in Sicily, we know little: but Strabo tells us that the district of Catana, thick with volcanic ash from past eruptions of mount Aetna, produced excellent wines.[131]

Plato had disapproved of both the tables and the beds provided for him by his kind hosts in Syracuse.[132] In Roman times, the most famous place in

Sicily for sexual pleasures was the old city of Eryx, built on a rocky island just off the north-west coast. The place was especially devoted to the goddess known to the Greeks as Aphrodite, to the Romans as Venus: there was an ancient cult centre of the goddess on the summit of the rock, supposed to have been founded by Eryx, son of Aphrodite, and embellished by Aeneas in the course of his travels; it had been maintained for many generations by the old *Sicani*, then by the Carthaginians, finally by the Romans.

> Consuls and praetors with business in Sicily, and all men of rank who stay there, on visiting Eryx, honour the holy precinct with generous sacrifices and offerings. Then, putting aside the dignity of their rank, they take full pleasure in the erotic games and the lovemaking, for only by this means, they believe, will their presence become pleasing to the Goddess.
>
> Diodorus 4.83.6

According to Strabo, a generation later, the number of women at the sanctuary, 'slaves of the Goddess' as they technically were, had declined.[133] Cicero's narrative of an episode of culture clash makes it clear that those who began as 'slaves' could amass wealth, buy their freedom, and continue to work in what was evidently a well established local industry.

> There is a woman called Agonis of Lilybaeum, a former slave of Venus Erycina. Before she encountered the quaestor Caecilius she was quite rich, a woman of substance. One of Antonius's naval captains requisitioned some of her slave musicians 'for the sailors'. Intending to confront the captain with the authority of the Goddess, she stated, as is always said in Sicily of all the slaves of Venus including those who have freed themselves from her service, that she and hers 'belonged to Venus' … Caecilius took jurisdiction, adjudged her a slave of Venus, sold her property and kept the proceeds. All Agonis had wanted to do was to keep a few slaves in the name and in the service of Venus: he took away all her property and even her liberty.
>
> Cicero, *Against Caecilius* 55–56

The most striking geographical feature of Sicily was the great volcano Aetna, permanently capped in cloud. After long quiescence Aetna erupted in 50 BC, the direct inspiration, apparently, for the anonymous scientific poem *Aetna*. Other eruptions followed: *undans Aetna* 'Aetna flowing like the sea' had thrown out lava, fireballs and molten rocks at Caesar's death.[134]

Below it flowed the cold waters of *herbifer Acis* 'grassy, herb-bearing Acis', on whose banks Polyphemus had once courted Galatea, and where Ceres had felled two tall cypress trees to serve as her torches in her frantic search for her lost daughter Proserpina.[135] One could identify, not far away, the harbour where Ulysses had landed. Closer to the great volcanic cone were the caves of the Cyclopes where Vulcan's work was done, and indeed there were rich sulphurous and bituminous springs hereabouts. The mountain was sometimes said to lie over the mouth of the giant Typhoeus: its eruption was his fiery breath.[136] Local people called the distinctive concave vents through which smoke and lava were ejected *crateres*, 'mixing bowls', likening them to bowls used for mixing wine with water, a central feature of Greek festivity: they were 'throats' or 'mouths' in common Latin (Lucretius 6.701–702), but it is the local term that has become widespread in modern languages.

It was a strange and numinous place. 'Here are vast terrifying vents descending to the abyss; here the mountain stretches, there it curls its limbs; here a profusion of rocks obstructs the path, in huge disorder' (*Aetna* 181–183). Such places showed the power that gods controlled, or that humans did not. Most of the time, fortunately for humans, it was held in check.

> Observe the worshippers on the topmost crest, where Aetna's interior is exposed to view. They placate the heavenly powers with incense in hopes that nothing will arouse the flames and that the abyss will yawn in peace.... If there is any breeze, it is too light to trouble the congregation, as the priest scatters the water and waves the torches with purified hands.... The air, utterly calm, stirs no cinder, not the smallest wisp of straw, no dry grass, no bits of chaff. The smoke rises vertically from those high aromatic altars, so peaceful is the place, so innocent of violence.
>
> *Aetna* 340–358

5   Aurora

Julius Caesar, during his campaigns in Gaul, had with him the large personal retinue that befitted a Roman proconsul, one who, already at this stage in his career, wielded patronage as none had done before. It was his custom to have dinner arrangements made separately for the 'Greeks' and the 'Romans' in his party.

This showed unusual sensibility – as might be expected from a man able to charm both Catullus and Cicero into friendship.[1] Conviviality was at the centre of both Greek and Roman cultural worlds: not merely the appreciation of wine and food, but the enjoyment of philosophy, literature, music and all the arts of entertainment; the observation, too, of fellow human beings, with the flirtations, courtships, friendship, love that may follow. But Greek and Roman conviviality were very different; those convinced of the moral rightness of the one would scarcely be at ease when participating in the other. 'It is not the Greeks' custom that women should recline in a *convivium* of men', said a Lampsacene father stiffly when the Roman administrator Verres hoped to meet his daughter at dinner (Cicero, *Against Verres* 2.1.66). Unease, embarrassment and inferiority threatened both Romans and Greeks in such clashes: Greeks, who, after all, were subjects in the Empire and risked a good deal in a stand on principle; Romans who could hardly deny that Greek culture was older and richer than their own.

Sensibility was not the end of it. Caesar showed that he could command the proper service of both a Roman *convivium* and a Greek *symposion* from the resources of his travelling household. By participating equally urbanely at both, as no doubt he did, he showed himself to be irreproachably Roman and at the same time to have the perfect mastery of intellectual culture that a Roman hoped to acquire in the Greek East.

> Well, Bullatius, how were Chios and famous Lesbos, and elegant Samos and Sardis, Croesus's capital, and Zmyrna and Colophon? Better than their reputation, or not so good? Were they all dull compared with the Campus and the river Tiber? Do you go for one of King Attalus's cities,

or – fed up with roads and seaways – do you fancy Lebedus? You know Lebedus: a village more deserted than Gabii and Fidenae.

Horace, *Epistles* 1.11.1–8

Travel in the East was still exhausting, as Horace suggests to his tourist friend, even if under Roman peace and after Roman road-building 'neither Cilician Gates ... nor inaccessible mountains ... cause terror' (p. 14). But cultural tourism had become, probably for the first time in human history, an attractive and almost 'popular' pursuit.

To visit famous sites and temples or to explore ancient works of art, we cross seas and lands, we tempt fate with our hurrying, we greedily dig up the falsehoods of early legend, we choose to travel through every nation. We admire the walls of Ogygian Thebes, happy to have travelled to another time. Now the Eurotas attracts us, the Sparta of Lycurgus; here is Cecropian Athens, celebrated in song. We admire the ashes of Troy, and measure the small burial mound of a great leader of men: 'Here lies untiring Achilles.' We attend to Greek paintings and sculpture, too: the Paphian's hair, dripping with the maternal moisture; the Colchian's children, playing in the shadow of their murderous mother.

Aetna 567–594, abridged[2]

The troubles and the rewards were great. 'I must make the grand tour to learned Athens, and let the long road wear away the pain of my love', writes Propertius. An unpractised traveller, he will sail the Adriatic and Ionian seas, praying to the gods who speak with the voice of the waves. He will land at Corinth's western harbour, Lechaeum, and from this peaceful bay go on foot across the narrow Isthmus.

Safe on the shore of the harbour of Piraeus, I shall climb Theseus's hill between the long arms [of the walls], and there in Athens I shall begin my cure, whether in Plato's grounds or in the gardens of learned Epicurus. Or I shall study the language that was the armour of Demosthenes; and the humour of Menander's plays; or classical paintings will distract my eyes, or craftsmanship in ivory and bronze.

Propertius 3.21.1–30

Propertius speaks of attempting to forget love in his studies. It is no surprise that, following the passage quoted here, the poem concludes with doubts whether forgetfulness is available. The love celebrated in the new poetry of Augustan Rome is not so easily forgotten. If an Augustan poet ceases loving, it is only so that he may hate with equal intensity, and in the consciousness that love may reassert itself momentarily. But the cures that Propertius prescribes to himself are not derisory. There is real exhilaration in the idea of drinking at the fount of culture, of pursuing the studies that had changed the lives of so many young Romans: for this, Propertius could leave Rome and could face the fearsome open sea voyage. So much that mattered had been said in Greek.

Greece had always seemed the source of culture: in a very early text, when Rome scarcely yet had a tradition of literature or books, Greek books in themselves are seen as things of power, magical objects that contain the future.[3]

As Rome grew in power, Romans found that they had more than one way to acquire Hellenism. The direct route was by conquest, as first demonstrated (Livy believed) by Vulso's army as it awaited a triumphal procession in Rome in 187 BC.

> The evidence was to be observed every day in the behaviour of his soldiers. The beginnings of foreign luxury were brought to Rome by the army of Asia. These soldiers were responsible for the first importation of bronze couches, costly upholstery, tapestries and other textiles, and pedestal tables and sideboards, then the height of fashion. It was at this time that cithara-girls and harp-girls and other festive amusements became features of dinner parties. The feasts themselves now began to be arranged with greater meticulousness and expense. The cook, cheapest and most despised of all slaves in our forefathers' times, increased in price. His work, once seen as servile, was now considered an Art. These, scarcely noticed by contemporaries, were the seeds of corruption.
>
> Livy 39.6

Having gained vast quantities of booty in Galatia, Vulso's army had spent a lot of it on the cultural pleasures of the Greek cities of Asia. Later armies and officials found that they could acquire their Greek culture *without* paying for it. 'The money, wives and children of allies, the works of art of temples and towns, the gold and treasures of kings' (Cicero, *De lege Manilia* 66) became fair game for seizure. If we appear to be too compendious in assimilating cultural tourism, 'university' study and the buying and stealing of works of art, we have the approval of Cicero, who from a less sophisticated Roman audience's point of view was perfectly correct in making the first and the last of these activities two points on a single scale of philhellenism: 'Statues, paintings and other works of art in Greek towns, which others think are there to take away, Pompey did not even bother to visit' (*De lege Manilia* 40).

Becoming Greek

Romans went to Greece to study the language at a high level and to learn and practise skills in logical analysis, writing and public speaking that they would afterwards apply in their use of Latin.

They already knew Greek: many had learnt it at home as young children (with the encouragement of private tutors, for this and allied trades were generally the prerogative of native Greek speakers). As the common language of the whole East, Greek was the first or second language of a great number of slaves in Roman and Italian households. We must guess that it was the lingua franca of many of these households, and particularly of certain professions carried on within them: cookery and the arts of entertainment, health and beauty, writing and tutoring. And Greek was a common language among many who exercised these trades in Italy and the West not as household slaves but commercially.

We know this because of the great number of Greek loanwords that became established in Latin, covering altogether an extremely wide subject field but centring on these trades. Slaves and freed slaves were likely to use more Greek loanwords than those of higher status; the evidence of Petronius[4] is confirmed by all other sources of information on lower-class spoken Latin, the vulgar Latin that was the direct ancestor of the Romance languages. More important for the subject of this book is that educated, cultivated and self-important Romans can easily slip Greek words into their Latin – and evidently in full awareness of what they are doing. In public and official circumstances they do it very little. Tiberius apologises to the Senate for inserting Greek technical terms, *monopolium, emblema*, in his addresses; Claudius is ridiculed as a *Graeculus* 'little Greek' for doing the same.[5] In other circumstances, educated Romans can do it a great deal, as Cicero does with the Greek tags and exclamations in his more personal and intimate correspondence. In what precise contexts do they need to help their Latin along with Greek, or with something that sounds like Greek?

In literary and scholastic matters, Greek comes naturally: *philologia, scholasticus*, scholarship; *poetae, sophistae, Homeristae*, the profession of literature (p. 128); *aenigma, ecloga, elegia, epigramma*, literary genres. But Rome derived other arts from Greece. For Propertius every example of artistic genius seems to be Greek, every example of military skill is Roman. Horace gives an ironic little history of the Greek arts and amusements, listing athletes, horses, ivory-carving, bronze-working, marble sculpture, painting, flute-playing and the performance of tragedy as successive enthusiasms of decadent Greece.[6]

Talk about any of these slightly un-Roman, wholly cultural pursuits, and Greek vocabulary comes naturally: the *theatrum* 'theatre', its shows, *acroamata*, and its public toilets, *aumatium*; its characters, *parasitus* the sponger, *hetaera* the courtesan; its personnel, *mimus, pantomimus, chorus* and *petauristarius* 'acrobat'; music and its modes, defined by Greek tradition and including 'simple Aeolian, querulous Lydian, solemn Phrygian' (Apuleius, *Florida* 4) not to mention lascivious Ionian and martial Dorian; an art gallery, *pinacotheca*.[7] Reject the Roman physical exercises of hunting the hare and breaking a horse and you 'become Greek', *Graecari*; your exercises and equipment will demand to be named in Greek, the *pilum* and the *discus*

(Horace, *Satires* 2.2.9–13), the *halter* or dumb-bell, the *ceroma* or prepared wrestling floor, yielding but yellow-staining to betray the fact of a fall, the *palaestra* 'exercise yard' – and of course the *palaestrita* 'trainer, masseur'.[8] Even your riding will be a little more luxurious and less Roman if you acquire a very Greek-sounding *ephippium* 'horse-cloth'.[9]

Medicine is a Greek trade and most of the troubles linked with physicians and their fellow professionals – *chirurgus* 'surgeon', *iatralipta* approximately 'physiotherapist' – are troubles with Greek names: *paronychia* 'whitlow', *cheragra, podagra* 'gout', *phrenesis* 'madness', *stomachum* 'indigestion': Horace neatly turned the theme of the *Iliad* from the sublime to the ridiculously Greek by defining it as *Pelidae stomachum*, Achilles' dyspepsia (*Odes* 1.6.6).[10] Most of those costly medical remedies have Greek names too, such as the dreadfully expensive *tisanarium oryzae* 'dose of rice gruel' (Horace, *Satires* 2.3.155). The business of cosmetics is equally Greek-sounding and equally expensive: *pixis* 'ointment pot', *diapasma* 'talc'.

The spectrum of men's dress corresponds to the spectrum of Empire. We know already of the naturally coloured grey-brown wools and the naturally waterproofed greasy cloaks that came from the West, *cucullus, sagum* – unassuming garb for unassuming people, slaves included. The *toga* is correct wear for the self-conscious Roman citizen and it was uncomplicated in its form and colouring. The Greek-sounding *synthesis* 'suit' is colourful, varied, studiously informal, and expensive – especially if it is a 'Tyrian suit' dyed with purple (p. 171). One wears a *synthesis* to dinner; one wears it at Saturnalia, when everyone is equal; but how un-Roman for the emperor Nero to appear in public in his *synthesis* at other times of year, as if he were not a citizen at all but a freed slave or a 'little Greek'![11] Accessories with Greek-sounding names were sexually ambiguous: a *Graeca mitella*, a simple woven headband would suit a pretty girl very nicely or it would label a eunuch priest (*Copa* 1: p. 18; Apuleius, *Metamorphoses* 7.8, 8.27). The four long Greek words in the first line of a poem by Martial (5.11),

> *Sardonychas, zmaragdos, adamantas, iaspidas uno*
> *versat in articulo Stella ...*

'Stella twirls *sardonyches*, emeralds, diamonds and jaspers all on the one finger' are quite insistent enough to pigeonhole their (male) wearer. A male reader immediately knows – I cannot speak for a female reader on this point – that Stella is one of those ridiculous extroverts who are inexplicably attractive to women. The same reader is thus not at all surprised to learn, from the next poem, that each stone or ring bore the portrait of a girl; though whether this was ten rival girlfriends, or whether it was Stella's wife and the Nine Muses or some analogous conclave, scholars disagree.

It is by now evident that in a literary Latin text Greek words, or words that sound Greek, are not emotionally neutral. A Greek accent gives a hint of luxury, a whiff of conspicuous consumption, a suggestion that one's

Roman ancestors would not have approved, and a feeling that male and female are not distinguished as definitively as they should be. If you keep an *analecta* 'slave to pick up fallen scraps of food' or punish him with a *colaphus* 'slap'; if you ride in a *chiramaxium* 'rickshaw', if you pay attention to a *pittacium* 'wine-label', if your house boasts a *hypogaeon* 'underfloor heating duct' or *thalamus* 'chambre' (the Latin word is *cubiculum* 'bedroom'), if your garden has a *daphnon* 'grove of bay trees' or a *hippodromos* 'ride', you are tending towards luxury. If your domestic equipment includes a *horologium* 'clock', *scaphium* 'chamber-pot' (the Latin word is *matella* 'pisspot'), *chrysendeta*, 'gold inlay utensils', *crystallina* 'rock crystal ware', *calices tepidique toreumata Nili*, 'engraved glasses from the warm Nile', you are trying to impress your guests. *Parapsides* 'starters', *epidipnides* 'afters', *apophoreta* 'presents to take away' and a *tricliniarchus* 'toastmaster'[12] are refinements unnecessary to old-fashioned Roman dinners. Earlier Romans enjoyed their meals without the interruption of *citharistae, cymbalistriae* 'lyre-players, girls playing the cymbals' and without the insistent hum of *symphoniaci* 'slave-boys providing background music'.[13]

There have been suggestions of sex in the undertones of these Greek loan-words. If one read Greek literature, one read also the sensual modern poetry of Callimachus and Philitas of Cos, poetry that aroused both boys and girls (Propertius 3.9.43–46);[14] one became familiar with Greek *hymenaea* 'wedding songs' and other erotic genres. Greek music extended to the suggestive performances of *Ionica* 'Ionic song and dance'.[15] Luxury architecture had in any case its Greek terminology, but Propertius's line of four Greek words evokes the full sensuality of the use of aromatic woods in the structure or furnishing of a lover's bedroom,

> *thyio thalamo aut Orycia terebintho,*

'a chamber in citronwood or in Orycian terebinth' (Propertius 3.7.49: p. 244). Greek words lend themselves to double entendre, like Martial's *kophon prosopon* 'walk-on part', literally 'dumb part', dumb in this poem because he is engaged in cunnilingus; likewise the terms *clinopale* (a joke by the emperor Domitian) and *epiklinopale* (if correctly restored to the text of Martial), which sound like wrestling holds and mean 'bed-wrestling'.[16] Greek took sex in its stride. It was the first language for medicine and music and also for love-making. Greek endearments are imagined by Martial as perfectly suited to a Roman *amica* 'lover' as she makes room in bed for her amorous boyfriend: *kyrie mou, meli mou, psyche mou* 'my lord, my honey, my soul'.[17] Greek words came to a man's lips when he wanted to characterise his lover's unconventional beauty.

> *nigra melichrus est, inmunda et fetida acosmos,*
> *caesia Palladium, nervosa et lignea dorcas,*
> *parvula, pumilio, chariton mia, tota merum sal,*
> *magna atque inmanis cataplexis plenaque honoris.*

balba loqui non quit, traulizi, muta pudens est;
at flagrans, odiosa, loquacula lampadium fit.
ischnon eromenion tum fit, cum vivere non quit
prae macie; rhadine verost iam mortua tussi.
at nimia et mammosa Ceres est ipsa, ab Iaccho
simula Silena ac Saturast, labeosa philema.

A black girl is '*couleur de miel*', an unkempt and smelly one '*inculte*', a dull-eyed one '*petite Athéna*', a tense and stiff one '*une daine*', a little one '*midge, une des trois Graces*, salty morsel', a big ugly one '*étonnante*, stunner', a stammerer is 'unable to speak, *elle bégaye*', a dumb girl is 'shy', a fierce, cross, loud-mouthed one is '*un flambeau*', a thin girl dying of inanition is '*petit amour*', and one who is '*délicate*' is coughing herself to death. A great busty woman is 'a real Ceres', a drunkard is '*une Silène, une Satyre*', a fat-lipped girl '*un baiser*'.

Lucretius 4.1160–1169

The Greek words used by Lucretius are represented by French in the translation. In this text Lucretius shows his usual sharp-sightedness. He adopts – for the purpose of argument – all the general Roman assumptions as to female beauty. The result bids to offend practically every reader; but then, Lucretius writes only for those who are capable of overcoming such emotions. The interesting point is that he uses the Greek words without remarking on the fact that they are Greek: he never *says* that Greek is the language in which the terminology is available. It is all the clearer, from his use of it in this context, that Greek came naturally to a Roman man in amatory contexts just as Martial (above) shows that it might come naturally to a Roman woman. The classic practical manual of sexual behaviour was in Greek – the work of Philaenis of Samos, now lost. The one significant known fragment is *Oxyrhynchus Papyri* 2891, and this fragment happens to include a passage recommending a man to use just such euphemisms as those exemplified by Lucretius in describing a woman who does not match the fantasy ideal.[18]

Latin writers make plenty more uses of Greek loanwords in sexual contexts. There are good Latin words for these things, but we find *corymbion* 'wig' because it is wanted for a pretty boy, *zona* 'belt' imagined as the way to clasp this boy to his lover, *strophium* 'brassière, breastband' for hiding heterosexual love-letters in, *sandalium* 'girl's shoe' handy for a comedy girlfriend to hit her lover with.[19] Arriving at the act itself, we have *automata* 'sexual movements', *pygesiaca sacra* 'the rites of sex' (Petronius 140), and *cinaedus* 'passive homosexual'; and to help the act along we have the most effective aphrodisiac known to Greeks and Romans, *satyrion, satureum* 'the satyr's drug, salep' (see p. 266).

In all the western Empire outside Italy we have come across only two places with a particular reputation for pleasures of a sexual kind – Gades and

Eryx – and both of them had Eastern links. The libertine or voyeuristic tourist of Roman times travelled east, in company with 'Myrtilus', a speaker in Athenaeus's dialogue:

> Don't we always choose the beautiful, even in inanimate things? So the Spartan way of life finds favour, a city where strangers are able to see young women naked; and on the island of Chios it is very pleasurable to stroll about the gymnasia and the running-tracks and to watch the young men wrestling with the girls.
>
> Athenaeus 566e

In Greece itself both Athens and Corinth had a venerable history of offering sex for money. As to the famous *hetairai* of Athens, there are plenty of these expensive, witty, independent women in the classic comedies, such as those of Plautus and Terence, that are set in Athens. Corinth's sexual reputation was as old as the fifth century BC, when Pindar addressed a charming poem to the sacred prostitutes of Aphrodite's temple there. The city's fame was recalled by Strabo and others, but as a matter of history. Rhodes, too, a wealthy centre of long-distance trade in Hellenistic times, had been a source of entertainers and, in comedy, of *hetairai*.[20]

The eastern Aegean offered more than memories of former pleasures in *concinna Samos*, 'elegant Samos', sacred to Juno, with its *Laura* 'Alley', a street of prostitutes whose foundation was attributed to King Polycrates;[21] whores of Samos figure in epigrams of Roman date in the *Anthologia Palatina*. The sexual temptations of the province of Asia, source of Rome's first supply of cithara-girls and harp-girls (p. 120) date back to the ancient Lydian kingdom, when Sardis was supposed to have already had a winding street of prostitutes, *Glykys ankon* 'sweet meander', not easy to escape from.[22] Eastern Anatolia offered several centres of sacred prostitution comparable with Eryx and Corinth.

> Comana is a populous city and is an important trading centre for the people from Armenia. When the Goddess 'comes out' people assemble there from everywhere to attend the festival. And so the inhabitants live in luxury, and all their property is planted with vines; and there is a large number of prostitutes, most of them dedicated to the Goddess. In a way the city is a lesser Corinth: a great many foreigners used to come there too to enjoy themselves, because of the large number of prostitutes sacred to Aphrodite.
>
> Strabo 12.3.36, abridged

If Egyptians were unhealthily wicked, as the Augustan poets were agreed (p. 172), it should follow that the 'pleasures of playful Nile' were particularly varied. Athenaeus recalls the *laura Eudaimonon* 'Street of the Blessed', in his own beloved Alexandria, where everything conducive to luxury was on sale.[23] These facilities were certainly an undertone in the Roman law students' riddle 'You can do half of it in Athens, all of it in Alexandria' (Seneca, *Apocolocyntosis* 8), even if the real answer to the riddle was that under local laws an Athenian man could marry his half-sister, an Egyptian could marry his full sister.

People of the East: slaves and others

Roman slaves came from all parts of the Empire and from beyond its borders. But Greek rather than Latin was the language of long-distance Mediterranean trade, including the trade in slaves. The Greek Aegean had long been a centre of the slave trade: Greeks had enslaved and sold one another assiduously in the course of their interminable petty wars of the fifth and fourth centuries BC; the strong market had attracted Carians, Illyrians and others who lived by piracy.

The slave trade was what most attracted the pirates to their way of life, proving exceptionally profitable. Slaves were easy to capture, and the market was large, wealthy and not very far away – Delos, that is, which could easily take in and send out ten thousand slaves in a day, whence the proverb, 'Trader: sail in, unload, all sold.' The reason was that the Romans, newly rich after their conquest of Carthage, required many slaves, explains Strabo (14.5.2), looking back to the second century BC. There was a large Roman community of traders on Delos, an island 'to which everybody, from all directions, brought merchandise and cargoes, an island full of riches, small, unfortified' (Cicero, *De lege Manilia* 55). Its sacred status – Delos was Apollo's island and held an annual festival to Apollo and Leto – contributed as much as its geographical location, 'ideal for those who are sailing from Italy and Greece to Asia. The international festival used to be a kind of commercial affair, and it was thronged by Romans more than by any other people' (Strabo 10.5.4). Rich Delos, full of Romans, was sacked in 88 and 69 BC and its trade did not come back. Under the early Roman Empire it was practically deserted.[24]

> O desert islands, morsels of land enclosed by the noisy belt of the Aegean wave: you have imitated Siphnos and parched Pholegandros, poor unfortunates. You have lost your ancient glory. Delos, once shining white, the first to encounter the doom of desolation, has taught you her ways.
>
> Antipater of Thessalonica 28 [*Anthologia Palatina* 9.421]

There had been other centres of the slave trade in Greece. Slaves were proverbially traded at the *Pylaia* festival at Delphi or Thermopylae, and that is why Dio (who should have known better) compared the old oral poet Hesiod, because he competed for the municipal prizes that keep so many poets in business even today, to a whoremonger who raises slave-girls at

home and then hawks them about at fairs such as the Pylaia.[25] At Calydon
in Aetolia, shrunken in Roman times but 'once a showpiece of Greece'
according to Strabo, something suggested to Plautus that there had been an
annual whore fair, *mercatus meretricius*, at the Temple of Venus. We know that
young Aetolian men sold themselves as mercenaries, so we may accept from
Plautus that their sisters sold themselves as prostitutes. Just so Cape
Taenarum, south-west of Sparta, was another place where prospective merce-
nary soldiers went to sell their services, and the fair Helen of Troy was once
rudely summed up as *Taenarius cunnus* 'a cunt from Taenarum'. The author
Apuleius traces his descent partly to Taenarum, meaning that he had Greek
slave ancestry, for no one lived at Taenarum. This stormy promontory far to
the south-east of Sparta was not within easy reach of the law, in common
with the remote and mountainous sites of many important trading fairs
ancient, medieval and modern. The same is true of Cape Sunium, south-east
of Athens, where somebody went to buy a slave girl in a play by Terence.
Under the Empire, Roman law encompassed all such places, and the Roman
peace put an end to the trading conditions that had suited the pirates,
leading to great changes in the old slave trade: but Greeks remained identified with it. Martial suggests the gift of 'a rosy youth from a Mytilenaean
dealer'.[26]

So it is natural that some Latin technical terms of slavery and the slave
trade are Greek in form or origin: *catasta*, the cage in which slaves were
displayed for sale (p. 268); *stigma*, the brand on the forehead with which
recaptured runaway slaves were marked (p. 212); *ergastulum*, the workhouse
to which recalcitrants were consigned (Columella 1.6.3). Greek words
seemed ideal – expressive and quite distinct from the system of names taken
by Roman citizens – to name a slave and to give a nickname or a literary
pseudonym to a lover. Horace gives us a raft of them, *Lydia, Tyndaris,
Leuconoe, Pyrrha* (the name Achilles had among the women), *Glycera, Lalage,
Chloe, Chloris, Lycoris, Pholoe, Myrtale, Myste, Lyde, Phryne, Neaera*: all these
Greek names for poetic women suggest romance or sex. Their foolish or
violent lovers have Greek names as well, *Telephus, Cyrus, Xanthias*. There is
even an *Inachia* (suggesting 'cow', since in mythology Io daughter of Inachus
was turned into a cow) abandoned for the boy *Lyciscus* 'little wolf'. Martial
likes to choose apposite Greek names too, *Phlogis* 'fire' for the girl with an
itch for sex, *Chione* 'snow' for the snow-cold girl, *Hypnus* 'sleep' for a sleepy
slave boy. There is no firm line between the literary names and the names
that people really used. *Lycisca* 'little wolf' was the trade name used by
Claudius's wife Messalina when she dabbled in prostitution (Juvenal 6.123).
Narcissus was a freed slave of the emperor Claudius and became his most
influential minister; *Lycinna* 'wolf cub' was quite possibly the real name of
the girl who taught Propertius about sex (Propertius 3.15.6), and many
similar examples are to be found not in literary texts but on tombstones
erected by mourning owners and lovers.[27]

Greeks, as I have argued elsewhere, were the people who began the whole business of local specialities and local excellence. We can look to Greece, and to no less a source than Apollo's oracle at Delphi, for an evaluation of Greeks both male and female.

> Of all the earth Pelasgian Argos is best. The Thessalian horses, Spartan women, the men who drink the water of fair Arethusa, but better still are they who live between Tiryns and sheep-filled Arcadia, linen-breasted Argives, goads of war. But you Megarians are not third or fourth or twelfth, in word or in count.[28]

Romans, when their views are canvassed, are both less discriminating and less complimentary. Horace talks of *Achivi uncti*, 'greased Greeks' (p. 139), Varro of *coma promissa, rasa barba, pallia trahentes* 'long-haired, smooth-chinned gown trailers' (Varro, *Menippean Satires* 311 Bücheler).[29] But we have seen that Romans looked to Greeks for the skills that would make them speakers and writers. Among the most successful, respected and well-paid of Greeks were the *sophistae*, 'lecturers, professors'. Working for themselves, employed by cities or in great households, many Greeks made their living as sophists, tutors, poets and philosophers from the beginning of the Empire to the final triumph of Christianity at the end of the fourth century.

The peoples of Anatolia are distinguished in Roman cliché by their trades as firmly as by their regional origins. From *Asia*, the Roman province, there are sexual slaves (p. 120). The fictional 'Trimalchio' of Petronius's *Satyricon* (75) had begun his career, after sale at auction in Rome, as his master's favourite boy (a position he held for fourteen years) and his mistress's lover. A Greek poet tells us of a later female counterpart to Trimalchio, 'the dancing-girl from Asia, the one who quivers all the way to her youthful finger-tips in her erotic postures' (Automedon 1 [*Anthologia Palatina* 5.129]).

Phrygia is the inland district of Roman Asia. Phrygia had already been a source of slaves to Greece in the fifth century BC; in Rome, Phrygian slaves could be conventionally insolent or conventionally timid, but their typical specialism was quite different from that of 'Asians', for *phrygio* already meant 'embroiderer' even in the very earliest Roman literature: 'I used to be a *phrygio* and I knew the trade well. Now I've left my needle and thread with the master and mistress' (Titinius, *Barbatus* 1 Daviault).[30] Further inland, in country that is now inhabited mainly by Kurdish speakers (perhaps they were already there) was *Cappadocia*, an independent kingdom in late Hellenistic times, annexed by Tiberius in AD 18. Cappadocians were often seen in Rome as slaves: in cliché they were recalcitrant, far from assiduous (it took six Cappadocian slaves to carry a litter), yet skilled bakers: for all we know, this is why Persius once describes them as *pingues Cappadoces* 'fat Cappadocians'.[31]

Syria, rump of the Seleucid Empire, became a Roman province in 64 BC. Its role, evidently still a source of great wealth, was as an entrepôt,

Figure 15   The most insubordinate of Syrian soldiers: Philip 'the Arab', who led a
revolt and became Emperor in 244. Marble bust from Shahba, Syria

Source   Photograph: R. Stoneman

exchanging the produce of the distant East for Mediterranean goods and
Mediterranean gold. And so, although Syrians emerge in Roman literature
as entertainers of various kinds (a real figure, the author of Latin mimes
Publilius *Syrus* who began his career as a slave; then also *Syrus*, a gladiator;
Syrus a clown; and the real little Syrian boys that Augustus found to be
diverting companions),[32] Syrians in the Roman Empire are much more typically traders and shopkeepers, like *Syrophoenix* the innkeeper in Juvenal's
eighth satire (p. 220), and like the former slave grown rich in trade who
butts in in his first satire:

> The praetor goes first, then the tribune. No, the freedman got there
> first. 'I was here first,' he says. 'Why should I be shy about keeping my
> place? Yes, I was born beside the Euphrates: can I deny it when my silly
> pierced ears give it away? But my five shops bring in four hundred
> [thousand sestertii]. What does the broad purple do for you, if Corvinus
> is driving migrant flocks of sheep in Laurentum country?'
>
> Juvenal 1.102–108

It is abundantly clear that Juvenal did not like Syrians, but from other
authors too we have the typical picture of a Syrian as a tradesman both obse-
quious and avaricious.[33] The reverse of this Roman stereotype is well

known. Aramaic speakers (*Syri* to Romans) were prominent in the long-distance trade of the Silk Road, instrumental not only in business but in spreading Christianity and Manichaeism to the great cities of central Asia and even, far beyond, deep into China. As Roman soldiers, meanwhile, Syrians were characterised in one view as 'mutinous, disobedient, seldom with their units, straying in front of their prescribed posts, roving about like scouts, tipsy from noon one day to the next, unwilling even to carry their arms' (Fronto, *Parthian Preface* [vol. 2, p. 209 Haines]) or, in brief, insubordinate.

There is a typical female counterpart to the male Syrian innkeepers, entertainers and independent-minded soldiers: a counterpart more favoured in Roman literature and just as widespread – at an even earlier date – in the

Figure 16   Syrian (or Roman) girl. Syrian painted glass beaker of the Roman period, found at the Kushan city of Begram (modern Afghanistan), now in Kabul Museum

Source   Photograph: Josephine Powell

Figure 17   Miniature bronze vessel from Lebanon, first century AD. The sides show
a frieze of female dancers holding hands. One of them is playing the lyre

Source   By permission of the Director General of Antiquities and Museums, Syria

world beyond. We have seen her already: *Surisca*, the 'young Syrian bar-girl,
her hair caught up in a Greek headband, trained to sway her quivering backside in time to the castanet, dancing tipsily, wantonly, in the smoky tavern,
smacking the noisy reed-pipes against her elbow' (*Copa*: p. 18). She represents a well-established trade, *ambubaiarum collegia* 'the companies of
flute-girls' as Horace describes them without approval but with accuracy.
They began to work in Rome as early as the first decade of the second
century BC.[34] At the end of the same century they had reached the Chinese
court of the Han emperor, for the 'skilled performers' obtained from
Nabataea and sent to China as a gift by the Parthian king, around 120 BC,
surely included Syrian dancing girls.[35] A further indication in literature that
these performers migrated east as well as west is found in the *Acts of Thomas*,
a Syriac work set in the first century AD and accurate in its historical ambience. It tells at length the story of the 'Hebrew flute-girl' whom the apostle
Thomas met by chance at dinner at a coastal city on the Persian Gulf. She
had a crush on him, as often happens to apostles in the apocryphal stories.
She played at his table for a long time, was entranced by the poem that he
improvised on the occasion, followed him to his inn, and is last seen crying

because he had departed on his reluctant mission to bring Christianity to India (*Acts of Thomas* 4–16).

Syri, then, are Syrians and Aramaic speakers in general, and this includes Jews: the two peoples are not always distinguished by Roman writers, though the special beliefs and practices of Jews are often noticed. We can read in some detail how this very distinct people, largely subject to Rome, viewed the Roman world.

Romans looked to Athens as a fount of wisdom, but in the Jewish stories it is often an Athenian who falls short. There was one Athenian who went to learn wisdom in Jerusalem, and after three and a half years he had still not got it right. He bought a slave who turned out to be blind in one eye.

'After three and a half years of study,' he exclaimed in disgust, 'I've bought a slave who's half blind!'

'By your life,' said the salesman, 'he's very clever and can see a long way.'

When the Athenian and his slave came out of the city gate, the slave said:

'Hurry and we'll overtake the caravan.'

'Is there a caravan ahead?' said his master.

'And there's a she-camel, four miles ahead, that's blind in one eye, pregnant with twins, and carrying two skins, one of wine, one of vinegar. The camel-driver is a gentile.'

'O one-eyed member of a stiff-necked tribe,' said his master, 'how do you know the camel is blind in one eye?'

'One side of the road has been grazed and not the other.'

'And how do you know it's carrying twins?'

'It lay down back there,' said the slave. 'I observed the impression of the two of them.'

'And how do you know it's loaded with one skin of wine and one of vinegar?'

'From the drips,' the slave replied. 'The drops of wine are absorbed in the ground; the drops of vinegar ferment.'

'And how do you know it's four miles ahead?'

'The mark of a camel's hoof can be observed for four miles behind it, but no further.'

'And how do you know the driver is a gentile?'

'Because he pissed in the middle of the road. A Jew would have gone to the side.'

Based on *Lamentations Rabbah* 1.1; *Talmud Babli, Sanhedrin* 104a[36]

Jews were perfectly conscious that their curious rules and customs aroused gossip. The strange business of circumcision demanded comment whenever a Jewish male bathed or made love; the refusal to eat pork was maliciously misunderstood as the worship of a *porcinum numen* 'porcine deity' in at least one source; the weekly observance of a day of rest and fasting was almost equally strange. And Jews came under the general classification of *Syri* as typical grasping innkeepers. Jews in Rome at the end of the first century were additionally condemned as beggars – 'the Jew who learnt to beg at his mother's knee' – and particularly as mendicant priests.[37]

An Egyptian would be *tinctus colore noctis* 'painted with the colour of night': this is why Martial talks of *fusca Syene* 'brown-skinned Syene', the city on the southern frontier of Empire where his presumably fictional 'rich friend Callistratus' had an estate.[38] The adjective *Memphiticus*, literally 'from Memphis' the old capital of Egypt, by this same connection of thought has eventually something of the night about it. It identifies colour more than geographical origin when Martial lists, among the lovers of a promiscuous Roman lady, 'Memphitic sailors from the city of the *Pharos*', which is Alexandria (Martial 7.30: p. 211). Alexandrian slave boys were perhaps a typical choice as attendants at dinner; both boys and girls, *Memphitides puellae*, are characterised as sacred and sinuous dancers;[39] and some found these youngsters attractive in their native costume, a pure white gown (*othone*), their long dark hair swept back to either side of the forehead – quite different from the style a Roman would adopt. Others (the debate comes from a fictional dialogue) applied to Egyptians the same stereotypes that are also used to characterise Africans from further south (p. 178): they were black-skinned, thick-lipped, thin-legged (Lucian, *The Ship* 2–3).

Among older Egyptians, Crispinus, Domitian's minister, is labelled by Juvenal (1.26) *pars Niliacae plebis* 'one of the rabble from the Nile', *verna Canopi* 'a home-bred slave of Canopus'. Egyptians, we may gather from the *Romance of Alexander* (A 1.3–4), were able to travel the Empire as fortune-tellers, easily identified as they sat at a street stall wearing that same typical Egyptian white *othone*; but there were impostors, and the fictional Olympias of the *Romance* was surely not the only client bold enough to ask one of these seductive astrologers whether he was really an Egyptian or not.

Transmarine wines

The division between the East and the West of the Empire recurs in several contexts: language is one, and wine is another. Here the reader's imaginative sympathy is required. We must begin with lists. They show that Mediterranean wines were already being ranked for quality – but they do not yet tell us how they tasted.

Those of the eastern Aegean islands had an ancient reputation. 'Now we shall deal with overseas wines in the same way', Pliny promises, having just set before the reader a hierarchy of the wines of the West. He mentions the venerated names of Thasos and Chios, then the fine Eastern wines of his own time.

Best liked is Clazomenian now that they mix less sea water in it. Lesbian tastes naturally of the sea. Tmolite is not liked as wine *per se*, but as a sweet additive through which the harshness of other wines is smoothed and at the same time matured: thus blended they give the impression of natural age. After these are classed Sicyonian, Cypriot, Telmessian, Tripolitan, Berytian, Tyrian, Sebennytic. The last-named is made in Egypt from the three grape varieties that are locally 'noble', *Thasios, aithalos, peuke*. Next to these in favour are Hippodamantian, Mystic, Cantharite, Cnidian *protropon*, Catacecaumenite, Petrite, Myconian.

Pliny 14.73–76, abridged

A century later we find another listing of good transmarine wines in the works of Galen, who had impressive qualifications for the task, being a native of the wine-producing region of Roman Asia and a careful and garrulous wine-taster. He writes for physicians who will be prescribing a regime for wealthy patients.

In Asia Minor and Greece and neighbouring provinces Italian wines are not to be found. Often the best wine to prescribe, of what is available in those parts, will be Ariusian (grown in certain districts of Chios) or Lesbian. There are three cities of Lesbos. The least aromatic and least sweet comes from Mitylene, more aromatic and sweeter from Eresus, then Methymna. Prescribe the 'unmixed', so called because there is no sea water mixed in. But they have not usually included sea water in the *best* wines of Lesbos or of Chian Ariusium, and, after all, it is the best wines that I am talking of.

Galen, *Therapeutic Method* 12.4 [10.830]

Galen lists more fine wines of the mid second century: Mysian, black Perperene, Nicomedian, black Aegeate, Aphrodisiaean, dry and sweet Tmolite, and the wine of Thera, which was one of the sweetest of all. 'Always try to get the best', he reiterates. Pliny wrote with the Italian market in mind, while Galen's list is addressed to those in Greece and Asia, and they are three generations apart; but reputations in the wine trade can be long-lasting. So it is no surprise that some names occur in both lists, and no surprise to find these same names cropping up again in less specialised sources, the ones that tell us what ordinary Roman wine buyers were talking about.

If we are to taste these wines we need to know of a classification only hinted at so far: the wines that were salted and spiced before bottling, and those that were not. None of the connoisseurs explains this: they expect us to know already that the bulk wines of the East intended for long-distance transport westwards were made with the addition of brine and other flavourings, which surely helped to stabilise them for their long sea journey. The

Figure 18   A collection of amphorae at the Bodrum Castle Museum, Turkey
Source   Photograph: R. Stoneman

typical salty wine was Coan. The invention was owed to the dishonesty of a slave: it was his way of fulfilling his target, so Pliny tells us, and it was one of the most successful examples of adulteration in the whole history of food. In addition to all its other attractions, Coan wine turned out to be a laxative.[40] Not only did other winemakers of the region imitate the procedure ('Rhodian is like Coan', says Pliny; 'Phorinean is even saltier') but the typical shapely amphoras of Cos were soon being manufactured at many sites across the Mediterranean, demonstrating that 'Coan wine' was actually made all over the place. Since salt would tend to conceal any native delicacy of flavour, this was easy to do. We have two recipes for it. One is in the old Roman farming manual by Cato;[41] the other in the Byzantine collection *Geoponica* (8.24), where it is attributed to Berytius, an author of Roman date.

> MAKING COAN WINE: Berytius. Some people boil 3 parts must and one part sea-water down to two-thirds. Others mix 1 cup salt, 3 cups *hepsetos*, about 1 cup wine must, 1 cup vetch flour, 100 *drachmai* melilot, 16 *drachmai* apples, 16 *drachmai* Celtic nard, into 2 *metretai* white wine.

The connoisseurs do not list Coan wine among the approved names – still less any of the imitations of Coan. In fact Pliny condemns a wine from the nearby Anatolian coast with the explanation that 'Ephesian is unwholesome because it is mixed with sea water and boiled must', the two major additives in Coan wine according to the recipes; and Clazomenian (unknown otherwise) had improved its reputation by reducing its brine content. No wine that we know to have been salted is given any further word of praise in Roman literature. Galen, as we have seen, carefully recommends the physician to prescribe Chian and Lesbian wines that are not mixed with sea water, with the reassurance that the best wines from both islands will be free of it.

Of the costly wines, those that relied on fermentation alone for their quality, most sources agree with Galen that Chian should be placed first. It was the acme of luxury, and commanded a higher price than Lesbian wines such as that of Mytilene. With ridiculous appropriateness, Horace's ambitious host 'Nasidienus' boasts of serving Chian wine and of getting his cooking vinegar from Methymna on Lesbos.[42] Chian wine had a mythological claim to be the oldest of all black wines; and at least two Chian districts were renowned. Ariusium was named by Pliny and Galen (above): it was a rugged and harbourless district that produced the best wine of Greece, Strabo agreed. Vergil, just to show that he can if he tries, in the course of his desultory list of wines names a type that is otherwise quite absent from all surviving sources, *rex ipse Phanaeus* 'Phanaean, the very king of wines', grown on the mountain or exported from the deep harbour of Phanae, not far south of the city of Chios (*Georgics* 2.98). Chian wine had been a rare luxury in Rome until the mid first century BC – and like many rare foods and drinks it had been taken on doctor's orders – until with the increasing lavishness of public festivity and patronage it became accepted as the expensive and luxurious choice for a 'transmarine wine'.[43]

Rhodian wine had its votaries: it was 'accepted by the gods and at second tables', said Vergil, *Georgics* 2.101–102. But most later judges agreed with Aristotle, whose deathbed decision was said to have been that 'both are excellent, but the Lesbian is the sweeter' (Aulus Gellius, *Attic Nights* 13.5). And though all transmarine wines were necessarily expensive in Italy, Lesbian was a moderate choice, less expensive and showy than Chian.[44] It was a tawny-coloured wine, *kirros*; both red and white wine turned naturally to this colour after lengthy maturing.

The same colour distinguished Aphrodisiaean and sweet Tmolite wine. The former of these two Anatolian wines grew on the slopes overlooking the Maeander valley, as did the Mesogite of Pliny's list; good they may both have been, but neither reaches poetry. Nor does the Perperene that Galen liked so much: it grew on the coastal slopes near Smyrna, *apud mare Zmyrnae*, where Varro (*On Farming* 1.7.6) said the vines cropped twice each year.

On the insecure basis of poetic reputation, the best vineyards of Roman Asia were those that looked down on the more northerly valley of the Hermus in which lay the old Lydian capital, Sardis. The vineyards of Tmolus, *Tmoli vineta*, south of Sardis, are practically a cliché.[45] Upriver to the east lay the strange volcanic region of Catacecaumene, literally 'the burnt-up country'. Here the plains were covered with ashes and the mountains and rocks were black as if from some great fire: it was the scene of Typhon's agonies, people said, and there was incessant volcanic activity. The inhabitants of Philadelphia found new cracks in their house walls every day. After one famous earthquake (so the story went) it was discovered that a traveller in slave-girls and his whole train of stock, who had been staying overnight in the inns at Carura, had all been swallowed up by the earth. The region was entirely treeless – but it was green with the vine that produced Catacecaumenite wine, one of the very best of the whole Empire.[46]

It is this wine-growing region of Roman Asia, rather than inland Phrygia narrowly defined, that Varro has in mind when he compares Italian vineyards with those of Homer's *Phrygia ampeloessa* 'grape-growing Phrygia'.[47]

Finally we taste the very sweet wines of the East, with Pliny's initial guidance and with the preliminary explanation that *mulsum* was spiced sweetened wine served as an aperitif (p. 141).

> *Psithium* and *melampsithium* are kinds of raisin wine with a flavour that is distinct and not wine-like; Scybelite, which comes from Galatia, has a flavour like *mulsum*, and so has the *aluntium* of Sicily … Greek raisin wine is classed highest, then Cilician, then African. The *psithia* grape (this is the Greek name: in Latin it is *apiana*) and the *scripula* are known to be used to make raisin wine in Italy and the western provinces too, after lengthy drying on the vine.
>
> Pliny 14.80–81

A second opinion, by the pharmacologist Dioscorides, fleshes out the Roman category of sweet wines:

> Wine made from sun-dried grapes, or from those dried on the vine and then pressed, is sweet and has the names Cretan, *protropos*, *pramnios* … The black, called *melampsithios*, is thick and nourishing, the white lighter, the intermediate has intermediate strength.
>
> Dioscorides 5.6.4

And to reinforce the nexus of related flavours and unrelated names, we can add information from Martial's modest gift poem (13.106), 'A Knossos vine, out of Minoan Crete, sends you this raisin wine. It is the poor man's usual *mulsum*!' to a curious and apparently illogical assertion of the lexicographer Pollux: 'Theran wine: the wine from Crete' (*Onomasticon* 6.2) and to Galen's evaluation of Theran and Scybelite wines as 'thick' and hence particularly nourishing. Like Perperene and Aegeate and the sweet wine of Cilicia, these were 'black' wines, 'naturally. You will find no wine both thick and sweet that is not black' (*On Good and Bad Juices* [6.800–801]).[48]

All these names are identified by one author or another as sweet wines: we have already cited Galen for the detail that Theran wine was one of the sweetest of all. What more? Pliny and Dioscorides together tell us that *psithium* wine was typical of the *psithia* grape, which was suited to semi-drying and to the making of very sweet wine: there was a 'black' kind (Greek *melas*), a white kind and something between. Pollux and Dioscorides together seem to be telling us that geographical names such as Theran and Cretan did not always mean exactly what they seemed. *Pramnios*, the wine name that came all the way from the *Iliad*, is linked with several contradictory place names in different sources and no one really knows whether it was originally a grape variety, a place, a style of wine-making, or something else. What we cannot fully do, two thousand years later, is to say with what precise flavours all these names were associated by Roman wine buyers. What we can do is to take them as overlapping categories and to explore what they had in common and how they differed.

First, they shared (or many of them shared) a flavour. What was the flavour of the *psithia* grape, distinct and not like that of wine? It has been concluded before now that this was the ancestor of the muscat grape of today, an important and distinctive group of varieties that does include both black and white kinds. The flavour that Pliny tried to identify was the musky flavour for which the nineteenth-century Russian court still looked to the sweet wines of Thera (Santorini), the flavour still familiar today from the wines of Samos, Lemnos and various places far from Greece.

Second, they shared natural sweetness. This was only available in ancient wine-making from the use of extremely sweet must, because only thus would fermentation cease before all the sugar in the must had fermented out: it would cease at about 16 per cent alcohol, above which yeast cannot survive. Hence these wines had typically undergone various processes that intensify the sweetness of the must. If made from semi-dried grapes, they are called *passum*, 'raisin wine'.

> Some make *passum* from any sweet, early-ripening, white grapes, drying the bunches in the sun till little over half their weight remains. Then they gently express the must. The more painstaking makers dry the bunches in this same way, pick the berries and soak them, without the stalks, in fine wine till they swell, and then press them. This style is considered better than any other.
>
> Pliny 14.81–82

If made from free-run must, they are called *protropum*, a Greek loanword in Latin:

> That is the name given by some to must that flows of its own accord before the grapes are trodden. This is put into jars at once and left to ferment out. Next year at the rising of the Dog Star it is cooked for forty days in the summer sun.
>
> Pliny 14.85

Greece

'We are in our prime,' Horace asserts with less than total conviction, 'we paint and sing and fight better than the greased Greeks' (*Epistles* 2.1.32–33). It was true that Greece was no longer in its prime. When Romans write about Greece they seldom have at the front of their minds the real contemporary state of Greece, its cities shrunken or abandoned, its wealth spent or stolen, its politics parochial, many of its people dependent on their Roman rulers. Greece in Roman literature is rather more Arcadian: the land of a Golden Age such as Hesiod had once described and the poet of *Aetna* re-imagined, when the luxury produce of Greek agriculture demanded no human labour – when 'the flow of Bacchus was the work of no feet but his own, and honey dripped from sticky leaves, and oil from the fat olive tree' (*Aetna* 13–14). In those days the sounds of hunting were heard across the mountains and valleys of Greece: this, too, is how Greece comes to mind. 'Enough of delays: Mount Cithaeron summons me clamorously, the hunting dogs of Taygetus, Epidaurus the tamer of horses, and the echoing voice of the forests resounds in assent' (Vergil, *Georgics* 3.42–45): could any Roman poet, conscious of the tradition in which he worked, refuse the call? Not Vergil, whose excuse this is for his failure as yet to write the epic of Rome's civil wars. Greece was the divine and powerful source of poetic inspiration – on Mount Helicon, home of the Muses, there was a tree the scent of whose blossom had the power to kill a man (Lucretius 6.786–787); to be more precise, Greece was the source of the poetic forms to which Romans were conscious of shaping their own inspiration. It is in this sense that Propertius 'bears Italian mystic objects in Greek dances' (3.1).

When Roman poets conjure up rural Greece, the image easily slips into that of a Golden Age. Arcadia, the secluded, mountainous region of the central Peloponnese, is the geographical root of the whole 'Arcadian' vision of pastoral felicity; it is wild country, inhabited by gods and spirits as much as by humans. The sounds are those of nature. Cities, their noise and their warfare are far away. 'The old Arcadians are said to have worshipped Pan, god of herds and flocks. He is everywhere in those mountains – witness mount Pholoe, and the Stymphalian waves, and Ladon hurrying to the sea with swift waters, and the Nonacrine heights ringed with pines, and tall Cyllene and the Parrhasian snows' (Ovid, *Fasti* 2.271–276). Features of this untamed landscape recur in other Roman texts. It is a real landscape, not an imaginary one, though Ovid had never seen it. Pausanias (8.25.13) said that there was no lovelier river than the Ladon in Greece or any other country;[49] as for the little city of Nonacris, Pausanias found it but no one now knows where. Even in Roman times only a few stones stood: 'In old times Nonacris was a little city of the Arcadians, named after Lycaon's wife. In our time it is ruins, and you cannot make much of them. Not far from the ruins is a high cliff: I do not know of any other so high. A river falls over this cliff, and the Greeks call it Styx' (8.17.6).

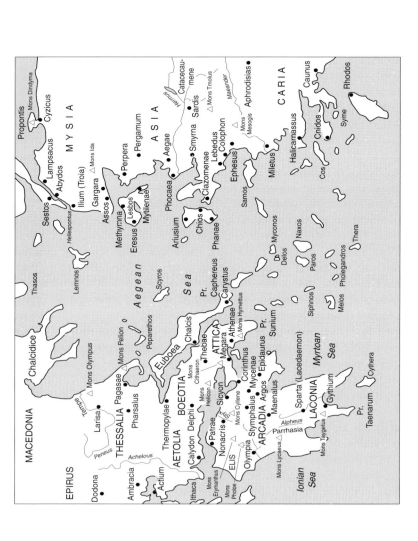

Map 7   Greece and the province of Asia

More especially dedicated to Pan (sometimes equated with Roman *Faunus*) was Maenalus. It was in the caves of this wooded valley of Arcadia that Pan would sit to wax the hemlock stalks – his prerogative, for no human might blow on hemlock pipes – on which he made his unearthly music. In this valley, more than in any other, poets imagined rustic Arcadian festivity, with women of Maenalus leading the dancers.[50] Also in Arcadia was the 'long mountain' Lycaeus, sacred to Apollo and supposed by some to be the birthplace of Zeus; and another mountain range, *dendrokomes Erymanthos* 'tree-topped Erymanthus' (Rufinus 6 [*Anthologia Palatina* 5.19.5]), where the mythical boar had been speared. Here the divine huntress Diana might be glimpsed, 'Diana ... happy in the rivers and the wooded crest that stands out on icy Algidus, or in the black forests of Erymanthus or of green Cragus' (Horace, *Odes* 1.21.5–8).

From its rural wealth Greece had had much to offer to Rome. Roman gardeners, more assiduous than any before in the development of new varieties, drew on centuries of market gardening in Greece: in the microclimates offered by the fractured terrain of Greece, local varieties of fruits, of vegetables, of vines, had gradually emerged, to provide plentiful material for Roman experiment and cross-breeding.[51] As to its own produce, Greece offered to the Empire the wine that we have listed above – but this came from Crete and the Aegean islands, not from peninsular Greece – and the simple and rustic luxuries that belonged to the stereotype we have already sketched. So Apuleius (*Metamorphoses* 1.5) assures us. 'I hunt about through Thessaly, Aetolia, Boeotia, for honey and cheese and all that line of grocery', announces a character in the story of the Golden Ass, and no confirmation is needed of the importance of Greek honey. It was the best in the Empire. 'The best honey is Attic, and the best of Attic the Hymettian', so the *Geoponica* asserts (15.7), adding more modest praise of Greek island honeys including Cretan and Calymnian. Hymettian honey, *mella Hymettia* from the sunny slopes of Mount Hymettus just outside Athens (and so *Cecropius mons*, the mountain of Cecrops), was a commonplace of gastronomy. With something of the aroma of the thyme that grew freely on Hymettus, it has probably varied little in flavour between Roman times and today. Thyme, it was recognised, gave the best aroma to honey. The very highest quality was called *akapniston* in Greek: it was taken from the hive without (as was normal) using smoke to drive off the bees.

Hymettian honey was traditionally demanded for one of the regular pleasures of Roman entertainment, the sweet aperitif that preceded a meal. Romans were told, and some at least believed, that a good *mulsum* also required the finest amber-coloured Falernian wine. The resulting colour, incidentally, was the brown of fish sauce and the brown of Canusian capes (Martial 14.127).[52]

Your best *mulsum* is mixed from new Hymettian honey and well-aged Falernian wine.

Macrobius, *Saturnalia* 7.12.19

Even in face of this uncompromising statement we may agree with Horace that it was going too far to refuse to drink Falernian at all unless 'diluted' with Hymettian honey (*Satires* 2.2.15).

Beside its simple culinary pleasures, Greece offered to the Roman world a commodity that was almost commonplace at home but much more highly prized elsewhere. Pliny gives a desultory but very informative history of Greek marble, observing that marble columns, imported at great cost to embellish rich Roman houses, were a feature of classical Greek architecture because in Greece marble was the obvious material to use. So it is not from earlier Greek texts, but from Roman ones that we hear of the famous quarries that sent Greek building stone to Italy. Mount Hymettus itself was one: its blue-grey marble would be less expensive, so Pliny implies, than Lucullean (note 56). He believed that the six twelve-foot Hymettian columns imported by L. Crassus, about 100 BC, were the first marble columns to be erected in Rome.[53] Not far off to the north Pentelic marble, from the Attic deme of Pentele, had its special fame.[54] Across the straits lay *undosa Carystos* 'billowy Carystus', at the southern end of Euboea. These reefs, *Carystea vada,* and the treacherous Cape Caphereus, were proverbial for shipwreck: it had been fatal in legend to many of the Greeks who had sailed to fight the Trojan War. The variegated marble of Carystus was tamed to Roman use.[55] Thasian marble was one of the three stones used in Nero's tomb (p. 176). Best known of all, from an island in mid Aegean, *Parium saxum* 'Parian stone' was a fine marble whose pure whiteness made it commonly used in classical Greek sculpture. But an even whiter stone, *lygdos, lygdinos*, was found on Paros 'in pieces no larger than a dish or a mixing bowl' (Pliny 36.62). This lucent marble made the ideal poetic comparison for a woman whose skin is perfectly white; and *Lygdus* is found as the name for a pretty slave boy, both in reality and in poetry.[56]

Spartani saxi 'Spartan stone', *Taenariae columnae*, 'columns from Taenarum' were imagined by Martial as ideal ornaments to an ideal *atrium*. This was green porphyry (verde antico) from the quarries of Taygetus, *Taygeti metalla*. It was hard to work but of a beauty that was fitting to decorate temples, so Greeks thought – or baths, so Romans thought. Strabo mentions a new quarry on mount Taygetus specifically catering to Roman demand: this was no doubt the quarry at Croceae described by Pausanias, the source of the 'Spartan stone'.[57]

Greek cities and islands

Greece is far better known than the other provinces of the Empire to Roman writers and readers, even to those who have never been there. Dalmatia and

Britain are desert regions on the literary map: most of Gaul and Spain are sparsely peopled. But Greek place names cluster in Roman literature, and they are names of places whose special character is mythological and historical rather than the result of contemporary wealth and trade. Crossing the sea from Brundisium, the traveller passed Corcyra, famous for its fruit trees – because on this island, around 1280 BC by the usual reckoning, had flourished the *Phaeacae silvae* 'Phaeacian woods' or more accurately the 'orchards of the King of Corcyra', *pomaria Corcyraei regis*,[58] or more accurately still 'the twice-bearing orchards of Alcinous and the boughs that stretch towards heaven, ever loaded with fruit' (Statius, *Silvae* 1.3.81–82), orchards so engagingly described in the narrative of Odysseus: 'there tall trees spread their leaves, pears and pomegranates and shiny-fruited apples and sweet figs and leafy olives, and their fruit never fails or falls short, winter or summer, all the year, but the West Wind, blowing, fertilises some and ripens others: pear upon pear grows old and apple upon apple, grapes upon grapes and fig upon fig' (*Odyssey* 7.112 – 121).

In Corcyra one should look out for good *polypus* (octopus, *Octopus vulgaris*), according to Ennius's curious gastronomic fragment. He borrows the detail from his Greek authority Archestratus, but he lived close enough to Corcyra to know for himself whether it was true. Having found it, one tenderises it before stewing: 'The octopus is to be beaten with twice seven blows', says the Greek proverb (*Suda s.v.*), and the Latin cookbook adds that it is to be simply spiced:

TO OCTOPUS. Pepper, fish sauce, silphium. Serve.

Apicius 9.5 [412 André]

Further south, the secluded mainland harbour of Ambracia, an easy and a regular landfall for travellers 'where the waves of the Ionian Sea are calmed' (Propertius 4.6.15–18), was a splendid place for seafood. 'Mitylene offers scallops: so does Ambracia, in large numbers, and great big ones too', said Archestratus (56 [Athenaeus 92d]), and once again Ennius takes his word for it; but then Ennius had probably tasted the well-reputed coquilles Saint-Jacques of Tarentum, just across the straits, and these are certainly what is meant by 'great big scallops', so much bigger than those known to Archestratus in the straits of Mytilenae. If more attractions than its seafood were needed, Ambracia now boasted a monument to Augustus's victory at nearby Actium.[59] South from here, the sea route approaches the entrance to the Corinthian Gulf; to its north, Calydon; to its south, Patrae, now becoming an important port. In the northern Peloponnese, Argos – *aptus equis Argos* of Horace (*Odes* 1.7.9), *Argos polypyros* of Varro (*On Farming* 1.2.7). Both these epithets, 'ideal for horses', 'fruitful in wheat', come straight out of ancient Greek poetry. So does the 'rich Mycenae', *Mycena ditis* of the *Priapeia* (75). In the real world Mycenae was a windswept ruin. Also in the Peloponnese, on the banks of the Alpheus, was Olympia, site of the historic

Figure 19   An imaginary sea well filled with luxury seafood. Each creature is
accurately depicted, but with no regard to overall scale: among others,
octopus and spiny lobster (centre), squid (right), two different dogfish
(mid right and lower left). Detail from a fourth-century AD mosaic in
the Museo Nazionale, Naples

Source   By permission of the Soprintendenza Archeologica per le Province di Napoli e Caserta

Figure 20   Left, *Pecten jacobaeus* (Coquille Saint-Jacques), typical of Tarentum and
Ambracia; right, *Proteoplecten glaber*, typical of Mytilenae

Source   Drawings by Soun Vannithone, from Alan Davidson, *Mediterranean Seafood* (2nd edn,
Harmondsworth, 1981). By permission of the author

Games. The sanctuary boasted the chryselephantine statue of Zeus by Pheidias, one of the seven wonders of the world.[60]

No longer noted as in classical times for its eels or for the delicate beauty of its veiled women, Thebes (Thebae) in Roman poetry summons up the ancient fame of its Cadmean walls, whose massive rocks were charmed into position by music; it is once more the *draconigena urbs* 'born from the dragon' because its first soldiers were born of dragons' teeth.[61] Chalcis recalls the continuous turbulence of the narrow Euripus; Delphi its sacred bay trees, its oracle of Apollo, and its well known position at the centre or navel of the world, *Delphi orbis umbilicum*.[62]

Megara, famously belittled by the Delphic Oracle (p. 128), had one claim to fame in the Roman world: a vegetable-growing town that had once depended on the Athenian market as the *suburbium* now depended on Rome, Megara had become a typical source of the reputedly aphrodisiac *bulbus* (grape hyacinth, *Muscari comosum*). 'Bring from Megara the fertilising seeds of the bulb that arouse men and arm them for intercourse with women', advised Columella in the verse section of his farming manual (*On Agriculture* 10.105–6). Once served to their customers by Athenian *hetairai*, bulbs remain a popular hors d'oeuvre in modern Greece, although they require long baking till tender (traditionally under hot ashes)[63] and, as an early Greek comedy had already emphasised, sympathetic seasoning: 'Look, if you please, at how highly the bulb is regarded for its extravagance: it insists on cheese, honey, sesame, olive oil, onion, vinegar, silphium. All on its own it is mean and sour' (Philemon 122 [*Epitome of Athenaeus* 64e]). The Roman cookbook suggests some Roman methods, inserting a quotation from a lost dialogue by Varro:

> BULBS. Serve in oil, fish sauce, vinegar, with a little cumin sprinkled over. – Or, mash and boil in water, then fry in oil. Make a sauce thus: thyme, pennyroyal, pepper, oregano, honey, a little vinegar and, if liked, a little fish sauce. Sprinkle pepper over and serve. – Or, boil and squeeze into a pan, adding thyme, oregano, honey, vinegar, concentrated must, *caryota* date, fish sauce and a little oil. Sprinkle pepper over and serve. Varro says: *What of bulbs? Boil them in water, I said, if you fancy knocking at Venus's door. Or serve them at dinner, as people do at proper weddings. But you may add pine kernels, or pounded rocket and pepper.* – Another way: serve fried bulbs in *oenogarum*.
>
> *Apicius* 7.12 [7.14 Flower and Rosenbaum, 305–309 André][64]

There are three cities of Greece that recur far more often than others in Roman literature. Of these three, Sparta (alternately *Lacedaemon*; its people usually *Lacones*) was most famous for its strange traditional way of life, to which Romans appealed as the authority for various forms of hardihood. One was the *ritus Laconum* 'Spartan routine' of the baths, for men only, that were built in Rome by Agrippa (p. 238).

> *aut claram Rhodon aut libidinosae*
> *Ledaeas Lacedaemonos palaestras …*

As he steels himself to celebrate the outlandish place names of his native Celtiberia, Martial (4.55: see p. 105) reminds the studious reader in these two lines of a couple of literary praises of Greek cities by his poetic predecessors. First he recalls Horace, who sang of 'bright Rhodes' (*Odes* 1.7.1). Then, with the 'Ledaean exercise grounds of indecent Lacedaemon', he alludes to the nude gymnastics in which Leda, like other Spartan girls, had taken part in the playful imagination of Propertius.

> We are taken aback at the rules of Spartan exercise, and especially at the girls' admirable regimen. There a young woman properly exercises her body in physical sports, wrestling naked with the young men, throwing a ball too fast for them to catch, spinning a nifty hoop; or at length stands panting, smeared with the mud of the wrestling floor, bruised in the rough pancration; or binds the leather straps to her brave fists, or swings and tosses the weighty discus, or races her horse around the ring, the scabbard bouncing against her snow-white thigh, a bronze helmet protecting her virgin head; or swims as the bare-breasted Amazon regiment swam in the waters of Thermodon; or maybe hunts with a pack of native hounds across the long mountain ridges of Taygetus…. Thus on the sands of Eurotas Pollux was to excel in riding and Castor in wrestling, and Helen is said to have armed for exercise just like them, breasts uncovered, and her divine brothers did not blush.
>
> Propertius 3.14

How right all this was, Propertius had gone on to argue. How much better Roman women would be for the freedom to bestow friendship or love that must surely have accompanied this practice of stripping and exercising alongside men – the very freedom that Roman men and boys possessed and tended to demonstrate at Agrippa's exercise ground on the Campus Martius.

There can be little doubt that Propertius is aiming an arrow of satire at Agrippa's resolutely male 'Laconian customs' (p. 238); the poem was written only a short time after his *pyriatorion Lakonikon* was built. For all that, there is a long literary history underlying the picture that Propertius had painted. It goes back to classical reality, the satire of Aristophanes, Aristotle's judicious criticism of Spartan women's 'excessive freedom', the notorious success of Cynisca at the Olympic Games.[65] Spartan women were famously 'the best', as pronounced by the Delphic oracle (p. 128). Their beauty was visible to all: unlike many other Greek women they were seen in public unveiled and – we may go as far as this with Propertius – lightly dressed, their hair perhaps tied back with a hairband *à la Laconienne*, a style all the more attractive for its careless simplicity (Horace, *Odes* 2.11.23–24: p. 246).[66]

For just as many centuries, Sparta had been famous for its race of hunting dogs, the *fulvus Lacon* 'tawny Laconian hound' and its *veloces Spartae catuli* 'swift Spartan puppies', alternatively named – but in poetry only – after mount Taygetus or after the town of Amyclae near Sparta, *Taygeti canes, Amyclaei canes*. This was one of the most admired breeds of the Empire,[67] differing from all others in some traits: Laconian bitches were said to carry their young for sixty-three days from conception, and to live eleven years (the males only nine) whereas the natural lifespan for other breeds was fourteen (Pliny 10.177–178).

The best of purple dyes was Tyrian, but Laconian was the best from Europe. It was the secretion of the shellfish called *purpura* in Latin (*Murex brandaris*), as was the dye used at Tarentum. *Laconicae purpurae*, in Roman poetry, are robes dyed with the Laconian purple that came from the harbour of Gythium, a town once enslaved to Sparta but freed by the emperor Augustus. Here heaps of discarded shells long remained as evidence of the ancient dyeing industry.[68]

Corinth is the second of the three famous cities of Greece in Roman literature. *Bimaris Corinthus* 'Corinth that stands on two seas' controlled the narrow isthmus that brought Adriatic close to Aegean.[69] So Propertius promises himself that on his way to Athens he will put in at the peaceful harbour of Lechaeum and from there walk across the Isthmus that separates sea from sea (p. 119). Ovid did the same on his sad journey into exile. The walk ended at *Corinthiacae Cenchreae*, Corinth's harbour on the Saronic gulf, where one took a second ship to continue East (Ovid, *Tristia* 1.10.9).

Not everyone has the fortune to go to Corinth, said the proverb: *non cuivis homini contingit adire Corinthum*, as Horace puts it in Latin (*Epistles* 1.17.36), and it was generally agreed that the truth of this had been demonstrated in the classical past in the cost of a stay at Corinth with its expensive prostitutes.[70] In Roman times, visitors went to trade, or to attend the Isthmian Games. Many did both at once. 'The Isthmian Games had always been well attended because of the special advantages of Corinth's site. The city was able to offer every kind of commodity that was carried there over two different seas. All of Asia and Greece came together for the fair', to abridge Livy slightly (33.32). Dio tells us how it was in the early second century AD.

> Many miserable sophists could be heard shouting and reviling each other round the temple of Poseidon while their so-called pupils fought with their fists. Writers were reading their nonsense aloud. Poets were reciting their verses to the applause of other poets; conjurors and fortune-tellers were showing off their tricks. There were countless

lawyers perverting the law and not a few pedlars hawking everything and anything.

Dio, *Orations* 8.9

The name of Corinth was immortalised among the luxuries of the Roman world for its bronze, *aes Corinthiacum*, a distinctive alloy that was rumoured to have been discovered by accident in the conflagration of 146 BC – but if this is so the oldest datable reference to what appears to be Corinthian bronze, in a literary letter of the third century BC (Hippolochus [Athenaeus 128d]), must be put down as a coincidence. Not unlike bronze of more recent times the true Corinthian alloy had a special smell, well known to connoisseurs. In Roman antiquarianism, 'Corinthian bronzes', *aera Corinthiaca, aera Ephyreia* were sought after. They might include fancy household objects, such as candelabra; little statuettes and full size statues; and even monumental structures. For example, all the gates of the Temple at Jerusalem were gilded, except the Gates of Nicanor, which were of Corinthian bronze – but this had gleamed like gold, so Rabbi Eliezer ben Jacob recalled after the Temple was destroyed.[71]

Athens and Sparta had once fought it out for the mastery of Greece. Sparta was now a mere provincial town. Athens, *intactae Palladis urbs*, the 'City of virgin Pallas', already noted as a centre of culture in the course of its third century BC decline, retained this status and continued to be the destination of Roman voyages eastwards. Athens was poetically *Cecropiae arces*, 'the heights, the acropolis of Cecrops'. Athens was the *locus gratus*, the 'beloved place' where student years had been spent and 'the most beautiful of all the cities that Zeus has brought into being'.[72] The city's protecting goddess, Pallas or Minerva or Athena, could be nicknamed *Cecropia puella* 'Cecrops's girl' because the mythical founder of Athens was king Cecrops. Many aspects of human culture had their beginning here: Athens was the origin of cereal crops, of law, of the philosopher Epicurus (Lucretius 6.1–6), and of tragic drama – or in Horace's allusive phrase *Cecropius cothurnus* 'the Cecropian buskin', since that was correct stage footwear in Greek tragedy (*Odes* 2.1.12). Admittedly the once-rich city was now poor.

Bring ten measures of charcoal, and you shall be a citizen, If you can bring a pig as well, you shall be Triptolemus himself. To your agent Heracleides you must give cabbage-stalks, lentils or snails. Possess yourself of these and you may call yourself Erechtheus, Cecrops, Codrus, whomever you will; nobody cares at all.

Automedon 5 [*Anthologia Palatina* 11.319], translation by Gow and Page

Its produce, apart from philosophy, is limited in Roman literature to honey (p. 141), to sheep perhaps, and to the ubiquitous *thymum* (thyme, *Coridothymus capitatus*) of mount Hymettus. This aromatic herb gave its special flavour to Hymettian honey. Along with wild greens such as rocket, thyme also served as a relish to set beside the bread of the very poorest of the poor students of the city.[73]

As with the cities of the mainland, so with the islands of the Aegean, fame in classical Greek history and poetry brings many places a casual mention in Roman literature even if they are quite insignificant in the context of the Empire. Cythera, for example, had from early times been sacred to Venus, the *Cytherea Venus* of Horace (*Odes* 1.4.5); so the wreaths of Venus's beloved myrtle that Roman women wore when they bathed in the men's baths on the first of April could reasonably be called *Cytheriaca myrtus*. Melos was known for the grey pigment *melinum*, used in women's cosmetics. No single author from Roman times talks of having tasted the wine of Naxos; yet Naxos remained memorable, from very early Greek poetry, as an island where wine flows at Bacchus's command. In the northern Aegean, Lemnos – *aestuosa Lemnos* 'stormy Lemnos', *tellus Hypsipylea* 'the land of Hypsipyle' because she had been queen when the Argonauts landed – was sacred to Vulcan, because this volcanic island was where he fell when Jupiter threw him down from Olympus. In Roman poetry, therefore, it was in Lemnian chains that the divine blacksmith caught his lascivious wife and her lover.[74] Thasos had once been famous for its wine, judged second best after Chian in the fifth-century Greek lists. Its grape variety, *Thasia vitis*, was one of those that had been transplanted to Italy; the grapes were small and the vine required planting in rich soil if it were to pay for itself (Vergil, *Georgics* 2.91). What happened to the wine? The answer seems to be that its flavour came to depend on the tricks of manufacture rather than on the grape. So it could be imitated, like Coan, and it was. Florentinus, the Roman author whose recipe follows, appears to have farmed in Bithynia – certanly not on Thasos.

> MAKING THASIAN WINE: Florentinus. We dry ripe grapes in bunches in the sun for 5 days; on the 6th at midday we put them, still warm, into must, with sea-water which has been boiled down to half, then remove them and put them in the vat and press them; then, after a night and a day, we put [the must] in jars. When it has fermented and cleared, we add a 25th part of concentrated must. After the spring equinox we transfer into smaller jars.
>
> *Geoponica* 8.23

Apollo's sacred island of Delos had once been a place of festival and frequent sacrifice. On this small and relatively barren island visitors had needed a regular supply of meat to buy for sacrifice. Originating in India, spreading by way of Persia, the domestic fowl (*Gallus gallus*) had rapidly become more widespread in classical and Hellenistic Greece, and it was natural that the people of Delos should have become specialists in poultry-farming. Pigs, sheep and oxen were costly to keep and could not be fully consumed at the sacrificial meal. These big animals were an occasional, lavish sacrifice; if used frequently, they would have produced a much larger supply of offal and cooked meats than the population of little Delos could consume. Chickens were cheap, easy to kill and draw, and could be roasted and eaten on the spot with little waste: no wonder Delos and its visitors had come to favour them. Desolate as the island had become under the Empire (p. 126), its ancient speciality was remembered in Petronius's phrase 'to dock with a Delian hand', that is, to castrate as one does a capon.[75]

Rhodes, once *euichthys* 'land of fine fish', was *clara Rhodos* 'bright Rhodes' to Roman poets. The city was sacred to the Sun (*Helios* in Greek, *Sol* in Latin): the colossal statue of Helios was still one of the seven wonders of the world, even though it had fallen into the harbour in the third century BC.[76] Rhodes was known in the Empire for its fighting cocks, Pliny tells us (10.48), and this is why Martial (p. 26) equips his flourishing landowner 'Faustinus' with Rhodian hens. There was something special too about *copta Rhodiaca*, Rhodian cakes (Martial 14.70): what? They may have been the urchin-cake or '*echinos*, as to which I say no more for the present: when you are with me we shall taste it made the Rhodian way and I shall try to explain more fully' (Lynceus [Athenaeus 647b]); or, given the lapse of four centuries between Lynceus and Martial, they may have been no such thing.

Lesbos, fairly called *nota Lesbos* 'famous' by Horace, *Lesbos euoinos* 'land of fine wine' by an earlier poet, had more claims to fame than the wines of Mytilenae, Eresus and Methymna – in increasing order of sweetness – that Romans continued to prize (pp. 134–6).[77] Methymna and Mytilenae were proud of the *pecten* (perhaps *Proteoplecten glaber*), smaller than the coquille Saint-Jacques but just as good in flavour. They were conserved in brine and exported;[78] if eaten fresh,

> grilled and served with vinegar and silphium they tend to loosen the bowels owing to their excessive sweetness; they are juicier and easier to digest if they are baked.
>
> Xenocrates 61–64, abridged

Lesbos had been the birthplace of personal love poetry in the work of Alcaeus and of Sappho, who could be called *Lesbis* 'the woman of Lesbos'.[79] Thus in some sense it was the homeland of sensual love, and *Lesbia* was a good poetic name for a mistress, whether the thought that was uppermost in her lover's mind was of the 'Lesbian girls with their trailing robes going to and fro being judged for beauty' (Alcaeus 130 Lobel and Page); or of the freedom of speech and action that Sappho, unique among women, had demonstrated in her poetry; or of the god Priapus's rule over the island (Petronius 133).[80]

Chios, too, was a land of luxury – the eponymous *vita Chia* 'Chian life' of Petronius (63). It produced the best of all transmarine wines (p. 136). Its 'golden lightly-dried Chian figs' (Martial 7.31: p. 27) were so well known that the word *Chiae* 'Chians' could be understood simply as 'figs'

(Calpurnius Siculus, *Eclogues* 2.81); they must have been something like the excellent figs that now come from Syme. And its gymnasia and racetracks attracted interest – if Athenaeus (p. 125) can be relied on – for the fact that young people of both sexes could be admired by the connoisseur of beauty as they were exercising.

Beside all that, Chios was the only significant source in the world, as it still is, of mastic, that most useful and aromatic substance, the resin of the Chian *lentiscus* (mastic tree, a variety of lentisk, *Pistacia lentiscus*). Mastic could be adulterated with pine resin, said Pliny; but genuine 'Chian white mastic', the best kind, sold for 10 *denarii* a pound in Rome in his time. To Greeks and to many Romans, the unique taste of mastic was indissolubly linked with the idea of fresh breath and clean teeth, just in the same way that the idea is linked with peppermint or spearmint in the minds of many modern westerners. That is why, while many woods could equally be used for making toothpicks, it is lentisk toothpicks that are specified in a gift-poem by Martial (14.22); for every part of the tree shares to some extent the aromatic quality of the resin. Apart from this primary use as a natural cleansing chewing gum, mastic contributed to the flavour of spiced wines – medicinal mastic wine and oil were made on Chios for export – and it was occasionally called for as a spice in cooking and an ingredient in compound medicines.[81]

Samos is best known to Roman archaeologists, as it was to many Romans, as the original manufacturer of a style of pottery that became ubiquitous on the tables of the Empire. 'Samian ware is still highly regarded for service at meals', writes Pliny, but he makes it clear that most of it no longer came from Samos. 'Its reputation is maintained today by Arretium and Surrentum in Italy, the latter for drinking cups only, and by Saguntum in Spain' (35.160).[82] The sweet wine of Samos was to be a Byzantine development, but Samos was already noted in Roman times for one gastronomic speciality, the *attagen Ionicus* of Horace (*Epodes* 2.54: francolin, *Francolinus francolinus*), a game bird for which the island was still noted in the eighteenth century but which is no longer to be found there today.

The reputation of Cos as the home of a kind of silk has the authority of Aristotle, who describes the life history of a moth that was found on the island. 'Certain women unwind the cocoons of these creatures', acccording to Aristotle, 'and afterwards weave a fabric with the threads. A Coan, Pamphila daughter of Plateus, is credited with this invention' (Aristotle, *Study of Animals* 551b13). The result may properly be called wild silk, and the distinction made in the *Digest* of Justinian, between *Serica* 'Chinese fabric i.e. true silk' and *bombycina* 'silk i.e. wild silk', is a valid one. Earlier Roman texts never set the two side by side: the fact that Chinese silk, too, was woven from the cocoons of moths was little known. Wild silk moths are called *bombyx* in Latin: Pliny (11.75–76) gives the fullest information on the manufacture, based partly on Aristotle. It seems likely that the silk moth of Cos was *Lasiocampa otus*, a large European moth that does weave a silky cocoon.[83] The business conducted by the ladies of Cos would have ceased to be of interest once the Chinese silk moth had been naturalised in Europe in the sixth century AD. Until then, *Coa vestis* or *bombycina vestis* 'a dress of Coan silk', perhaps a *tenue pallium* 'thin shift', was a most sensuous and revealing garment for a beautiful woman. The adjectives *levis, tenuis* 'light, thin' are often called upon; *lubrica Coa*, 'slinky' or 'sinuous', is Persius's version.[84] 'In her Coan silk you can see her as well as if she were naked', Horace bluntly advises (p. 261), talking of the evaluation of prostitutes, and we are reminded of the *nebula linea* 'woven cloud' in which, according to Publilius Syrus, women paraded as if naked and of the wisp of wild silk that is the only garment of a pretty dancer in a pantomime described by Apuleius.[85] 'Dress me in Coan silk and I shall be an easy-going girl', Propertius (4.2.23) imagines the effigy of the changeable god Vertumnus to say. Elsewhere the same silk-loving poet sees himself nobly resisting the temptation to seduce 'a girl who shines through her Arabian wild silk' (2.3.15), a reminder that wild silk came from the Near East as well.

Crete, the largest Greek island (Map 8), is naturally more complex than others in its literary profile.[86] Cretan dogs – or 'Dictaean', after the mountain in central Crete where Zeus was born – *pugnaces Cretes* 'fighting Cretans' were a respected hunting breed, fleet-footed in mountain terrain, but they hunted more noisily than Carians and had a wild look and a stubborn streak.[87] Cretan men had once been famous as archers, *Kretes toxophoroi* (Pindar, *Pyth.* 5.41). Pliny knew a reason why. The reeds that were used as arrows in Crete were especially suited to their purpose, having a greater distance between knots than other reeds and being malleable when heated. These arrows are prominent in Roman poetry, *Cretaea sagitta, Cydonia spicula, calami spicula Gnosii*; Vergil even provides an African nomadic shepherd with the unlikely accoutrement of a Cretan quiver. The learned Claudian knew another reason: Cretan goats' horns were made flexible by heating and turned into bows.[88]

The old harbour city of Cydonia, later Khania, in western Crete, had two significant exports. The quince (*Cydonia vulgaris*), the aromatic apple-like fruit called by the Romans *cotoneum*, is known in Greek literature from the sixth century BC. The Latin name derives, by way of an intermediary language, from Greek *kydonion {melon}*, literally 'apple of Cydonia'. Using the Greek name, Calpurnius Siculus calls them *cerea Cydonia sub tenui lana* 'quinces, waxy beneath their soft down' (*Eclogues* 2.91). Quince orchards and nurseries of Roman date have been identified in the fields around Cydonia.[89] Romans knew the flavour of quince best in quince wine, the *kydonites* of Dioscorides:

> It is also called 'apple wine'. Remove the seeds from quinces and chop them as if chopping turnips. Pour 12 pounds into 1 *metretes* [6 gallons] grape juice; [leave to ferment] for 40 days. Strain and bottle.
>
> Dioscorides 5.20

In later times the most widespread use for this fruit has been in what the Byzantine Greeks called *kydonaton* 'quince paste, marmalade', still popular in several Mediterranean countries. The first recipes for this go back only to the sixth century AD, but it is a linear descendant of classical quince honey, *melomeli*, for which a recipe follows:

> Remove the seeds from quinces and pack them as tightly as possible into a jar that is then filled with honey. It is ready to use after a year. It tastes like honey wine, and has the same dietary effects.
>
> Dioscorides 5.21

The sweet wine of Cydonia, *passum Creticum* 'Cretan raisin wine', appears to be a novelty of Roman times, first mentioned as a component of a compound drug by Scribonius Largus and then as something worth drinking by Pliny and Martial (p. 137). It increased in favour through early medieval times.[90]

It was a long time since Crete had had a hundred cities, if indeed it had ever truly been *Krete hekatompolis*, 'Crete of the hundred cities' as in the *Iliad*. It was this Homeric epithet that came to Horace's mind, none the less, when ruminating on Antony's possible flight path in his attempt to escape the victorious Octavian. Antony had actually given large estates in Crete to his royal mistress Cleopatra not long before. These estates reverted to Octavian – Augustus – on his victory and Cleopatra's death, and they may well have formed the basis of an Imperial monopoly in the medicinal herbs of Crete.[91] The island had already been well known for the quality and efficacy of its herbs, the *Cressae herbae* of Propertius, when Theophrastus was compiling the *Study of Plants* in 310 BC; even in his time there were some who said that in leaves and stems and all parts above the roots they were the best in the world. Some of them, such as the two gynaecological drugs *dictamnon* (dittany, *Origanum dictamnus*) and *tragion* (perhaps *Hypericum hircinum*) could be found nowhere else. Dittany leaves, pounded in water, would bring on labour; *tragion* was used to promote lactation and to cure breast ailments.[92]

The full development of the trade in Cretan medicinal herbs has been tentatively dated to the time of Nero, whose physician Andromachus came from Crete. Galen describes it in full vigour. 'Many herbs are imported every summer from Crete: the plant men that the Emperor maintains there send great trays full of them not only to the Emperor himself but to the city at large' and to some provincial markets too. They were gathered whole 'so that everything is present, plant, fruits, seeds, roots, juice' and loosely enveloped in rolls of papyrus. The rolls were packed into baskets woven from withies of the agnus castus (*Vitex agnus-castus*). The herbalists of Rome bought Cretan herbs by the basket. The rolls were labelled on the outside sometimes just with the name of the particular species, sometimes also with the district of origin – and if this was *Pedias*, said Galen, the quality was likely to be best of all.[93] *Pedias* is modern *Peza*, now a wine appellation, the green, well-

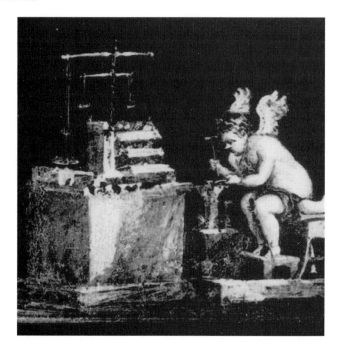

Figure 21   Cupid as pharmacist, with medicine cabinet and delicate equipment for weighing and blending herbs, spices and other simples. Detail of wall painting from the 'House of the Vettii', Pompeii

Source   Photograph © Roger-Viollet, Paris

watered district of hills and valleys south-east of Knossos. Crete remains justly celebrated within Greece, and even in a wider context, for the health-giving properties of its wild herbs.[94]

Galen cannot resist observing that the Imperial pharmacists always preferred the Cretan dried supplies of such plants as *polion* (ja'adah or hulwort, *Teucrium polium*), *hyssopon* (hyssop, *Hyssopus officinalis*), *thlaspi* (perhaps shepherd's purse, *Capsella bursa-pastoris*), *helleboros melas* (black helle-bore, *Helleborus niger*), *chamaidrys* (germander, *Teucrium chamaedrys*) and *chamaipitys* (perhaps herb ivy, *Ajuga iva*). If presented with the fresh plants these timeservers would not have recognised them. But he himself had found fresh specimens of all these growing wild in the country round Rome, and they were better than the Cretan ones except after a very wet spring.[95]

North from Greece

The mountainous territories that lie north of classical Greece (Map 7) have a slightly different character, in Roman literature, from that of the ancient lands – the old city states – to their south. Thessaly (poetically sometimes

Haemonia) is a lowland plain whose classical capital was *Larisa opima* 'wealthy Larisa'. At Pharsalus, to the south, Caesar had gained his great victory over Pompey in 48 BC, a victory that gave its catch-title *Pharsalia* to Lucan's epic of the Roman civil war. It was indeed true, as Eumolpus had expressed it in his little epic in Petronius's *Satyricon*, that Romans had 'coloured the Thessalian shores with the blood of men'. These plains nourished the finest breed of horses in Greece. So the Delphic oracle (p. 000) had asserted; and a 'pure white Thessalian horse' or 'quadruped of the Thessalian hills' remained the typical fine horse to Roman writers.[96]

The Thessalian plain is entirely surrounded by green mountains: the land traveller and his horse encounter all the landscapes so musically listed by Apuleius in the text just cited, whichever the route of their approach. *Ardua montium et lubrica vallium et roscida caespitum et glebosa camporum emersimus*: 'We had surmounted steep hill tracks, slippery stream beds, dewy mountain pastures and soft meadows' (p. 17). The greatest of those encircling mountains is Olympus, Vergil's *frondosus Olympus* 'leafy Olympus', home of the Greek gods. Just north of this sacred peak lay the gorge of Tempe, equally lush and green, through which the river Peneus reached the Aegean, having irrigated the Thessalian plains. There were fine vineyards along the eastern coast, perhaps managed from the olive-rich island of Peparethos in Roman times; the modern appellation is *Rapsani*.[97] Catullus gives Thessaly its classic profile of slightly supernatural fertility in his description of a mythical wedding feast.

> All the flowers that the fields bear, that Thessaly engenders in her high mountains, that the prolific breeze of warm Favonius engenders beside a rippling river – all these Chiron brought, plaited together in garlands. Permeated with the joyful aroma, the house itself laughed. Now the river god Peneus is here, leaving the green-growing vale of Tempe and her girdle of overhanging forests to the songs of the dancing wood-nymphs of Haemonia, and he is not empty-handed: he has pulled lofty beeches up by the roots, and tall straight-stemmed bay trees, with a swaying plane and a slow-growing poplar, sister to burnt Phaethon, and a wind-tossed cypress.
>
> Catullus 64.279–293

Crete, as we have seen, was the best single source in the Mediterranean for medicinal herbs, and exported them in quantity. Second best, many said, were the slopes of mount Pelion in south-east Thessaly. It is no coincidence that the centaur Chiron, native of Pelion and one of the visitors at the wedding feast, was a skilled herbalist according to the mythical tales, gathering his herbs on the slopes near Pagasae.[98] But the reputation of Thessaly in matters medicinal was far more equivocal than that of Crete. Can you laugh at dreams, supernatural terrors, miracles, witches, ghosts in the night, and Thessalian omens? asks Horace rhetorically (*Epistles* 2.2.208–209).

Certainly the superstitious Horace himself did not laugh at them; nor did many of his Roman readers. Witches, like physicians, made great use of medicinal herbs – indeed the two professions were not as wholly distinct as Galen would have liked to think. Thessaly was famous for its herbs, but it was even more famous for its witches. 'You are a young man and a stranger in town, or you would recall that you are in Thessaly, where witches nibble at the faces of corpses to get ingredients for their magic craft', the fictional Lucius is warned (Apuleius, *Metamorphoses* 2.21). The warning goes unregarded: it is by Thesssalian witchcraft that he is turned into an ass, the central theme of the story.

Epirus, the even more mountainous region west of Thessaly, had been important in Greek religion for the ancient oracle of Zeus, a voice that came from a sacred oak tree in forested Dodona in the district called Chaonia. Apollo, too, had a sanctuary there.[99] Since the oak recalled Dodona, the acorn – mankind's prehistoric food – might be poetically *Chaonia glans* 'Chaonian acorn'. Vergil extends this logic further, taking the Achelous river of southern Epirus as typical of rivers; hence the pure water that people used to drink before wine was invented becomes *Acheloia pocula*, 'cups of Achelous' (Vergil, *Georgics* 1.8–9). A Molossian breed of dogs, from an inland district of Epirus, had been well known as long ago as the sixth century BC, when (according to later sources) King Polycrates had imported them to Samos among other selected animal breeds and plant varieties. The *acer Molossus, levis Molossus* 'swift, light Molossian' is still apparently respected in Roman times.[100] Oricum, a harbour in western Epirus, was a source for the wood of the terebinth tree (*Pistacia terebinthus*). Terebinth resin is an aromatic, and terebinth wood is itself aromatic: some believed it was the very wood from which incense must come. Costly and distinctively patterned, it was especially used for veneering and marquetry: for a game board, for example, in Petronius's fiction. Orician terebinth is the choice in Vergil's *Aeneid* for a finish that will be further inlaid with ivory. Propertius borrows the idea from Vergil, instancing *Orycia terebinthus* in the panelling or furniture of a lover's bedroom.[101]

To the north-east, even Macedonia's very few Hellenistic specialities are entirely forgotten in Roman literature, though the wine of Greek Chalcidice is not.[102] It is astonishing that a kingdom which had recently exerted power on a world scale should have imposed nothing of itself on the general literary consciousness beyond the names of Philip and Alexander – these, of course, recurred in the names of the great cities that both founded – and the Macedonian *kausia* 'broad-brimmed hat' that offered 'shelter in a snowstorm, helmet in battle'.[103] But this national garment redresses the balance. It had spread thousands of miles by the second century BC. To the east it was worn by Bactrian monarchs in the splendid series of portraits on their Greek-style coinage, by means of which they asserted their solidarity with those of their subjects who traced their origins to Macedonian settlement. Meanwhile, to the west it was introduced to Rome (Latin *causea*). It is known as headgear in some of Plautus's comedies, though these admittedly are not set in Rome. The *causea* was still around as a sun-hat in the Rome of Martial's time. You might well need one in the Theatre of Pompey, where the awnings could not be erected if it was windy.[104]

From the viewpoint of classical Greece, Macedonia and Thrace had shared an important characteristic with Thessaly: their lush fertility, seen in literature in occasional rumours of twice-bearing fruit trees or ridiculously high-yielding crops, and in Pindar's celebration of Thrace 'of abundant grapes and of fine fruit'. This commonplace emerges once more in Roman literature in Pliny's fond belief that Maronea in Thrace had really once produced a wine so strong that it needed to be diluted with twenty parts of water (as Odysseus had asserted); for Pliny's trusted source 'Mucianus, three times consul' had recently been able to taste a wine almost as strong while touring in the district: 'each pint was mixed with eight of water; it was black in colour, fragrant, and became fuller with age'.[105]

Like all neighbouring regions, Thrace (Map 8) is seen in Roman poetry from a thoroughly Greek point of view. Only when regarded from Greece is the north wind 'Strymonian'; and *Strymoniae grues* 'the cranes of the Strymon' make no geographical sense where Vergil inserts them in his *Georgics* (1.120). But these particular cranes spent the summer in the shallow waters of the river Strymon, in western Thrace, and overflew the Aegean twice a year, a symbol of the changing seasons to Greeks and to all in this poetic tradition.[106] They offered Vergil the poetically localised cranes that he required; four centuries later, they provided Claudian with an epic simile in which he not only names their summer habitat but also appeals to the legend of their battle with the Pygmies of deep Africa: 'when the cranes leave their summer home of Thrace clamorously to join issue in doubtful war with the little farmers – when they desert the Strymon for warm-watered Nile – the Λ traced by the speeding line stands out against the clouds and the heaven is stamped with the figure of their flight' (Claudian, *War Against Gildo* 474–478).[107]

We may wonder what thoughts were uppermost in Ovid's mind when he said goodbye to his heavy baggage at a harbour on the northern coast of the Aegean and struck northeastwards across Thrace (*Bistonia* sometimes in poetry, after the name of an ancient tribe). His ship continued by way of the Hellespont into the Black Sea, but 'it was my desire to cross the Bistonian plains on foot' (*Tristia* 1.10.23). Did he expect Thrace to be rich and fertile – and cold too, *gelida Thrace*? It was all of these in the literature that Ovid knew; it was all these things in reality when compared with Greece, but not when compared with central Italy. Tired of wintry seas, did he hanker for the valley route that ran alongside the Hebrus river, cold and pure and recently imagined as *Hebrus nivali compede vinctus* 'Hebrus, bound in a fetter of snow'?[108] Was he, with his eye for religious ritual, anxious to see something of what he actually did see on his winter walk northwards through the passes of *gelidus Haemus* 'icy mount Haemus'?

'I have seen the Sapaei, and those who live in the snows of Haemus, offer the entrails of dogs to Artemis', Ovid wrote afterwards in the *Fasti* (1.389–390), and it was on this occasion that he saw it. He had, surely, wanted to observe Thracian religion at first hand; and what he observed differed from the stereotypes of Greek and Roman poetry. His reading had told him not of the dog sacrifices but of the *impia Thracum pectora* 'savage breasts of the Thracian women', the *matres Ciconum* 'mothers of the Cicones' and their nocturnal orgies. 'In remote mountains you bind the hair of the Bistonian maidens with vipers for hairbands', said Horace rhetorically to the god Bacchus (*Odes* 2.19.18–20). All these peoples, to Roman poets, were the same: *Thraces*, *Bistones*, *Edoni*, *Bisaltae* and even *Cicones*, the long-vanished tribe that Odysseus claimed to have fought. Their womenfolk, whether maids or mothers, were all Bacchantes, all engaged in nocturnal orgies to the honour of the wine god. It was at the hands of such women as these that Orpheus had died, mythical lyric poet and musician at the sound of whose lyre Thracian wild beasts were charmed into docility, Thracian rivers were stopped in mid-flow.[109]

Their menfolk were also known to drink themselves to madness, whence Horace's *furiosa Thrace* 'mad Thrace'. It was regarded in classical Greece as a matter of fact that the drinking of neat wine, as notoriously practised by Thracians and Macedonians, would lead to insanity.[110] That led in turn to fighting: 'it is a Thracian habit to fight with the cups that are meant for pleasure' (Horace, *Odes* 1.27.1–2), and keen Thracian horsemen had begun to fight for Rome as long ago as 110 BC. Incidentally, a poet of hunting gives us *Strymonius Bisalta* as a breed of horse, a 'Bisaltian from the Strymon', while Vergil has an idea that the Bisaltae of northwestern Thrace are wild enough to drink milk curdled with horses' blood.[111]

Thracian pugnacity led also to the *Thraex* 'Thracian' becoming a recognised type of gladiator, armed with a sabre and small shield and often matched against a *mirmillo*.[112] *Thraex erit*, 'he'll turn gladiator' says Horace of a spendthrift left with no other means of support (*Epistles* 1.18.36).

The Hellespont was 'the strait that separates Sestos from Abydos', 'the straits that flow between the neighbour towers';[113] it is often mentioned in Roman poetry with a reminiscence, direct or indirect, of Leander (*Abydenus iuvenis* 'the boy from Abydos'), who swam the strait at its narrowest point, between these two cities, for his nocturnal meetings with the beautiful Hero (*Thressa puella* 'the Thracian girl'). For one poet the whole long waterway becomes *Leandrius Hellespontus*. Leander himself, from his very first appearance in surviving poetry, serves as the typical young man in love.[114] Still, the Hellespont had something further to offer, as indicated in Catullus's *ora Hellespontia, ceteris ostriosior oris* 'shores of the Hellespont, more oysterous than other shores' (Catullus fragment 1). Archestratus, doyen of gastronomes, had already given a similar opinion: 'Aenus has big mussels, Abydos oysters' (56 [Athenaeus 92d]). His rough Greek hexameter was reproduced by Ennius, as usual it seems, in even rougher Latin: *mures sunt*

Aeni aspera{que} ostrea plurima Abydi, 'at Aenus mussels and at Abydos rough-shelled oysters are most plentiful' (*Hedyphagetica* [Apuleius, *Apology* 39.2]). And so the narrows where Leander swam are most appropriately called 'the jaws of oyster-bearing Abydos', *ostrifera Abydos*. Oysters (*Ostrea edulis*) abound, in fact, all along these coasts; Cyzicus, commanding the Propontis, is *Cyzicos ostreosa* and the city that faces Byzantium is *ostrifera Calchedon*.[115]

The Asiatic city of Lampsacus gives the Roman Hellespont a sexual resonance. Priapus was sometimes *Hellespontiacus Priapus* in Roman poetry: for Lampsacus in particular was *tuta ruricola deo*, 'guarded by the rustic god', the god of the erect phallus who was worshipped (Martial asserts) by *Lampsaciae puellae*, the girls of Lampsacus.[116]

Above the Hellespont lay the Propontis; above that, the narrower, more treacherous straits known in ancient times as *Bosporus*. In myth this had been the site of 'the clashing rocks', *Symplegadae*, whether we place these fearsome landmarks in the strait itself or beyond its northern end, where the entrance to what we now call the Black Sea is marked by treacherous rocky islets, the *instabiles Cyaneae* 'mobile Cyanean rocks'. It was not forgotten that these difficult straits had marked the Phoenician sailors' furthest north: the 'vast Black Sea', *vastus Pontus*, had awaited Greek maritime enterprise.[117] Byzantium commands the southern entrance to the Bosporus: thus 'the Byzantine harbours hold the gate to the Pontus. This place is the vast threshold of the twinned sea' (Ovid, *Tristia* 1.10.31–32), the twins being the Propontis and the Pontus, imagined as a temple of two chambers with a threshold between.

Even by the fourth century BC the unrivalled position that Byzantium commanded had led to a certain insouciance among its population. The historian Theopompus had summed it up as a transshipment port. Its people spent their time at the market and the harbour; they were lecherous and habituated to drinking in taverns. It should be noted that respectable Greeks in general did not get drunk or close deals in taverns but in one another's houses; Byzantines, if they did these things in taverns, would naturally appear to Theopompus to be 'lecherous'. He was quite right, at all events, that the city served as a transshipment port, controlling the trade between the Pontus and the Aegean and enriching itself in the process. It was also a great exporter of salted tuna, sometimes called *cybium*. On its long migration from Pontus to Atlantic the *tunnus* (tunny, *Thunnus thynnus*) has no choice but to pass this way.

> The Horn, which is close to the Byzantians' city wall, is an inlet extending about sixty stadia westwards. It resembles a stag's horn, being split into several inlets – branches, as it were. Into these the young tunny stray, and they are then easily caught because of their number and the force of the following current and the narrowness of the inlets. They are so tightly confined that they can even be taken by hand. These creatures

originate in the marshes of *Maiotis*. When they get a little bigger, they swim out through its mouth in shoals, and are swept along the Asian coast to Trapezus and Pharnacia. That is where the tunny fishery begins, though it is not a major activity, because they have not yet reached full size. As they pass Sinope they are more ready for catching and for salting. When they have reached the Cyaneae and entered the strait, a certain white rock on the Calchedonian side so frightens them that they cross to the opposite side, and there the current takes them: and the geography at that point is such as to steer the current towards Byzantium and its Horn, and so they are naturally driven there, providing the Byzantians and the Roman people with a considerable income.

Strabo 7.6.2[118]

A much-respected delicacy on classical Greek menus, the salted tunny of Byzantium was enjoyed by Romans too. Horace gives us *Byzantia orca*, a barrel from Byzantium, containing tuna pickled in strong-smelling brine (*Satires* 2.4.66); *Apicius*, centuries later, tells us with what sauce to serve the contents.

SAUCE FOR SALTED CATFISH, BONITO AND TUNNY. Pepper, lovage, cumin, onion, mint, rue, walnut, *caryota* date, honey, vinegar, mustard, oil.

Apicius 9.10.8 [9.11 Flower and Rosenbaum; 428 André]

Statius varies the menu, giving us a fleeting savour of 'Byzantine chub mackerel' (p. 215): this, too, must have reached Rome smoked or salted.

In spite of occasional political upsets, Byantium continued to prosper. Eventually refounded by Constantine the Great as *Constantinopolis* it would become the eastern capital of the Empire, often described as the 'New Rome'. After a century of this new status its people were as insouciant as ever, 'youngsters avid for sex, and old reprobates whose great glory is gluttony and whose pride is to have achieved variety in their corrupt banquets.'

Their hunger is only aroused by costly meats, and they tickle their palates with foods imported from overseas, the flesh of the starry fowl of Juno, or (if they can get it) the green bird that can speak, supplied by the dark Indians. Not the Aegean, not deep Propontis, not the marsh of Maeotis can sate their appetite for foreign fish. They love perfumed clothes. Their greatest pride is in raising a laugh with a silly joke, and in their own far from manly beauty. Their chins are smooth, and even their *Serica* feel heavy to them. The Hun and the Sarmatian may be at our gates; their minds are on the theatre. They despise Rome and care only for their own houses, which I hope the Bosporus washes away. They are well-schooled dancers; they are connoisseurs of charioteers.

Claudian, *Against Eutropius* 2.326–341[119]

They were not all lacking in the higher sensibilities. Agathias, historian, poet and anthologist from sixth-century Byzantium, is one of the earliest writers of many who have tried to encapsulate a little of the beauty in and around the city. This is his 'Letter to Paulus Silentiarius while staying *peran tes poleos* [across from the City, at Pera] to study Law'.

> Over here the soil is already green with spring shoots and is ready to reveal the ripe generosity of the fruit-garden. Over here the mother hens cluck to their new chicks under the shady cypresses, and the linnets chirp shrilly, and the tree frogs croak, skulking in the rough brambles. What pleasure is in all this for me? I would rather hear your voice than Apollo's lyre. As a matter of fact I am torn by two desires, to see you, my good friend, and to see that sweet heifer: I am smouldering, I am obsessed with her. But the Law keeps me over here, far from my slim gazelle.
>
> Agathias [*Anthologia Palatina* 5.292][120]

To which Paulus drily replied: 'Passionate Love knows no Law ... what kind of love is it, if a mere arm of the sea can keep you away from a girl's body? Leander showed the power of love by his swimming, careless of night and storm. You, my friend, could alternatively take the ferry' [*Anthologia Palatina* 5.293].

Asia and its hinterland

Attalus Philometor, the last of the Attalid kings of Pergamum, in western Asia Minor, was a strange man. He took a special interest in medicinal and poisonous plants – a well-chosen hobby for a paranoid monarch. He sowed them and tended them himself in his palace garden, and made it his business to gather their juices and fruits as they came ripe; he is further said to have mixed edible with poisonous plants and sent these special salads as presents to his friends.[121] Whether for this reason or another, Attalus eventually found himself without heirs, and the disposition that he made for his kingdom after his death was also strange. He bequeathed it to the Roman people.

To the Roman economist this was a good thing. The income of the Attalid kings, while remaining proverbial (Horace, *Odes* 1.1.11–14: p. 6), now flowed towards Rome.

> The income from other provinces is scarcely enough to make it worth our while to defend them, but Asia is so wealthy, so fertile that in the richness of its harvest, the variety of its produce, the size of its herds and flocks and the quantity of its exports it exceeds every other country.
>
> Cicero, *De lege Manilia* 14

The Roman moralist considered Attalus Philometor's bequest a bad thing

(Pliny 33.148). Once annexed, the kingdom of Pergamum (Latin *Asia*, so called because at this date it was the only Roman possession on the continent of Asia) had to be governed and defended. Its wealth became a continual temptation to Roman soldiers and administrators: Asia was even the cause of Rome's moral decline (p. 11).

> That lovely country and its pleasures soon softened the soldiers' warlike spirits. This was where Roman soldiers first learnt to make love, to be drunk, to enjoy statues and pictures and embossed plate. They stole them from private houses and public buildings; they plundered temples and polluted everything, sacred and secular
>
> Sallust, *Catiline* 11.5–6

Reading Sallust is a rough ride. The reader jibs at accepting from him that Roman soldiers did not know how to make love or to be drunk before the campaigns in Asia; and dares to wonder whether it was a wholly bad thing if they now learnt to appreciate art. Yet his train of thought is subliminally persuasive, and the key to it is in the soft pleasures that begin this rapid descent into total corruption.

The way of life of ancient Lydia (Hellenistic Pergamum; Roman Asia) had been regarded in classical Greece as excessively soft and luxurious, for all that Lydians had somehow managed to win an empire of their own and had later won distinction as soldiers within the Persian Empire. What was wrong, exactly, with *ingens Lydia* 'monstrous Lydia'? Its wrongness is encapsulated in a Greek legend expanded by Roman poets, the story of Omphale, the Lydian princess who took Hercules as her slave. How did she use him? She treated him as a maid, making him play with her soft Ionian girls, setting him to spin wool, and smacking him if he made knots or broke his threads.[122] For this and no more overtly sexual act she is characterised as *lasciva Lydia*, 'lascivious Lydienne': she had made Hercules effeminate, and to do that to a man was sexually improper.

This is the correct Roman view of the pleasures of Asia[123] and what they do to men. Asia continued to be the source of slaves skilled in ministering to the new pleasures (p. 128); and Horace's phrase, *pingues Asiae campi collesque* 'the fat fields and hills of Asia' (*Epistles* 1.3.5), fair enough in its evocation of the province's agricultural fertility – its wine, for example – evokes also its lazy luxury. The Etruscans of Italy, supposed on one theory to have originated in a migration from Lydia, were also fat (p. 76) and outlandish in their sexual relationships (p. 265).

Asia was a land of great rivers: thus, in Latin poetry, an inhabitant of Asia might be characterised as the *Lydus septifluus* 'Lydian of seven rivers'. Its mineral wealth sparkled in the streams of *auro turbidus Hermus* 'Hermus, cloudy with gold', and in those of its tributary, *Pactolus aureas undas agens*, 'Pactolus rolling its golden waves'. This last was 'the Lydian river [*Ludon flumen*] that flows below the walls of Sardis, carrying the gold from which the king's ingots were moulded' (Varro, *Menippean Satires* 96, 234 Bücheler). That king was Croesus, independent Lydia's last monarch, never to be forgotten as a byword for wealth. The river Pactolus in fact provided a fairly consistent mixture of gold and silver – about 27 per cent of the latter: this mixture was called in Greek *elektron*, the same term that is used for 'amber'. The third river of Asia, equally well known in its own way, was *Maeander totiens redeuns eodem* 'Maeander who so often retraces his steps'.[124] Local people used to bring lawsuits against the god Maeander for shifting his bed and so changing their boundaries without permission. When they win, Strabo explains, the god pays his fines out of the ferry tolls.

Lydia had been regarded in Greece as an originator of the arts and the practices of luxury.[125] Pliny tells us that one of these Lydian inventions was the dyeing of wool: and Lydia is indeed noted in classical Greek literature for its *phoinix* dye (madder, *Rubia tinctorum*). In Latin this is the *cruor* 'blood red' of a poem by Martial (p. 106). The *Sardiana tapeta* 'hangings from Sardis' of Varro's *Menippean Satires* (212 Bücheler) are more luxurious than this, however. King Attalus of Pergamum had added a further variation to Lydian colourings: he was the inventor of a kind of cloth of gold. In Latin, garments of woven gold were known in his honour as *Attalicae vestes*, and gold curtains as *Attalica aulaea*;[126] and it is to this costly material that Varro probably referred. It was in the news, for Attalic gold curtains or hangings graced the Porticus Pompei in Rome (p. 235), then newly built.

Two kinds of stone originating in Asia make their way into Roman poetry. Almost two hundred miles inland, in the mountains of Phrygia, lay Synnada and the nearby quarries of Docimaea. Synnadic marble, the *Phrygius lapis* of Horace, was white with red flecks. Very large blocks of it came to Rome, for Rome was extravagant enough to pay the very high cost of transport from Synnada to the Aegean coast.

> Phrygian marble, purple clothes brighter than Sidon, the Falernian vine, Achaemenian *costus*: none of these will comfort one who mourns. So why should I build a high hall in a new style, raised on pillars, just to attract envy? Why exchange my Sabine valley for more troublesome riches?
>
> Horace, *Odes* 3.1.41–48

Yet the Basilica Aemilia, in the Roman Forum, had been restored with just such pillars of Phrygian stone.[127] And then there was the remarkable *sarcophagus* stone. We have nearly forgotten the meaning of this name now: it means 'flesh-eating'. Found near Assos in the Troad (Map 7), it was evidently a kind of lime, and was used in two quite different ways. In tombs it hastened the decomposition of flesh, with the appearance indeed of eating the corpse and turning it to stone. And the sharp edges of *sarcophagus* rendered it suitable for making strigils, needed by every healthy Roman to scrape off the oil and dust of exercise;[128] hence, in a gift poem by Martial (14.51), strigils are 'sent by Pergamon'.

The box thickets (*Buxus sempervirens*) of the Phrygian mountains were known in Rome for the use of this wood in making a musical pipe, *Phrygius cornus, barbara tibia, barbara buxus, Celaenaea buxus, buxus Berecyntia Matris Idaeae* 'Phrygian horn, barbarian boxwood flute, Celaenaean boxwood, Berecyntian boxwood of the Idaean Mother'. Its liquid, wailing notes[129] were heard in the Phrygian or Barbarian musical mode and in particular in Phrygian religious rites, so outlandish to Romans: the worship of Cybele or the Great Mother, *Magna Mater, Mater Phrygia, Mater Cybeleia*, notably on mount Dindyma (p. 165), and the rites in honour of Attis, centred on Celaenae near Apamea in Phrygia. In emulation of Attis, Cybele's devotees castrated themselves, having drunk, it was said, of the intoxicating waters of the river Gallus. These mendicant eunuch priests were called *galli*, a local term apparently, occasionally used in Latin of other eunuchs and sometimes punned with *gallus* 'cock' or *Gallus* 'Gaul'. [130]

We return to the coast of Asia – that is, to the eastern shore of the Aegean, settled by Greeks for many centuries before the Roman annexation – and we follow it from south to north. Caria offered figs, commonly named after the whole region or after 'thirsty Caunus' where they were dried and from which they were exported: these figs were *Caricae* or *Cauniae*.[131] The coastal city of Cnidos was famous for Praxiteles' statue of the love goddess, Greek *Aphrodite*, Latin *Venus*, visible from afar in an unusual temple that was open at both sides so that the goddess's naked beauty could be admired from every angle. Lucian tells us that 'obscene terracotta objects', *kerameutike agelasia*, were sold to tourists.[132]

Miletus had been known for its sheep as long ago as the sixth century. Their wool remained famous in Roman times. Although said by some to be surpassed even within the province of Asia by the black wool of Laodicea and by the colour-dyed Colossian wool, *Milesia vellera* – simply *Milat* in Aramaic – were still widely regarded as the best in the Empire: so they must be the very quality that the Land of Israel would produce in the time of the Messiah, according to the teaching of Rabban Gamaliel the Elder.[133] Cloaks made of Milesian wool shared this high reputation: blood-red, madder red, was their typical colour. Proverbial for unbridled luxury and linked by reputation with the titillating *Milesiae* 'Milesian tales' of popular literature, Miletus was equally famous as the birthplace of the venerable philosopher Thales.[134]

At Ephesus you visited the 'great temple of Artemis', one of the seven wonders of the world; there were others along this coast, the fallen Colossus of Rhodes, the *Mausoleum* or tomb of Mausolus at Halicarnassus.[135] North again from Ephesus, passing Smyrna and the Perperene vineyards that look across the straits at Lesbos, one entered *Troas*, the neighbourhood of Troy (Latin *Troia* and *Ilium*). This region goes under many names: geographically it belongs to *Mysia*, the southern shores of the Hellespont and Propontis and their hinterland; *Phrygia*, though that properly belongs to the interior mountains of Asia;[136] *Dardania*, serving as a poetic doublet for Troas; and often *Ida*, the mountain range lying south and east of the Trojan plain. Mysia, and in particular Gargara, the southern slopes of Ida, are among the districts that offer rich harvests. Ida itself is *amoena fontibus Ida* and *aquosa Ida*, 'watery Ida, pleasant with its springs', both epithets drawn from Homer's *Ide polypidax* 'Ida with many springs'; it is also 'tree-clad Ida' on whose meadows Jove slept with Juno, from whose valleys the same Jove seized his cupbearer Ganymede, in whose glades Paris had judged the three goddesses for beauty, Paris who was destined to become *Troica mentula* 'a prick from Troy' in a blunt summary of the Trojan story found among the poems called *Priapeia* (68.9–10). Ida was a source of pitch (produced by burning 'Corsican pine', *Pinus laricio*), proverbial for its stickiness. Troy itself was a matter of history, and references to its rivers – cold Scamander, slippery Simois – are nods to the *Iliad* rather than to contemporary Asia.[137]

The one major city in Mysia was Cyzicus, 'the city of the Cyzicenes, the most famous in Asia and our staunchest ally there' in Cicero's superlatives, clinging to the shore of the Propontis and therefore 'oyster-rich Cyzicus'.[138] 'Cold Cyzicus has been your delight these many years', Propertius writes to an absent friend, 'the isthmus that floats on the water of Propontis; and Cybele of mount Dindyma, her image carved in a vine stock' (3.22.1–3). Why 'cold'? Only because of a nominal connection with the far north: Cyzicus stood on *Arctonnesus*, a peninsula that was joined by a sea-washed isthmus with the Asian mainland. The ancient image of Cybele was on Arctonnesus, 'on a rocky height under the shade of oaks, taller than any other trees thereabouts'. Celebrants performed the rites of Cybele wreathed in oak leaves; so, at least, the Argonauts did in Apollonius's Hellenistic epic. From its connection with the worship of Cybele, honoured in the Phrygian musical mode, the mountain on Arctonnesus is *ululantia Dindyma* 'wailing Dindyma'; and because her priests castrated themselves *Dindymus* is used twice by Martial as the name for a eunuch or a homosexual.[139]

East of Cyzicus Roman Asia bordered on the province of Bithynia (in poetry sometimes *Thynia*) in northwestern Anatolia. The Roman governor's capital city was Nicomedia, 'the wholly beautiful city of the Nicomedians',[140] and under the early Empire he was generally responsible for Pontus – the northeastern coast of Anatolia – as well. Hence one of the odd geographical conflations of Roman poetry. Why does Horace speak of Bithynian ship timbers, *Bithyna carina*? It is because the timbers came from the pine forests (*Pinus nigra var. caramanica*) of Pontus. 'The only thing we needed was shipbuilding timber', a military leader reported of the preparations for an expedition on the Black Sea, 'and there is plenty of that in Pontus, as you know' (Arrian, *Black Sea Expedition* 5.2). Horace knew this perfectly well, but either name would serve: Roman administration had made them synonymous. Elsewhere he can compare a ship with a *Pontica pinus, silvae filia nobilis* 'Pontic pine, daughter of a noble forest'.[141] A second forestry resource of Pontus was box-wood, *buxus*. This came from Amastris, and especially from the virgin box forests around *buxifer Cytorus* 'box-growing Cytorus'.[142]

Map 8   Eastern half of the Roman Empire

Northern Anatolia was important in ancient times as it still is today for its fruit and nut trees. The filbert (*Corylus colurna*) was in fact called *karyon Pontikon* 'Pontic nut' in Greek, and Statius alludes to this with his *quicquid nobile Ponticis nucetis* 'finest harvest of the nut orchards of the Pontus' (p. 231). The old Greek colony of Cerasus was linked by name with the sour cherry, Greek *kerasos*, Latin *cerasus* (*Prunus cerasus*). This fruit had been transplanted to Greece in early classical times, but did not reach Italy (it was said) until the first century BC.[143]

The further districts of Anatolia are less heard of in the literature of the Empire. The mountain forests of 'green Cragus' where Horace imagines Diana hunting (p. 141) are in coastal Lycia. Much further east, Cappadocia offered a breed of horses called *Cappadoces*, and a kind of lettuce too.[144] Lycaonia and other inland regions of Anatolia were known for their herds of *onagri* (onager or wild ass, *Equus asinus*). On the north coast, somewhere in Pontus, the 'naked Chalybes' of early Greek history once mined their iron. Their literary reputation outlived them by centuries.[145]

It is in Anatolia that we begin to encounter Eastern aromatics. The otherwise insignificant town of Selge, in the high borderland between Pamphylia and Galatia, was important for its storax (usually *styrax* in Latin). This gum was the result of the attack by worms on a tree (*Liquidambar orientalis*, a relative of the American sweet gum) that grew here plentifully. It was collected and sold either pure or mixed with the sawdust of the tree, the latter form being less powerful in use but more fragrant immediately. It was poorer than the better known Syrian storax (p. 170), but women used it to perfume their hair. The author of *Ciris* calls this west Anatolian form *Idaeus storax*: I know no other evidence that it was found on mount Ida.[146]

The best saffron in the world, *Corycius crocus*, *spica Cilissa* 'Cilician stamen', grew in coastal Cilicia at the Corycian cavern, an awe-inspiring cauldron-like depression in the limestone, irrigated by a river that emerged from a natural spring in the rocks and after crossing the basin disappeared underground once more. Among the luxuriant vegetation plots had been established to grow the *crocus*, the purple saffron crocus (*Crocus sativus*). The aromatic consists of the dried stigmata of the flower: it is a spice that will always be expensive because its collection is so laborious. Saffron is a very ancient Mediterranean commodity. Pliny observes that it is one of the flowers named in the *Iliad*, and we can now take its history back six centuries further, for Minoan frescoes from Knossos and Akrotiri show the picking of saffron.

By Romans saffron was burnt in sacrifice. It was mixed with sweet wine and the resulting sticky mixture was sprayed liberally about at theatres, filling the air with costly fragrance (p. 235). It was used to give a red tinge to the hair by women who 'wished they had been born in Germany or Gaul', says Tertullian disapprovingly. Saffron was also used in a subtle and seductive aromatic oil, *crocinum*, that could be applied to the hair on more private occasions to encourage sensuality and poetry. 'The perfume-pot shall tease our nostrils with saffron oil', writes Propertius; and it might still do this even when empty, for murrine ware, itself slightly aromatic, was good at absorbing other aromas. The best *crocinum* used to be made in Soli, near Corycus; but Rhodian *crocinum* was better in Pliny's time, he says. Typical additives included wine, *cinnabaris* and *anchusa* (alkanet, *Anchusa officinalis*), the last two to adjust the colour.

Corycus was not the only source of saffron. 'Mount Tmolus sends saffron aromas', said Vergil, and possibly he was right; Pliny adds the Lycian mount

Olympus, the island of Thera and the neighbourhood of Centuripa in Sicily. But cultivated saffron, wherever grown, was not as powerful as the wild kind.[147]

Cilicia made sweet wine and grew fruit trees of high enough quality to be worth transplanting to Rome.[148] The province also had a speciality of felt-making. Saul of Tarsus, the Christian St Paul, was a *skenepoios*, a tent-maker, and he made them of felt, naturally – that was the usual fabric for the purpose among the nomadic Arabians also. Because Cilicia was identified with felt, items made of felt in other parts of the Empire were also *cilicii*, like Martial's *udones cilicii* 'felt slippers' made in Africa from Cinyphian goathair (p. 110).[149] Beside its felt manufacture Tarsus was known for its river Cydnus, dangerous but not fatal to Alexander the Great, 'fine and clear, safely deep, pleasantly swift, delightful to swim in and cool in the height of summer. Even if he had known that he would catch a fever from it, I think Alexander would still have taken his swim' (Lucian, *On the Hall* 1).

Syria

Syria came to the Roman Empire as the last remaining territory of the Seleucid kingdom that had once stretched from western Anatolia all the way to the Indus valley. In its shrunken form it was still a rich region.[150] Syria's varied produce came partly from its own climate and its famous fertility, and partly from a very long period of development of botanical gardens and parks and experimentation with crop varieties, one result of which was the *Syria* pear (p. 65). The origin of these developments can be traced to the Assyrian and Persian empires – particularly the latter – and the tradition was continued under the Seleucid monarchs. The enthusiasm for gardening and fruit-growing was shared by many others than the reigning houses. Rabban Johanan ben Zakkai taught his Jewish pupils, 'If you have a seedling in your hand and they say to you, 'Look, here comes the Messiah!' go and plant the seedling first and then come out to meet him' (*Avot de-Rabbi Natan*, second recension, 31).[151] Beside this native wealth in fruits, vegetables, wine and aromatics, Syria was at a trade crossroads: here the goods of the East were transferred into Mediterranean ships – whether they had come by way of the Persian Gulf and the Euphrates, or the Red Sea and the desert road to Petra – and the rare produce of the West was transferred to caravan for its journey eastwards. The early Chinese commonly equated Syria with Rome, regarding it as the actual source of the Roman produce that reached them; just so, writers of the Roman Empire describe as 'Syrian' or 'Assyrian' several of the costly commodities that actually came to Rome by way of Syria from much further south or east, such as myrrh (p. 184), asafoetida (p. 189) and *malobathrum* (p. 198).

For Syria's own fruit, climatic conditions were crucial. It was said in later times that in first-century Palestine a worshipper of the Roman gods set a problem for the great teacher Johanan ben Zakkai:

'We have festivals, and so do you. We have the Kalends, the Saturnalia, and the Emperor's Accession Day; you have Passover, Pentecost and Tabernacles. What is the day that we both celebrate?'

'The day when rain falls,' said Rabban Johanan ben Zakkai. 'It is said: *The meadows are clothed with flocks, the valleys mantled with grain; they raise a shout, they break into song.* And what follows that text? *A song, a psalm. Raise a shout for God, all the Earth!*'

Deuteronomy Rabbah 7.5[152]

One of the most famous of Syrian fruit varieties is the damson. Its modern English name is a reminder of the fact that it came to ancient Rome from the territory of Damascus. To Romans these small, sharp-flavoured plums were *Damascena* or *Syriaca pruna* 'Damascus plums, Syrian plums'. They were best known to the Romans not as a transplanted variety but as exports from Syria, 'all that devout Damascus grows on its boughs' – thus as dried fruits.[153] Martial's gift poem is written to accompany a present for Saturnalia: 'A JAR OF DAMSONS. Accept plums wrinkled with the decay of foreign old age: their use is to relieve the burden of a stuffed stomach' (13.29). He writes elsewhere of 'pointed jars of ancient damsons' (5.18), and it must be admitted that prunes are not everyone's idea of youthful beauty, salutary though they may be to the stuffed stomach.

A second fruit that grew in Syria and came to Rome in dried form was the date. There were two different kinds of dates that were familiar in Rome, called *caryotae* and *Thebaicae* (for the latter see p. 174). We know they came from different provinces: *Thebanae*, by their name, were clearly Egyptian, while as to *caryotae* we are admonished by Varro, 'You know, of course, that the Syrian *careota* palms will fruit in Judaea but won't fruit in Italy?' (*On Farming* 2.1.27). *Caryotae*, then, came from Syria and Palestine. They were the dates that were gathered in king Herod's rich palm groves and in the plantations that surrounded Jericho; they were the product of 'the palm-growing hills of Idume', 'Idume rich in its palm orchards' in Palestine. It was with these, among other sticky delicacies, that Domitian's guests were pelted at his Saturnalia party (p. 231). And Varro is quite right that the date palm (*Phoenix dactylifera*) needs a consistently high ambient temperature, much higher than that of Italy, if it is to bear fruit. What we do not know is how the Theban dates and the *caryotae* differed; but they must have differed in some way if there was to be any point in serving them side by side at dinner parties, as was done, for example, at Trimalchio's fictional feast (Petronius 40). Since *caryotae* were used frequently as ingredients in cooking we may suppose that they were a fully dried date, with more concentrated flavour.[154]

Among the aromatics named in Roman literature as Syrian, the most important that truly came from this region is *opobalsamum*, now known both as 'balm of Gilead' and 'balsam of Mecca', the resin of a tree named *balsamum* in Latin (*Commiphora opobalsamum*). Although many authors believed it native to Palestine or Syria,[155] it had actually originated in southern Arabia and had been transplanted to Jerusalem and Jericho in very ancient times – the seedlings had been brought by the Queen of Sheba, so the story went, on her visit to Solomon. The Jews, as they faced defeat by Roman troops, tried to destroy these admirable and valuable trees (so Pliny says) but the Romans prevented the destruction. As a result, balsam trees were required to be present in Rome at the Judaean triumph of Vespasian and Titus: whole trees, carefully transported, were displayed on the ceremonial floats. 'The balsam tree is now a Roman subject, and pays tribute just like the people who tend it', observed Pliny (12.112) with his habitual dry sententiousness.

The choicest and most expensive of all the gums, *opobalsamum*, 'very sweet in taste', was an ingredient in the hair unguents that were used by Roman men: 'a fashionable man combs his curled hair neatly, always smells of balsam and cinnamon ...' says Martial disapprovingly (3.63). Balsam was the evanescent smell that Martial's sensitive nose detected in empty ointment jars (p. 264). It was also employed in costly medicines. It was not only the gum that was marketed. The seed (p. 175), the seed husk and also the wood of the balsam tree, *xylobalsamum*, were sold for their aromatic qualities, even the wood fetching 6 *denarii* a pound in Pliny's time.[156]

Styrax was a second Syrian aromatic, a sticky red gum. The storax tree of Syria (*Styrax officinalis*) produced a better quality than the Anatolian supply, which was from a different tree. It was used in medicine: 'a small dose dispels melancholy, but a larger one causes it', says Pliny (24.24). It cost 17 *denarii* a pound.[157]

A third Syrian aromatic is *galbanum*, the sap or resin of a *Ferula* species, used medicinally and as an ingredient in compound unguents: it grew on mount Amanus in north-western Syria, says Pliny, and it only cost 5 *denarii* a pound. Its yellow colour – it is *luridum galbanum* to Calpurnius – and its sweaty texture were unforgettable. Galbanum is still in use: it comes from *Ferula galbaniflua* and is now collected only in the neighbourhood of Hamadan in Iran. In ancient times galbanum travelled widely – Lucan is right with his *peregrina galbana* 'far-travelled tears of galbanum' – not only westwards to Rome but also eastwards to China, and Chinese texts confirm what we gather from Pliny: there were two sources of supply, Syria and Persia.[158]

The *bitumen* of the Dead Sea (the sea was known from this product's Greek name as *Lacus Asphaltita*) and the *cedri* or cedars of Lebanon (*Juniperus excelsa*), also well known products of the region, are less significant in Roman poetry than the fruits and aromatics.[159]

The great metropolis of Syria was *Antiochia*. As the Seleucid capital Antioch had been 'a famous and populous city, thronged with scholars and very active in higher education' (Cicero, *For Archias* 4). Under the Empire it lost little of its importance, and remained 'the fair city of the Antiochenes' (*Epitome of Athenaeus* 20b); and not far off was Daphne, with the great sanctuary of Apollo Daphneios.

The inland city of Jerusalem, capital of Judaea in southern Syria, achieves little notice in Roman poetry – though it is the *Solymae perustae* 'scorched Jerusalem' of Martial (7.55). Syria's other literary cities were Tyre and Sidon. *Cadmea Tyros*, so called as the homeland of the mythical Cadmus, son of Agenor, who had founded Thebes and brought the alphabet to Greece, was the principal source of the finest of all purple dyes and so of fine clothes. Tyrian purple, 'all that wicked Tyre collects in its Agenorean copper', was in origin the secretion of a purple-shell, Latin *murex* (*Murex trunculus*). The living shellfish having been smashed with a single blow, the dye was extracted and applied – a process demanding skill and attention – in copper vats. The most admired effect was of the hue of clotted blood, but darker in shade.[160]

The product is so important in Rome that poetry offers several names for it. We find *Sidonium ostrum, Tyrium ostrum, ostrini colores* 'Sidonian shellfish, Tyrian shellfish, shellfish dyes'; then *lanae Tyriae, muricibus Tyriis iteratae lanae, rubentia Tyrio suco*, 'Tyrian wool, wool twice-dyed with the Tyrian murex, tinged red with the Tyrian juice'. With an access of puritanism, Vergil insists that wool ought to be white, not dyed with 'Assyrian poison'. Few Romans agreed. Togas were white, of course – official Roman citizen attire, abandoned with relief whenever custom allowed – but even togas had their purple stripe. The simpler garments that non-citizens wore about Rome, citizens too when they could get away with it, were brightly coloured, typically with the range of colours to which the Tyrian shellfish dye could be adjusted. These were *Tyrii cultus, urbica Tyrianthina* 'Tyrian wear, a double-dyed Tyrian city suit', fine and costly gear to be contrasted with rough Gaulish woollens. But other garments were admired in Tyrian purple: a tunic, a cloak, a headdress. There could be no richer colour in which to drape a bed, and Cicero expected to shock his audience when he told them that *conchyliata peristromata* (a luxurious Greek phrase this, 'shell-dyed drapery'), once part of Pompey's vast wealth, were now being used 'as bedding in slaves' quarters' because Antony had gambled them away (Cicero, *Philippics* 2.67). Double-dyeing, either twice in purple (*iterata*), or in another hue reinforced with purple (*Tyrianthina, amethystina*), increased the cost and the beauty of the result.[161] There were many cheaper dyes than Tyrian: 'wool dyed without the use of purple is not unattractive, but if you set it beside Tyrian stuff you will see the difference and reject it, as Ovid observes', said Quintilian (12.10.75), using the distinction to get across a literary point and alluding to Ovid, *Remedies for Love* 707.

The great island of Cyprus was a place for shipbuilding, hence the *trabs Cypria* 'Cyprian keel' – meaning a ship – in a sequence of geographical allusions by Horace (p. 6). 'Cyprus ... can from its native resources build a merchant ship from the keel to the topmost canvas, and launch it fully equipped', explains Ammianus (14.8.14). It was also the birthplace of Venus and the backdrop of that famous icon in which she is pictured wringing her hair as she rises from a seashell.[162] She was worshipped here at Paphos and in the 'tall groves of Idalium'; her poetic by-names include *Cypria, Paphia,*

Idalia; her son Eros can be *Idalius puer* 'the Idalian boy', her favourite doves *Paphiae columbae, Idaliae volucres* 'Paphian doves, Idalian birds' and her planet *Paphia lampas* 'the Paphian luminary'.[163] Possibly with the island's Venereal connection in mind, Martial urges both pleasure and caution on an addressee in Cyprus:

> As you recline in the flowery meadow, where a stream rippling between sparkling banks stirs the pebbles, and all your troubles are far away, may you crush ice into your black measure [of wine], your brow red with tender garlands, with just one boy lover and just one most innocent virgin girl to tickle your fancy. But do be careful, my dear Flaccus, of the excessive heat for which Cyprus is famous.
>
> Martial 9.90

Egypt

Egypt had been the proximate source from which Greek literature came to Rome. There were other libraries, there were other centres of literary creation and scholarship, there were Hellenistic poets who never accepted the patronage of the Ptolemies: but without Callimachus, the library in which he worked, and the writers in his circle, the literature of Augustus's Rome would have a very different complexion. Yet Roman writers seldom attribute their literary ancestry to Egypt, and it comes as a slight surprise when 'Eumolpus', at the opening of the surviving fragment of Petronius's *Satyricon* (2), observes in the course of his little cultural tour that the art of painting had come to Rome from Greece by way of Egypt.

To Romans, in spite of this heritage, Egypt[164] had symbolised danger and threat. Even the land route from Syria to Egypt by way of Pelusium, the 'narrow sandy approach to Egypt through Arab country' (Aristides: p. 14), had been one of the riskier roads of the Mediterranean coasts. But the ancient kingdom was finally tamed: the 'land of Memphis', *Menphitis tellus*, as it had once been (Memphis being the native capital before the foundation of Alexandria) was now *viridis Aegyptus* 'green Egypt', and its fertility was put to Roman use.[165]

Noxia Alexandrea 'poisonous Alexandria', a land most apt for treachery; Memphis, so often stained with the blood of Roman defeat. The two great cities stood for Egypt's last challenge to Rome, a challenge that poets of Augustus's early years looked on with horror. Barking Anubis, the dog-headed deity, against Jove; sistrum against trumpet; *baris* 'Delta punt' against *rostra Liburna*, Augustus's swift warships. Had the battles gone the wrong way, Antony's effeminate mosquito-nets (*conopia*)[166] would have softened the sharp skyline of the Tarpeia, and his Egyptian queen would have sat in judgment on the Capitol among the trophies of Marius's victories, along with the diseased herd of unhealthily wicked Egyptians with whom she threatened Rome's ruin.[167] Cleopatra is not named by Augustan poets:

Figure 22   Mosaic from Ostia showing fish, amphorae and palm trees: products of Egypt

Source   Photograph: R. Stoneman

they dare only to call her *femina, mulier, Aegyptia coniunx, regina* 'the woman, the Egyptian wife, the queen', not unlike the great detective recalling his dubious battle with the formidable Irene Adler of 'A Scandal in Bohemia': *to Sherlock Holmes she is always* the *woman.*

Poisonous Alexandria was also the 'golden city of the Alexandrians' (*Epitome of Athenaeus* 20b) and *Alexandri clara urbs*, the 'glorious city of Alexander', wide and beautiful, vast and yet crowded with humanity.

> I entered by the Sun Gate, as it is called, and was instantly struck by the splendid beauty of the city, which filled my eyes with delight. From the Sun Gate to the Moon Gate – these are the guardian divinities of the entrances – led a straight double row of columns, about the middle of which lies the open part of the town, and in it so many streets that walking in them you would fancy yourself abroad while still at home. Going a few hundred yards further, I came to the quarter called after Alexander, where I saw a second town; the splendour of this was cut into squares, for there was a row of columns intersected by another as long at right angles. I tried to cast my eyes down every street, but my gaze was still unsatisfied, and I could not grasp all the beauty of the spot.
>
> Achilles Tatius 5.1[168]

The province that Augustus won in his defeat of Antony and Cleopatra was unique in the Empire. It boasted the Pyramids whose summits reached the stars, and the great Pharos, the lighthouse of Alexandria, that seemed to rival them in height. These were two of the seven wonders of the world, and a natural wonder to match them was the Nile, flooding its valley and renewing the fertility of Egypt every year.[169]

> It is the centre of their existence – their river, their land, their sea, their lake; it is strange to see close together the boat and the hoe, the oar and the plough, the rudder and the winnowing-fan. Where you have sailed, there you sow; for the river has its due seasons, and the Egyptian sits and waits for it, counting the days. Nor does the Nile ever deceive.
>
> Achilles Tatius 4.12, abridged

That fertility was at its greatest in the Delta,

> where sluggish Nile pours forth its waters, and the lucky tribe of Pellan Canopus farm their lands, patrolling them in painted boats; where the borders of quiver-bearing Persis press close, and the river that flows all the way from the dark Indians empties through its seven mouths, making Egypt green with its black silt.
>
> Vergil, *Georgics* 4.287–294

Green Egypt kept Rome supplied with wheat by way of the great grain ships. Of its many other crops the 'Pelusian lentil' and 'Pelusian flax' manage to get into poetry.[170] Bottle gourds (*Lagenaria vulgaris*) grew well here, and *Apicius* offers a typical recipe.

> GOURD ALEXANDRIAN FASHION. Drain a boiled gourd, season with salt, arrange in a dish. Crush pepper, cumin, coriander seed, fresh mint, asafoetida root. Moisten with vinegar. Add *caryota* date, pine kernel; crush. Blend with honey, vinegar, fish sauce, concentrated grape juice and oil. Pour the whole over the gourd. Bring to the boil, season with pepper and serve.
>
> *Apicius* 3.4.3 [75 André]

Up river, Thebes in southern Egypt gave its name to a kind of date, *Thebaicae*, perhaps juicier than *caryotae* (p. 169) because less thoroughly dried. They were served at Trimalchio's fictional feast; they could be given as presents at Saturnalia; and for some medicinal purposes they were better than *caryotae*. And then there was Egyptian wine. Roman poets did not know that vintages were being labelled as early as the death of Tutankhamun, but they did know that Cleopatra's mind was fuddled with Mareotic wine (Horace, *Odes* 1.37.14), product of a vine – *Mareotis alba* – that was recommended, according to Vergil, for planting in light soil. The Saite wine of Egypt is one of the seven appellations of the empire separately listed and priced in *Diocletian's Edict*. Egyptian beer, the *Pelusiacum zythum* of Columella, was equally venerable in age, but few Romans drank it.[171]

Egypt transmitted many spices and aromatics to Rome, but it produced few of them: the *spicifer Nilus* 'spice-growing Nile' of Martial (10.74) is one of the more misleading of poetic epithets and Statius's 'incense or pepper from the Nile' (p. 215) is equally unhelpful. Most came from Africa, India and beyond to the Ptolemaic ports of Berenice, *Leukos Limen* and *Myos Hormos* on the Red Sea, to be transshipped to Alexandria, taxed – at 25 per cent in Roman times – and sent on their way across the Mediterranean.

From Egypt itself came *acacia* (Egyptian thorn, *Acacia nilotica*), source of gum arabic, used less as an aromatic than as a vehicle for face paints.[172] The Nile valley and north-western Arabia grew *myrobalanum*, the ben nut (or behen nut or horseradish tree, *Moringa spp.*).

> The kind that grows in Arabia is called Syrian, and the nut is white; that of the Thebes district is black. Syrian produces the better oil, but Theban in greater quantity.... Manufacturers of perfume press oil from the shells only, but druggists use the nuts too. They pound them while adding small quantities of hot water.
>
> Pliny 12.100–103

Further supplies came from Eritrea (*Trogodytica*) and Sudan (*Ethiopia*), the latter producing very pungent, oily nuts. To Romans, ben oil was a costly unguent used on the hair.[173] Other oils were made in Egypt: their sources included *balanites* (zachum oil or Egyptian balsam, *Balanites aegyptiaca*) and *cnecos* (safflower, *Carthamus tinctorius*). Although Egyptian olive oil, the 'Memphis oil' of Galen, was agreed to be of low quality, the wealth of perfumed oils and other aromatics made Egypt an important source of unguents, simple and compound:[174] 'By Isis, my friend, if only you remember to bring me some of those little salt fish from Egypt, or aromatic oil from Canopus, or an ibis from Memphis – and one of the pyramids if you happen to have room in your ship' (Lucian, *The Ship* 15). Pliny offers several formulae. Here are two:

> Later the *Mendesium* became popular, made of zachum oil, pine resin and myrrh. *Metopium* has now overtaken it. This is bitter almond oil, pressed in Egypt, to which are added verjuice, cardamom, ginger-grass [*Cymbopogon schoenanthus*], sweet flag [*Acorus calamus*], honey, wine, myrrh, seed of balsam of Mecca, galbanum and terebinth resin.
>
> Pliny 13.8[175]

Egyptian drinking glasses, *calices tepidique toreumata Nili* 'engraved glasses from the warm Nile' were a true luxury, appreciated by the Roman rich for their very fragility – a proportion broke in the course of manufacture, and they were easily cracked by hot water. The sensible man would use earthenware.[176] Another valuable product was *polymita* 'damask', a kind of twill in which several differently-coloured warp threads were interwoven with the weft. This had once been a Babylonian speciality, but the product of the Egyptian comb, *pecten Niliacus*, was now preferred. To demonstrate his master's wealth Trimalchio's meat-carver wore a damask cape, *alicula polymita*.[177] Egypt was the source of an Imperial necessity in *papyrus*, product of a plant (*Cyperus papyrus*) that grew in *papyrifer Nilus*. It was sufficiently expensive that alternatives were in use for keeping temporary records, slips of alder bark in the northern provinces, potsherds in the south. Papyrus made a fine gift, *chartae, chartae maiores, chartae epistolares* 'sheets, large-size sheets, writing sheets', and the large size deserved to be appreciated all the more if they were the gift of a poet, because he must have been strongly tempted to scribble all over them instead.[178]

Several distinctive types of stone came from Egypt. *Thebanus ophites* 'Theban serpentine', only available in small pieces, was patterned like a snake (according to Lucan, who is never predictable, snakes were patterned like serpentine). There were two kinds, one hard and dark, the other soft and white. Both, said Pliny, might be worn as amulets, and would relieve headache and the symptoms of snakebite. The white serpentine was used to make boxes, and also mortars for the grinding of medicinal drugs.[179]

Pinguis onyx 'fat onyx', as Martial calls it because of its greasy feel, is what is now known as onyx marble. It too was found near Thebes, and it too came in small pieces.[180] Thus Latin *onyx* (Greek *alabastron*) came to mean a 'perfume jar': the ideal use for onyx marble, says Pliny, was to contain perfumed oils because this impervious substance kept the aroma fresher than any other. This explains Horace's *nardi parvus onyx* 'a little onyx jar of nard', Martial's *Cosmi siccus onyx* 'an empty onyx jar of Cosmus's wares' (his favoured perfumier), and, with just that slight verbal imprecision that we might expect of Propertius when in love, *murreus onyx* 'a murrine perfume-jar', though in truth the jar could be either murrine ware or onyx marble, not both![181]

The 'columns from the Egyptian sands' that are mentioned in Seneca's *Letters* (115.8) are of the magnificent red porphyry from the Eastern Desert.

> It is in Egypt too that the red glow of porphyry is at home ... the quarries can supply solid blocks of any size required. The emperor Claudius, through his agent Vitrasius Pollio, first brought this stone to Rome and had it used for statuary, but the innovation was not widely approved, and no one has done so since.
>
> Pliny 36.57

Pliny does not mention the fact, but Egyptian porphyry was one of the three stones used in Nero's tomb:

> Nero was buried by his nurses Egloge and Alexandria and his girl-friend Acte at the Domitian family burial plot: it is on the Hortuli hill and can be seen from the Campus Martius. The base of his tomb is of porphyry, on which stands an altar of Luna marble, with a perimeter wall of Thasian marble.
>
> Suetonius, *Nero* 50

Although red porphyry statues soon fell out of fashion, red porphyry was used in great quantity in building, as is evident from the enormous investment made by the Imperial government in developing the convict labour quarries at *mons Claudianus* and *mons Porphyrites* and transporting the stone by caravan, Nile barge and Mediterranean ship to distant Rome.[182]

We have already seen the *ibis* (*Threskiornis aethiopica*) briefly mentioned, Egypt's 'sacred ibis that comes to assist the farmer' (Macer 6 Morel), that is, to protect him against snakes.[183] The most famous of the animals of Egypt were surely its *crocodili* (*Crocodylus niloticus*) or in poetry *Niliaci feri* 'Nile beasts'. Thirty-six of the creatures were killed in the Circus Flaminius in the games of 2 BC; Domitian, an extravagant showman, in due course produced crocodiles for his Circus games as well. Roman ladies must have covered some of the considerable cost of getting crocodiles safe to Rome: it was their belief that crocodile dung, *crocodilea*, would remove facial blemishes and redden their cheeks. Crocodiles had first been seen in Rome at the games held by M. Aemilius Scaurus when he was aedile in 58 BC. He showed five crocodiles and one hippopotamus, having excavated a temporary pool for them.[184]

6 Barbaricum

Africa

Afra genus begins the characterisation of the slave Scybale in the poem *Moretum* attributed to Vergil, 'African in origin, and her whole body betrayed her native land: crinkled hair, thick lips, dark colour, big chest, sagging breasts, small stomach, thin legs, wide-stepping' (*Moretum* 32–35). The caricature is not unique to Vergil. It denotes people whose ethnic origin is well beyond the Roman sphere, people who came to the Middle East and the Mediterranean world largely as a result of slave-raiding. This business centred on Egypt, and continued, with some interruptions, from Pharaonic times down to the early twentieth century.

In truth more than one physical type was recognisable – hence the *Aethiopes utrique* 'both kinds of Ethiopians' of Apuleius (*Metamorphoses* 1.9). It is not surprising that Apuleius, himself a North African, should be the writer who makes this point. Neither type would have been close to Apuleius's local knowledge, however, for few if any slaves came to Rome from across the vast Sahara. One ethnic type was drawn from populations living south of the kingdom of Nubia, in the upper Nile valley and the eastern fringes of the Sahara; 'in general they have very black skins, flat noses and frizzy hair, especially those living along the river', says Diodorus (3.8.2). The other type represents the slaves bought by long-distance seaborne traders along the Indian Ocean coast, particularly from the Somali port of Opone, which, says the *Periplus* (13), supplied 'finer quality slaves, most of which go to Egypt' rather than to Arabia, Parthia or India. The peoples immediately south of Egypt, the *exusti Nubae* 'burnt Nubians' themselves and the nomadic Bedouin of the Eastern Desert, were rather less likely to fall into Roman slavery, and the same is true of the Berber peoples of the Sahara.[1]

But in Roman literature a generalised *Aethiops* or *Afer* emerges, and both names are used interchangeably. The physical type is again seen through Italian eyes in the episode in Petronius's *Satyricon* in which Encolpius and Giton disguise themselves, ineffectively, as Ethiopian slaves. Encolpius begins by proposing that they borrow ink from the poet Eumolpus to colour themselves 'from hair to toes'.

'Why not? [asks Giton sarcastically.] And circumcise us to disguise us as Jews, and pierce our ears like Arabs, and chalk our faces so that Gaul will take us as one of her own. As if colour would make the difference! A lot of things have to be consistent if a deception like that is going to work... Do you think we can give our lips that ugly swollen look? can we crinkle our hair with curling tongs? can we cut scars on our faces? can we make our legs bandy? walk flat-footed? give ourselves African beards?'

Eumolpus is in favour, however, and Giton is overruled. They let him shave their heads and add painted brands to their foreheads to make them look like recaptured runaways (Petronius 102–103). In lavishly supplied Roman households 'Ethiopian' slaves might be considered ideally employed as bath attendants.[2]

The trade route southwards from the Egyptian ports on the Red Sea brought to the Empire many other riches in addition to slaves. In the early third century BC Ptolemy Philadelphus had founded the port of *Ptolemais Theron* 'Ptolemais of the hunts', on the Red Sea coast of modern Sudan, as a centre for the capture of elephants (*Loxodonta africana*) for his army. India was well known to have elephants as well – and larger ones, the Romans believed – but most elephants in the Roman world came from Africa. At the time of the *Periplus*, about AD 50, Ptolemais still exported a bit of ivory but the elephant supply was now controlled by the kingdom of Axum, further south.[3] The elephant is named in Roman poetry in reminiscence of its earliest appearances on the Roman scene, in the armies of Pyrrhus of Epirus whom the Romans fought in Lucania (so *Luca bos* 'Lucanian ox') and in the army of Carthage (so *Libyssa belua* 'Libyan beast'). These terrifying, snake-handed creatures with towers built on their bodies (*turrito corpore*) had been first taught by the Carthaginians to brave the wounds of battle, according to Lucretius (5.1302–1304). Romans demanded elephants for the Circus, and noted that *Libycus dens* 'Libyan tooth, ivory' was strong enough to bear the weight of a bull, if elephants were pitted against bulls in the arena. But very often the tusks alone were wanted. The elephants of northeastern Africa were already being hunted down for ivory.[4]

Eastern Africa offered Rome four other strange beasts. The *hippopotamus* (*Hippopotamus amphibius*) had once been native to Egypt. By Roman times it had long since retreated southwards, but hippopotami were kept in captivity in Egypt, as they had been for more than a millennium already. When they were wanted for the Roman Circus, it was from Egypt that they came.[5] The *rhinoceros* or *bos Aegyptius* 'Egyptian ox', a more recalcitrant beast, was hunted somewhat further south; *color buxeus*, says Pliny, 'it is of the colour of boxwood', from which we know that Rome had seen the white rhinoceros (*Ceratotherium simus*), the largest living land mammal excepting the elephant. Its fierceness made it popular in Rome, but it was not easy to capture and transport. A rhinoceros with one horn was displayed by Pompey in 55 BC; Augustus displayed one, and a hippopotamus too, in his triumph over

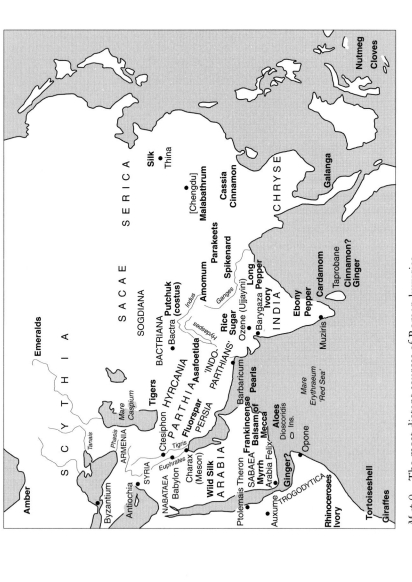

Map 9 The most distant sources of Roman luxuries

Cleopatra in 29 BC, and publicised the rhinoceros further by showing it at the Saepta before the triumphal procession. Domitian's Circus games, as described by Martial, included a rhinoceros that fought with a bull.[6] We are reminded that the audience expected the animals that were displayed in the Circus to be killed before their eyes, no matter how rare and valuable: for one of Martial's gift poems is written to accompany a *rhinoceros*, a rhinoceros-horn flask, a unique and extremely valuable gift. Does this mean that the Emperor himself had something to do with the Saturnalia gifts for which the gift poems in Martial's book 14 were written? He, as proprietor of the beast in question, could have ordered the creation of the object that Martial describes: '*RHINOCEROS*. As we saw not long ago in the Master's Ausonian arena, this rhinoceros dealt with a bull as if it were a straw dummy. Now the *rhinoceros* is yours' (Martial 14.53). Any such costly container was sure to be used for perfumed oil or ointment: in this case a poem by Juvenal confirms it, for he describes the *rhinoceros* being used when washing.[7] A *camelopardalis* (giraffe, *Giraffa spp.*), rarest of the three since its habitat was further south, was seen once or twice in the Roman Circus.[8] Few Romans ever saw an ostrich, *struthio-camelus* (*Struthio camelus*) but their eggs were of high repute in medicine.[9]

One important aromatic came to the Mediterranean from north-eastern Africa. *Zingiberi* (ginger, *Zingiber officinale*) is native to south-east Asia or Indonesia, but Roman sources insist that it was farmed in *Trogodytica* (Eritrea) and southern Arabia. Although some such statements are mistakes, this need not be. Ginger actually is grown now in Eritrea and Ethiopia, and it is perfectly possible that it was transplanted there early in the history of ocean trade because ginger has been customarily grown in pots, for use as a food flavouring, by Indian Ocean mariners.[10] The Greek and Latin name, first found in medical works by Celsus, Scribonius Largus and Dioscorides in the first century AD, is a direct loan from the Pali *singivera*, itself a loan from Tamil. Since both Pali and Tamil were used in Sri Lanka in Roman times, it is no surprise that Ptolemy should confirm that ginger was already grown in *Taprobane*, Sri Lanka. The source of Ethiopia's ginger plantation was Sri Lanka; the source of that was somewhere in south-east Asia.[11] Both Pliny and Dioscorides combat the popular notion that ginger was the root of the pepper tree. It cost 6 *denarii* the pound in Rome, Pliny tells us (12.28). The recipes in *Apicius* call for ginger (*gingiber*) rather sparingly, principally in tonics and digestives; Dioscorides, by contrast, suggests that preserved ginger was eaten as a delicacy, expensive though it must have been.

Ginger is a different plant from pepper, grown mostly in Trogodytica and Arabia, where they make much use of it fresh, as we use leeks, boiling it for soup and including it in stews. It is a small tuber, like galanga [*Alpinia galanga*], whitish, peppery in flavour and aromatic. Choose roots that are not worm-eaten. Some producers pickle it, to preserve it, and export it in jars to Italy: in this form it is very nice to eat, pickle and all.

Dioscorides 2.160

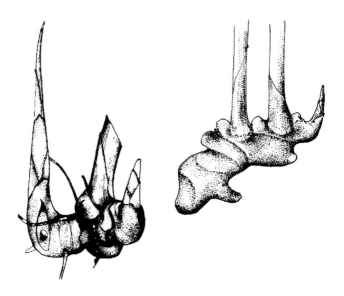

Figure 23   Left: *Alpinia galanga* (galanga); right: *Zingiber officinale* (ginger)

Source   Drawings by Soun Vannithone, from Phia Sing, *Traditional Recipes of Laos* (London, 1981). By permission of Alan Davidson, publisher

Arabia

Across the narrow Red Sea lay the country that above all others in the world Romans considered 'happy, blessed'; at least they named it so, *Arabia Felix* in Latin, *Arabia Eudaimon* in Greek. It takes a leap of imagination for us to comprehend this. The Arabian desert was and is an inhospitable place. Roman military operations in Arabia had not been especially successful. The essential point, however, was that southern Arabia (*Sabaea*, Biblical 'Sheba') produced frankincense and myrrh, two of the most typical aromas of Roman divine ritual and festivity. Bolder poets were able to trace frankincense and myrrh to the imaginary, utopian island of *Panchaea* in the Indian Ocean. In fact the harvesters of aromas were in southern Arabia: the *extremi cultores* 'most distant of farmers' of Vergil, the *odorati Sabaei* 'aromatic Sabaeans' of Statius, the *dociles Sabaei* 'peaceful Sabaeans' of Claudian – and why should they not be peaceful? The 'hitherto unconquered kings of Sabaea' whose conquest Horace had eagerly anticipated were destined, in the event, to remain free from Roman laws and taxes.[12]

Nabataea was the focus of the trading caravans that crossed the desert, and transmitted these and many other aromas to the Mediterranean world. A kingdom with a settled capital in the remarkable city of Petra but with a largely nomadic and trading population – the *mitra velatus Arabs* 'turbaned Arab' – Nabataea had in pre-Roman times competed with Ptolemaic Egypt to transmit the products of the Indian Ocean spice trade to the West. The competition had led to some incidents of piracy in the Red Sea;[13] and large quantities of spices had actually taken the route from the Nabataean Red Sea port of *Leuke Kome* 'white village' (Map 8), by caravan to Petra, and thence through Syria to the Mediterranean coast, which is why, as we have seen, some Indian aromas are called 'Syrian' in Roman texts. When Nabataea at last was annexed peacefully and became part of the Empire under the name of *Arabia*, it was true, as Aristides said, that Rome was the master of 'cargoes from India and even from Arabia Felix' (p. 272); and for the first time the emperor was able to charge import duty on the whole trade equally.

For Romans and their gods, these aromas accompanied worship, feasting and love-making. Arabia, whose whole harvests were spices, whose cooking fires were the wood of the incense and myrrh trees,[14] must be permanently happy – 'There is a happy, far-off land in the extreme east, where the great gate of heaven stands open ... this grove, these woodlands are the home of the matchless phoenix', wrote the anonymous author of the poem on the *Phoenix* (1–2, 31). If, rising from her fragrant ashes, she rebuilds her nest with the fragrances of Arabia and of the Nabataean camel caravans, the phoenix must be a happy bird indeed,

> collecting the spices and aromas that the Assyrian gathers, the rich Arab, that are harvested by the Pygmy peoples or by India, or that grow in the soft bosom of the Sabaean land. She collects cinnamon, the perfume of far-wafting *amomum*, balsam of Mecca mixed with *folia*; there is also a slip of gentle cassia and of Egyptian thorn, and the rich teardrops of frankincense. She adds the tender spikes of downy nard and the power of Panchaea's myrrh.
>
> *Phoenix* 79–88

The full range of these perfumes, 'all that the solitary bird amasses in her nest', might seem excessive if combined in a man's hair oil, but aromas such as frankincense or myrrh were by association aphrodisiac to Romans.[15] From here also Romans bought their aloes, a medicine proverbial for its bitterness, juice of *Aloe perryi*, found on the island of Socotra and marketed on the Arabian coast.[16]

Latin *tus*, Greek *libanotos*, frankincense, is a gum from the tree *Boswellia sacra*, which is unique to southern Arabia (modern Oman), though one of the Ptolemies had tried to transplant it to Egypt. Two similar species, *B. carteri* and *B. frereana*, grow in Somalia and produced what the mariners called 'Far-Side incense', *libanos peratikos*: this was also exported to Rome. The best quality white frankincense cost 6 *denarii* the pound[17] but it was a 'trick of the spice trade', *fraus Seplasiae*, to falsify true frankincense with the white drops that occur in the exudate of the pitch pine (Pliny 16.40). From the earliest literary records onwards, frankincense typified Roman pagan worship. 'Address Janus, Jove and Juno with incense and wine', the elder Cato instructed his readers (*On Farming* 134). Because of its ubiquity, frankincense occurs in varied phrases in Roman poetry: we hear of *Panchaia pinguis turiferis harenis* 'rich Panchaea with its incense-bearing shores', and of *Panchaei ignes* 'the Panchaean fires' that are in fact the smoke of incense on Roman altars. The prized substance was gathered by *turilegi Arabes* 'the incense-gathering Arabs'; or, when poetry required, it was supplied by the Euphrates or by *turifer Indus* 'the incense-bearing Indus'.[18]

Murra or *myrrha* is myrrh, the resin of the tree *Commiphora myrrha* that grows in south-western Arabia and in Somalia. The mythical Myrrha had tricked her father into sex, and was turned into the myrrh tree as her divine punishment (Propertius 3.19.15–16). Qualities and prices of myrrh varied astonishingly; 12 to 16 *denarii* was usual, but the very best *stacte* could fetch 50 *denarii* the pound.[19] The aroma of *olens murra, fulva murra* 'aromatic, yellow myrrh' (on occasion *Orontea murra, smyrna Syrie* 'myrrh from Syria, from the river Orontes') was linked in Roman thinking with funerals – but also with more convivial and erotic contexts. It might flavour wine. It formed part of a perfumed oil applied to an attractive woman's hair: 'Tell smart Neaera to hurry and tie up her myrrh-scented hair, and if that awful doorman holds her up, damn him' (Horace, *Odes* 3.14.21–24).[20]

To a Roman poet, even the nomads who kept Arabian sheep are people of many aromas (Propertius 3.13.8). The Arabian desert is pictured more realistically by one of the earliest and greatest of Arabian poets, Imr al-Qais: 'away in the dry hollows you may see the dung of antelopes spattered like peppercorns' (Imr al-Qais, *Mu'allaqa*).[21]

Armenia

Romans did not understand Armenians. It was said that the *Armenius fugax* 'Armenian, inclined to run away' had run away on one occasion from the much-admired Germanicus (*Consolation to Livia* 389), but there turned out to be a real difficulty in interpreting what Statius neatly calls *suspecta fides aut fuga vera ferocis Armenii* 'the doubtful faith or real flight of the fierce Armenian'. To bring the idea closer to something that can be expressed in English, there was difficulty in deciding whether he will adhere to an agreement, and whether, having begun to run away, he will not fiercely turn to ambush his pursuer (Statius, *Silvae* 5.2.40–41). Through the early centuries AD Armenia was the subject of dispute between two powerful and at times brutal neighbours, Rome and Parthia (later Persia). Survival had demanded that the *crine decorus Armenius* 'neat-haired Armenian' be no more honourable or predictable than these.[22] Armenia was a rugged place in the shadow of the *inhospitalis Caucasus*, subject to bitter cold and paralysing snows in winter: snows here had troubled Lucullus and Antony in the course of their campaigns, still fresh in memory when the Augustan poets were characterising Armenia and its mount Niphates, *rigidus Niphates* 'icy', *arduus Niphates* 'steep', *volvens saxa Niphates* 'rolling rocks'.[23] Yet even the sterile forests of the Caucasus, battered by the wind, provide pine for ships, cedar and cypress for houses (Vergil, *Georgics* 2.440–443).

In a late fifth-century Armenian work, the *History* of Lazar P'arpec'i, the same landscape is seen rather more sympathetically. The context is the division of Armenia, in 387, between Rome and Persia, and the consequent flight of King Arshak to the West. The finest Armenian lands had fallen to Persia, 'the illustrious province of Ayrarat, which produces all varieties of plants and crops'.

> Its plains are extensive and abundant in game; its encircling mountains are beautiful and rich in pasture, and they abound with deer and gazelles. Streams flow from the heights to water the farmlands below. Needing no irrigation, these provide for the numberless population of the capital an abundance of bread and wine, vegetables as savoury and as sweet as honey, and various types of olive. The rolling hills and plateaus are so colourful with flowers that at first glance they seem to be bright cloths scattered with abandon. The wonderful aroma of the flowers revives, refreshes and reinvigorates hunters and shepherds who live in the open. Every root and plant useful in medicine is to be found there: they are made into healing ointments and medicines.
>
> Lazar P'arpec'i, *History* 7

Lazar goes on to list gold, copper, iron and precious stones, sugar-cane, silk-worms; then game birds, notably 'partridges and pheasants that murmur sweetly, that love the craggy places and lurk among the rocks, and others fat of flesh and sweet in taste that dwell among the reeds and hide among the bushes and thickets'; then onagers, wild goats, stags and hinds, boars. Huntsmen and fishermen, in this earthly paradise, exchange their catch generously with one another, and are especially generous to strangers. Thus 'one can see at everyone's meal piles of game heaped up one on other, with their heads set out in order; giving festive pleasure to those assembled to eat the fish and meat'.[24]

Varying strongly from the inhospitable Roman image, this is indubitably Armenia. We observe the wealth of game, already noted by Xenophon in his retreat with the Ten Thousand; in particular the onagers, typical of eastern Anatolia in Roman texts (p. 167), and the pheasants whose Latin name, *phasiani*, links them with the river Phasis in Colchis, modern Georgia, where travellers saw them congregating in vast numbers.[25] And we notice the wealth of medicinal plants. This, too, links neatly with Greek and Roman texts, in which *impudica Colchis* 'shameless Colchis' evokes Medea and her deadly skill with drugs, *venena Colcha* 'Colchian poisons'.[26] She was believed to have relied on *Colchicum* (meadow saffron, *Colchicum sp.*), as well she might. This plant deserves Lazar's praise as well as Roman poets' blame. Common in Armenia and Georgia, it produces colchicine, which is in current use as an effective treatment for acute gout, but is also a dangerous poison. 'I describe it carefully so that it will not be taken in mistake for grape-hyacinth', writes Dioscorides (4.83). Deaths resulting from similar mistakes, as well as from deliberate poisoning, are on record.[27]

Parthia and Persia

> The grave lords of the Parthians were still, and the quiver-wearing populace seethed with eagerness to see, and the Persian women, eyeing their handsome visitor, sighed with a secret fire. The treaty is sworn at altars fragrant with heaps of incense and with the Sabaean harvest. Magi took blessed fire from the sanctuary and slaughtered calves by the Chaldaean rite. The King's own hand makes the libation from the jewelled cup, and invokes the mysteries of Bel and Mithras who guides the wandering stars. And when they went hunting in company with him, who was quicker than Stilicho at spearing lions? Who could shoot the striped tigers at greater range?
>
> Claudian, *Stilicho's Consulship* 1.54–66

Claudian imagines the scene at the ceremonial surrounding the conclusion of a treaty between Rome and Persia: not just any treaty but the very one, signed by Stilicho on Rome's behalf in 387, in which eastern Armenia was ceded to Persia, occasioning the lament that is quoted above for the lost province of Ayrarat. Claudian's scene and his principal characters are drawn with some truth and with admirable learning: we shall explore a few details.

Stilicho had crossed the *flumina hostilia* 'enemy rivers' of an earlier propaganda, the *rapidus Tigris* 'swift Tigris' and *altus Euphrates* 'deep Euphrates', *Medum flumen* 'Median river';[28] thus he had reached Babylon, the scene of the ritual, the city through which the great Euphrates flows, built by the legendary queen Semiramis. Its walls were wide enough for two chariots to drive abreast; these walls were one of the seven wonders of the world, and another were the hanging gardens, built by Nebuchadnezzar in imitation of the *paradeisoi* 'parks' of highland Iran to please his Median wife.[29]

The Parthian capital was not Babylon but Ctesiphon, 'ennobled with palm groves and equally with orchards of olives, apples and other fruits' (Pliny 6.131). A third major city of Mesopotamia was the river port near the head of the Persian Gulf, Charax, otherwise '*Maishan*, where is the resort of the merchants of the East', otherwise '*Meson* the great, that lies on the shore of the sea' (*Acts of Thomas* 108, 111), planted by Alexander beside the sea and successively rebuilt by a Seleucid and an Arab monarch, but 'now 120 miles from the coast, so we are assured by the Arab ambassadors and by our own merchants who have been there' (Pliny 6.138–141).

To Romans the *Persae, Medi* and *Parthi* were conventionally the same people – proprietors of an uncomfortably powerful kingdom with which Rome shared a border. To Augustan poets they had been *graves Persae* indeed, not only 'grave' but also 'threatening': they had invaded Syria while Romans were occupied at Philippi, and who was to say they would not seize a moment to advance further? So we find *horribilis Medus* 'the frightening Mede' and *Parthi Latio imminentes* 'the Parthians, threatening Latium'. Horace describes himself as 'more deceitful than the Parthians' for going back to poetry after promising to leave it alone (*Epistles* 2.1.112). Parthian deceitfulness, like that attributed to the Armenians, was a strategy of war. *Sagittiferi Parthi* 'the Parthians, armed with arrows', *pharetrata Persis* 'quiver-wearing Persia', *fugax Parthus* 'the Parthian, inclined to run away' would turn their backs in flight, retaining the *Medus acinaces* 'Median scimitar', discharging the famous 'Parthian shot' at the moment of escape, only to turn again and attack the unwary pursuer. Western men had considered themselves to be attractive to Persian women at least eight centuries before Stilicho's embassy.[30]

Few Romans were privileged to meet a Parthian or Persian of the ruling class. By contrast, it was easy to meet a *Chaldaeus* 'Chaldee'. There were two kinds of Chaldee: the hereditary caste of priest-scientists who had built up their real and impressive knowledge of the movements of the stars and planets in the great temple of the god Bel (in ruins in Roman times) at Babylon; and the astrologers who used this knowledge to predict the future for money, and lived for over a hundred years, eating barley bread to sharpen their vision ([Lucian] *The Long-Lived* 4–5). The first group disapproved of the second. The fortune-telling Chaldees turn up in Greek, Aramaic and Latin literature in the second century BC, suggesting a rapid diaspora. At almost the same moment the Jewish historical romance of *Daniel* tells of their legendary presence at the Babylonian court and their private language, and Cato is advising that a farm manager in inland Campania should be forbidden to consult them – to 'try out Babylonian calculations', *Babylonios temptaris numeros*, as Horace expressed it later.[31]

Iranian rituals are solemn and strange in Roman eyes. Ovid imagines the horse sacrifices of Persia (*Fasti* 1.385–6); Martial depicts the *pilleati Parthi* 'fez-wearing Parthians' kissing their painted kings' shoes (10.72). But hunting, a royal enthusiasm pursued by Near Eastern monarchs since very early times and one to which the Persian *paradeisoi* were well adapted, was an enthusiasm that Westerners such as Stilicho could share.

Tigres (tigers, *Panthera tigris*), such as the one that diplomatically submitted to Stilicho's missiles, were hunted not in the game parks of Parthian and Persian kings but in the wild. They were native both to central Asia and to India: 'dark India fears its striped tigers', said Seneca (*Phaedra* 344), and the first tigers seen by Romans came as a gift from an Indian monarch to Augustus while he was in Samos in 20 BC. The tigers of Iran were found most commonly in the northern province of Hyrcania, *Hyrcanae tigres*;[32] north again from here the stormy Caspian Sea bounded Parthian and Persian territory.[33]

As early as Plautus's plays, around 200 BC, Persia was known to have a mountain made of gold. Parthia's wealth remained an accepted and enviable fact. *Gaza* 'treasure' was a Persian loanword in Latin.[34] The colour of imagined Parthian scenes comes not only from the glitter of gold and the flames of the fire altar, but also from Persia's 'fine fabrics and purple dyes', 'dyed tents', 'Babylonian garments' and simply *Babylonica*. This term by itself denotes rich embroidered drapes and coverlets; the kind of thing that a lover's wealth could all too easily be spent on, according to Lucretius.[35] The Babylonian needle, *Babylonos acus*, had once been the chief maker of *polymita*, 'damask', a kind of twill in which several differently coloured warp threads are interwoven with the weft.[36] Wild silk was also produced in the neighbourhood of the Persian Gulf, *Arabia bombyx, Assyria bombyx*.[37]

More often seen in Rome than Parthian gold were the pearls that came from its Persian Gulf shoreline and from the shores further east that belonged to Indo-Parthian and Kushan kingdoms. These waters are *gemmiferum mare* 'the jewel-bearing sea' and *rubrum salum* 'the Red ocean' because *mare Erythraeum* 'Red Sea', as an ancient geographical term, covered the modern Red Sea, Indian Ocean and Persian Gulf. To Romans, the harvest of these seas consists of *lacteae gemmae* 'milky jewels' that enrich the far-off Arabs and Indians; they are *lapilli Erythraei* 'Red Sea gems', *cari litoris Indici lapilli* 'costly gems of the Indian shore', or more fully 'all that the black Indian finds in Erythraean seaweed', and Romans use them to mark the good days on a calendar.[38] To a Sogdian prince, supposed composer of the 'Hymn of the Soul' that is embedded in the *Acts of Thomas* (108), they are 'pearls from the land of the Kushans'.

It was from Parthia that Rome imported its drinking cups carved from fluorspar, *murrina*, a highly prized and very costly ware that served to enhance Parthia's reputation for wealth. The carving of such vessels requires repeated heating, in the course of which the fissile substance must be impregnated with a resin to prevent splitting. Difficult to make and easy to break, fluorspar cups were lustrous rather than gleaming, and their typical colouring, *maculosa murra* 'mottled murrine', was in shades of purple and red. The resin would add an aroma to the wine and to the act of drinking from the cup. Several resins might be used with slightly different effect, but myrrh – whose source was not very distant – was probably often chosen. A lingering scent of myrrh would explain the Latin name, and would also give support to Pliny's remark 'there is something to be said for the flavour they impart', because wine aromatised with myrrh was liked by Romans. Fluorspar was used for perfume jars too: Propertius talks of a *murreus onyx*, 'murrine perfume-pot' (p. 167) as a reminder that onyx marble was another appropriate material for making them.

Murrine vases first reached Rome in the booty of Mithridates' defeat in

63 BC. Nero spent a million sesterces on just one of these symbols of Roman luxury, and Petronius, in the course of his last day on Earth, smashed another just so that Nero should not have it (p. 000).[39]

Persians profited from their proximity to the sources and the routes of the spice trade: they used aromatics liberally in worship, festivity and medicine. The adjectives *Assyrius* and *Achaemenius*, applied by Roman writers to spices to which they properly do not belong, remind us that some eastern aromatics, including spikenard (p. 196) and putchuk (p. 197), reached the West by way of the Persian Gulf and Syria; *amomum* (p. 197) came by an even more northerly route. Strabo had heard that aromatic shrubs were so common in eastern Iran that Alexander's troops had used them for tent coverings, while Pliny gives a recipe for the Parthian *regale unguentum* that demonstrates the range of aromatics with which the king of the Parthians was believed to anoint his brow. They include all three of those just listed – another excellent reason for Roman poets to call them 'Persian'.

> The Royal Perfume, so called because formulated for the Parthian kings, comprises ben-nut oil, putchuk, *amomum*, cinnamon, *comacum* [unidentified], cardamom, spikenard, zatar [*Origanum syriacum*], myrrh, cassia, storax, ladanum [*Cistus creticus*], balsam of Mecca, sweet flag [*Acorus calamus*], ginger-grass [*Cymbopogon schoenanthus*], wild grape, tejpat, *serichatum* [unidentified], henna [*Lawsonia inermis*], thorny trefoil [*Calycotome villosa*], galbanum, saffron, nut-grass [*Cyperus rotundus*], marjoram, cloves [*Syzygium aromaticum*], honey, wine.
>
> Pliny 13.18[40]

The eastern edge of the Parthian empire was the source of a most important aromatic, though not one likely to be included in a 'royal unguent'. On their expedition of conquest in the north-eastern satrapies of what was then the Persian or Achaemenid Empire, the soldiers of Alexander the Great had made a providential discovery. 'He crossed the mountains to Bactriana by ways that were barren but for a little shrubby terebinth, so short of food that they had to eat their horses and so short of wood that they ate them raw; but with the raw meat their digestive was silphium, which grew plentifully' (Strabo 15.2.10).[41] At first thought to be identical with the famous silphium of Cyrene (p. 110), this central Asian spice was soon recognised as something different: however, it could be substituted for silphium in cookery. Some preferred it, though Galen considered it 'rather windy' and Dioscorides knew exactly why true Cyrenaic silphium was better. 'The Cyrenaic, even if one just tastes it, at once arouses a humour throughout the body and has a very healthy aroma, so that it is not noticed on the breath, or only a little; but the Median and Syrian are weaker in power and have a nastier smell' (3.80).

There was in truth only one Eastern kind, variously distinguished by

Romans as Syrian, Median, Armenian and Persian. It is what we now know as asafoetida or hing, the resin of *Ferula asafoetida*, a plant found only in Afghanistan. Not long after Dioscorides' time, when silphium became extinct, asafoetida came into its Roman inheritance. It was now in heavy demand both medicinally and in the kitchen. The demand raised the price, and it was necessary to note that (like Persian galbanum) asafoetida might be adulterated with *sagapenum*, the far less magical resin of *Ferula persica*.[42] Still called *silphium* or *silfi* or *laserpicium* in *Apicius*, asafoetida is required in well over half of all the recipes in that collection. Appropriately, it figures prominently in

> PARTHAIN CHICKEN. Open the chicken at the rear and spreadeagle. Crush pepper, lovage, a little caraway, moisten with fish sauce, blend with wine; arrange the chicken in a Cumaean dish and pour the sauce over it. Dissolve fresh asafoetida in warm water, pour over the chicken as you cook. Season with pepper and serve.
>
> *Apicius* 6.8.2 [6.9.2 Flower and Rosenbaum; 238 André]

Asafoetida possesses a remarkable aroma, combining something of leek and something of onion with much that is neither: it well earns the name of 'devil's dung' in some modern languages. Roman cuisine would have been a very different thing without it.

Several of the fruits now grown in Europe had originated in central Asia or had been developed in Assyrian and Persian gardens, but Roman poets did not know the history of all of them. Few remembered that the pistachio had come to the Mediterranean from eastern Iran. It was first brought to Italy by Vitellius, father of the Emperor, who served in the Levant in the late AD 30s, but it spread so quickly, grafted on hospitable *Pistacia* or *Prunus* stocks, that it soon seemed native.[43]

Poets did remember that *Medorum silvae* 'the forests of the Medes', the 'very rich land' of Media, had transmitted westwards the noble *malum citreum* or 'citron' (*Citrus medica*). Its Hellenistic Greek name *melon Medikon* 'Median apple' was a permanent reminder of the fact. 'There are three parts of this fruit', Galen explains, 'the acid in the middle, the flesh around this, and the skin on the outside. The latter is an aromatic, attractive not only for its scent but also for its taste' (*Properties of Foods* 2.37 [6.618]). Scarcely palatable in spite of their aromatic peel, citrons are sovereign against poison-wielding mothers-in-law, Vergil observes (*Georgics* 2.126–136). Vergil's source on the citron is the *Study of Plants* of Theophrastus, who mentions the citron's qualities as poison antidote, though not the mothers-in-law. Continuing to embroider freely, Vergil adds that the leaves of this huge tree can scarcely be detached by the most violent wind, and its flowers are extremely hardy.[44]

The peach (*Prunus persica*) by its Greek and Latin names, *melon Persikon, persicum*, betrays an origin in Persia. Persia seems really to be where this fruit was first developed from a wild species: it was from Persia that the Chinese also learnt of the juicy yellow peach, providing the evocative title – *The Golden Peaches of Samarkand* – of Edward Schafer's study of the exotics of Tang dynasty China. By the first century AD peaches were established in Italy, thanks to Roman grafting skill; the Pompeiian still life that includes a half-eaten peach is well known. It had been difficult to establish them at Tusculum, said Pliny, but from there they certainly supplied the Roman market.[45] They were only eaten fresh: 'some fruits will not take drying', said Galen, 'as mulberries, watermelons, muskmelons, peaches and the like' (*On Good and Bad Juices* [6.785]).

India

The 'wealthy Indians', *Indi dites*, were wealthy with gold, mined, according to venerable legend, by ants, the *Inda formica* of Propertius.[46] They occupied one of several countries that Romans could convincingly describe as *ultima terra* 'the last land on Earth', whose eastern shore was the first to be illuminated each day by the rising sun. Its great rivers included *pulcher Ganges* 'beautiful Ganges', and the tributaries of the Indus – of these, 'fabulous Hydaspes' gets into poetry most often, though it had been on the banks of the 'resounding Choaspes' that the Hellenistic poet Nicander had imagined pistachio trees flourishing – and the Indus itself after which the whole country was named.[47] The Indus was sometimes strangely imagined as identical with the Nile, so that Vergil can describe 'the river that flows all the way from the dark Indians, emptying through its seven mouths, making Egypt green with its black silt' (p. 174).

There were fine women in India: the god Bacchus himself, on his fabled expedition there, had brought back 'captive girls of outstanding beauty'. European women, in return, fetched a high price in India: the *Periplus* lists 'slave musicians and beautiful girls as concubines' with fine wine and other Western luxuries for which the great royal palace, normally at Ozene (Ujjāyinī), would pay well. The women of this court were widely famed. The classical poet Kālidāsa, writing about 400, imagines a cloud's eye view of the garden terraces of royal Ujjāyinī: the dancers almost too tired to flirt and flutter their fans, till suddenly all the girls dash for cover, scared by a playful fork of lightning.[48]

Indian males were occasionally seen as slaves in Rome, such as the well-named *fuscus Hydaspes* 'swarthy Hydaspes' who takes his part as a waiter, a rare and expensive one, in Horace's *Satires*; Tibullus, too, talks of swarthy men, roasted by the Indian sun, serving as slaves. Indians are *colorati* 'dark-coloured', sometimes even *nigri* 'black', like those who form part of the clientele of 'Caelia' in Martial's epigram ('you're fucked ... by black Indians from across the Red waters': p. 211). Sometimes they are *depexis crinibus Indi* 'straight-haired Indians'. Owing to the climate under which they live they have especially hot constitutions: when they try such a strong drink as wine they immediately became drunk, and are driven twice as mad by the wine as Greeks or Romans would be (Lucian,

Figure 24 Royal women. Detail of the ivory lid of an Indian casket of about AD 400, found at the Kushan city of Begram (modern Afghanistan), now in Kabul Museum

Source Photograph: Josephine Powell

Nigrinus 5). Yet somehow the *imbellis Indus* 'unwarlike Indian' is supposed to be threatened by a Roman attack on Parthia and is unfairly pictured as unable to make headway against Augustus in the East. The match was never played.[49]

'The green bird that can speak, supplied by the dark Indians' (Claudian, *Against Eutropius* 2.330–331: p. 160) was among the creatures that made the long voyage westwards to Italy. This *psittacus* was a parrot, and specifically the Indian ring-necked parakeet (*Psittacus krameri*), though other talking species were occasionally met with and given the same Latin name: Aelian (*Nature of Animals* 16.3) describes a better talker, 'the size of a starling and brightly coloured ... called *kerkion* by the Indo-Greeks' that was probably the mynah (*Gracula religiosa*). Prized for their imitation of human speech, *psittaci* were kept as pets and taught to say *chaire* or *have*, the daily greeting in Greek or Latin, or even *Caesar have* 'hail Caesar!' Pliny is certain that parrots are 'indecent in their speech when drunk', a criticism no bird deserved from a human being.[50] Martial writes a poem (14.73) to accompany the gift of a parrot, an especially clever one that had taught *itself* to say *Caesar have*! In Petronius's gift poem for an identical occasion, the parrot speaks.

> The Indian land gave birth to me, beside that purple shore where white day returns to the newly illumined earth. Raised there to divine honours, I have here exchanged my wild vocabulary for the accents of Latium.
>
> Petronius fragment 31.1–4

Not every Roman believed, with Lucretius (2.537–539), that India was

Figure 25   A pair of parrots harnessed to a toy farm cart. Detail of the 'Dionysian mosaic' at Cologne, Roman Germany

Source   By permission of the Römisch-Germanisches Museum, Cologne

protected from invasion by an 'impenetrable ivory wall', but all could understand his epithet 'snaky-handed', *anguimanus*, for Indian elephants (*Elephas maximus*).[51] Few of these came from India to Rome, but a white elephant spoken of by Horace (*Epistles* 2.1.196) as appearing in the theatre suggests that some, at least, did. India was the major source, however, for Rome's ivory, at least when it came in the form of full-sized tusks, *Indicum cornu, Indicus dens, dens pecudis Indicae, Indum ebur* 'Indian horn, Indian tooth, the tooth of the Indian herd, Indian ivory'. African elephants had been hunted down to the point at which the supply of ivory was faltering. Indian ivory was used – in Roman poetry – for false teeth; for luxury writing tablets; for a fancy cashbox; for a medicine chest; for a birdcage; and for a set of knucklebones, an expensive toy, but worth their cost if they were winners.[52]

India was rich in precious stones – Claudian imagines its warriors camping in gem-studded tents – and exported several kinds of gems to Rome. They include the red or brownish-red *sarda*, in modern terms two varieties of chalcedony known as carnelian and sard. Romans believed these had come first from Sardis in Lydia, because of their name, and also believed that there were Arabian and Persian kinds. All these actually came from India. Many Romans wore signets of carnelian or sard;[53] and 'chalcedonies from the Indians' are named in the 'Hymn of the Soul', composed as by a Sogdian prince, in the *Acts of Thomas* (108). *Onyx*, as the name of a gem, applied to fiery red, horn-coloured and black stones, also from India. More distinctive were the *Indi sardonyches*, as Martial calls them. The Roman *sardonyx* was a naturally occurring union of *sarda* and *onyx*: in modern terminology it was 'a banded chalcedony containing at least one layer of carnelian'. Pliny describes its appearance 'like flesh superimposed on a human fingernail, both parts of the stone being translucent', and identifies Scipio Africanus, who died in 183 BC, and the Emperor Claudius, as two male fashion-setters who wore sardonyx signet rings.[54]

The dense, black wood known in Latin as *hebenum* 'ebony' was sometimes said by Romans to come from India alone, but Lucan – an amateur of obscure geographical and ethnographical detail – is quite right that there was an African source also, in the upper Nile valley, and that Egypt's supplies had come from here. The main African species is *Diospyros melanoxylon*; the main Indian one is *Diospyros ebenum*. Ebony was exhibited in Rome by Pompey in his triumph over Mithridates in 61 BC; but ebony had been seen there before, for when the college of priests dined about 70 BC under Caesar's presidency, the couches were of ebony.[55]

'They arrive with gold and depart with pepper', wrote the Tamil poet Tāyan-Kaṇṇanār (*Āgam* 149.7–11), speaking of the Roman traders who were to be seen at the port of Muziris in southern India. He was right. Pliny, not long before him, had lamented the great quantities of Roman gold coin that were shipped eastwards to buy these transitory aromas, equally necessary in high Roman society as flavourings, as medicines and as perfumes. '100 million *sestertii* a year go from Rome to India, China and the [Arabian]

Peninsula' (Pliny 12.84). And the businesslike author of the *Periplus* 'Sailing guide to the Indian Ocean', a trade manual compiled around AD 50, shows that for merchants on the India route 'gold and silver coin' were commodities like any other, acceptable at some ports and not at others, a necessary cargo for most ships making for India because they were just about the only predictable bulk Roman export of adequate value to be exchanged for a shipload of aromatics.[56]

Pepper was rightly singled out by Tāyan-Kaṇṇanār. This, more than any other spice, was what the Romans wanted from India. If India merchants treated coin as a commodity, the Caesars treated pepper as a currency, storing vast quantities of it, perhaps never to be used, in the Roman treasury. There were two kinds of pepper, according to the Greek botanist Theophrastus, and he was right. From north India came the pungent spice known in Greek in full as *makropeperi*, in Latin as *piper longum* (long pepper, *Piper longum*). This in the early Hellenistic world was the usual kind of pepper, because the Indian Ocean monsoon sailings had not yet begun and the natural route of supply was from north-west India to the Persian Gulf. So Prakrit *pippalī* 'seed of long pepper' was borrowed into Greek as *peperi*. When the Ptolemies and then the Romans developed the monsoon sailings, they began to buy the round pepper of southern India (black pepper, *Piper nigrum*) in larger quantities. Regarded as a new version of the same spice, it retained the same name, Latin *piper*, though its Indian names are different.[57] In Pliny's time both kinds were available but the rarer, more powerful long pepper cost 15 *denarii* the pound, the ordinary black pepper only 7 *denarii*. Nowadays long pepper is scarcely obtainable outside India. White pepper, which in fact is shelled black pepper, was thought by Romans to be a third different kind, milder than black.

Gourmets and assiduous doctors might prescribe one kind rather than another, but generally people talked about *piper* and listed it in recipes as if only one kind were in normal use.[58] We have quoted from Diphilus of Siphnos the oldest evidence of the use of pepper as a condiment in the Greek and Roman world (p. 65) and must add that Diphilus was a doctor and his intention was dietary. Similarly, pepper is wanted in Petronius's *Satyricon* (138) in a cure for impotence. But the peppered egg yolk and peppered fish sauce that occur elsewhere in this text (32, 36) provide nothing but expensive flavour, an excuse for one of the host's intimate friends to whisper to his neighbour, 'Don't think he ever needs to buy anything. It's all home-grown: wool, wax, pepper, if you ask for hen's milk you'll get it' (38). *Piperatum*, a cold sauce or dip to serve with side-salads, made good use of the flavour:

> Pound pepper, steeped overnight, and add fish sauce to form a smooth, muddy *piperatum*.
>
> *Apicius* 2.2.8 [56 André]

The use of *bacae* (juniper berries, *Juniperus communis*) in late Roman cookery is itself an indication of the popularity of pepper, for they are a cheap pepper substitute.[59]

Apart from pepper, the greatest of the aromatics of India were not flavourings so much as perfumes and medicines. One with a long history was spikenard, sometimes inaccurately called *Assyria nardus*, *Achaemenia nardus* 'Assyrian, Persian nard' in poetry. Spikenard consists of the spike or ear that grows from the rhizome of *Nardostachys jatamansi*, a plant of the southern slopes of the Himalaya. In the West there were alternatives to the costly spikenard of India, 'Syrian nard' perhaps *Valeriana sisymbrifolia*, 'Celtic nard' *Valeriana celtica*, and others; but the really high prices, 100 *denarii* the pound, were fetched by the the 'tender spikes of downy nard' that travelled to Rome by way of Barygaza (in modern Gujarat) or the mouth of the Ganges.

Why did Romans want spikenard? It contributed to the aroma of dining and festivity, as is shown by two very different sources less than a century apart. In both, we hear of a perfumed oil to anoint the brow, and of a carved onyx marble jar (see p. 176) in which it is kept. Horace explains:[60]

> It's a dry summer, Vergil, you pursuer of well-born boys! If you fancy tasting a Calene vintage, you must earn your wine with nard: one little onyx pot of nard will get you a jar now lying in a Sulpician warehouse, generous enough to give new hope and effective at washing away the bitterness of troubles. If you are eager for these pleasures, come quickly and bring your fee: I don't see you soaking up my wine if you come empty-handed.
>
> Horace, *Odes* 4.12.13–23

Figure 26   Mosaic depicting the poet Vergil, now in the Bardo Museum, Tunis
Source   Photograph: R. Stoneman

Thanks to a religious biography from the eastern Mediterranean we can sharpen this picture. 'While he was staying at Bethania in the house of Simon the Leper, reclining at dinner, a woman came with an *alabastron* of costly spikenard perfume. She broke open the pot and poured it over his head'. Afterwards there was complaint about the waste of money, and Jesus said, 'Let her alone ... she has prepared my body for burial' (Mark 14.4–9), a clever response: if her intention had been to improve a festive occasion and to honour an admired teacher or prophet, it was equally true that costly perfumed oils anointed the dead.[61] Festivity and death were not far apart (p. 43). At Sulla's funeral in 78 BC, the procession included a model of the great man himself – preceded, as in life, by a lictor bearing the consular fasces – all made up in cassia and frankincense (Plutarch, *Sulla* 38); and 'experts say that Arabia does not produce as much spice in a year as the emperor Nero burnt in one day along with the body of his beloved Poppaea' (Pliny 12.83).

Other Indian specialities can be dealt with more briefly. *Oryza* (rice, *Oryza sativa*) was a costly commodity to be prescribed by well-paid doctors to rich patients as an ingredient in medicinal gruels.[62]

Amomum is an ancient aromatic that seems to have reached the Roman world by an inland trade route from northern India, if indeed it is 'Nepaul cardamom', *Amomum subulatum*, now regarded as a poor substitute for cardamom. It had the appearance of a tiny bunch of grapes with leaves around: the best, red in colour, fetched 60 denarii the pound. Romans generally traced amomum to Pontus, to Armenia, to Commagene on the border between Syria and Parthia, and to Media; it was the *Assyrium amomum* of Vergil and Martial, and one of the juices that nourished the phoenix according to Ovid. Scarcely a single author connects it with India; the *Periplus* does not even mention it.[63]

Putchuk or kusth, as it is now known, was *Eoa costos, Achaemenius costus* 'Eastern, Persian costus' to Roman poets. It was Persian in a sense, being marketed at Barbaricum, at the mouth of the Indus, the port city of what was a Parthian-ruled state in the first century AD, Indo-Parthia to numismatists. Putchuk came from 'the highlands' (*Periplus* 39, 48), that is, from Kashmir, where the kusth plant (*Saussurea lappa*) now grows and is 'still used for scenting shawls', says J. G. Frazer. With a 'burning taste and exquisite odour' (Pliny 12.41) putchuk was an inexpensive aromatic in the Roman Empire, only 5½ *denarii* the pound, and was used in the cheaper medical prescriptions and magical formulae.[64]

Beyond India

Few Romans knew the east coast of India – even the author of the *Periplus* had perhaps not been there – and fewer still knew the coasts beyond. The products that came to Rome from these distant lands are the subject of continual confusion to Roman writers.

First a highly prized aromatic – *casia* and its best variety, *cinnamum, cinnamomum*. There were 'many sensational speculations as to the origin of the cinnamon of the ancients', wrote Berthold Laufer: Herodotus traces it to Arabia, Theophrastus specifically to Sabaea. Two assiduous enquirers, Strabo and Pliny, suggest a more distant origin. Neither of them explains his views clearly, but both suggest a source on some distant coast of the Indian Ocean. Possibly the Roman supply came from Sri Lanka, from which fine cinnamon (*Cinnamomum zeylanicum*) comes now. The more likely hypothesis is that it came from cultivated trees of *Cinnamomum cassia* and of *Cassia* species grown in Yunnan, Guangdong and mainland south-east Asia; it came by sea from Indochina. The geographer Ptolemy locates a people named *Trogodytai* on the eastern shore of the Bay of Bengal. These, according to Pliny, bought cinnamon from neighbouring *Ethiopes* and carried it 'over vast seas on rafts which have no rudders to steer them, no oars to push them, no sails to propel them, indeed no motive power at all but man alone and his courage'. But all that is certain is that Roman merchants bought their cinnamon in the ports of Somalia.

After their journey cinnamon and even cassia were so extremely expensive in Roman times that they were scarcely used in food. They were a valued medicine. Galen tells of making up an antidote for the emperor Marcus Aurelius using cinnamon that had come in a 'box shipped from the land of the barbarians, four and a half cubits long, in which was a whole cinnamon tree of the first quality'; the imperial dispensary stored cinnamon, acquired in this form, for many years (*On Antidotes* [14.63–65]), an indication of its fabulous value. Apart from this, cinnamon and cassia were a concomitant of divine sacrifice and of funerals. They were also a prized aroma in perfumed oils such as the hair oil of the 'fashionable man' defined by Martial (p. 170). They 'corrupted' good olive oil, says Vergil fastidiously – but see page 196 for a more intimate relationship between Vergil and luxury perfumed oils. He imagined 'fresh cassia' in Egypt; Propertius calls it Arabian, and Statius talks of *rara cinnama* 'rare cinnamon' as the harvest of the *odorati Sabaei* 'aromatic Sabaeans'; Apuleius knew of a cinnamon trade from India. The litterateurs, in other words, faithfully reflect the geographers' various opinions.[65]

Horace names *malobathrum Syrium* as one more of those perfumed oils for the brow or the hair. This aromatic had perhaps once reached the Mediterranean by way of Syria, but, like others, it actually came from much further off. Latin *malobathrum*, by way of Greek *malabathron*, had been a loanword from Sanskrit *tamalapattra* 'the dark leaf', a name used occasionally of tejpat leaf, which comes from a tree (*Cinnamomum tamala*) related to the sources of cinnamon and cassia. It seems that the sixteenth-century scientist García de Orta was right to identify *malobathrum* with tejpat. In ancient times it came to the ports at the mouth of the Ganges from the mountains of Sichuan or Yunnan. The *Periplus* (65) describes, carefully though without full understanding, the gathering of tejpat leaves into balls of different grade

and the silent barter between collectors and traders that marked the beginning of the long journey of *malobathrum* from the east Asian mountains to
the Roman West. At some stage it was processed into oil for use in
perfumes; Pliny prices the oil at 60 *denarii* the pound.[66] The whole leaf was
also known in Rome and used in ritual and in cookery, generally under the
simple name *folium* 'the leaf': to Martial it is on one occasion (11.18) *Cosmi
folium* 'the leaf you buy from Cosmus', a dealer in aromatics whose name
occurs over and over again in Martial's epigrams like a commercial break.
Tejpat is occasionally called for in the recipes of *Apicius*: it is an optional
ingredient in the 'Cumin sauce for oysters and shellfish' (1.29.1–2; p. 65).
To assist the unfamiliar cook it is helpfully called there, in full, *folium mala-
bathrum* 'tejpat leaf'. In medieval medicine this leaf was *folium Indicum*
'Indian leaf'.

In modern terms, then, the source of both cinnamon and tejpat is 'China'.
It is not surprising that no Roman sources see it that way. At the time of
which we speak, Chinese language and Chinese government had only
reached relatively recently the regions where the *Cassia* species grow.
Chengdu, capital of Sichuan, whose fertile wealth is first celebrated in the
Shu Capital Rhapsody of the learned Zuo Taichong around AD 300, is a long
way from the Chinese heartland and was quite distinct from the northern
cities in its culture and in its range of natural products. Among these,
cinnamon and tejpat alone had reached Europe; oranges (*Citrus aurantium*)
and Sichuan pepper (*Zanthoxylum spp.*) were still to come. In exchange,
Sichuan already grew grapes and pomegranates transplanted from the
West.[67]

China

To the north-east, the end of general geographical knowledge was reached
with the rich region of Bactriana and its greatest city, *ultima Bactra* 'Bactra,
the most distant'. This had been the limit of Semiramis's rule, and in a more
reliable historical frame the approximate limit of Cyrus's and of Alexander's.
Augustan poets saw it as the potential limit for the Roman Empire in
turn,[68] though Horace, for example, was also able to imagine Augustus
going even further, eventually to lead in triumph to the Capitol 'conquered
Chinese and Indians from the Eastern shore'. The great historian Sima Qian
was right, after all, that after the exploration and opening of the Silk Road,
around 125 BC, 'all the barbarians of the far west craned their necks to catch
a glimpse of China'![69]

From somewhere in central Asia, it was supposed, the Parthians got their
finely decorated quivers, and perhaps bows, and perhaps arrows: they are
Chinese arrows to Horace, a Chinese bow and quiver gracing the King of the
ancient Persians in Chariton's historical romance, 'accoutrements from the
barbarian country beyond Parthia' to Aristides.[70]

In general, Roman writers knew scarcely anything of the *Seres* or Chinese, whose country lay far to the east of Bactra. The author of the *Periplus* (64) had heard, far inland from the mouth of the Ganges, 'under the North, in some outer region where the sea ends' of a very large inland city, called *Thina*, from which silk and silk fabrics were carried overland by way of Bactra. 'It is hard to get to this Thina: only a few people ever come that way'. Silk is the only Chinese product that generally made its way to the Roman market and into Roman consciousness. Greek and Roman authors did not generally know that Chinese silk was woven from the cocoons of the silk moth (*Bombyx mori*), but Pausanias, in one of his odd but indispensable asides, manages to get it right.

> The threads from which the *Seres* make their cloth do not come from a plant but have another origin entirely. There is a little creature in that country whose name in Greek is *ser* (the *Seres* themselves have a different name for it), about twice the size of a big beetle, but otherwise resembling spiders that make webs under trees, and like them having eight legs. The *Seres* keep them, making suitable houses for them winter and summer, and the work the creatures do is to spin a light thread, winding it around their feet.
>
> Pausanias 6.26.6–7[71]

Like the *bombycina* 'wild silk' of Cos and Arabia (p. 151), *Serica* 'Chinese stuffs, true silk' were costly, aromatic (either perfumed or associated with occasions on which perfume was worn), light, feminine and sensuous; 'even their *Serica* feel heavy to them', writes Claudian of the fops of Constantinople, and Seneca would have preferred not to look at young women 'in silk dresses, if dress is the word. Truly nothing shields their bodies, nothing guards their modesty: they are naked'.[72]

Scythia and Dacia

Scythia was the northern edge of the world. This vast region ran from an undefined border with China all the way to the mouth of the Danube on the western Black Sea coast – thus corresponding to modern Russia with some of central Asia. Scythia lies 'under the Bear' – the arctic constellation, that is – and it may be imagined ever thick with ice and snow. There was pleasure, akin to that experienced by modern science fiction writers, in following up the logic of this idea: deer trapped in the snow would meekly await the huntsman's knife, bronze vessels would split, wine would be served with an axe. This would not be grape wine, incidentally, but a brew made from the fruit of the *sorbus* (serviceberry or sorb, *Sorbus domestica*), enjoyed in their cosy underground dugouts by those resilient Scythians (Vergil, *Georgics* 3.349–383).[73] The more typical lifestyle of southern Scythia – the great Eurasian steppe – was nomadic.

The nomads pitch their felt tents on the wagons on which they spend their lives. Around the tents are the herds from which they get their milk and cheese and meat. They follow the grazing herds, ever shifting to find pasture; in winter they are around the marshes of the Sea of Azov, in summer in the steppes.

Strabo 7.3.17

The *profugi Scythae* 'homeless Scythians' were, like other nomads, unpredictable.[74] Lucian observed that a fly leads a nomadic, predatory life *à la Scythienne*: wherever night overtakes her she finds her dinner and her bed. But dining like the Scythians offers a temptation to be always shifting to richer pastures (Lucian, *The Fly* 9; *Symposium* 13), and sure enough the *Scytharum bellicosissima gens* 'very warlike Scythian people' were continually raiding the settled lands to their south.[75] Once Romans had established the Danube as their frontier, the task of repelling Scythian incursions fell to Roman soldiers and their commanders.

Ego nolo Caesar esse,
ambulare per Britannos,
Scythicas pati pruinas,

so Florus teased his imperial pupil, 'I don't want to be Caesar, to walk among the Britons, to be frozen by Scythian frosts' inviting the riposte that is quoted on p. 219 from an emperor, Hadrian, who had worked on both of these frontiers.

One unfortunate Augustan poet was able to explore the truth of the poetic picture of Scythia at first hand. It was to Tomis (see Map 8) that Ovid was banished, not far south of the Danube mouth. He had not enjoyed the last few days' sail along the wild, rocky *laevus Pontus, sinister Pontus* 'left shore of the Black Sea'.[76] 'The land to my left is barbarous, habituated to greed and robbery, full of blood and murder and war' (*Tristia* 1.11.31–32). Whatever his secret crime, it had offended Augustus too bitterly to be forgiven even by his successor, and Ovid died at Tomis in AD 17, 'the Milesian city' because it had been a Greek colony founded from Miletus (1.10.41) but Greek was no longer its everyday language. Roman administration had not spread across the Balkans as it later would, and Tomis was *in media Barbaria*, isolated in a Barbarian land.

There is nothing further off than this except cold, and enemies, and the waves of the frozen sea. Roman territory extends no further than this along the left shore of the Black Sea: Basternae and Sauromatae are its neighbours. This is the last country under Italy's rule, scarcely clinging to the edge of your dominion.

Ovid, *Tristia* 2.195–200

The poet's loneliness and frustration, almost palpable in the *Tristia* 'Laments', do not weaken his descriptive power. He allows us to see a little of the lands across the Roman frontier: the Carpathians and Transylvanian Alps, *fera Scythiae Sarmaticaque iuga* 'wild mountains of Scythia and Sarmatia' (1.8.40); the Danube delta, *Scythiae paludes* 'marshes of Scythia' (3.4.49); the bleak steppes of Dobrogea and Bessarabia that 'will not bear fruit ... you may see the plains in their nakedness, without a leaf, without a tree' (3.10.73–75); and 'the meagre resources of the countryside – its cattle and its creaking carts' (3.10.59).

'They keep out the biting cold with pelts and stitched breeches: only the face is exposed.... Their beards gleam white, coated with frost' (3.10.19–20), so he tells his faithful correspondents, far away in Rome, concerning Tomis, its winter climate and its peasant neighbours. He is not concerned to lighten the gloom. But Ovid is an honest poet, if there are any such, and has to admit that things begin to look a little better when the snow begins to melt in the spring sunshine, when those dreadful squealing axles can no longer make their way straight across the frozen Danube, and the first ships mark the beginning of the sailing season. In an outpost like Tomis the poet was not alone in 'hurrying to meet and greet the captain, to find out his destination and his name and his home port. But it will be strange if he is anything but a local man, one who sails our own waters: not many seamen from Italy reach us here' (3.12.27–37).

In summer Tomis was defended from the rough people to the north by the wide Danube, but – even poets in Rome knew this – the Danube freezes in winter (3.10.4). When that happens, then 'across the bridge of ice, while the waves glide beneath, the Sarmatian oxen pull their barbarous carts' (3.10.33–34), and most of them, most of the time, were on their way to market. When there was any fighting, only 'the guard on the wall and the town gate keep back the hostile *Getae*' (3.14.41–42). The *Danuvius* or *Hister* is a river of many poetic names: turbid, rolling its yellow silt, as wide as the Nile, it is *Danuvius rapax* 'greedy Danube' like the raiders who crossed it, *ultimus Hister* 'the most distant', *horridus Hister* when it freezes, *septemplex Hister* 'sevenfold Danube' where its seven channels form a delta.[77]

Little more than a notional boundary in Ovid's time, the Danube was destined to form Rome's frontier in eastern and central Europe for centuries. More distant Scythian rivers occur in Roman poetry, *saxosus sonans Hypanis* 'rocky and noisy Hypanis', *Tanais nivalis* 'snowy Tanais', the latter, perhaps, being the *Scythicus amnis* 'Scythian stream' of Horace.[78] These remained outside Roman experience; but the Danube was at length sufficiently tamed to send *carpa* (carp, *Cyprinus carpio*) to the imperial table, or at least to that of Theodoric, Gothic king of Italy (Cassiodorus, *Variae* 12.4). Apart from this Scythia sent little else to Rome except *Scythae zmaragdi, Scythici ignes*, 'Scythian emeralds, the flames of Scythia'. It was not only Martial who saw the green gleam of emerald as like fire: Statius, also, wrote of 'emeralds flowering with secret fire'. None was purer or more faultless, said Pliny. Scythian emeralds were as much better than other emeralds as emeralds are better than other gems.[79]

We have already noted, in Ovid's usage, other names than 'Scythian' for the people of this vast region. Towards the end of the Empire, Claudian lists an unholy alliance by which his hero was not frightened, 'the dreadful yell of the advancing *Alanus*, the nomadic ferocity of the *Chuni*, the *Gelonus* with his scythe, the *Geta* with his bow, the *Sarmata* with his club' (*Stilicho's Consulship* 1.109–111); further on he gives us the '*Saces* in his painted tent' (1.152–160). Divided from one another by thousands of miles and by almost a thousand years, these fearsome peoples come together in literature. The Geloni are half-Graecised Scythians out of Herodotus's *Histories*, otherwise absent from the historical record, but to Roman poets they are *ultimi Geloni* 'most distant Geloni', drinkers of milk curdled with horses' blood, and Augustus by his eastern campaign of 30 BC is imagined to have confined their wanderings within narrower frontiers.[80] The Sauromatae or Sarmatae, in Herodotus, were nomadic Scythians of the eastern steppes. They do re-appear in later history, eventually settling along the northern bank of the middle and lower Danube. This *fera gens* 'savage people', if such they were, *vagus Sarmata* 'the wandering Sarmatian', migrated in large numbers to Italy under the later Empire.[81] Some had involuntarily arrived there earlier: having battled with the Romans across the Danube, Sarmatae were available as slaves in Martial's time (p. 212) and were already suited to shepherding Tiburtine sheep. The Alani are first heard of in the first century AD, when they crossed the Caucasus to raid Armenia and Parthia. Later they threatened Roman frontiers too.[82] They were famous for their horses – not least because the emperor Hadrian had one, *Borysthenes Alanus, Caesareus veredus* ... 'Borysthenes the Alan, Imperial mount' and commemorated its death in the *Epitaph for Borysthenes* of which that was the first line. The warhorse was appropriately named after one of the rivers of Scythia. 'The Alan tethers his Sarmatian steed at your door', Martial had already written (p. 211) to a promiscuous Roman lady. The *Sacae*, definitely an Iranian people, never came close to Roman borders but were known to have invaded the formerly Greek dominions in central Asia. The horse-mounted *Chuni truces* 'cruel Huns' had probably migrated from further east than any of the others when their 'nomadic ferocity' burst on the Roman scene in the late fourth century AD.[83]

The fifth name in Claudian's list is that of the Getae, whose language was the everyday speech of Ovid's Tomis. They were not Scythian nomads but a settled people, inhabiting both banks of the lower Danube and thus straddling the Roman frontier: appropriately Martial (11.3) tells us of a *rigidus centurio* 'frozen centurion' reading his poems while guarding the Empire in *Geticae pruinae* 'Getic frosts'. In Roman literary tradition Getae are classed with the Scythians by geographical proximity, the vagueness of poets, the force of Ovid's poetry, all reinforced by the fact that another people with a very similar name arrived precisely here in the third century and, just like pastoral nomads, threatened the Empire's frontiers. These were the Goths: they are sometimes *Gothi* to historians, but very often *Getae* to poets. Though 'flaxen-haired' like Germans, they are *pelliti* 'skin-clad' and they ride in wagons just like the *Getae* of Ovid[84] whenever the frontier is breached, 'when unrest at home drove barbarian hordes over groaning Rhodope and the now deserted North had poured its tribes in wild confusion across our borders, when all the banks of Danube poured forth battles and broad Mysia [Moesia] was rutted by Getic cartwheels, when flaxen-haired hordes covered the Bistonian plains!' (Claudian, *Panegyric on Honorius' Fourth Consulship* 49–54, translation after M. Platnauer).

Dacians are not confused with the rest of the peoples from beyond the Danube. The *Dacus asper* 'harsh Dacian', the 'Dacian far from our world', the 'Dacian whose pleasure is to tip his arrows with the poison of his native land' (Silius 1.324–325) is formidable in a quite distinct way. Martial might say of a treaty made in Domitian's time that the northern bank of the Danube was *iam nostra ripa* 'now *our* bank' and that the river's waters had been enslaved.[85] That was eventually true, but not until, after two hard-fought campaigns, Trajan had driven Dacia (approximately modern Romania) to capitulation. For these campaigns written sources are scanty, but a pictorial narrative – Trajan's Column – makes up the lack. A detailed depiction of the river Danube and the Roman defences opens the narrative sequence. Later Trajan is shown sacrificing, and in the background is the new permanent bridge, one of the greatest of Roman feats of engineering, by which the river was tamed.[86] But Dacia itself was only conquered when Trajan captured its royal stronghold, one of the greatest architectural complexes of Europe in its time. Its formidable size is conveyed on the Column by making the curving lines of its walls extend continuously around almost a whole circuit. The fortress's temple precinct, an impressive feature to modern visitors, is not shown: the Column dares only to depict Roman divinities and those such as the river god Danuvius who did not oppose the Roman conquest. The Romans starved the defenders out, but victory came only after the Dacian king Decebalus had shared out among his companions a mysterious liquid – the 'poison of his native land' of which Silius had written.[87] Dacian skill with medicinal plants is further signalled by the inclusion of Dacian glosses in the expanded versions of Dioscorides' *Materia Medica*.

Germany and the far north

The Rhine frontier was just as often threatened as the Danube (see Map 6); Roman interaction with Germany was no less full of incident than that with Scythia.[88] Such incidents were the stuff of legend: the migration to southern Gaul and Italy of the Cimbri, stopped by Marius in 101 BC; Augustus's bold attempt to reduce Germany 'to the form of a province', dramatically halted by the destruction of Varus's army in AD 9. Border warfare continued through every century of Empire, warfare from which numerous Roman commanders earned triumphs and several members of the Imperial family gained the surname *Germanicus*, beginning with Augustus's nephew whose German victories were soon followed by his early death:

> *Nec tibi deletos poterit narrare Sicambros,*
> *Ensibus et Suevos terga dedisse suis,*
> *Fluminaque et montes et nomina magna locorum*
> *Et siquid miri vidit in orbe novo.*

'He shall never tell you how he massacred the Sicambri, and how the Suevi offered their backs to his swords; nor of the rivers, the mountains, the place names that carry such weight, the wonders that he saw in that new world' (*Consolation to Livia* 311–314). Domitian took the name *Germanicus* in 83 after triumphing over the Chatti, and even renamed the month of October *Germanicus*, a change that did not stick.

The final result was very different from anything foreseen by Romans of the late Republic and early Empire. *Fera Germania caerulea pube* 'wild Germany with its blue youth' (blue? its young men were perhaps blue-eyed rather than blue-painted like the Britons) seemed eventually not so strange and fearsome as it had to Horace, to Propertius and to Ovid – who talks of *Germania rebellatrix* 'Germany fighting back' in AD 10 after the shocking defeat of Varus.[89] Those fierce blue eyes, *truces et caerulei oculi* (Tacitus, *Germany* 4) were soon perfectly familiar in the Roman provinces and even in the city of Rome itself.[90] After continual migration, individual and *en masse*, peaceful and warlike, by the fifth century the Rhine frontier was little more than a memory. Arable farming had spread on the east bank; people and animals crossed without formality; Romans could hunt in the Black Forest.

> The traveller looks at the two banks of Rhine and wonders which is the Roman side. The Sali and the Sygambri till their fields; the Chauci do not object to Belgic cattle pasturing; Gallic herds cross the Elbe and graze the lands of the Franks. It is safe to hunt in the vast silences of the Hercynian forest, and in those groves once made fearsome by antique superstition Roman axes now fell trees that were once the object of pagan worship.
>
> Claudian, *Stilicho's Consulship* 1.222–231

Claudian gives no sign of awareness that the balance of power was also shifting.

> We sent no fleets against the Franks, but they are at our feet. We did not crush the Suebi in battle, but they obey our law. Who would believe it? Bold Germany serves us before any war trumpet is sounded.
>
> Claudian, *Stilicho's Consulship* 1.189–192

But within a few more decades it would be clear to all that Germans were commanding rather than serving in what had been the western Empire.

German ethnic names are common enough in Roman poetry, and they have differing associations. From the Rhine delta the *auricomus Batavus, russus Batavus* 'golden-haired, red-haired Batavian' is a typical German, typical enough to imitate in a children's toy mask[91] and the *auris Batavus* 'Batavian ear' is typically untrained to pick up Martial's Spanish-Latin wit (Martial 6.82). Batavians are familiar because the Roman army had crack cavalry regiments recruited on the German frontier and called *Batavi*, the Batavians being renowned horsemen (Dio Cassius 55.24). Next to them in the Rhine's flood plain were the 'swampy Sicambri', *paludosi Sicambri*. A formidable enemy in Augustus's time, these *caede gaudentes Sygambri, torvi Sigambri, indomiti Sicambri* 'slaughter-loving, grim, unconquerable Sicambri' were to become *deleti Sicambri* 'massacred Sicambri' after their defeat by Germanicus.[92] Eastwards the *flavi Suebi, genus Suevi acre* 'flaxen-haired Suebi, a harsh people' are to be found at the beginning and at the very end of Roman history, repeatedly defeated, repeatedly formidable. Ausonius's slave girl Bissula, in whose memory he wrote a pretty sequence of poems, was – he says – a Suebian, 'child of a family and a hearth far across the icy Rhine, knowing the birthplace of the Danube' (*Bissula* 17–18), and like most of her compatriots *oculos caerula, flava comas* 'blue-eyed, fair-haired' (26). *Rutili* 'red-haired', some authors say.[93]

The *persona Germana* 'mask of a German' is a Saturnalia gift for a child, in Martial's poem. Just such a mask can be seen in the British Museum.[94] For a lady, the equivalent gift, but a much more expensive one, is *Arctoa de gente coma* 'a hairpiece from a northern people', *Rheni nodi* 'knots of hair from the Rhine', *Teutonici capilli*, 'hair of a Teuton' or of one of several other peoples, the *crinigeri Chauci* 'long-haired Chauci' for example. Both sexes wore their hair long – warriors of the Suevi and Sicambri wore it tied in a knot over the right temple

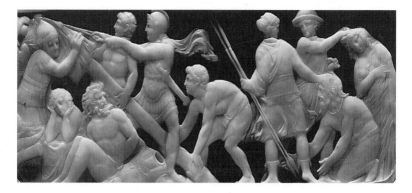

Figure 27   Erecting a trophy and herding long-haired prisoners of war. Detail from the 'Pannonian Triumph of Tiberius' on the onyx Gemma Augustea

Source   By permission of the Kunsthistorisches Museum, Vienna

– and this long hair, shorn from prisoners of war, fetched a high price in Italy, where most people's hair was naturally dark and to have blonde hair was many women's ambition.[95]

Curiously, a second means to achieve the desired result was on offer from the same region: *spuma Batava, spuma Chattica, pilae Mattiacae*. This 'Batavian foam', as it is most often called, was a soapy substance, supplied moulded into balls, that cleaned and lightened the hair, giving it a reddish or fair colour. It was compounded of ash and fat. If made with too high an ash content it would not only bleach but dissolve the hair, a catastrophe that seems actually to have happened to Ovid's 'Corinna' (*Amores* 1.14). The safe way was to use it to enhance or highlight a light-coloured hairpiece rather than one's own hair, as Martial advises:

HAIR. Chattic foam puts fire in Teuton ringlets: you'll be better dressed in captive hair.

Martial 14.26[96]

The frontier river itself – the *barbarus Rhenus* of Propertius – provided a Roman luxury at the end of the Empire, the pink-fleshed *ancorago* or *salmo* (salmon, *Salmo salar*),[97] a match for Danubian carp that was served at the Gothic king Theodoric's table (Cassiodorus, *Variae* 12.4). From the far side came a breed of dog, the *volucres Sygambri* 'flying Sicambrians' (Grattius 202).[98]

The most exotic product of Germany was *sucina*, amber, the resin of ancient pine trees in which insects were sometimes entombed. This precious commodity was brought to Rome from the Baltic shores. Amber used to be warmed in the hands in order to perfume them with a barely perceptible, delicate aroma[99] – Martial writes of the 'scent of amber warmed in a virgin's hand' (p. 264). The colour that was most prized was called 'Falernian' after the wine. It was translucent with a soft glow, and most pleasing of all if it had something of the lightness of boiled honey (Pliny 37.47); the best indication we have of the colour of Falernian wine.

The far north and north-west of Europe scarcely emerge from the fog and ice into Roman consciousness. Beyond the Ocean was Britain – and some other islands, one of which was famed only for its unattainability, *ultima Thule*, another perhaps unfairly for its snow, *glacialis Hiverne* 'icy Ireland'.[100] St Patrick himself, once a young shepherd kidnapped from Roman territory, had unpleasant memories of the weather here – 'nearly a hundred prayers a day, and almost as many at night when I was out in the forests and on the mountain. Before daybreak I used to wake up to prayer, in snow, in frost, in rain' (Patrick, *Confession* 16). To Romans, in spite of the conquest of Britain, the tidal Ocean and all that lay beyond it would remain fearful. The expedition along the north German coast undertaken as part of Germanicus's German campaign inspired a powerful evocation of the terrors of the outer sea, quoted by the elder Seneca from a narrative poem now lost. These sailors were truly at the edge of the Roman world.

The day and the sun are still visible, ever further behind them. They are banished beyond the limit of the known world to go boldly through forbidden darkness to the border of the universe and the very edge of the earth. The Ocean that bears beneath its sluggish waves monstrous creatures, savage whales, hounds of the sea – the Ocean rises against their captive vessels, and the mere noise of the breakers has power to terrify them. They believe their ships to be mired in slime, their course to be beyond the reach of any favouring breeze, and each one of them to be consigned by unfeeling destiny to be torn in pieces by the monsters of the sea. One among them, high on a tall prow, fighting to breach the opaque air with his warlike eyes yet able to discern nothing of the disappearing world, expels the pressure on his chest with these words: 'Where are we bound? Day itself abandons us: the everlasting darkness of these frontiers conceals from us the world that we have left. Are we in search of another population, living under the other pole of heaven, and another world untouched by the winds that blow in ours? No! The Gods demand otherwise. They will not allow mortal eyes to see where the universe ends. Why do we rape with our oars this sea that is not ours, these forbidden waters? Why break the silence of the abode of the gods?'

Albinovanus Pedo [Seneca, *Suasoriae* 1.15]

7   Saeva urbs

We now return to the city to which all the luxuries of the Empire and the world were drawn and where they were all consumed, to 'Rome, surveying the whole world from her seven hills – Rome, the locus of empire and of the gods (Ovid, *Tristia* 1.5.69–70).[1]

The 'seven ruling hills' and similar phrases occur often as poetic by-names for Rome.[2] None of the cities that Romans knew could claim such a remarkable physiognomy. Cicero may tease his Roman audience with the idea that the wide streets and regular plan of Capua would have been better for all concerned, but no one can fail to sense the local pride with which he depicts Rome's idiosyncrasies.

> When they set Rome with its ups and downs, its attics and overhangs, its streets which are not exactly straight, its alleys which are extremely narrow, against their own Capua, very well laid out on a very level site, they will laugh and make fun of us.
>
> Cicero, *On the Agrarian Law* 2.96

The city had grown at random, without any long term plan; those who built had been 'never masters of the future, always slaves to the past', and building took place unceasingly as a consequence of 'collapses, fires and continual buying and selling: because they buy in order to demolish and build afresh' (Strabo 5.3.7).

The city's fractured terrain had once been farmland and hill pasture: its narrow streets reminded the thoughtful walker of their early history as country lanes. Cows had once grazed the *herbosa Palatia* 'grassy Palatine'. A couple of huts had occupied the *arx* that was now the Capitol. As to the low-lying districts: the smoky Velabrum had once been a marshy pool, a frontier between exogamous villages, 'where, on a holiday, a girl destined for the farmer's approval would be rowed across to meet her young man, and would bring home on her return the gifts of the countryside – cheese and a white sheep's snowy lamb' (Tibullus 2.5.23–38). Such images grew out of the easy combination of Rome's evocative contours with the legends of the city's foundation. That event was firmly dated in Rome's own tradition; every detail was lovingly recorded. But there was also an old story that Rome was a Greek colony. And Jews, for their part, said that on the very day on which King Jeroboam presented the two golden calves the first two huts of Rome were built, though they could not be made to stand until water from the Euphrates at Babylon was fetched to mix with the mortar. The site on which they were built had formed from silt that gathered around a Nile reed that the angel Gabriel had planted on the day on which Solomon married Pharaoh's daughter: thus two sins of Israel led to the foundation of the empire that would destroy Israel – not without contributions from the two earlier empires where the Israelites had been captive.[3]

Athenaeus gave Rome a most striking epithet, *the Romaion ouranopolis* 'the heavenly city of the Romans'. Rutilius puts the same thought more explicitly, in an apostrophe to his fellow-citizens. 'You offer to the conquered equal shares in your own justice, and thus you have made what was a world into a single city.... The stars that watch all things in their unceasing motion have never seen a fairer empire' (65–82). We shall encounter other expressions of the view that Rome, in its own citizen body, in its population, in its wealth, in the variety of its merchandise, encompassed the whole world. Meanwhile we shall not lose sight of the fact that Rome was *iniqua Urbs, saeva Urbs* 'the unjust city, the savage city', in Juvenal's trenchant phrases (1.30–31, 3.8–9): in both texts the adjective is divided from the noun by a line-break, as Juvenal plays on the shock effect of characterising thus the metropolis of which he and his readers were citizens.

Rome's remarkable size was enough to arouse wonder: it was 'a city so populous that Polemon the Rhetor calls it an epitome of the world'. So it was that Galen had managed to assemble four cases of a very rare type of dislocation by questioning the doctors at Rome, Portus (*to Limen*) and Ostia. It was not surprising that Hippocrates had never seen such a dislocation; after all, the cities where he worked were no bigger than a single neighbourhood [*amphodos*] of Rome.[4] But in truth it was not merely Rome's size that made it unique: it was the endless variety of its people. We need only recall for a moment the voices of shopkeepers and hawkers calling their wares 'each in his distinctive accent' by which the sensitive Seneca was prevented from working (p. 218). These cries were in varieties of Latin or Greek, the two great languages of the Empire, as familiar to Seneca as to those who walked the streets of Rome. The languages spoken by visitors were far more varied.

> What people is so distant or so barbarous, Caesar, as to send no visitor to your city? The Rhodopean farmer comes from Orphic Haemus; the Sarmatian, fed on the blood of his horse; he who drinks the first waters of the new-found Nile; the rider of the waves of furthest Tethys. The Arab hastens, the Sabaeans hasten, and the Cilicians colour the city with their clouds of saffron.

> Martial, *Spectacula* 3

Thracians (of mounts Rhodope and Haemus) and Cilicians were from within the Empire; others from well beyond its borders. Martial does not mislead us. All were to be seen in Rome – the foreign visitors less frequently but for at least four reasons: as captives to be displayed in a Triumph; as slaves; as merchants; and as diplomats. Martial may aim at a German slave, or perhaps rather at a German trader, when he writes: 'The *Marcia* flows here, not the Rhine. Don't get in the way, you savage German, don't keep this boy from the generous fountain. The conqueror's water supply should not slake a captive's thirst while a citizen is pushed aside' (11.96). As if to show that the mention of 'Sarmatians' in the previous quotation is no random fancy, a few years after it was written the Dacian king Decebalus's brother Degis visited Rome (Martial 5.3) in the course of the emperor's negotiations in 89 to settle the Danube frontier. Domitian bestowed a diadem on him, an act regarded by him, though no doubt not by Decebalus, as signifying Roman supremacy. Finally, the effect in bringing strangers to Rome of the city's greed for exotic luxuries, for use in pleasure and in ceremonial, is signalled in the last two examples in the quotation from *Spectacula*. The Sabaeans supplied Rome's frankincense and myrrh and the Cilicians (as Martial says himself) its saffron.

He finds no difficulty in imagining that these travellers, whether from within the Empire or from beyond, partook of the city's pleasures.

> You put out for Parthians, Germans and Dacians, Caelia; you don't mind sharing a bed with Cilicians or Cappadocians; you're fucked by Memphitic sailors from the city of the Pharos, and by black Indians from across the Red waters; you don't mind the cocks of circumcised Jews; the Alan tethers his Sarmatian steed at your door. You're a Roman girl: don't you fancy any Roman pricks?
>
> Martial 7.30

One senses irritation here very much like the irritation shown by Catullus at the thought of sharing the sexual favour of 'Lesbia' with a grinning Celtiberian who brushes his teeth with his own urine – an irritation expressed in a poem (p. 86) that the Celtiberian Martial certainly knew.

Throughout Roman literature, from the beginning to the end of Empire, there is an ambivalence – a natural ambivalence, let us admit – concerning the inexorable extension of citizenship. It was this, more than anything, that had turned Rome into the world city, and as just one example it had turned the semi-barbaric Celtiberians of Catullus's view into the better-than-Italian Roman Celtiberians of whom Martial was one. Greeks, Gauls, Spaniards, Britons, all were turning up as citizens (Seneca, *Apocolocyntosis* 3). *Religiosa patet peregrinae Curia laudi* ..., wrote Rutilius, 'the sacred Senate House is open to newcomers' success, and does not count as foreign those who are properly its own. They enjoy all the power of the order to which they belong' (13–15). This had truly been a unique feature of the Roman state: Rutilius, who saw it in decline, recalls it with appropriate pride.

The slave population of the city was large and varied. Slaves had very different histories, like the two late Imperial ministers, Eutropius and Hosius, unsympathetically described by Claudian:

> legs bruised from the black iron, faces branded … a cook and a pimp. Both their backs were furrowed by the whip, but these two slaves were not from the same school! One was forever changing hands; the other had been a houseboy, reared at a Spanish hearth.
>
> Claudian, *Against Eutropius* 2.343–344

The infliction of pain was the ordinary way to assert authority over a slave, hence these 'backs furrowed by the whip'; one might legally show ownership of a slave by calling eye-witnesses to beatings that one had inflicted (Seneca, *Apocolocyntosis* 15). The brands (*stigma*) imply that the two men, while slaves, had tried to escape. Recaptured runaways risked having their foreheads branded – though it was not impossible later to erase or disguise a brand.[5] Persistent escapers and other recalcitrants risked relegation to a chain gang, hence the 'legs bruised from the black iron' of the quotation. Chain gangs were used in heavy labour of various kinds: at mills, in road-building, in farming. They comprised some of the most intelligent of the Roman slave population – 'a vineyard worker must be not only strong, but also clever, which is why vineyards are often tended by a chain gang' (Columella 1.9.4) – doomed to a hobbled life and, often, an early death.[6]

In the extract from Claudian, 'houseboy' stands for the Latin *verna*, whose precise meaning is 'slave born and brought up in the household'. Horace pictures for us the imagined sale of a *verna*, one who has been taught some written Greek and – not that he has actually been taught music – can provide a song at his owner's drinking party (*Epistles* 2.2.7–9). *Verna* in Latin is packed with undertones. A *verna* is *procax* 'impudent', *garrulus* 'chattering', *contumeliosus* 'argumentative' and most often *urbanus*.[7] There is a world of meaning in this one word. Are we to translate it 'smart'? The man so characterised is a city boy, wise to Rome, perhaps a little cocksure, and certainly respected in his own circle, which is exactly what Martial insists is *not* the case in a poem addressed to an imagined *verna* who is supposed to think too much of himself (p. 222).

Slaves might originate from any province of the Empire, Italy included: there, as elsewhere, children were sold into slavery to relieve family debt.[8] They might also come from across the frontiers, whether as prisoners of war or in the course of trade. Martial hints at the variety on offer (7.80): don't give 'Marcellinus' a Sarmatian boy, he advises, one who used to play with his hoop on the frozen Danube – Marcellinus has already seen plenty of those, having fought on that frontier: give him a rosy youth from a Mytilenaean dealer, or a Laconian whose mother has not yet sent him for whipping (too young, that is, to have undergone the Spartan *rite de passage*). But I'll send *you*, Martial promises, a captive from the Danube, ideal for shepherding Tiburtine sheep. He reminds us elsewhere that the large-scale slave trade had some effect on Roman family lines, a matter of principle that was traditionally supposed to be close to the heart of every head of a Roman citizen household.

> Marulla has given you seven non-heirs, Cinna. They aren't yours or any of your friends' or neighbours': conceived in the slave-cells and the outhouses, every one is a witness to their mother's degradation. This young Moor with the crinkly hair is trying to tell us that his father is your cook, Santra. The boy with the snub nose and thick lips is the very image of Pannychus, your wrestling-master. Anyone can see your baker, Dama, in the third youngster's bleary eyes. This fourth one, with his pansyish forehead and his girlish face, is the son of your lover boy Lygdus, so you can bugger him too if you like and it won't be incest. And of course this one with the pointy head, and big ears flapping like a donkey's, is without a doubt the child of your fool, Cyrta. The two girls, one black, the other red-haired, belong to Crotus the musician and Carpus the farm manager. You could have had a family as numerous as the Niobids, if only your Coresus and Dindymus weren't eunuchs.
>
> Martial 6.39

Low Rome

In our exploration of the city of pleasures we cannot do better than follow Tibullus's guidance. Why, after a glance at the villages atop the *Arx* and *Palatia*, did he choose the marshy Velabrum, lying between the two, as the setting for his two-line love story of archaic Rome (p. 209)? The *Cloaca Maxima*, Rome's great sewer, now meandered underground here in a massive vaulted tunnel. The Velabrum was no longer a marsh but a busy city district. But there was no forgetting that it really had been a village boundary, as in Tibullus's story: along its south side the *Vicus Tuscus*, the 'Etruscan village or neighbourhood', recalled by its name Rome's early ethnic complications.

Cheese had been an ideal gift for Tibullus's archaic courtship. Rome's best smoked cheese now came from the crowded hearths of the Velabrum.[9] 'Cheese is not suited to every hearth or to every smoke, but the cheese that imbibes the smoke of Velabrum has the true flavour', according to Martial's gift poem (13.32). If the Velabrum really was the *locus celeberrimus Urbis* 'most famous locality in the City', as Macrobius insists (*Saturnalia* 1.10.15), it can only have been as a shopping centre, the focus of trade in food and wine from early times at least to the early Empire.[10] Along the Tiber bank, to the west, were old place names that evoked the food trade of the middle Republic – *Forum Holitorium* 'Vegetable Market', *Forum Boarium* 'Cattle

Market'. The Vicus Tuscus, to the south-east, was perhaps the greatest shopping street of all. Horace talks of 'the fishmonger, the fruiterer, the poulterer, the perfumier and all the unholy crowd from the Vicus Tuscus' (*Satires* 2.3.227–228). Later 'expensive silks from the Vicus Tuscus' were a gift that Martial expected a rich mistress to demand.[11]

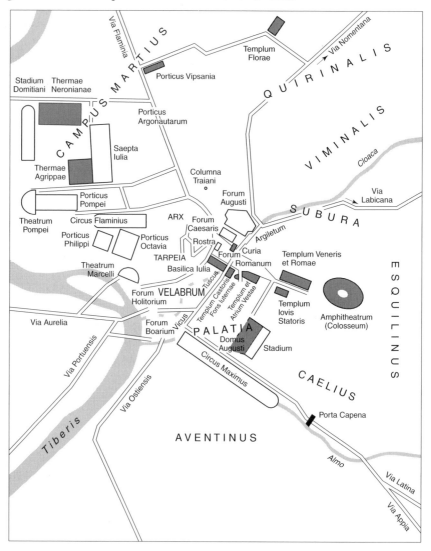

Map 10   Literary landmarks of central Rome

Those who strolled north along the Vicus Tuscus would find themselves crossing the *Forum Romanum*, the traditional centre of Rome's public life (p. 223). Directly north of that had been an open space called *Macellum* on which, in 179 BC, was built the city's central covered market for meat and fish.[12] It was as wealthy as three other extremely wealthy places, the golden mountains of Persia, the legendary vineyard of the *ager Caecubus* and the Capuan market *Seplasia* (Varro, *Menippean Satires* 38 Bücheler). But it was demolished by Augustus. To make way for his civic centre, the Forum Augusti (p. 224), the old central market was moved from the heart of the city – a step with incalculable social consequences, imitated by town planners in London and Paris more recently.

A kite-shaped field along the east side of the *Macellum* had been early Rome's 'claypit', *Argiletum*. A lane ran through this north-eastwards, gently rising, following the valley bottom between the Viminal and the Esquiline. In the later Republic and early Empire this was no lane but one of Rome's busiest streets. Here, until a rebuilding under Domitian and Nerva, bookshops clustered.[13] Martial, for the best of reasons, is anxious to tell us so.

> No doubt you're often going up the Argiletum [he addresses 'Lupercus']. There's a shop opposite Caesar's Forum with every upright covered with writings, front and back, so that you can run through all the poets in a moment. Look for me there. You needn't ask Atrectus (that's the shopkeeper's name) – he'll hand down from the first pigeon-hole, or the second, a Martial smoothed with pumice and finished in purple, five *denarii* to you.
>
> Martial 1.117

Not far off was a competitor, Secundus, a 'paperback shop' as it were, where you could buy Martial not in old-fashioned roll but in new-fangled volume form. It was 'behind the threshold of Peace and the Palladian Forum' (Martial 1.2), and that puts it in the Argiletum. Somewhere nearby, we may guess, were stalls where unwanted secondhand books met their usual Roman fate – to be sold to grocers or cooks (Martial 6.61.7–8) and to end up 'soaked by Libyan olives, used for wrapping incense or pepper from the Nile, or for cooking a Byzantine chub mackerel' (Statius, *Silvae* 4.9.10–13).

The ancient lane through the Argiletum, having entered the valley between Viminal and Esquiline, reached a village called *Subura*. Not just any village: Subura made up one of the four old city tribes of Roman citizens and, in an alternative and traditional list, it was actually one of the Seven Hills of Rome, though it is not a hill at all. By the middle Republic, Subura had become a centre of Rome, the place where Hannibal should have planted his banner had he made the city his own.[14] It remained one of the two or three focal points of the city that we are re-imagining – and the one in which most people were most at home. Martial, praising his country-woman, the Celtiberian 'Marcella', for her perfect Romanity, remarks that she has no rivals among women born either in the heart of Subura, *in media Suburra*, or on the Capitoline Hill. It was in Subura that Julius Caesar, as a young man, bought his first house. Subura was the intimate valley, modestly shielding itself from strangers' view, that Rutilius recalled to his mind's eye as he gazed at Rome from the Janiculum: 'I like to trace the lines of the hills to the limit of vision and to be led on by my pleasure-seeking eyes to the favourite places that they think they can still see' (p. 20).

From the edgy perspective of the Danube frontier, with his eyes turned away from the amoral pleasures of the City to focus on its benign gods and possibly merciful Caesars, Ovid is able to imagine Rome as *placida urbs Quirini* 'the tranquil city of Romulus'. No one ever described Subura so. This is *fervens Subura, vigilax Subura, clamosa Subura* 'seething, wakeful, clamorous Subura'. It is in the streets of Subura that Martial, himself now retired in far-off Bilbilis, imagines his fellow-satirist Juvenal still pacing restlessly. The fastidious Juvenal, as keen as Martial to catalogue City life but less keen (it appears from his poetry) to partake of it, answers with 'I'd rather choose Prochyta itself than Subura!'[15] We can see as clearly why women who had lovers loved Subura as why Juvenal claimed to hate it. It was busy and noisy, day and night; it was intimate and anonymous. Well-known and respectable citizens either set themselves up as moral censors or they strolled through Subura in the late evening: never both.

In one of his most evocative poems, 'Cynthia' reminds Propertius of their early 'stolen pleasures', *furta*. She was someone else's, therefore; Propertius at that time was one of the 'adulterers barked at by the dogs of Subura' of whom Horace spoke (*Epodes* 5.57–58). Cynthia used to climb out over her windowsill to meet young Propertius, and it was through the streets of 'wakeful Subura' that they wandered together (4.7.15–20). If the decisive Sulpicia wanted to be in Rome with her lover –

> It's my bloody birthday and I shall have to spend it moping, without Cerinthus, in the dreadful country. 'What could be nicer than the city? Is a country estate the place for a girl, a farm at Arretium, a cold river? You worry about me so much, cousin Messalla; there are times when women shouldn't travel.' If I do not get my way, and I am forced to go, my thoughts and my desires stay here in Rome.
>
> Sulpicia 2[16]

– she surely had in mind this same district of Rome. This, surely, was where 'Cynulcus' accused 'Myrtilus', in Athenaeus's dialogue (567a), of 'wallowing in the taverns, my dear professor, with your friends – your girl-friends I mean'. It was in these streets that the young emperor Nero would wander incognito. Sometimes he dressed as a slave: a slave was freer than an emperor in Subura. After dusk he would snatch a felt cap or leather hood, go down to the hot food shops and range the city looking for fun, sometimes getting into fights, calling in at taverns and brothels, even breaking into shops. Like Nero long before him, Gallus, the wild nephew of Constantine the Great, also used to go around the streets and shops incognito at night. Fluent in

Greek, he would get into conversation and query people's feelings towards 'Caesar' – towards himself, that is. But these parts of Rome were so well lit at night that they were 'as clear as day'. Gallus began to be recognised rather frequently, and got himself into difficulties.[17]

Subura was not Rome's market centre, but it offered shops and stalls where all the foods grown in Rome's hinterland and some of the best from elsewhere in the Empire were waiting to be bought, 'barnyard birds, eggs of the same, golden lightly-dried Chian figs, baby offspring of a bleating goat, olives too young to bear winter, parsnip just tinged with early frost'. In that poem (quoted more fully on p. 27) and again in the next, Martial plays with the thought that no Roman really needed to have fresh food grown and sent in at great expense of labour from his own country farm.

> No Massylian serpent guards my fruit-trees; I have not the royal orchard of an Alcinous. My garden is both safe and fertile in its Nomentan fruit; my leaden apples fear no thief. Accept this waxy fruit of my own harvest, grown for me in the heart of Subura.
>
> Martial 10.94[18]

If there was gourmet fish on sale in Subura, Juvenal knows why. *Lupus* (bass, *Dicentrarchus labrax*) was a costly delicacy, much favoured by Roman epicures, who paid especially high prices for the ones caught at Rome in the reach of the Tiber 'between the two bridges',[19] although 'you cannot possibly tell whether that gaping bass is Tiberine or from open sea; landed between the bridges, or out off Ostia' (Horace, *Satires* 2.2.31–33). It is no longer certain which are the 'two bridges', but the cavernous *Cloaca Maxima* must certainly have debouched into the Tiber close at hand. Now the stroller along the Vicus Tuscus, across the Forum, up the Argiletum and into the heart of Subura has had the *Cloaca* under his feet almost the whole way: this sewer was the current incarnation of the stream that once flowed through the rural valley between Viminal and Esquiline. So a sewer under Subura was the real lair of Rome's favourite bass, *vernula riparum* 'home-born slave of the Tiber banks', fattened on all the excrement of Rome (Juvenal 5.104–106).

One side of the night-life of Subura is personified by the *Suburanae puellae* 'girls of Subura'. Whores lived here: they leaned out of Subura windows to entice passers-by; they 'sat', to attract customers, in the main street of Subura that served also as its local market.[20] There were brothels here – visited by Nero on his jaunts – that offered pleasure in the narrow space of an *inscripta cella* 'alcove with a price list', carefully screened: 'Even a whore keeps witnesses away with her curtain or lock; there are few spyholes in the Summummian brothel' (Martial 1.34). If one did not care for privacy, there were dark alleys.[21] 'Did he not make the streets safe for you?' asks the author of an *Elegy for Maecenas* (1.23–25) rhetorically: the great man had served as city aedile, responsible for crime prevention. 'Did anyone rob you, while you

Figure 28   Bread shop. Wall painting from house VII.3.30, Pompeii

Source   By permission of the Soprintendenza Archeologica per le Province di Napoli e Casert

were making love, on some dark night? Was anyone so savage as to stab you?' And so a young man in a new, adult white toga could learn a lot in an exploration of Subura, with complaisant friends or under the guidance of a *Suburana magistra* 'female professor from Subura'.[22]

The more convivial side of Rome's night-life is represented by the taverns and hot food stalls. These were more than a nocturnal luxury: they were also a daily necessity in a crowded city many of whose poorer inhabitants could not possibly have risked lighting a cooking fire in their tenements. In the streets of Subura, and Velabrum too no doubt, you could buy *asse vinum, asse pulmentarium* 'wine for an *as*, snack for an *as*' (Varro, *Menippean Satires* 316 Bücheler); or, as Martial would have it (1.103: p. 244), *asse cicer tepidum constat et asse Venus* 'hot chickpea costs an *as* and sex costs an *as*'. The noise and the aroma of Rome's street food began before sunrise – 'Get up! The baker is selling the boys their breakfast, and the crested birds of dawn are singing all around' (Martial 14.223) – and continued throughout the day to irritate such sensitive souls as the younger Seneca with 'a patissier's varied cries, and a sausage-vendor and a sweet-seller and all the proprietors of cook-shops selling their wares, each in his distinctive accent' (*Letters* 56.2). Seneca might easily have added to his list the salesman who 'hawks milk-by-the-measure [*lac venale*] noisily through the city' (Calpurnius Siculus, *Eclogues* 4.25–26). But we hear most about the sausages, *candiduli divina tomacula porci* 'divine sausages of nice white pork' of Juvenal, *ferventia tomacula* 'sizzling sausages' of Petronius,[23] *fumantia tomacla* 'smoking sausages' of Martial; and about the hot chickpea soup, with Martial's 'man who sells chickpea soup to a crowd in the interval' (p. 222). Everybody fancied these things sometimes: even the gourmet's jaded stomach 'pines to be revived with ham and sausages and all the rest of the stuff that comes in smoking hot from the filthy *popinae*', as Horace (*Satires* 2.4.59 – 62) learns from the elaborate gastronomic rules retailed to him by 'Catius'. And the highly respectable Sidonius imagines retreating to a boozy inn in whose smoky kitchen 'aromatic saucepans give off the scent of sausage and thyme and juniper berries, and the steam of stewing pots mingles with the smoke from spitting frying pans' (p. 83); this is in Gaul, not in Rome, and the juniper berries are the very first textual evidence of a distinctively Gallic cuisine.

Everybody ate street food, even emperors. It was slightly less respectable to eat and drink in the *pervigiles popinae* 'ever-open cookshops' (Juvenal, below) – this epithet means that they were open all night, presumably. Hadrian, in reply to his tutor (see p. 201), pretended to disapprove of them –

> *Ego nolo Florus esse,*
> *ambulare per tabernas,*
> *latitare per popinas,*
> *culices pati rotundos:*

'I don't want to be Florus, to stroll among the taverns, to lie around the cookshops, to pick up the fat fleas'. Some of the less-admired Caesars, such as Nero and Gallus, were certainly among the clientele; and some of Cicero's opponents, such as Mark Antony (p. 39) and Catiline, who shortly before his attempted revolution had got into deep water with *aes alienum contractum in popina* 'loans arranged in taverns' (Cicero, *Against Catiline* 2.4). Customers who spent too long in these places might be labelled *popino*, an habitué of bars; *lurco, ganeo*, a glutton; and in Rome of the fourth century 'many of the lowest and poorest sort spend their whole nights in taverns' (Ammianus 14.6.25). Yet they were important enough in respectable people's lives for the *Mishna* to give instructions on the formalities of tavern eating for Jews.

> If two groups are eating in one house and one can see the other, they associate themselves in inviting one member to say the blessing for all: otherwise each party does so for itself. One does not bless the wine until water has been mixed with it.
> … one does not bless a lamp or aromatics belonging to heathen.
>
> *Mishna Berakoth* 7.8, 8.6

Juvenal, in his sternest mood, gives us something of the ambience (even Juvenal himself must have visited one *once*).

But whenever Lateranus fancies a visit to the all-night cookshops, the host *Syrophoenix* (he lives at the Idymaean Gate), shiny with respectful *amomum*, runs to welcome his guest's approach, greeting him as 'Master', maybe 'King', and Cyane hurries along with her legs on view and her wine-by-the-measure.... Lateranus is an old man but he's still hanging around the bathhouse wineshops and the curtains with the price tags. Yes, send to Ostia for him, Caesar, look in the big cookshop there: you'll find him lying alongside some brawler, in among sailors and thieves and runaways, with hangmen and coffin-makers and the silent cymbals of a supine priest of Cybele. There all are equally free, all drink from a common cup, the couch is barred to no man, the table as close to one as to another. What would you do if you found one of your slaves among them, Ponticus? You'd send him off to Lucania or your Tuscan *ergastula*.

Juvenal 8.158–180, abridged[24]

The women of the taverns, like Cyane here and Surisca in the poem *Copa* (p. 18) and the 'pipe-playing slut' of Horace (p. 25), were hard-working people. They were musicians, dancers, waitresses and prostitutes. The 'curtains with price tags' that come into Juvenal's mind are those of alcoves in brothels (p. 217); to him, as to Horace, cookshops and brothels are all one.

The bars and taverns in and around the great Baths were the nearest thing that Rome had to restaurants. In some you could choose either to sit or to recline; and in some you could spend serious money (Martial 5.70), while the snacks available in others would be converted into a full meal only by a miser: 'Aemilius gulps down lettuce, eggs, chub mackerel at the Baths. "I never dine out", he says' (Martial 12.19). In some you could demand a certain level and variety of cuisine for which the ordinary cookshops had no time at all. Not everyone thought they were a good thing.[25] But the Greek–Latin phrase book attributed to Pollux, written in the second century AD and intended for Romans of some wealth and sophistication, helpfully sets a scene in a restaurant of this kind.

Mix wine for us: we'll recline. First give us beetroot or gourd. Add fish sauce to that. Give us radishes and a knife: serve an *oxygarum* with lettuce and cucumber. Bring a trotter, a black pudding and a sow's womb. We'll all have white bread. Add oil to the salad. Scale the pilchards and leave them on the table. Give us mustard, shoulder and ham. Is the fish grilled? Carve the venison and the wild boar and the chicken and the hare. Slice the cabbage. Carve the boiled meat. Serve the roast. Give us a drink.... Bring the turtle-doves and the pheasant: bring the udder, and let us have some *allec*. Let's eat: just right. Give us the roast sucking-pig. That's very hot: carve it for us. Bring honey in a jug. Bring a fatted goose, and some pickles. – Give us water for our hands. Do you have any yoghourt? Bring us that, with honey, and halva. Cut it into slices: we'll share it.

Pollux, *Phrase Book* c. 21–22[26]

In the breathless and overstuffed form of a phrase book – a single party would hardly order quite so much – Pollux manages to tell us a good deal of what food was to be looked for in a Roman restaurant in the second century, and of how it was expected to arrive at the table. If we care to mix this evidence with the recipes of *Apicius* we may serve beetroot 'dressed with mustard, a little oil and vinegar' (3.11.2), gourd *à la mode d'Alexandrie* (recipe on p. 174), radishes with *piperatum* 'pepper sauce' (3.14: see p. 195), trotters with pepper, fish sauce and asafoetida (7.1.5), sow's womb rolled in bran, marinated in brine and baked (7.1.6); and sow's udder stuffed with a very expensive pounded mixture of sea urchin, pepper and caraway, baked, and served (as Pollux's speaker, canonically, insists) with *allec* and mustard (7.2.2). Cabbage demands at least a generous splash of fresh olive oil;[27] better is the perennially popular cabbage recipe traceable to Mnesitheus of Athens, a physician of the fourth century BC. A version is given by Cato (*On Farming* 156) for taking before a drinking party to prevent drunkenness. Mnesitheus's original recipe is repeated by Oribasius, physician to the emperor Julian in the fourth century AD (*Medical Collections* 4.4.1). *Oxymeli*, required in this recipe, is honey vinegar made by 'simmering honey till it foams, discarding the scum, adding enough vinegar to make it neither too sharp nor too sweet, and boiling again. For use, mix with water, just as you would mix wine with water' (Galen, *Staying Healthy* 4.6 [6.273]).

> Cabbage should be sliced with the sharpest possible iron blade, then washed, drained, and chopped with plenty of coriander and rue: then sprinkle with *oxymeli* and add just a little bit of asafoetida. You can eat this as an appetiser.

The traffic and the trade in the streets of central Rome competed for every inch of space. Shops had crowded on to the pavements, wine-jars were chained to the base of columns – chained to discourage snatch theft; barbers, cooks and butchers all conducted their business on what were supposed to be the footways: passers-by were forced to walk in the muddy road, till Martial's temporary hero Domitian ruled against these encroachments (Martial 7.61), and that surely had only temporary effect. The pedestrian needed to stay alert.

> A contractor, hard at work, hurries by with his mules and his crew; a great big crane swings a rock and then a beam; a mournful funeral

tangles with some farm carts; a mad dog clears off, and here comes a muddy pig. Just get on with writing your poetry!

says Horace hopelessly to himself (*Epistles* 2.2.72–76). He evokes the exciting clash of funerals and farm carts, and the resulting cacophony of horns and trumpets and wailing and shouting, again on a second occasion (*Satires* 1.6.42–44).

With great men so anxious to embellish their city, blocks of marble on their way through narrow Roman streets were a recurrent hazard (Tibullus 2.3.43–44). Martial gives us a vignette of himself on the way to pay a respectful call. 'I have to struggle up the High Path on the Subura slope, up those forever dirty, slippery cobblestones: I can hardly get by for the long mule-trains and all those marble blocks hauled along with ropes' (5.22.5–8). Mule trains and rope haulage are part of the same picture: wheeled traffic was largely banned from central Rome in Martial's time. The large quantities of marble required because of Domitian's building projects (and Martial would never complain of those in Domitian's lifetime) had to move on sledges, like nearly everything else that was too bulky to go on men's backs or in mule packs.

We have already heard something of the noise of Rome from Horace and Seneca. Martial, too, indicates that it was hard to bear.

> You want to know, Sparsus, why I'm off so often to dry Nomentum to visit my cottage's dirty Lar? People without money haven't the space to think, or to be quiet, in the City. Schoolmasters kill you in the morning, bakers at night, coppersmiths' hammers all day long. Here's the bored exchange clerk clinking a pile of Neroes on his dirty counter. There's the beater of Spanish gold bashing his worn stone with a mallet. The fanatical crowd of Bellona never stops, nor does the talkative sailor with his bandaged body, nor the Jew who learnt to beg at his mother's knee, nor the bleary-eyed match-seller.
>
> Martial 12.57[28]

High Rome

It is from such vignettes that we realise the variety of trades to be met with in Roman streets and alleys. Martial addresses a home-bred slave, *verna*, who thinks himself typically *urbanus* 'smart':

> I'll tell you what you are. You're a *verna* – yes, just like the pedlar from across the Tiber who swaps sulphur-matches for bits of broken glass, or the man who sells chickpea soup to a crowd in the interval, or the professional snake-charmer, or the salt-dealer's boys, or the cook from the tavern touting his smoking sausages, or the bad graffiti-writer, or

the naughty trainer of dancing-girls from Cadiz, or the unstoppable whine of an ageing queer.

Martial 1.41

Roman poetry has naturally no consistent point of view: but no single poet has a consistent point of view, for no poet is on his honour to write always from his own heart. With Martial here and Horace in unguarded moments and Juvenal more often, we shall now adopt the supercilious point of view, looking down on the world and its business from the Seven Hills and the Forum that was Rome's public meeting place.

The street scene contrasts strongly with that of the anonymous Subura. Here the noble and wealthy 'use another man's voice to greet their acquaintances: one is supposed to be grateful for a mere glance' (Lucian, *Nigrinus* 21). The crowd of clients and slaves in attendance on the great included a *nomenclator* whose task it was 'to nudge him with his elbow and make him offer a hand for kissing' (Horace, *Epistles* 1.6.49–55) and discreetly to evaluate relative status.

> Some expect kowtowing. Not just a formal obeisance, Persian fashion; you must go up, bow, display by your very attitudes the abjectness of your spirit, kiss the man's chest or his right hand – thank goodness at least *they* don't kiss *us*! – and in doing this you are the envy and admiration of those even less privileged than yourself.
>
> Lucian, *Nigrinus* 21

Horace, keen-eyed but modest, preferred to stroll independently of hangers-on – not that he had many.

> I go wherever I fancy and I go on my own. I ask the price of greens and flour. I stroll about the lying Circus, and the Forum as the sun sets; I hang around the fortune-tellers; then off home to a dish of leeks, chickpeas and flatbread. Three slave-boys serve my dinner; there are two cups and a ladle on the marble slab, a cheap casserole, an oil flask and a dessert dish, all Campanian ware.
>
> Horace, *Satires* 1.6.111–118[29]

The centre point of his stroll is the *Forum Romanum*. It would be *Forum triste* 'tiresome Forum' to Martial (Martial 5.20): it was by attendance on great men that poets such as Martial made their living. Horace was slightly luckier: he was secure in his patron, and was only troubled by the occasional obligation to take the patron's role and to promise some help to clients of his own.

The real importance of the Roman Forum was that it was the centre of public politics and law, *in quo omnis aequitas continetur* 'the place where all of justice is contained' (Cicero, *Against Catiline* 4.2), and this in a society fascinated by the nature and the mechanisms of law. It was from the *Rostra* at the north-western corner of the Forum, the Rostra 'left to us by our ancestors decorated with naval spoils and the prows of captured ships' (Cicero, *De lege Manilia* 55), that Tribunes traditionally addressed the Roman people: adjacent was the *Curia*, the Senate's regular meeting place. So long as news and political talk was free,[30] the Rostra was where news began, and, as Horace puts it, 'The chilling talk spreads from the Rostra to the *compita*' (*Satires* 2.6.50).[31] Here, and later in the *Forum Augusti* under the statue of *iuris peritus Apollo* 'Apollo expert in law' (Juvenal 1.128) – so called because he overheard so many lawsuits – by demonstrating their skill in real public speaking Roman students reaped the just reward for study that had taken place possibly among the colonnades of the adjacent *Forum Caesaris*. In this way the Forum in Rome played the same part played by the gods and nymphs of Greece, the patrons of poetry. These, however, could offer their acolyte no reward, beyond, possibly, kisses (Martial 1.76). Advocacy in the Forum, by contrast, was the route to wealth and influence. To the Forum came those young men from all over the Empire who planned to exercise their citizen rights, to plead and to harangue with more-than-Italian eloquence and not-quite-Italian accents.

The Forum was Rome's financial centre too. On its southern side was the Basilica Iulia or *Iulia tecta*, begun by Caesar and completed by Augustus: this is where banks were established.[32] Close by, at the Forum's south-eastern angle, was an unprepossessing wall built originally to keep sacred a spot that had once been struck by lightning. This was called *Puteal* 'the Precinct', and it was where you negotiated loans. 'Roscius wants to meet you *ad Puteal*' hints that Roscius wants a loan; if you are 'worried about the Forum, the Precinct and the First of the Month' you have worries about the repayments on a loan of your own.[33]

Finally, the Forum was Rome's religious centre. At its eastern end was the Temple of Castor and Pollux (*Templum Castoris*), beside which was the *lacus Iuturnae, fons Iuturnae* 'Iuturna's pool or spring' where the twin gods paused to water their horses after their supernatural appearance to fight for Rome at the battle of Lake Regillus.[34] Eastwards again were the *monumenta Regis templaque Vestae* 'mementoes of the King and the temple of Vesta', *opus Regis placidi* 'the work of the peaceful King', an ancient complex piously identified with king Numa: at the centre of this was the little *Regia* or 'palace'. 'This tiny place, holding up the Atrium of Vesta, was at that time the great palace of the unshaven Numa' (Ovid, *Fasti* 6.263–264) – it was well known that archaic Romans shaved once every market day. The Temple, a very holy place, was tended by the Vestal Virgins, whose devotion to celibacy and guardianship of the perpetual Fire were compensated by their luxurious lifestyle in the often-enlarged *Atrium Vestae* 'antechamber of Vesta'.[35] Many of Rome's holiest places lay along the *Sacra via* 'Sacred Way' that began near the site of the Colosseum, passed through the Forum from east to west, and rose steeply to the *Arx*; it was 'sacred' because every month certain holy objects were carried this way to the Arx, and every month the augurs left the Arx this way to perform their ritual (Varro, *On the Latin Language* 5.47). Ovid, writing from Tomis, imagines a guided tour, beginning from the Forum and following the Sacred Way eastwards.

> 'This is the Forum of Caesar', said my guide. 'This is the Sacred Way, so called from the rites. This is Vesta's house, guarding the Palladium and the Fire. This was the tiny palace of ancient Numa.' Turning to the right he said, 'This is the gate of the *Palatia*. Here is Stator: at this very spot Rome was founded.'
>
> Ovid, *Tristia* 3.1.27–32[36]

The same route is followed, a century later, by a copy of Martial's verses on their way to a patron's house.

> Say hello for me, obedient book: I'm sending you to Proculus' well-swept hearth. You want to know the way? I'll tell you. Go by Castor, next door to white-haired Vesta and her virgin establishment, and then climb the Sacred Hill to the [gate of the] venerable *Palatia*, where many a statue of the Great Leader shines. At the massive radiance of the Colossus, proudly surpassing the wondrous work of Rhodes, go straight ahead. As you reach the house of sodden Lyaeus, just where there stands a shrine of Cybele with a painted Corybant, turn left ...
>
> Martial 1.70[37]

Temple-going, then, is one of the pleasures of high Rome; and temples are everywhere in the City. When Martial wants to tell the reader where he lived while writing books 5 and 6 of his *Epigrams* in about the years 90–91, he points immediately to his neighbour *rustica Flora*, his nearest temple (5.22): in a sense he had made 'country girl Flora', healthily unashamed of sex, his patron goddess (*Epigrams* 1 preface). Similarly the temple of 'sodden Lyaeus' and the shrine of Cybele serve as landmarks on Martial's route just quoted. No one will suppose that Greek and Roman temples served only for sacrifice. The *Templum Opis* 'Temple of Wealth' on the *Tarpeia* was, appropriately, where Caesar's 'bloody treasure' had been deposited, and from where Antony abstracted it as soon as Caesar was safely dead (Cicero, *Philippics* 1.17, 2.93). Ovid, remembering Rome from a thousand miles away, remembers – and wishes sadly that he might renew – his visits to the three public libraries of Rome in his time, of which two were in temples. He and his books are now banned from all three. He begins his dream-journey at Augustus's library in the Temple of Apollo.

> Among the columns of foreign marble were the Children of Danaus and their barbaric father with drawn sword; and all those matters that ancient and modern men of learned spirit have invented are set out

openly for those who wish to read them.... But I searched in vain, and the keeper of the holy place told me to leave those halls. I found another temple, not far off, beside a theatre, but it too was not to be entered by me. And even Libertas would not allow me to reach her rooms, the first that were opened to scholarly books.

Ovid, Tristia 3.1.61–72

Apollo's temple was on the 'high Palatine', *alta Palatia*, close to Augustus's own house (*Domus Augusti* on Map 10). The library was in the *porticus* 'cloister', surrounded, as Ovid remembers so clearly, by narrative paintings of the myth of the Danaids. Latin and Greek texts were shelved separately and, as Horace urges his fellow littérateurs, there was still plenty of room for more Latin poets.[38] Ovid's second visit is to the library in the *Porticus Octavia* in the Campus Martius; finally he applies to the oldest of the three, the library presented by the historian Asinius Pollio to the Temple of Liberty, perhaps on the Aventine.

Some temples naturally gathered special activities, more or less obviously relevant, around themselves: the flower market at the Temple of the Lares on the Sacred Way in Rome, 'where many wreaths are twined by clever hands' (Ovid, *Fasti* 6.791); the stalls selling 'obscene terracotta objects' to tourists at the temple of Cnidian Aphrodite (Lucian: p. 164); the enthusiastic guides or priests on the steps of the temple at Gnatia, ready to demonstrate to credulous visitors that incense would miraculously melt there without fire (Horace: p. 63).

Observances varied endlessly, from the simple placing of a garland of wheat at Ceres's temple door (Tibullus: p. 22) to the individual visits by devotees that made the Temple of Isis in Rome such a good place to pick up girls, to penances and pilgrimages undertaken as fulfilment of a vow: 'a woman whose prayer has been answered is often seen bearing a burning torch' along the twenty-mile road from Rome to Diana's shrine at Aricia (Ovid, *Fasti* 3.263–272: p. 44).[39] Not all offerings to the gods were costly or troublesome. Every April at the *Vinalia*, says Ovid, Venus demanded from the whores who worshipped her 'lovely water mint and her very own myrtle, and chains of rushes interwoven with rose': they went in procession on that day to the temple of Erycina at the Colline Gate (Ovid, *Fasti* 4.865–872). But some expense was generally required on foods, wines or aromas. 'Bring living turf, boys, lay down aromatic boughs, set out incense and a saucer of two-year wine: she'll come easier if I offer a victim', says Horace (*Odes* 1.19.13–16) and the reader may decide whether 'she' is Venus to whom the offering is made, or Glycera with whom Horace hopes to spend a pleasurable night, or sex itself. The sacrifice is not elaborate, but the incense is really costly. Such exotics had become a natural part of sacrifice. Just so, the spiced and honeyed cakes that were frequently offered were luxuries to those who offered them, even if they might eventually be all too mundane to the priests and attendants of the temple. 'Like the priest's runaway slave', says

Figure 29   Ceremonial before a temple of Isis. Detail of a wall painting from
Herculaneum

Source   By permission of the Soprintendenza Archeologica per le Province di Napoli e Caserta

Horace elsewhere, 'I'm tired of cake; I need bread, not *placentae* soaked in honey' (*Epistles* 1.10.10–11).[40]

Of all Rome's ceremonies none was grander than the Triumph in which the spoils of Roman victories were paraded through the city. The route of the procession began in the *Campus Martius*, passed through the Velabrum, entered the Forum and climbed the last steep curves of the Sacred Way to the temple of *Juppiter Optimus Maximus* 'Jove Greatest and Best' on the *Arx*. This precipitous twin-peaked hill is the 'Capitoline' on the maps: *Arx* and *Tarpeia* usually in poetry. These *sacrae Arces, dominae Arces, Tarpeias Arces* 'sacred, ruling, Tarpeian rocks'[41] commanded Rome and the world, more so with every new Triumph, until at last as Jove looked out from the *Arx* there was nothing for him to see that was not Roman (Ovid, *Fasti* 1.85–86). Triumphs had their own reassuring ritual: the white bulls of Clitumnus whose privilege was to lead the procession (p. 21), the golden chariot in which the victorious general rode, the golden 'Etruscan crown' that he wore (p. 75), the attendant whose only task was to remind him with a whisper that he was mortal, and the rowdy soldiers who sang scurrilous songs of him and his victories, having been kept hanging around in Rome in advance with too much money and nothing to do but get into trouble.[42]

Several of the costly luxuries of the Roman world had first become known in Rome through their display at Triumphs. Among these were the bronze couches, the tapestries, the cithara-girls and harp-girls of Asia, all displayed in 187 BC (p. 120). A rhinoceros was shown in Pompey's Triumph of 55; a rhinoceros and hippopotamus together took the starring role relinquished by Cleopatra in 29 (p. 179). Balsam of Mecca trees from the royal garden of Jerusalem were carefully transported to Rome for the Judaean Triumph of Vespasian and Titus (p. 170), and Vergil hints (below) that date palms from Syria had already been seen in some recent Triumph. Ebony wood, seldom seen in Rome, was exhibited by Pompey in his Triumph over Mithridates of Pontus in 61 (p.194). This is a reminder that the original function of Triumphs was to display captives and booty: in this case, costly timber from Mithridates' royal store. Ebony grows nowhere near Pontus, but that was irrelevant.

The power that Triumphs held over Rome's poetic imagination must be accepted as the explanation for a very strange circumstance. The best existing description of a Triumph is written by a poet who did not see the event. Tiberius's Pannonian Triumph is described in loving detail by Ovid from exile, 'thanks to you, Fame, through whom I saw the triumphal procession though imprisoned among the Getae'. Rome had scarcely room for the multitude of visitors. The victor was showered with applause and with rose petals. It had rained, but now the sun shone, and the freshly rinsed Forum sparkled with reflections from the gold of the captured trophies. Great numbers of enemy troops marched by with chains about their necks: many were generously spared death, including their leader Bato (Ovid, *Letters from Pontus* 2.1).

Writers who tell us that they saw images of captured cities and provinces borne on triumphal wagons (p. 6) are telling the simple truth. So is Propertius, a spectator in 29, who saw Cleopatra running away to the shallow streams of fearful Nile, and saw the 'servant of Romulus' putting chains about her wrists, and watched as her arms were bitten by the sacred asps, and saw the shady path of sleep engulf her body (Propertius 3.11.51–54). On the basis of tableaux of the Cleopatra story, displayed on floats, he allowed his imagination full play. So it was that the Triumph made real for him the conquest of Egypt and the longed-for humiliation of its barbaric queen. And indeed she had had no other route but suicide to escape the destiny of leaders who opposed Rome in war and were defeated. Had she lived, she herself would have walked the triumphal route, enslaved and chained, to be butchered or magnanimously spared when the procession reached Jove's temple.

Other poets go further in imagination. Horace sees 'as yet unviolated Britons' paraded in chains on the Sacred Way in a Roman Triumph (p. 85): he sees it almost a century before Claudius achieved it. He imagines Augustus leading 'conquered Chinese and Indians from the Eastern shore' in triumph to the Capitol (p. 199): no Roman ever did. And there are two separate evocations of a Triumph that was perhaps deserved, but never took place: that of Germanicus for his German campaign completed in 11 AD. The celebration was about to begin, thought Ovid: he could already hear the crackling of the incense; he could see Germanicus riding high in his Sidonian purple, and the German leaders dishevelled, chained, humbled; he could see the pictures of lakes, mountains, forts and rivers that had been filled with savage slaughter and drenched in German blood (Ovid, *Tristia* 4.2). Well, it did not come true. Germanicus had 'turned barbarian backs in flight, and earned a Triumph that Romans never saw': his consolation would surely be to lead a triumphal procession in heaven (*Consolation to Livia* 18–19, 332–335).

One last triumph of the Roman poetic imagination is Vergil's own. At the opening of book 3 of the *Georgics* he imagines himself in the role of conqueror, leading the captive Muses of Greece in triumph to his native Mantua, shaded by Idumaean palms. He will place a marble temple in the green meadow beside the Mincius: it will be Augustus's temple. Vergil the victor, bright in his Tyrian purple, will lead a hundred chariots, with Greek athletic games going on around. His head wreathed in olive leaves, Vergil will lead his Triumph to the temple, sacrifice the white bulls and review the painted scenes of Britain and its people (p. 85) and the temple doors carved with Indian and Egyptian victories. He will display the conquered cities of Asia, that famous Armenian river Niphates, a Parthian loosing his parting shot, and trophies from both ends of the conquered world (Vergil, *Georgics* 3.10–39). It is a dream sequence whose logic changes almost with every line. Its connecting link is the poet's privilege. So long as the real conqueror, Augustus, is raised to the only imaginable greater height – that of God – the poet may safely claim the right to triumph, for it is the poet who records and preserves the conqueror's achievement. The imagined triumph turns into the epic of Augustus's victories that Vergil eventually never wrote, and back again into the celebration of empire and conquest that Triumphs truly were.

Triumphs were the greatest of all the entertainments that Rome derived from its conquests. But all the public entertainments of Rome drew on the resources of the Empire, even the very smallest. There were of course performers who made a living by gathering a curious crowd in the crowded streets of the capital. There were snake-charmers,[43] a profession that specially belonged to Marsians from central Italy. Their magic also allowed them to cure snakebite and to charm an aching tooth (p. 69). There were story-tellers: Apuleius's *Metamorphoses* presents itself to Latin readers as a story-teller's text, beginning with the African author's apology to his audience 'should there be anything strange and foreign', *siquid exotici ac forensis*, about his style (1.1): and indeed its eloquence is not that of Cicero. *Forensis* was the right word, suggesting, like modern French *forain*, those who come to town from a distance, those who are here for the fair. The whole Empire came to Rome. There were jugglers and acrobats, probably mostly from Greece and the province of Asia. 'Days ago, in front of the *Stoa Poikile* at Athens, I saw an itinerant juggler swallow a cavalry sword, point first, and then, after he'd been round the audience for small change, he swallowed the business end of a lance, and leaned back with the handle sticking out of his mouth, and a good-looking soft-limbed boy climbed up the handle with snaky movements' (Apuleius, *Metamorphoses* 1.4, abridged): such displays were to be seen in Rome as well. Itinerant dancers, colleagues of those who appeared in the Circus and in taverns, performed erotic routines ancestral to the belly-dances of the modern Levant. Their skills included teasing the audience with obscene language (Martial 10.3.2). Among the most admired were the slave dancing-girls who came from Gades, and Telethusa may have been one of these (see also p. 107), 'Telethusa the itinerant dancer, out there with no skirt on, pushing her arse higher and higher, her fluid thighs shimmering' (*Priapeia* 19.1–4). The verb *criso* is the technical term in Latin for the mesmerising rapid vibrations of thighs and buttocks that are the defining element of this dance routine – 'as if her arse is a winnowing-basket' (Lucilius 330).[44]

The most varied and the most typically Roman of entertainments were the Games. These were at first presented in the old *Circus Flaminius* and the later *Circus Maximus*. Long and straight, these had been designed for the chariot races that were a part of Roman life for hundreds of years. It is the races that Vergil calls to mind in the terrifying image of spreading war that closes book 1 of the *Georgics* (509–514): 'Unholy Mars rages over the whole earth. It is as if a chariot, bursting from the starting-gate, gathers speed inexorably from lap to lap: the driver, tugging at the reins, is carried on helplessly, and the team does not respond to the bit'.

In due course, vast, circular open theatres were built specifically for the Games. There was Nero's wooden *Amphitheatrum* of AD 57 (Suetonius, *Nero* 12; Tacitus, *Annals* 13.31), so called because its oval shape resembled a double theatre entirely surrounding the stage; then the greater *Amphitheatrum*, better known now as *Colosseum* and acclaimed as the eighth wonder of the world (p. 12).[45] These spawned a large number of imitations: eventually all provincial towns of any pretension had to have an amphitheatre.

The Emperor's box commanded the arena, and the front rows reserved for upper ranks (*senatores, equites*) had unrivalled views, but visibility was excellent even from the 'wedges' of seats rising skywards. Comfort was limited: you took your own cushion; in fact chopped reed was called *tomentum circense* 'circus stuffing'[46] If you were wise, you took some refreshment too, 'like the *eques*, drinking during the show, to whom Augustus sent down a message: '"I go home when I want to have a meal." "Because you needn't worry about losing your seat," said the *eques*' (Quintilian 6.3.63). But lead *tesserae* 'tickets' were given out to citizens – *equites* got ten tickets – as entitlement to wine in generous measure. The Games themselves were presented by annual magistrates, and eventually by Emperors; the tickets, an idea first used by Agrippa in 33 BC, were a way of apportioning further generosity[47] and thus of buying additional popularity. The Games brought many citizens – and many others – together for a whole day or for days on end, drunk with wine, sated with beauty, with thrills and with blood, galvanised by the roars and applause that could be heard all over the city and well beyond.[48]

With childlike enthusiasm Statius tells us of the *Saturnalia* entertainment arranged for a temporarily grateful citizenry by the emperor Domitian.

Off with you, father Phoebus, stern Pallas, and all the Muses: you're on holiday. We'll want you back on the first of January. Saturn, loose your fetters. Come here you three, drunk December, rude Fun, indecent Joke! Help me tell about the fine day and the bibulous night that our cheerful Caesar arranged for us.

Scarce had Dawn got out of bed when sweets began to rain down on us, a rare dew distilled by the rising East Wind. The finest harvest of the hazel orchards of the Pontus and of the fertile hills of Idume, all that devout Damascus grows on its boughs, all that thirsty Caunus dries, all fell in profusion: there was a veritable shower of little cheeses and fritters, Amerines not too smoked, must-cakes, and enormous *caryotis* dates from invisible palms [like rain from a sunny sky, Statius assures us.] A second 'audience', at least as good-looking and well-dressed as we who were sitting down, now threaded its way along every row. Some carried baskets of bread and white napkins and more elaborate delicacies; others served languorous wine in brimming measure: you would think each one a divine cupbearer from Mount Ida. The same table served every class alike, child, woman, *plebs*, *eques* and *senator*: freedom had loosed the bonds of awe. You yourself – most gods could not have managed this! – you, Caesar, condescended to share our feast.

Among these glories and exotic luxuries, the pleasures of the arena flitted by all too quickly. Here was the unwarlike sex, untrained in swordsmanship, but vicious enough to put up a manly fight! you would think Thermodon's bands were battling wildly beside Tanais or barbarous Phasis; and there a bold battalion of dwarfs dealt out wounds and threatened death; and the cranes, waiting to swoop on random prey, saw in amazement that the dwarfs were fiercer than themselves.

Now, as the shades of night draw on, what excitement about the distribution of presents! Here come the girls whose price is not too high; here you can find every variety of act that delights a theatre audience for skill or beauty, a troupe of busty Lydiennes clapping their hands, Gades complete with cymbals and castanets, a competing chorus of Syrians, the theatre people and the people who exchange sulphur matches for broken glass. In all this racket, great clouds of birds swoop suddenly down through the air, birds from holy Nile and frozen Phasis, birds that Numidians capture under the watery South Wind.

Scarcely was azure night invading the world, when through the darkness a shining ball of fire, brighter than the flame of the Gnosian crown, fell right into the arena. The sky was ablaze with sparks; darkness was completely banished; languid Peace fled away, and, observing this, lazy

Figure 30 Syrian musicians in terracotta. The woman on the left beats a drum, the
one on the right plays a double flute. From Roman Syria, first century
AD

Source By permission of the Director General of Antiquities and Museums, Syria

Sleep ran off to some other cities. Who, finally, could describe the scene
that ensued, the wild partying, the merriment, the food that no one had
to pay for, the broad rivers of wine? I'm beginning to feel weak. Caesar's
wine was too much for me, and it's time I staggered off to bed.

Statius, *Silvae* 1.6, abridged[49]

It was appropriate to the spirit of Saturnalia that all classes should be
treated alike. Perhaps *equites* did not get their usual allowance of ten wine
tickets on this occasion. The partying seems to have been Domitian's main
concern: at any rate Statius says rather little about the show. He pays more
attention to the attendants, the attractive boys – like Ganymede, Jove's
cupbearer from mount Ida – who served wine, and the troupes of theatricals
and allied trades – 'Gades' means the dancing girls of Gades – who did the
distribution of presents.

We need to know more of the typical programme than Statius tells us
here. To begin with the less grandiose: Apuleius, in the *Metamorphoses*
(10.29–35), describes fictional Games at Corinth in the province of Achaea.

They include a Pyrrhic dance, that is, a sword dance by boys and girls in armour; an erotic pantomime; the public execution of a murderess; and a hunting display. In Petronius's *Satyricon* a forthcoming show is discussed at Trimalchio's fictional dinner. The magistrate presenting the Games is putting together a programme beginning with a series of fights to the death among gladiators,

> not a professional team but freedmen mostly ... he'll give them top quality steel and no escape, an axeman in the middle where everyone can see.... He's already got some vicious types and a woman charioteer – and Glyco's bursar, who was caught having it off with his master's wife: you'll see fighting in the audience between puritans and lover-boys, all because Glyco, the mean fellow, has condemned his accountant to the wild beasts. It's giving himself away. How is it the slave's fault? he did what the slut told him to. She's the one who deserves to be tossed by a bull. Well, if you can't flog the ass you flog the saddle.
>
> Petronius 45

As an actual example of the more elaborate shows, we may instance the memorial games at the dedication in 29 BC of the temple of Julius Caesar in the Forum. Patrician boys played the Troy game, Patrician men competed on horseback and in two-horse and four-horse chariots, and a Senator, Q. Vitellius, fought as a gladiator. Great numbers of wild and tame animals were killed, including a rhinoceros and a hippopotamus: the latter had never been seen in Rome before. There was a battle between platoons of Dacians, 'a Scythian people more or less', and Suebians (Dio Cassius 51.22.4–6).

In Rome, gladiatorial shows were always on the programme – the axeman's task, in the quotation from the *Satyricon*, being to carry out in full view of the audience the frequent death verdict on losing gladiators. An occasional variation was to see women fighting, and we should add that in Statius's piece, quoted above, 'Thermodon's bands' are the legendary Amazons, fetched in to make it clear to the reader that in Domitian's entertainment the 'unwarlike sex' fought bare-breasted.

Wild beast shows were also a universal feature. They were not always violent. Martial tells us of performances resembling modern circus shows.

> When the leopard's spotted neck bears a light yoke, when evil tigers submit to the whip, when stags bite on golden bits, when Libyan bears are tamed with bridles, when a boar as big as the one that Calydon bred submits to a purple muzzle, when bad-tempered bisons pull carts, when the elephant is ordered by his black trainer to do a girlish dance and obeys – who would not think that the show is produced by the gods?
>
> Martial 1.104

An imagined rural visitor to Nero's wooden amphitheatre, forerunner of the Colosseum, is impressed not only by the gold, ivory and marble fittings but also by the white hares, boars, elks, buffalos, aurochs, bears, seals and rhinoceroses that are displayed (Calpurnius Siculus, *Eclogues* 7.23–38, 45–84). 'I saw white deer in Rome, to my astonishment, though I did not have the chance to ask what land or island they came from', Pausanias tells us (8.17.4). But the audience rather expected danger and death. Bull-leaping, a risky sport, is described by Martial (5.31). Hunting displays were given: Juvenal (1.22–23) suggests one in which a woman hunter appears bare-breasted, as if playing Artemis or Atalanta. We learnt from Dio Cassius (above) that the rhinoceros, hippopotamus and other beasts shown in 29 BC were killed in the course of the Games; he tells us elsewhere (55.10) of 260 lions killed in the Circus, and 36 crocodiles in the Circus Flaminius, at the Circensian Games in 2 BC.

In the text quoted above from the *Satyricon*, 'Glyco's bursar' is condemned to death by his cuckolded master. Wild beasts commonly played a part in the public executions that were a regular and expected feature of Games programmes. *Who* was executed would depend on circumstances. The fictional Glyco might have been better advised to avoid gossip and kill his slave privately: but the magistrate needed someone to be thrown to the wild beasts, and a slave, already destined for death, would evidently do. The form of death was infinitely variable. The murderess in the *Metamorphoses* is condemned to mate with an ass in the arena: a lion is then to be released on the scene and will probably kill both the ass and the woman. Neither half of this grisly plot is to be blamed on Apuleius's imagination. Martial's *Spectacula*, a short series of poems inspired by Domitian's Games, praises the Emperor for showing that the myth of Pasiphae was true: in other words, he had had a condemned woman mated with a bull in the arena. Martial also records a combat between an armed woman and a lion (the woman won); and a criminal provided with wings, like Daedalus, and launched above a cage of bears (the bears won). The geographer Strabo saw Selurus, leader of a shepherd revolt in Sicily, executed as part of a Games programme. He was placed on a high scaffold representing mount Aetna: it collapsed, carrying him down into a pen of wild beasts hidden beneath.[50]

For a long time, under the Republic, the streets and the Forum were the locations even for such elaborate entertainments as plays. But at last, on the Greek model, theatres were built. There were three by Augustus's time; in literature we hear most often of the oldest of them, the *Theatrum Pompei* built by Pompey in 55 BC. It was, of course, open air: no one thought of a roofed theatre. But the Roman audience had never been trained to sit in the same place, in the sun, for a whole day together. Awnings were added, there-fore – providing unplanned shelter for vagrants, who spent the night under them. Lucretius helps us to visualise these awnings,

> yellow, scarlet and maroon, stretched flapping and billowing on poles and rafters over spacious theatres. The crowded auditorium below and

the stage with all its scenery are made to glow and flow with the colours of the canopy. The more completely the theatre is hemmed in by surrounding walls, the more its interior, sheltered from the daylight, is irradiated by this flow of colour.

Lucretius 4.75–82, translation by R. Latham

We might deduce from this, and from Martial's striking simile (p. 263), that the awnings at Pompey's theatre could not safely be erected on a windy day: other texts assure us of the fact.[51] A fine spray of saffron-tinged wine imparted a Cilician aroma and an aura of lavish expense to Roman theatres. On whether the sticky jets were directed at the stage only, or at the audience as well, the sources are not unanimous,[52] but we can be sure that 'the whole auditorium was filled with the fragrance' (Apuleius, *Metamorphoses* 10.34). Syrian dates were available as snacks, *notae caryotides theatris*, 'dates as we know them at theatres' (Martial 11.31).

An additional luxury at Pompey's theatre was the adjacent *Porticus* in which the audience could shelter on a rainy day. It was a rectangular cloister embellished with curtains of cloth of gold, *Attalica aulaea* (p. 163), and with works of art. Leisurely strollers promenaded along the shady walks through its gardens – *vetus Pompei umbra*, 'Pompey's old shade'; *in Magni ambulatione*, 'strolling through Magnus'. It turned out to be an excellent place to meet members of the opposite sex – and remained unaccountably more popular than newer public gardens.[53]

The proper entertainment for the theatre was the play: in Greece, after all, this is what theatres were for. The classic Roman five-act plays of the second century BC were still performed a century and more later, repeatedly revived by public demand. These and most forms of drama known in Rome were influenced by Greek models. But the Roman audience was, it would appear, not like the Greek. Would a classical Greek audience even have understood Martial's reference to 'the sound made by voices and hands in the full theatre when the audience sees Caesar suddenly arrive' (Martial 6.34)? The Roman readiness to be distracted, the demand for incessant incident, interludes, thrills and strange animals must somehow be satisfied. No author or producer could afford to forget the boxing match and the tightrope dancer who had drawn the audience away from the first performance of Terence's *Hecyra*: and none would, for the African author's disillusionment is on record for all time.[54]

So it is that Roman theatre-goers had many things beside plays to command their attention. People who spend whole days on entertainments will dream – Lucretius asserts – of 'watching acrobats and lithe-limbed dancers, hearing the liquid song of the cithara and its eloquent strings, seeing the same packed theatre and the colourful show of the stage' (4.980–983). Connoisseurs of the stage – equally four centuries later – will be found arguing 'which boy can do the best somersaults, or bend over backwards and sweep the marble floor with his long hair, or turn his body into the most perfect curve; which boy has the most expressive fingers or the most sinful eyes' (Claudian, *Against Eutropius* 2.359–362). Tragedies and comedies, given in classically standardised costumes and in traditional masks, were rivalled, and perhaps almost pushed off the stage, by two less hidebound forms, mime and pantomime. Mimes were plays without masks or choruses and following none of the rules of plot and taste laid down by the critics: they relied on low farce and tales of adultery, and 'impressionable girls are there watching, and boys, and their mothers and fathers; most of the Senate's there' (Ovid, *Tristia* 2.501–502). The mime *Laureolus* by Catullus (not the poet) culminated in the villain's crucifixion on stage – a scene utterly alien to the classical genres – making it possible, at a revival in AD 80, for a condemned criminal to be substituted for the actor in this scene and to be crucified in earnest (Martial, *Spectacula* 7). Pantomimes were mimes with song and dance: their appeal was aesthetic and erotic. Words mattered little: the 'plots' were familiar tales and tableaux from Greek mythology, like the pantomime of the Judgment of Paris in Apuleius's *Metamorphoses* (below). So pantomimes could be performed before very large audiences, at the amphitheatre or the circus, as well as in theatres. There were 'variety' acts too: clowns such as the *grallatores* who performed on stilts; erotic dancers like 'Quintia' who, in this probably fictitious epigram, dedicates her cymbals and castanets – accoutrements of the dancing girls of Gades – to the appropriate deity.

> Quintia, the people's favourite, well known in the great Circus, unrivalled in the seductive vibrations of her buttocks, offers you, Priapus, her erotic armoury – her cymbals and castanets and the drum that she beats. In return, grant her always to please the crowd, and to make every member of the audience share your own rigidity!
>
> *Priapeia* 27

Actors (*mimi, pantomimi*) were largely of slave origin and from many provinces of the Empire; some, by contrast, were Roman citizens who had lost their fortunes. Actors of both sexes were classed legally as *prostituti*, because 'it is by an immoral arrangement that they give away control of their bodies': so Cassiodorus explains the matter (*Variae* 7.10) to a newly appointed *Tribunus voluptatum* 'Lord Chamberlain' of the late fifth century. He has his eye on the women, though, when he adds, 'you are placed in control of *prostitutae*: be careful to be chaste yourself.' Cassiodorus's technicality is not the only reason for the general equation of actors with prostitutes. Many shows aimed for erotic appeal; performances both male and female were evaluated sexually; actors of both sexes were said to be promiscuous, sometimes extravagantly so. They were occasionally involved in high scandal, as when the *pantomimus* Paris – an Egyptian, incidentally – was crucified by Domitian in 82/83 because he was suspected of an affair with the empress Domitia Longina: as if to confirm the suspicion, it was said to have been because of this that Domitia eventually joined the conspirators who assassinated Domitian in 96.[55] The sources insist that women performers, in particular, played to arouse the male audience and succeeded in doing so. In the theatre and circus, as in sideshows in the street, actresses and dancers such as the Quintia and Telethusa of the *Priapeia* (above and p. 230) were seen almost naked.[56]

New Rome

Their public buildings, aqueducts and baths were the most distinctive of the legacies of Roman cities. Rome herself had much to catch the eye: no one would overlook the temples on the *Arx*, the Imperial residences on the *Palatia*. But at Rome too the observant eye was immediately caught by the aqueducts and baths – and by other new and lavish public buildings that rapidly turned the *Campus Martius* 'Field of Mars' from an open place for military exercises into a theme park.

Strabo, in Augustus's time, singled out the water supply of Rome and the public buildings on the Campus as two striking features of its urban landscape. Grandiose development continued through the first century AD, assisted elsewhere by the great fire of 64 upon which Nero rebuilt, but here on the Campus Martius by the fire of 80 that made room for Domitian's projects.

> *Quid Nerone peius?*
> *Quid Thermis melius Neronianis?*

'What could be worse than Nero? What could be better than Nero's Baths?' asks Martial (7.34), as if to demonstrate to later detractors that he was quite well aware of the moral complexities of autocracies such as the one under which he wrote: for it was Martial too who asked without any irony, concerning Domitian's developments, 'Under which ruler has Mars's Rome been larger or more beautiful?' (5.19).[57] Towards the end of the Empire Rutilius, poetically addressing the metropolis itself, places the emphasis where Strabo did.

> Your glittering temples dazzle wandering eyes – I could think them truly the houses of the gods – and what of the streams suspended on aerial arches, higher than the rainbow's reach? One might call them mountains raised to the stars, Giants' work as Greece would say. Rivers are diverted into your precincts and concealed under ground; the great Baths swallow up whole lakes. Your walled gardens are irrigated by streams of your own: they echo with the babble of local springs. Thus a cool breath refreshes the summer air; a healthy thirst is relieved by clear

waters.... What of the groves enclosed by vaulted cloisters, where Rome-bred birds frolic with varied song?

Rutilius 95–113

Of Rome's many aqueducts poets tell us at least of three: 'Nymphs who live in Latium and the Seven Hills,' calls Statius (*Silvae* 1.5.23–28), 'you who bring new waters to Tiber, who love the headlong *Anien* and the Virgin of the swimming pool and the *Marcia* that brings Marsian winter and snow; you whose diverted wave rises to precipitous height and is distributed upon innumerable arches'. Statius's *Anien* is the old *Anio vetus* aqueduct. His *Marcia* is *aqua Marcia*, to other poets *Marcius umor, Marcius liquor*, the 'Marcian water that will last for ever', 'the generous fountain; the conqueror's supply' of water that was well worth queuing for, good for drinking, good to mix with this year's wine, wonderful for swimming in. The generous Marcia watered some of the artificial grottos in private pleasure gardens.[58] Statius's 'Virgin' is *Aqua Virgo*. Built by Agrippa in 19 BC, this was an underground conduit beginning eight miles east of Rome and coming to the surface in the Gardens of Lucullus. From there it ran as an aqueduct to Agrippa's new Baths (*Thermae Agrippae*) in the Campus Martius. It was *Virgo gelida, gelidissima, cruda*, the 'cold, very cold, raw Virgin', good for bathing in. Hearty young men washed their oiled limbs in Virgin water after exercise.[59]

The practices of bathing and the social life of the Baths were very different things in Cicero's time and in Martial's. Under the Republic, Romans were rather prudish about taking a dip. 'It is our custom that grown-up sons do not bathe with their fathers, nor sons-in-law with fathers-in-law', says Cicero (*On Duties* 1.129), giving us a hint elsewhere (p. 270) of the feeling of slight impropriety produced by any such mixing of the generations. Plutarch, a later writer dealing with a slightly earlier period, says the same thing in historical perspective.

Cato never bathed with his son. This was normal with the Romans. Fathers-in-law did not bathe with sons-in-law, either: they were shy of stripping and being naked together. Later they learnt to do this from the Greeks. In return they have now infected the Greeks with the idea of men and women bathing naked together.

Plutarch, *Cato the Elder* 20.8

The first part of this moral landslide, the mixing of the generations, probably came with the partly Greek-inspired system of healthy afternoons of exercise and bathing that Agrippa assiduously encouraged in his sports complex – as we would call it – on the Campus Martius. All went together, the exercise ground, the hot baths and the cold *Virgo*. The whole structure is named by the later historian Dio Cassius (53.27) *pyriatorion Lakonikon* 'the Laconian steam bath'. Dio explains that Agrippa called it Laconian because stripping off and rubbing down with oil were in those days seen as particularly Spartan practices. Some explanation was certainly needed, and Dio's will roughly fit the facts. Bathing was already popular in Agrippa's Rome, but the exercise ground idea was new and borrowed from Greece. However, the idea of a three-stage routine at the Baths is not Greek; it is typically Roman. This idea arises precisely now, and it comes from the combined facilities that Agrippa devised and provided. Agrippa and Augustus were concerned with healthy exercise for young men, and 'Laconian' was a name intended to get the scheme across. Propertius's outrageous vignette of naked Laconian *girls* at exercise (p. 146) will have failed to amuse Agrippa. By Martial's time (6.42: below) the 'Laconian' idea was embedded in Latin: *Laconicum* was a steam bath and *ritus Laconum*, 'Spartan customs', were equated with absorbing dry vapour, drinking the cold *Virgo*, swimming in the *Marcia* and not having much time for women.

The second idea in Plutarch's sequence – that the two sexes might bathe together – had not occurred to Agrippa. Even in Martial's time Agrippa's baths were still for men only (11.47). But meanwhile, at other bathing establishments, women had begun to bathe alongside men, and not only in the course of the occasional time-honoured festival. There was, about this same time, a new luxury craze for sea water pools, *piscinae marinae*. Bathing in brine was supposed to be healthy, and Nero had a sea water pool in his vast palace, the *Domus Aurea*. This fashion may have had something to do with the mixed bathing idea; after all, men and women bathed together in the sea. Martial, at any rate, talks of a sea water pool as potentially a location for sex, and he is not alone in thinking so.[60]

The great public baths are not alone in attracting poets' praise. Possibly a more club-like atmosphere was to be enjoyed at the private baths? Possibly a more select clientèle attended? Rome had many of them, lavishly appointed, we are told, by developers who found them a profitable investment.[61] Here the waters of Latium or of the cold Marsian country mirrored the colours of polished marble from far across the Empire; and in these baths, too, you could bathe in accordance with 'Spartan customs'.

> Bathe in the baths of Etruscus, Oppianus, or you will die unclean. No waters will caress you like these: not the spring of Aponus, unkind to girls, not soft Sinuessa nor prized Baiae. Nowhere is there such perfect peace; light itself lasts longer there. The quarries of Taygetus give of their greenness; marbles cut deep by the Phrygian and the Libyan vie in varied colours. Rich onyx marble exhales its dry breath; serpentine glows with a thin flame. If you like it the Laconian way, you can dip in the dry steam, then in the raw *Virgo* and the *Marcia*. They shine so palely and so still that you would think there was no water there at all, and you were seeing the white Parian marble of an empty bath.
>
> Martial 6.42, abridged

Elements of this pretty picture recur in other descriptions. Statius, too, gives us a swimming bath, a tasteful one where there was no room for the marble of *undosa Carystos* or of Thasos, no room for onyx marble or serpentine from Egypt (p. 176); instead there was yellow *purpura* cut from the marble quarries of Numidia, and the stone of Synnada that was stained with the blood of Attis himself, and white stone from Tyre and Sidon, and just a little of the green porphyry of Laconia that contrasted so nicely with the red of Synnada. And there was no plebeian bronze: all the fittings were of silver (*Silvae* 1.5.34–41). In *Hippias or The Bath* Lucian tells us of a new bath designed by Hippias and just completed: the location is some unknown city that Lucian was visiting as lecturer (5). Here, in what we must regard as a triumph of Imperial interior decoration, the marbles of Empire are colour-coded, and other texts confirm that the coding was standard.[62] The cold bath is, how appropriately! in cool green porphyry of Laconia; the warm bath and the lounge in comfortable red Synnada marble; the steam bath in yellow Numidian marble whose colour glows in the generous sunlight of this well-lit room.

We began our exploration of the Campus Martius with Agrippa's Baths. In Martial's catalogue of Rome's pleasures, *Campus, porticus, umbra, Virgo, Thermae*, 'Campus, cloister, shade, *Virgo*, Baths' (5.20) Agrippa accounts for two, and the Campus for three more. Of these three, the open space itself takes first place, *gramen Martium* 'the grass of Mars', *apricus Campus* 'the bracing Field', so firmly identified with young men's martial exercises that a singlet – as worn on these occasions – is called *campestre* 'Field wear' and the exercises are *proelia campestria* 'Field battles'. The young men concerned included – in Agrippa's time – Rome's short-lived youth brigades, the *Collegia Iuvenum* in whom Augustus invested so much effort.[62] For one such youngster Horace claims to have felt an unrequited tenderness: 'At night in my dreams sometimes I catch and hold you, sometimes I pursue you, as a bird, over the grass of the Campus Martius, or – unyielding boy! – in the voluble waters' (Horace, *Odes* 4.1.37–40). Horace plunged in only in his dreams, but the athletics of the Campus might indeed in summer be pleasantly varied with a dip in the Tiber, relatively clean at this point since it had not reached Rome's built-up area.[63] Indeed the notorious Clodia, object of Cicero's forensic scorn, was said to have chosen her house specifically for its view of this reach of the Tiber, enabling her to select future lovers from among the young swimmers.

The other pleasures of the Campus are 'the cloisters, the shade' – a fair summary of many of its new buildings. One such, the first of them in fact, was the *Porticus Pompei* attached to Pompey's Theatre (p. 235). There were soon others too: gardens surrounded by colonnades, pleasant and fashionable places to stroll and meet and talk and place bets on horses and chariot-races. Among them was the *Porticus Europae* or *Agenoris puella* 'Agenor's daughter' – that is who Europa was – with its leisurely crowd, its box hedges and its painting of the Rape of Europa. It was hot in the afternoon.[64] The *Porticus Argonautarum* also has a nickname, *dominus levis primae carinae*, 'flighty captain of the most ancient keel': this is Jason, leader of the Argonauts. Here one paused to study paintings of the story of Jason and Medea.[65] The *Porticus Vipsania* is called *laurus Vipsanas* 'the Vipsanian bay tree' so it must presumably have been planted with bays.[66] The *Porticus Philippi* stood before the Temple of Hercules and the Muses. You bought wigs and German hair here,[67] and 'there's no shame in buying it: we see it on sale openly, before the eyes of Hercules and the Virgin Choir' (Ovid, *Art of Love* 3.167–168).

Something slightly different was the fancy rebuilding of the old *Saeptum*. This was where the *Aqua Virgo*'s arches ended, just beside Agrippa's Baths. The Saeptum had been a paddock, a voting enclosure and a fairground before the elaborate reconstruction by Agrippa and Augustus that left it surrounded by grand colonnades. Under the Empire it was still a place for shows and fairs, including occasional displays of wild animals, occasional gladiatorial games.[68] But the surrounding colonnades became luxury shopping precincts, and in later texts they gain the onomastic upper hand: the singular *saeptum* 'paddock' has become plural *Saepta*, and it means 'arcades'. Many of the products of Empire were on sale in these boutiques to those with plenty of money to spend.

> Eros has tears in his eyes as he gazes at mottled murrine cups, at boys, at higher grade citronwood. The poor fellow sighs from the bottom of his heart that he can't buy the whole *Saepta* and take the lot home; and so do others, though their eyes are dry. Most of them laugh at his tears — and secretly share them.
>
> Martial 10.80

Martial, like Ovid, is one of the more honest of poets; sometimes he is almost honest to himself. He could not afford a spending spree at the *Saepta* but these luxuries that 'Eros' covets were three of the very things that Martial wanted too. He would surely never own a murrine cup (p. 000); higher grade citronwood and really luscious slave boys were far beyond his means. But the two latter items recur again in a list of objects that he appraises in a richly furnished house, 'couches encrusted with first grade tortoiseshell, solid Maurusian citronwood of a weight rarely seen, silver and gold on a fancy tripod, and boys standing to attention whom I wouldn't mind being slave to' (Martial 12.66); and then again we read his clever sketch of Mamurra's enjoyable day at the *Saepta*. Could Martial himself have done this — or was he too well known to be able to get away with it? Mamurra 'paced all about the *Saepta*, where golden Rome sets out her riches. He inspected the soft slave boys: he ate them with his eyes. Not the ones they display in the shop fronts, but those upstairs in the special cages; those that ordinary people, my sort of people, never see'. He looked at the table-tops — the ones that were wrapped up; he looked at the ivory — off the top shelf; he looked at a tortoiseshell couch (*hexaclinon*), which he decided was too small for his citronwood table; he looked at the Corinthian bronzes, and

Figure 31   Cupid as jeweller. Detail of a wall painting from the 'House of the Vettii', Pompeii

Source   Photograph © Roger-Viollet, Paris

as a true connoisseur he tested them by the smell; he looked at statues, and decided they were not by Polyclitus after all; he looked at rock crystal vases, and was sure they were really just glass; he looked at murrine vases, and scratched them to test that they were genuine; he looked at emeralds, pearls, *sardonyches*, jaspers – but they were overpriced. And then he just bought a couple of cups, and carried them home *himself* (Martial 9.59).

8   The use of Empire

'Jewels, marble, ivory, Etruscan figurines, paintings, silver, clothes dyed with Gaetulian purple: some will never have them, and one or two don't even want them', wrote Horace (*Epistles* 2.2.180–182). Horace placed himself in the second category. Perhaps he was right that such people were rare.

> I was right not to raise my head above the parapet, Maecenas, glory of the *equites* ... I am better as the owner of what others despise, poor amidst great wealth, than if people said that I stacked away in my barns all the produce of the agile Apulian's plough. True, a stream of pure water and a wood of a few acres and the certainty of a harvest do not seem a more generous fortune than the brilliant command of fertile Africa. Calabrian bees bring me no honey, and Bacchus is not maturing in Laestrygonian jars for me, and I have no greasy fleeces fattening in Gallic pastures, but still I have no crying needs – and if I did want anything more, you would give it to me, wouldn't you? I will better stretch my small income by shrinking my ambition, than by trying to join the kingdom of Alyattes to the Mygdonian plains. Those who want things, lack things.
>
> Horace, *Odes* 3.16.18–39[1]

Modest as his requirements were, even Horace speaks sometimes of consuming the products of Empire: the Greek wine jars in which he bottled his own Sabine wine; the Falernian and Massic vintages that he enjoyed on occasion; the sensuous nard oil that he expected Vergil to bring to a party for which he himself would supply the wine; the attentive boys and the easily-distracted girls who – in his poetry – often wait upon him. Our purpose in this final chapter is to weigh how Romans used the wealth that Empire brought them.

The art of dining

It is in the arts of food and love – the arts of human interaction – that we shall finally appraise the value that Romans placed on the products of their Empire.

One could dine very cheaply in Rome and leave the Empire alone. Martial imagines such a lifestyle, though not for himself. 'From a bowl of ten olives more than five are left for next time; a single serving provides two dinners; you drink the thick dregs of red Veientan; hot chickpea soup costs an *as*, sex costs an *as*' (Martial 1.103). This food and wine is all Italian, like Horace's homely dinners of beans, cabbage and bacon, at which his guests could drink as much or as little wine as they wanted, mixed with as much water as they wanted, and the slaves could have what was left over (*Satires* 2.6.63–76, and see p. 223). Few other literary meals are so limited geographically. Even a simple picnic – as imagined by poets, Horace and Martial included – requires one or two exotica, whether these are Greek courtesans in Italy, Italian wines in Greece, perfumed oils redolent of the further East, or costly mountain ice.[2]

From the beginning of Roman literature to its end, no writer doubts that aromas are central to the pleasure of dining and entertainment; and if we care to ask *why* they are so central, we shall find few direct answers to such an unnecessary question. Plutarch, though, makes a speciality of asking and answering questions that his contemporaries thought obvious or silly: he is one of the few who bother to give a reason. Why do we add aromatics to wine? (why do we burn aromatic oil at dinner? he might have added); why do we spread the floor with aromatic foliage, bugloss, verbena, maidenhair fern? (and why do we spray theatres with saffron?) Plutarch's answer applies to all four questions, not only the two that he asked himself. It is to give a certain pleasurable feeling and enthusiasm to the guests – just as Helen did for Menelaus's guests (*Rules for Health* 132b).[3] Thus, with a single sweep of the pen, one of the world's great cultural relativists turns Helen of Troy from a slightly threatening expert on sleeping draughts to an aromatherapist and installs a Homeric pedigree for the Roman quest for spices and perfumes. We may add that medical writers ascribe very specific health-giving effects to individual perfumes: textbooks of perfumes, parallel to those on the 'properties of foods', once existed, though only a few fragments survive.[4]

Such effects were not looked for only in the dining room. Bedrooms, too, are more hospitable to 'pleasurable feelings and enthusiasm' if they are aromatic. We already know of the woman's bedroom imagined by Propertius, furnished in aromatic 'citronwood and Orician terebinth', *thyio thalamo aut Orycia terebintho* (3.7.49). For a more fully imagined scene we must look to Syriac literature: 'her bedroom is bright with light, and breathes the aroma of balsam and all spices, and gives out a sweet smell of myrrh and tejpat. Inside are myrtles strewn on the floor, and all kinds of scented flowers' (*Acts of Thomas* 6).

In poetry and literary prose, the importance of aromas in conviviality is such that picnics and parties may be described at which no item of food is mentioned – only the wine and the aromatics. If a dinner is narrated, aromatics are almost sure to appear in some way. Now these aromatics may be simple and home-grown, like the examples that Plutarch gave (above).

'Our feast shall not lack roses, vigorous celery, fleeting lilies' (Horace, *Odes* 1.36.15–16). 'What joy it is to light upon virgin springs and drink their waters', adds Lucretius. 'What joy to pluck new flowers and gather for my brow a glorious garland from fields whose blossoms were never yet wreathed by the Muses round any head' (1.927–930 = 4.2–5, translation by R. Latham). The virgin springs are there to be tasted, and the idea of tasting leads Lucretius at once to picnic, to conviviality. In that context virgin aromatic flowers, too, are wanted: this is Lucretius's chain of thought. As Propertius in turn makes clear (3.10), food, wine, aroma and love all work together to produce the effect of pleasure. Thus, in the far-off Golden Age, when life was simple, young men would bring to their girls baskets of fresh-fallen quinces, purple blackberries, violets that they had picked with their own hands, white lilies, grapes in bunches, and birds with bright plumage. To these gifts their girls responded with wanton embraces in the long grass, where lovers lay covered only by a deerskin and shaded by a low-boughed pine (3.13.25–46). Poetry, too, may be expected to emerge from scenes like these. 'Rose petals shall fall around my neck, wines that flowed from Falernian presses shall be poured out, our hair shall be three times anointed with the Cilician stamen, and the Muses shall stir the thoughts of reclining poets' (4.6.72–75).[5]

In the centuries of Empire the local aromas of Italy were still wanted. Martial sends a gift of roses, bought at market, and naturally supposes that his friend will wear them as a wreath.

> Were you born in the fields of Paestum or of Tibur? Did Tusculan country blush with your blossom? Did a manageress pick you in a Praenestine garden, or were you once the glory of rural Campania? My friend Sabinus will like you better as his wreath if he thinks that you came from my own Nomentan farm.
>
> Martial, 9.60

Horace advises myrtle: 'A myrtle wreath suits you as you serve, boy, and it suits me as I drink under my modest vine' (*Odes* 1.38.6–8). And this tells us that it was necessary for those who served to be perfumed and wreathed, no less than the reclining diners and drinkers.[6]

It is Horace again who reminds us – he is actually writing literary criticism, and using this familiar image as a metaphor – that the exotic perfumes can perfectly well be dispensed with altogether. 'If, at a good dinner, the musicians are off key and the aromatic oil is off and the honey served with the poppy seeds is Sardinian, we are annoyed, because we could have managed without these things' (*Art of Poetry* 375–377). The perfumed oil and the rest are optional: if they are not to be good, it would be better not to have them at all.

Optional they may be, but most convivial occasions – in literature – do seem to expect the exotic aromas as well as the flowers and wreaths. We recall Horace's demanding 'a little pot of nard' from Vergil as contribution to a party at which Horace supplies the wine (p. 196). 'Why shouldn't we boldly lie under a tall plane tree, or indeed this very pine, our grey hair wreathed with roses, our foreheads dabbed with Assyrian nard, and drink while we can? Let the wine-god drive away our nagging worries', he writes elsewhere, as if to reassert the beneficial influence of aromas – as well as wine – on luckless mortals.

> Come on, boys, who'll be the first to get spring water to cool off our cupfuls of this fiery Falernian? Who'll go and fetch from home that elusive whore, Lyde? Tell her to be quick, and bring her ivory lyre, and if her hair's a mess just do it up with a hairband *à la Laconienne*.
>
> *Odes* 2.11.13–24

And at the home-grown and cheerfully sensual *Floralia*, where wild aromatic plants and flowers contribute so much to the atmosphere, the celebrant's hair will still be redolent of exotic scents.

> I was going to ask why there should be greater wantonness and wilder games at Flora's festival; but then I realised that she is not a severe goddess and her gifts are aimed at pleasure. Foreheads are wholly girt with woven crowns, and the decorated table is covered with rose petals. A celebrant dances, drunkenly, his hair bound with linden fibre, and experiences the sensation of unlimited wine; another sings, drunkenly, at the unyielding threshold of his lovely girlfriend, and his hair, plastered with aromatic oil, is bound with soft garlands. Nothing serious is done when the brow is wreathed; those garlanded in flowers do not drink water; while your water, Achelous, was not yet mixed with the juice of the grape, there was no pleasure in wearing roses; Bacchus loves flowers, Bacchus loves the wreath, as you can tell from the stars of Ariadne.
>
> Ovid, *Fasti* 5.331–346

To return to the perfumed oils applied to the body and the hair, Pliny gives a desultory history of the changing fashions in these. He identifies rose as the single essence that was most often used, and we know of the towns in Italy whose speciality it was to supply roses to the Roman market. But Pliny makes it clear that people normally used compound perfumes, always incorporating scents from far beyond the Empire's frontiers. And we know that these are the costly scents that assert themselves when poets are being specific about perfumed oil: 'the scents of the phoenix's nest', balsam of Mecca, *amomum*, cinnamon, cassia, tejpat and nard. We might expect there to be differences between the sexes in the choice of aromas, but it is difficult to demonstrate them from the texts: possibly *amomum* was preferred by men; possibly cinnamon by women;[7] we hear of a seductive slave girl *cinnama flagrans et balsama rorans* 'fragrant with cinnamon and dewy with balm' (Apuleius, *Metamorphoses* 2.8). 'The highest praise of a perfume', Pliny concludes, 'is if a passing woman who is wearing it distracts men who are otherwise engaged. For this, people are prepared to pay more than 400 *denarii* a pound!' (13.20).

And now the food, *ab ovo usque ad mala* 'from the hard-boiled egg to the apples'. This, famously, was the way that Horace summarised the 'one thing after another' school of epic poetry (Horace, *Satires* 1.3.6–7): once more his allusive style of literary criticism assists us, for here he gives us the alpha and omega, the traditional first and last of the Roman menu.[8] How do the literary menus draw on the resources of Empire?

Among the several occasions for meals conjured up by the author of the *Daily Conversation in Greek and Latin* attributed to Pollux, one shows us a host entertaining a group of friends to an informal supper (80–84). Two aperitifs are offered, the wine-based spiced *conditum* or a concentrated grape juice, mixed with hot or cold water as each guest chooses. There is a small dish of boiled mallow. Mallow (*Malva spp.*) was a typical garnish, rather like lettuce leaves in perfunctory English catering; but you can eat mallow if you fancy, and here a slave is sent to see if there is any *piperatum* 'pepper sauce' (p. 195) to help it down.[9] Then two cold courses: foie gras, thrushes, lettuce and bread; a *salsum* (salt meat or fish), sardines, young broad beans eaten pod and all; then hot dishes, fowl *rapatum* with fish sauce, roast chicken, *offae*, *copadia*, roast sucking pig; alongside these a platter with endive, radishes, mint, green olives and new cheese, truffles, mushrooms.[10]

As with the restaurant scene from the related *Phrase Book* (p. 220) we may expect a meal outlined in a language lesson to be rather overstuffed. But the author is not making a literary point, for or against fine flavour, fresh farm food or Eastern spices: that is why we have taken it first. The setting is Rome and all the foods named might have come from Rome's neighbourhood, except perhaps salt fish. But their cooking demanded exotic flavourings in almost every case. Most lavish of all in its demands is *conditum*, the spiced wine aperitif that supplanted *mulsum* (p. 141) at some time perhaps in the second century. Apicius's is by no means the most highly spiced version: the manuscripts of Oribasius offer two recipes requiring several additional aromatics,[11] to which Byzantine sources add more.

A NEW CONDITUM. 15 lb honey are put in a bronze jar already containing 2 pints wine, so that you boil down the wine as you cook the honey. This to be heated over a slow fire of dry wood, stirring with a stick as it cooks: if it begins to boil over it is stopped with a splash of wine; in any case it will simmer down when the heat is taken away, and, when cooled, re-ignited. This must be repeated a second and a third time; then it is finally removed from the brazier and, on the following day, skimmed. Next 4 oz ready-ground pepper, 3 scruples mastic, 1 dram each tejpat leaf and saffron, 5 roasted date stones, and also the flesh of the dates previously softened in wine of the same type chosen above and of sufficient quantity to give a smooth purée. When all this is ready, pour on 18 pints smooth wine. If the finished product [is bitter], coal will correct it.

Apicius 1.1

We must consider the aperitif further. Wine was usually mixed with hot, recently boiled, water, a healthy additive. Some liked to add cold water instead, but fresh cold water could cause gastric ailments, for reasons we understand better than the Romans did. The emperor Nero's great invention was to boil the water, then to bottle it and chill it in snow. This produced more-or-less sterilised cold water to add to wine, a real contribution to human happiness. But it was an expensive process: it was only worth mixing the result with first-rate wines.[12] Most of those who liked cold wine there-fore continued to add fresh water to it. If they could afford snow, they simply added that. So Martial talks of a small cup of Falernian – it would be small, considering the cost of summer snow in Rome – with snow melting in from a *saccus nivarius* 'snow bag' suspended above.[13] Alternative systems were to put lumps of ice in your wine, or to put the snow in a *colum nivarium*, a kind of colander, and to pour the wine through it: Setine wine, another expensive one, is Martial's example this time. Snow was also some-times used as a garnish on food.[14]

Daring now to explore a dinner of the most lavish kind, we move briefly into the realm of history. What follows is real (or is reported as real: never trust documents). It is the menu of a dinner enjoyed by the college of *pontif-ices* 'priests' of Rome, a most august body, upon the inauguration of Lentulus as *Flamen Martialis* between 74 and 69 BC. About eleven priests were present, including Julius Caesar, who possibly presided as *rex sacrorum* 'king of the celebration', and his brother Lucius who as augur had conducted the formal ceremony. 'The dining room was furnished with ebony couches' (the first appearance of ebony in Rome: p. 194). The men reclined in two circles. Respectably forming a third circle were Lentulus's wife (a priestess) and his mother-in-law and four Vestal Virgins.

> For hors-d'oeuvres sea urchins, as many raw oysters as they wanted, palourdes, mussels, thrushes under a thatch of asparagus, a fattened chicken, a *patina* of oysters and palourdes, black piddocks, white piddocks. Then more mussels, clams, sea anemones, blackcaps, loin of roe deer and wild boar, fowls force-fed on wheatmeal, *Murex trunculus* and *Murex brandaris*. The dinner was udder, the split head of a wild boar, *patina* of fish, *patina* of udder, ducks, roast teal, hares, roast fowl, frumenty and Picentine loaves.
>
> Macrobius, *Saturnalia* 3.13.10[15]

This is an excellent demonstration both of Roman gastronomy and of

Caesar's tasteful generosity, if indeed he presented the meal. Yes, tasteful, even though the varied richness of the hors d'oeuvres is slightly staggering. Some of the shellfish must have been pickled, since not all were found near Rome, but otherwise everything in this list will have been fresh. Italy, by way of Rome's markets, had provided of her best. The contribution of the Empire and the wider world is passed over in silence, as is appropriate on a traditional, indeed archaic, Roman occasion. Unknowable to us, this contribution will certainly have been there – in incense and other aromas appropriate to sacrifice; in flavourings, especially pepper, no doubt present in practically all the dishes; and perhaps in wine. Caesar liked to vary the wines at his dinners, Pliny tells us:

> At his triumphal dinner as dictator, Caesar provided an amphora of Falernian and a jar of Chian to each circle ... but at the feast in his third consulship it was Falernian, Chian, Lesbian, Mamertine – the first time, apparently, that four kinds of wine were served at a dinner.
>
> Pliny 14.73

The alternation between Italian and Greek – *citra mare nata* and *transmarina*, 'born on this side of the sea' and 'overseas' – was classical;[16] and to Roman drinkers Greek wines, specially treated to withstand the long journey, had something of the sweetness and weight that sherry and port have for us. They were expensive, too.

> Greek wine used to be so prized that one would serve just one cup each at a dinner. On the wines that had primacy in his youth M. Varro writes: 'As a boy L. Lucullus never saw a fine banquet at his father's at which Greek wine was passed round more than once. Himself, on his return from Asia, he distributed more than a hundred thousand jars as gifts. C. Sentius, praetor in our own time, said Chian wine was never seen in his house until prescribed him by a doctor for his heart.'
>
> Pliny 14.95 – 97

Enough of fact. We needed these real dinners under our belts before taking on all too briefly the literary menus of Rome.[17] The little genre of menu-poems has a feature that is dangerously attractive to literary critics. Just as there is a world of allusion behind poetry, so there is a world of food to which the menus allude, and we scarcely know enough of the food to understand the allusions. 'If you are suffering from a sad bout of eating-at-home, Toranus', writes Martial to a perhaps fictional friend, 'you might as well come and be hungry with me'.

> If you like to take an appetiser, there's cheap Cappadocians and heavy leeks. A slice of tuna will be hiding under the halved eggs. Green cabbage, just picked from the cool garden, will be served on its black

dish, to be taken with oily fingers, with a sausage lying heavy on snowy porridge, and a pallid bean and pink bacon. If you want the rewards of the second tables, shrivelling grapes will be set before you, the pears that bear the name of the Syrians, and chestnuts, baked in slow steam, the creation of learned Naples. You will make the wine good by drinking it. If, after all this, Bacchus as usual stirs your hunger, noble olives will come to your aid, newly borne on Picene branches, and the boiling chickpea and the warm lupin. It's a meagre feast, who could deny? but you will tell no lies and hear none, and recline at peace with no forced smile.

There'll be no host reading to you out of a thick book, and no girls from naughty Gades, endlessly enticing, their sexy thighs shimmering in well-schooled motion; just clever little Condylus, playing something cheerful on his pipe. That's our dinner.

'You'll go in after Claudia: name the girl you want to go in before me', Martial (5.78)[18] concludes, incidentally showing us – as no other source happens to do – that Roman diners, like the more formal of British ones, ritually mixed themselves up before 'going in'. 'Cappadocians' are a kind of lettuce: we know this from Columella, but we would guess it anyway from the order of items. Lettuce always comes at the beginning: it helped the digestion if you took it early in the meal.[19]

Here we are on firm ground. There is nothing bad about Martial's menu, nor is there anything specially good about it except that he promises not to read his poetry. Nothing comes to market from further away than Picenum and Naples; the Syrian pears and Cappadocian lettuces are varieties transplanted to Italy, not fresh imports. In one way this is not the meal that Toranus or Martial would have had alone. It is fuller, more elaborate; it is a dinner for three friends got up out of everyday supplies, all the way to the cheap *fervens cicer et tepens lupinus*. At the end of a much more sparing meal we remember Martial's pricing of *cicer tepidum* at an *as* (p. 244); we recall, too, Horace's own meal at home, 'leeks, chickpeas and flatbread' with a few trimmings perhaps: there must have been something to keep three slave boys busy (p. 223). Beans or peas or chickpeas are the filler and at the same time the *pièce de résistance* of a really simple Roman meal. So a rabbi helpfully advised Jews who were the guests of gentiles: 'Pieces of bread are a great sign to guests. So long as the guests see the pieces they know that something more is coming after them; when they see a whole loaf and beans they know that nothing else comes after them' (*Tosephta Berakoth* 4.14). So beans and peas alternate with patisserie in the mind of Juvenal's 'secret glutton who sings the praise of beans, who loudly orders pea soup but whispers to the boy for *placenta*' (*Satires* 11.58–59): they are alternative endings to a meal.

The excuse for such an unexciting invitation as Martial's was that Toranus would eat even less excitingly at home. In a second poem Martial begins to

Figure 32   Bread found in an oven at Pompeii

Source   By permission of the Soprintendenza Archeologica per le Province di Napoli e Caserta

sketch a similar low-grade meal, with a similar diffident invitation – then feigns to realise that it is not good enough, and pretends he has just been describing the hors d'oeuvres. 'You'll dine nicely, Julius Cerealis, if you're my guest. Come if you have nothing better. Keep the eighth hour free. We'll bathe together: you know Stephanus's baths are next door.'

> First you'll get lettuce, good for moving the bowels, forced leek shoots, a young tunny bigger than any thin chub mackerel, garnished with egg and sprays of rue; more eggs, fried over a gentle flame; cheese smoked at a Velabran hearth; olives that have felt the frost of Picenum. So much for the appetisers – ah, does that phrase get you interested at last? If I go on lying you might come: fish, shellfish, udder, plump barnyard fowls and plump marsh birds, the kind of thing that even Stella rarely serves.

'I'll promise more: I won't recite to you', the modest poet finally assures his guest (Martial 11.52). Again, his marketing has demanded nothing from further away than Picenum. Not many years later, Pliny the Younger issued a literary invitation *after* the event, with a menu no more lavish in its attractions. 'PLINY GREETS SEPTICIUS CLARUS: You promise, but you don't turn up to dinner, I'm afraid! There will be a price to pay: you owe me an *as*, no less'.

> All ready were a lettuce each, three snails, two eggs, porridge, with *mulsum* and snow (and yes, you must count in the snow, right in the first line, because it melted away on the plate), olives, beetroot, gourds, *bulbi* and a thousand other things no less appreciated. You would have heard comic actors or a poetry reader or a lyrist, or, such is my generosity, all

three. But you chose to go to someone else's for oysters, sows' wombs, sea urchins, and girls from Gades.

'How much we should have played, laughed, learnt! You can get more elaborate food in plenty of other houses, but nowhere more cheerful, more simple, more carefree', Pliny says modestly (*Letters* 1.15.1 – 4). Pliny's is a true philosopher's dinner: we can all agree that Septicius Clarus has made the wrong choice. But look at the price demanded from the poor fellow, immortalised for ever as the one who didn't turn up; compare it with Martial's prices on page 244. How can Pliny claim to have spent so very little on his fresh but not exactly mouth-watering menu? There is only one answer: it is all supposed to come from his own farm, all but the snow with which the *mulsum* 'honeyed wine aperitif' is chilled. Everything that Septicius Clarus enjoyed at his alternative venue cost serious money, not least the dancing-girls (p. 107).

Martial had already laid claim, in one of his several poetic menus, to a fertile kitchen garden. 'Are you with me, Stella, Nepos, Canius, Cerealis, Flaccus? But there are only six of us, and *Seven makes the sigma*, so let's invite Lupus'.

> The farmer's wife has brought me queasy mallows and all the varied wealth of the garden, to wit antaphrodisiac lettuce, bareheaded leek, breathy mint and lubricious rocket. Chub mackerel, rue-flavoured, shall be topped with sliced eggs; there shall be a tunny udder dripping with brine: and those are the appetisers. Our modest dinner, served on a single table, shall be a kid stolen from the jaws of a beastly wolf, meat-balls (requiring no carver's knife), builders' beans and tender sprouts; to these I shall add a chicken and some ham left over from my last three dinners. When you are full I shall give you juicy apples, and wine out of a Nomentan flagon, without lees, at its best in Frontinus' second consulship.
>
> On top of these, jokes without bitterness, freedom that need cause no worry next day, and nothing you might wish unsaid: my guest will talk about the Greens and Blues, and our drinking will not get anyone into trouble.
>
> Martial 10.48[20]

Juvenal's *Satire* 11 launches into criticism of gourmets who spend vast sums of money on exotic food; and then takes the farm-fresh menu idea to its logical conclusion, inviting the reader to a properly Roman dinner with no single ingredient bought at market. His menu is quoted on p. 1, with its milk-fed kid, wild asparagus, preserved grapes, 'Signine pears and Syrian pears' and freshly picked apples.

These literary dinners aim to display the host's wealth (or poverty) and possession of (or failure to possess) a country farm. Their gastronomy is at a

Homeric level: home-grown food, not merely fresh but practically still alive, is what they boast of. It was to cater to such boasts that the special trade in spring lambs and kids existed. In a throwaway word or two, these dinners betray the fact that a real gastronomic tradition exists all the time in the background. 'Nomentan' wine gives us an easy benchmark: readers know it, and they know we are not overspending; anyway they know we have a cottage in Nomentum, by virtue of which, like Horace with Sabine, we are fully entitled to like Nomentan wine. Pears? along with Juvenal or Martial (above) let's drop in the names Signine and Syrian, catchwords as impressive and commonplace as 'William'[21] in France or 'Conference' in England. Olives? they will be Picene, picked at the beginning of winter not too far from Rome; yes, some say that Greek olives, if conserved in oil, are better than Italian, but more important is that young olives are better than old.[22] We really do notice the bittersweet aroma of rue (*Ruta graveolens*: who could fail to notice it?) so we'll mention that;[23] the bitter taste of lovage, equally strong and even more ubiquitous than rue in the Roman kitchen, is not so distinctive individually and no poet ever mentions that. Cheese is thoroughly Roman, since the best smoked cheese is smoked in Velabrum: we'll list that, or perhaps one of the mountain cheeses, a *meta* of Sassina. In fact the variety of cheeses available on Roman markets was astonishing, but good well-known respectable names, like Wensleydale or *Cantal*, do best in poetry.[24] One more thing: that dangerous moment at the beginning of the meal, when any Romans who are over-fed feel temporarily uncertain of their appetite, requires some dietary massaging. We'll show that we know the true nutritional qualities of our appetising vegetables, mallow (to be helped down, the reader will remember, with pepper sauce: p. 247), lettuce, mint and rocket. The last-named, an unassuming peppery salad leaf (*Eruca sativa*), is 'lubricious rocket' to Martial (above), a reminder that aphrodisiac qualities were assigned to numerous foods.[25] In his teasing letter to his absent guest Pliny claims to have served no fewer than three aphrodisiacs, snails, eggs and *bulbi*, the grape-hyacinth bulbs whose name is linked with Megara (p. 145). Why so many? Had it come to Pliny's ears that Septicius Clarus failed to satisfy the girls from Gades?

Roman gastronomic traditions were really extensive and highly detailed: the literary dinners give us small snippets, discreetly dropped in where wanted. It is precisely in this that they differ from the utterly disastrous dinner of Nasidienus (Horace, *Satires* 2.8), from the tiresome gastronomic lecture of Catius (Horace, *Satires* 2.4) and from the showy, but not especially good, dinner of Trimalchio (Petronius 26–78): at those equally fictional events, gastronomy obtruded, spoiling the food and spoiling the fun.

We agree with Statius (p. 267) that it does not matter 'how the Phasian bird differs from the crane of wintry Rhodope, what sort of goose has the largest liver, why a Tuscan boar is tastier than an Umbrian'. It will be a 'female white goose, fattened on juicy figs', by the way. It does not matter if hares' forelegs are the best portion (Horace, *Satires* 2.8.88–93) since hares are

Figure 33   Fragment of a Roman fresco with peacock
Source   By permission of the J. Paul Getty Museum, Malibu, California

rare and luxurious food anyway. Peacocks were costly enough[26] – Pliny (10.45) could name the first Roman who killed a peacock for food and the first who force-fed peacocks – without the fancy for eating peacocks' brains (Suetonius, *Vitellius* 13.2). It does not matter whether one presents a specially large *mullus* (red mullet, *Mullus spp.*), fashionable and ridiculously expensive as the large ones were: it will only have to be cut into portions at table (Horace, *Satires* 2.2.33–34).[27] Do one's guests need to know that a *murena* (lamprey, *Petromyzon marinus*), a dangerous delicacy from Roman fish farms,[28] has been 'caught when pregnant: after spawning the flesh is inferior'? Still, 'Nasidienus' is right to take care over the sauce:

> This is my sauce for lamprey: Venafran oil of the first pressing, Spanish fish sauce, five year old Italian wine to be added during the cooking (if adding after, Chian will serve better than any other), white pepper, and vinegar from the vineyards of Methymna. My own innovation is to add green rocket and bitter elecampane [*Inula helenium*].
>
> Horace, *Satires* 2.8.43–53

Horace's satire is usually accurate: we can be sure that Nasidienus's sauce works with lamprey, and that some first century BC gastronomes had been as precise as he is about the selection of ingredients.

Discreetly or not, food and wine and aroma displayed the wealth of

Empire. So did the festive setting, 'the tables splendid with citronwood and ivory, the couches covered with golden drapes. The ample cups were of different workmanship, but all of equal costliness: you might drink from engraved glass, carved rock crystal, brilliant silver and gold, amber wonderfully sculpted, or marble' (Apuleius, *Metamorphoses* 2.19). The ears were meanwhile amused or deadened – in certain houses – by chamber music, the continual piping, humming or singing of attendant slaves and of others in the background whose sole task this was, *symphoniaci pueri*.[29] This was not something new: it was a fashion inherited by Romans from Etruria. 'It is one of their luxuries, Alcimus tells us, that the Etruscans do their bread-making and their boxing and their whipping all to the music of the flute' (Athenaeus 518b). One hopes the background music ceased when actors or poetry readers were called on to perform. As in classical Greece, after dinner could turn into a literary occasion, whether in a self-consciously literary coterie like that of the future emperor Tiberius when he was on campaign in Asia (Horace, *Epistles* 1.3) or simply because that was the best time to read some kinds of poetry. 'I don't write for the hungry: the wise move is to eat and drink and then read my stuff. Wiser still, go to sleep and take it to be a dream' (Ausonius, *Bissula* 13–16).[30]

Diners reclined – the cup of wine to their right, the perfumed oil ready to their right hand to be applied to their own brow or to a favoured attendant's.[31] Privileged guests might come attended by 'shadows', lucky clients of a powerful patron: the host's own clients helped to make up numbers. Like the *parasitoi* of Greek comedy, the *clientes* of Rome are easy to mock. Their reward for assiduity and luck is dinner, which does them little good, after all. 'How much they eat and drink that they didn't want! How much they say that they shouldn't!' After a long evening of polite backbiting they finally leave, tired and emotional, picking the menu to pieces, grumbling that the host is a skinflint or a spendthrift; 'the alleys fill up with them, vomiting, fighting around the knocking-shops'. By dawn they are in bed and ready to call for a doctor (Lucian, *Nigrinus* 22).

Whoever invited them all, it was still the host's duty to place the diners,[32] perhaps bringing together 'those who like wine, those who like sex – not only who *suffer the goad of love for boys* as Sophocles puts it, but also those who itch for women and for girls: burnt by the same fire they will cling closer to one another ... unless, by Zeus, it is actually the *same* boy or the *same* girl that they fancy' (Plutarch, *Symposium Questions* 1.2). At a big dinner, a host might well serve the best food and wine only to the table at which he entertained his favoured guests.[33] 'When I'm invited to a meal, now that I'm no longer on the payroll, why don't I get the same meal as you? You swallow fat oysters from the Lucrine lake, I suck at a mussel and cut my lip. You have champignons, I swallow pig-mushrooms. You square up to turbot, I face a gilthead. A fat-arsed golden turtle-dove fills you up, I'm served a magpie that died in a coop' (Martial 3.60). Horace envisages a more intimate and a more equal occasion, one at which nine (later it might be seven) diners reclined around a single table.

> If you don't mind lying on Archias's couches, if you aren't afraid of a meatless dinner served in dishes of modest circumference, then I expect you as my guest, Torquatus, at home, at sunset. You'll drink wine that was drawn off in Taurus's second, between marshy Minturnae and Petrinum-under-Sinuessa; at least, you will unless you have a better one, in which case send it over. The hearth is already gleaming, the furniture is ready dusted for you ... I am the best man to ensure – and I will – that no stained cover and no dirty napkin is going to wrinkle your nose; that you can see your face in every cup and every plate; that no one will repeat, outside, what is said among trusted friends; that neighbour is well matched to neighbour. I shall get Butra for you, and Septicius; Sabinus as well, unless a prior engagement or a better girl prevents him. There's room for some 'shadows', but it is a very small dining room: smelly goats not wanted. Write me back how many you're bringing ...
>
> Horace, *Epistles* 1.5[34]

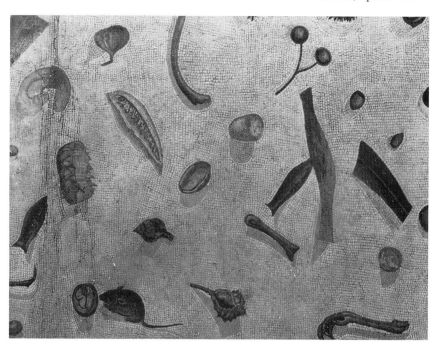

Figure 34   On a floor strewn with the remains of a dinner, a mouse investigates a walnut. Detail from a *trompe l'oeil* mosaic from Roman Italy, now in the Vatican Museum

Source   By permission of the Monumenti Musei e Gallerie Pontificie, Archivio Fotografico, Vatican City

Figure 35   Fresh grapes, apples, apricots, pomegranates, pears; and the stemmed glass bowl is a real luxury. To the right, an amphora suggests wine, and a lidded pot overflows with conserved fruit. Detail of wall painting from Pompeii

Source   By permission of the Soprintendenza Archeologica per le Province di Napoli e Caserta

The art of courtship

'No Roman thinks it wrong to take his wife to a dinner party' according to the biographer Cornelius Nepos (*Lives* preface), a risky generalisation, as we learn from a scene of gritty realism in Petronius's *Satyricon* (67): the noisy public argument between Trimalchio and his loving wife Fortunata as to whether she will join Trimalchio's guests at dinner, rather than supervising the kitchen as she wants to do. Still, at dinner among the more cultured Romans, men and women mingled; and in a society in which wealth and patronage outweighed most other values, such gatherings gave opportunities for courtship and seduction.

Very few women were, legally, free to dispose of themselves; but a *tutor* (a legal guardian, a husband, a father, a man who keeps a lover) might be angling for favours from a patron, or might be in debt to a businessman. Such a man could find it convenient not to notice his honoured guest's advances to a wife or daughter. Horace confirms, with characteristic bluntness, that this is one reason for the perceived increase in adultery in Roman families at the beginning of the Empire.

When a girl grows up, what does she most like to do? she learns Ionic dances, she studies the Arts, and all of her to her tender fingertips dreams of forbidden love. Soon, at her husband's drinking parties, that girl will be ready for younger men. Not that she will be choosing a secret lover, while the lights are out, to share her stolen pleasures; she'll be called for openly, and off she'll go upstairs, under her husband's eyes: it may be a shopkeeper, it may be a Spanish ship's captain whose prosperity buys her disgrace.

Horace, Odes 3.6.21–32

He takes the family viewpoint here: he is against adultery. Tibullus and Ovid give us the opposing point of view. They explain with care how to pursue a secret love affair at a dinner party under the eyes of a woman's *tutor*. Neither shopkeepers nor ships' captains, they were simply of higher status than men against whom they played – or imagined playing – this power game.[35]

Elsewhere Horace's attitude towards secret love affairs is more avuncular. 'Now is the time to be off to the *Campus*, the city squares, and your assignation; now for the soft whispers after dark, the quiet laugh that tells you she is waiting, hidden, in a cosy corner, the token that she will snatch from your arm or your unruly finger' (*Odes* 1.9: see also p. 39). The seizing of a token is not the least threatening move in this game; as in the classic comedies, it may reappear one day in the company of a love-child. The Campus Martius, the shady portici there, the Games, the theatre, the temples (especially the Temple of Isis) and later the mixed baths: all these are places to meet and flirt. Temples were a location with Greek antecedents, since religious processions and temple worship were among the few occasions at which the secluded damsels of Greece, real and fictional, could be seen and fallen in love with.[36] We hear of the nocturnal meetings, too: of young men throwing pebbles at the shutters of a girl's bedroom, or less secretly of a mother playing the go-between; of a girl thrown out of doors naked because her man came home unexpectedly and caught her with an adulterer (Rufinus 14 Page [*Anthologia Palatina* 5.41]); of a girl tiptoeing to her lover, stepping across a sleeping watchman; of Cynthia climbing out over her windowsill into Propertius's arms.[37]

What is a man's profile of the woman who is open to courtship? Horace, above, is not alone in fingering the Arts as an influence on her. Propertius (p. 123) agrees, with his mention of the modern poetry in Greek that inflames girls. He's in favour of it: he himself will write the kind of book that can be always lying on a stool, always being picked up and read as a girl lies alone, waiting for her lover (3.3.18–20). To turn to history for a moment, Sallust, in exploring the social background of Catiline's conspiracy, talks of women like Sulpicia who knew Greek and Latin literature, who were better at singing and dancing than a respectable woman had any need to be; of women who had made money in their youth by prostitution, but later could not keep up their income and ran into debt. They were easy prey for Catiline; their husbands could be persuaded to join as well, and they would be good at stirring up the urban slaves (Sallust, *Catiline* 24–25).

Women's freedom of choice is the other reason for the apparent prevalence of adultery. This freedom is a hard thing for male poets and philosophers to deal with. It is dangerous to moralists, promising to libertines. It is Romulus's fault – the so-called 'rape of the Sabines' was a mass elopement, a bad example to set – but it is also the fault of sensual Greek-inspired poems and paintings (Propertius 2.6). Ironically, it was by contrast with Greek cities, such as Athens, that Romans could correctly estimate the greater degree of freedom that Roman citizen women possessed. Some were ready to take what some men regarded as the male role in courtship, to make the advances, to make the running. The sex manual of Philaenis could be imagined as a source of practical sexual information for a Roman woman (*Priapeia* 63.17). Hurry up and live, girls (advises a *Menippean Satire* of Varro: 87 Bücheler), while youth still allows you to play, eat, love and steer the chariot of Venus! We hear in literature of women who played the active role even more fully, practising athletics and wrestling, cutting their hair so as to be free to travel. Prejudice aside, an 'Atalanta' might be just the right kind of partner for a really virile man, *vir viracius* (Varro, *Menippean Satires* 225 Bücheler).[38]

At the other end of the spectrum of freedom, more than one poet agonises over what must really have been a dilemma for some: is it right to fall in love with a slave girl? Horace drily mocks men who do, teasing a lovelorn friend, offering the mythological support of Achilles, who was captivated by the *serva Briseis*, Telamonian Ajax, who was attracted to *captiva Tecmessa*, Agamemnon, who led in triumph his *virgo rapta* Cassandra – three nobly born prisoners of the Trojan War. He kindly suggests that a modern *Phyllis* will equally turn out to have noble barbarian parents, a credit to any son-in-law – and concludes with frank appraisal of her 'arms, her face, and her gently rounded calves' (Horace, *Odes* 2.4), because, in Horace's poetry, slave girls were for sex, and that was a simpler matter. 'If you're feeling stiff, and there's a slave-girl or a houseboy at hand, available for screwing, what do you do? Hold back?' (*Satires* 1.2.116–118). Others betray a more complex view than Horace will approve – but sex remains paramount. So we hear of *Lycinna*, a slave girl in Propertius's family presumably, who first taught him about sex; *heu nullis capta Lycinna datis* 'I gave her no presents but Lycinna was all mine', says the poet with a sigh (3.15.6). We read of Fotis, described by the hero of Apuleius's *Metamorphoses* as *forma scitula, moribus ludicra et prorsus argutula* 'pretty, playful and very sharp' – his host's slave girl with whom he spends a torrid night (2.6–7).

A slave and a free woman are appraised in different words: for the slave it will be the comfortable diminutives and the non-literary *scita, scitula* 'pretty' of Plautus and Apuleius. She is *lepida, dicacula* 'amusing, a good talker' and her hands are *floridae, roseae* 'flowery, rose-pink'.[39] Horace will have her *candida, recta, munda* …, 'fair-skinned, well-proportioned, nicely presented but not so as to pretend to be taller and whiter than nature made her' (*Satires* 1.2.123–124),[40] and he cites the free-thinking philosopher Philodemus in his support – a ploy less usual in a verse argument than in a prose one. The poem that Horace means is no longer known – surely not the epigram quoted on p. 24 – but Rufinus probably agrees with it:

> I prefer a slave girl to the great ladies: illicit fun is no better when it's expensive. *They* smell of myrrh, and they sniff, and they have servants there in the bedroom. A slave is just herself, her own scent and her own charm; her bed is just her bed, always ready and it doesn't ask for a tip!
>
> Rufinus 5 Page [*Anthologia Palatina* 5.18]

Beside the spectrum of freedom there is also a spectrum of profitability. Somewhere on it comes the woman who is called *amica* 'girlfriend' by her lover but *meretrix* 'tart' by his father (Horace, *Satires* 1.4.49). We shall survey this spectrum with Martial's help.

> You're a man of iron, Flaccus, if your cock can stand when your girl asks you for half a pint of fish sauce or a couple of bits of tuna or a small mackerel, and isn't sure if she's worth a whole bunch of grapes, and if her maid proudly brings her some *allec* on a red earthenware saucer she eats it up quick, or when she's wiped her brow and got over her diffidence she might dare to ask for five fleeces to make herself a little cloak. I want my girl to demand a pound of tejpat perfume, or a few emeralds with sardonyxes to match, and to insist on the best silk bought in the Vicus Tuscus, or ask for a hundred little *aurei* as if they were coppers. Do you think I'm going to give them to her? I'm not. But that's what I want her to think she's worth.
>
> Martial 11.27

In Roman poetry there are women who expect, for their friendship, costly gifts from all of the Empire and beyond. To be such a woman's lover may be a status symbol, but she will consume one's inheritance, transmuting it into Babylonian brocades, Greek embroidery from Elis or Ceos, gay slippers from Sicyon, emeralds set in gold, Tyrian drapes that will soon show the wear and the stain of lovemaking, drinking parties, entertainments, perfumes and garlands (Lucretius 4.1123–1133). There are also said to be women who demand too little.[41]

> The fair Phyllis gave herself to me for a whole night, wide open, nothing barred, and in the morning I was wondering what present to give her: a pound of Cosmus's perfumed oil, or of Niceros's, or a bale of Spanish fleeces, or ten of the yellow ones with Caesar's head on – when Phyllis put her arms around my neck and gave me a kiss as long as a doves' wedding and said 'Can I have a bottle of wine?'
>
> Martial 12.65

There are women who will state a price for sex but will give good measure, enthusiasts who will take two or three men at once – like Cleopatra, famous in Roman propaganda for her sexual avidity, imagined by Propertius lying between two of her slaves, being screwed (*trita*) by both.[42] 'I want the girl who's easy, who floats around in a shift; I want the girl who let my boy have her on the way here, I want the girl who will let me have it both ways for a second *denarius*, I want the girl who can manage three men at once. The one who demands a fortune and uses long words I'll leave to the prick from fat Bordeaux' (Martial 9.32). There are even said to be women who might not want a present at all.[43]

There are women who work in brothels; slaves, mostly, though they might earn enough to buy their freedom.[44] There are women who work in dark alleys or in tombs (p. 31). All these will show openly what they have to offer; even with the more expensive of them, 'there's nothing in the way. In her Coan silk you can see her as well as if she were naked: nothing wrong with that thigh, not a bad leg; backside just right for size' (Horace, *Satires* 1.2.101–103).

Well placed on the spectrum of profitability are the women who know how to get what they want, such as the one imagined by Philodemus:

> Hullo.
> Hullo to you.
> What's your name?
> What's yours?
> Don't be so forward.
> Don't you, then.
> Do you have a date?
> If anyone wants me.
> Have dinner with me tonight?
> If you like.
> Right. How much do you want?
> There's no deposit.
> Strange thing to say.
> You can decide how much to give me when we wake up.
> Fair enough. I'll send my boy for you. Where will you be?
> I can't say.
> When will you come, then?
> When you want me.
> I want you now.
> Lead the way.
>
> Philodemus 4 [*Anthologia Palatina* 5.46]

There is also a spectrum of beauty – of attractiveness to men, of conformity with the male ideal of a beautiful woman. When a writer talks of a woman *toto iactans e corpore amorem* 'whose whole body expresses love' what fantasy picture does he see? Since it is Lucretius (4.1054) who supplies this text, it is fair to add that appreciation of beauty is not necessarily lustfulness. Rabban Gamaliel, Paul's Jewish teacher, as he walked on the Temple Mount at Jerusalem, once caught sight of an attractive woman – not that it was his practice to look at women, but the path was narrow and he could not help himself. 'Blessed is He who has such handsome creatures in his world,' said Gamaliel – not that he was enthralled by her beauty, for it was his practice when he saw a fine donkey, camel or horse to utter the same blessing (*Tosephta, Avodah Zarah* 3.10).[45]

The attractive woman is likely to be fair-skinned, *candida*. A *candida puella* is to be shared by Catullus and Varus. Horace's 'Glycera' is of a purer colour – that is, a purer white – than Parian marble. The prejudice was so widely shared that some used euphemisms in describing a dark woman: 'if she is blacker than Illyrian pitch they call her tawny [*fusca*]' (Ovid, *Art of Love* 2.657–8); very often Greek euphemisms, as Lucretius makes clear (p. 124). The girl that wants Martial, so he teases 'Procillus', is 'fairer than a well-washed swan, than silver, than snow, than a lily, than privet': this last simile is out of Ovid, from Polyphemus's praises of Galatea. Martial, bluntly and unconventionally, is – he says – in love with a girl 'blacker than night, than an ant, than pitch, than a jackdaw, than a cicada' (1.115).[46] Philodemus, seldom conventional, asserts a similar choice: 'Philaenion is little and dark, but curlier than celery, with skin softer than down, and a voice more enchanting than Aphrodite's girdle, and she'll do anything and sometimes doesn't charge. I want to go on being Philaenion's lover, O golden Aphrodite – until I find one even better' (8 [*Anthologia Palatina* 5.121]).

Horace's 'Pyrrha' has *flava coma* 'flaxen hair' (*Odes* 1.5.4) and so does a cheap prostitute – from Germany, Scythia or Gaul – in a satire of Juvenal (p. 31). But they are not praised for it. Blonde hair was evidently important to the Roman women who bought German hair. When young they affected fair hair; when white-haired with age, they wanted it black (Tertullian, *On Women's Dress* 2.6–7). By male poets, no distinguishable significance is attached to hair colour. Yet Apuleius, Horace and Martial (p. 263) care about hair.[47] In Apuleius's imagination, before lovemaking a woman 'releases her hair into joyful abandon, like the picture of Venus rising from the waves' and, as if increasing the resemblance, she covers her sex with her hand (Apuleius, *Metamorphoses* 2.16).

There is approval of a face *nimium lubricus aspici* 'so sexy I daren't look' (Horace, *Odes* 1.19), of a tongue whose touch is like nectar in a kiss with open lips (Apuleius, *Metamorphoses* 2.10), and of eyes *fulgentes* 'smouldering' (Horace, *Odes* 2.12) or alternatively half-closed, moist, tremulous, languid with desire (Apuleius, *Metamorphoses* 3.14); of soft flesh – *mollior et cycni plumis et lacte coacto* 'softer than swansdown, softer than clotted cream' in the rustic similes of Polyphemus (Ovid, *Metamorphoses* 13.796). An attractive woman's arms are *candentes, teneri* 'shining white, tender'; her back *eburnea*, 'ivory-white'; even her shoulders stunningly white, for, unlike a man's shoul-

ders, they will seldom see the sun. Her tender skin is easily marked: it may
well show love-bites, or bruises inflicted by a violent lover or a jealous
master. Her breasts are firm, well-disciplined, even when *gymna peridromados*
'free of their breastband'; they are not over-large, 'so that there is just
enough for my hand to hold and to hide'; the nipples and areolae are dark-
coloured, so Horace suggests.[48] Her legs are youthful, straight,
well-proportioned;[49] her hips shapely – from Ovid's *quantum et quale latus*
we learn that quality mattered as much as quantity – earning her the Greek
epithet *euiskhios* 'fine-hipped'; her bottom *automate saleuomene* 'standing out
determinedly' yet tremulous.[50] Her tummy is *planus* 'flat' and smooth. Her
mons Veneris may be *glabellum* 'hairless' (but depilation is not for old
women, says Martial); her sex is *hyaloi isos, hygrometopos* 'glassy, moist'.[51] And
her vagina will differ totally from Martial's description:[52]

> Lydia is as baggy ... as the wide-meshed nets they catch wild thrushes
> with, or the awnings of Pompey's theatre when the South Wind doesn't
> catch them, or a bracelet that fell off a sick queer's wrist, or a mattress
> divorced from its Leuconian stuffing, or a poor Briton's second best
> trousers, or the wrinkled throat of a Ravenna pelican. They say I fucked
> her in a sea-water pool. I thought I was fucking the pool.
>
> Martial 11.21

It will not reduce the ideal female's attraction if her dress is loose, loose
enough to reveal her breasts when she reclines at a dinner (Tibullus 1.6.18).
That is a less trivial point than it seems: the lascivious Omphale, treating
Hercules as one of her maids, makes him, too, dress in loose clothing (*Elegies
for Maecenas* 1.69–86). As to aromas, 'Lucius' in the *Metamorphoses* will talk
of a lover's *inhalatus cinnameus*, 'cinnamon breath' (2.10), and Martial,
mourning a little slave girl, will recall her as 'choicer than Erythraean pearls,
the polished tusk of the Indian herd, the first snows, an untouched lily; her
hair nicer than the wool of a Baetic flock, than the bunches from the Rhine,
than a golden dormouse; her mouth fragrant as a rose-garden of Paestum, as
the first honey of Attic combs, as a tear of amber warm from the hand ...'
(Martial 5.37).

How do these measures of ideal attraction apply to boys? The poets' ideal
will have 'softer skin than any silly woman' (Horace, *Epodes* 11.24) and will
rival women in his lack of body hair. He will have *khrotos eupnoios* 'aromatic
skin' whose colour – this seems the first essential – will be *marmorea, niveus,
nive candidior* 'like marble, snowy, whiter than snow' or even *tes lygdou
leioteron* 'smoother than Parian *lygdos*' which was very white as well as
smooth. *Lygdus*, as a slave boy's name, reasserts this quality. His face, in
particular, will be *candidus* 'white', his forehead not too high, his cheeks like
the down on quinces, blushing with modesty, his lips as red as Paestan roses,
attracting the lover to exchange sips of wine with him. His hair will be long
and (says Martial) straight.[53] A boy might curl his hair and end up looking

like a *Maura puella* 'Moorish girl'; the god Priapus, like Martial, would disapprove (*Priapeia* 45). His buttocks will feel warm by comparison with a woman's (Strato [*Anthologia Palatina* 12.7]). We will leave Martial, once more, to describe the aroma of his breath.

> The faint smell of balm given off by scent-jars that were emptied yesterday, the smell of the last breath that wafts from the saffron spray, the smell of apples ripening in the winter chest, the smell of a field luxuriant with spring trees, the smell of silk from the Palace presses of the Empress, the smell of amber warmed in a virgin's hand, the smell (but only from afar) of a broken jar of dark Falernian, the smell of a garden that attracts the Sicanian bees, the smell of Cosmus's flasks and the hearths of the gods, the smell of a garland just fallen from hair rich in unguent: why list them all? They are not enough. Mix them, then, and that is the sweet smell of my boy's morning kisses.
>
> Martial 11.8.1–12[54]

Boys should not be masturbated, says Martial, a keen pederast to judge from his poems, as this matures them too quickly; their sweat begins to smell, their body hair and beard to grow, and it's no longer fun to look at them. They soon decline in any case. Their skin reddens with wind and dust, their hair coarsens and they begin to take an interest in girls; a real enthusiast could fantasise about the girl lucky enough to be the one who makes such a boy into a man.[55]

We must ask, too, what makes a man attractive to women. Sulpicia had wanted her lover to come to her, she writes: 'importuned by my *Camenae*, the goddess of Cythera has brought him to my lap'. Now that he is there, she wants her love to be broadcast to all, 'and anyone who says she has not known pleasure may tell the story of mine'. How does she want him to be?

Sulpicia demands that 'Cerinthus' be as bold and as intense as she herself. 'I will not write anything in sealed tablets for none but my man to read: I enjoy having been bad, and I don't care to pretend to be good. They will say that I am no better or worse than he is' (Sulpicia 1 [Tibullus 3.13]). Her 'goodness', as I translate it, is Latin *fama*, a woman's reputation among men – a matter of great importance to Roman men, but not to Sulpicia. In a later poem she seems to mock her man for caring about the risks he ran by an affair with a citizen's daughter, but the poem is difficult: the *toga* may be the whore's not Cerinthus's. Her pride, not his, was at stake: 'Look out for your *toga*, then: take a wool-working slave as your whore, and never mind Sulpicia daughter of Servius. Those who care for me care most of all that I am not supplanted by a love you will not speak of' (Sulpicia 4 [Tibullus 3.16]). Most painful was the knowledge that his love for her did not match the intensity of her own feelings. The one regret that she admits to in her few remarkable poems is that 'yesterday I let you spend the night alone – I was trying to pretend I was not on fire' (Sulpicia 6 [Tibullus 3.18]). Thank goodness for Sulpicia, because without her it would be impossible to write, from Roman literature, of the qualities that women looked for in men: needless to say, men's views on the subject are unhelpful.

The Empire did not create all these stereotypes. On the contrary, it subverted them. Just occasionally, we can see the result in literature. The girls of Italy match the stereotypes, but *habet quiddam helcysticon provincialis formonsula uxor*, 'a lovely young married woman from the provinces has something *attrayant* about her' (Varro, *Menippean Satires* 176 Bücheler). 'You see a tender girl of stunning whiteness; you see a brown one; you fancy both. You see a girl with a Grecian look, you see a Roman; both are equally fascinating' (Propertius 2.25.41–44). The boy who attracts a man's love will be unusual indeed, if, as Martial once demands, he is 'whiter than snow' yet 'from the banks of the Nile'; but that is his origin, in Martial's fantasy, because Egypt produces more wickedness than any other province and Martial wants him wicked (4.42). Egypt gave birth to the seductive and decadent Cleopatra, we remember. Ovid imagines Ariadne outraged by Bacchus's preference for one of the young and beautiful Indian girls that he had brought home as captives from his fabled Indian expedition. The Cretan Ariadne, who describes herself as *fusca* 'brown-skinned', thus finds herself supplanted, shockingly, by one who is not paler than herself but darker, of the colour one would wish on one's enemies (*Fasti* 3.493–4). Can one fancy a *lupa barbara picta mitra* 'barbarian slut in a coloured headscarf'? wonders Juvenal (3.66). She is certainly Greek or Eastern, in Juvenal's image, because of the Greek words surrounding her. Some could fancy her, as Juvenal knew well: Propertius, in a mood of rejection, will look for a Syrian woman 'who walks the *Sacra via* in muddy shoes, and doesn't mind you approaching her.... I'll take the girls that the Euphrates and the Orontes send me' (3.23.15–22). What of the *flava lupa*, 'flaxen-haired slut' who emerges from a tomb beside the Appian Way in another allusion by Juvenal (p. 31)? A prostitute working in a tomb is unlikely to be able to afford a German hairpiece. She herself, then, is Gaulish, German or Scythian, from the northern edge of the Empire, and she finds customers.

Already in the second century BC Rome was enhancing her sexual repertoire. 'A compulsion to impiety will overtake them', say the *Sibylline Oracles* (3.184–186). 'Male will have intercourse with male. They will set up boys in brothels'. As to the origin of these practices, some might attribute them to Rome's Etruscan heritage. To observant Greek eyes the Etruscans had been very odd in their sexual behaviour at dinner parties,[56] even odder than the Greeks themselves. But Paul considers it a consequence of the failure to honour God that Roman women 'have exchanged natural for unnatural intercourse, and their men, abandoning natural intercourse with women, are burnt by desire for one another, misuse one another, and pay the penalty for perversion in their own bodies' (*Romans* 1.26–27).[57] Martial, by contrast, accuses an unnamed 'circumcised poet' from Jerusalem of the same practice, as if it were typically Eastern (11.94). Sallust had considered it a result of the luxury that emerged out of Rome's Eastern conquests that 'men were violated like women, and women offered their bodies to all' (*Catiline* 13).

Variety was not all. The quality of Roman sexual experience was adjusted by new aphrodisiacs. The old standby, the 'Megarian bulbs' of Cato, Varro and Columella (p. 145), was rivalled by *satyrion* or *satureum* 'salep', the root of *Orchis mas*, gathered then and now on the slopes of the Mysian mount Olympus.[58] It is 'sweetish to the taste; the larger of the pair of tubers, taken in drinks, increases libido, the smaller represses and forestalls it. They are also eaten baked, like *bulbi*' (Galen, *Properties of Simples* 8.15.17). Their wealth even enabled Romans to follow the well known precept concerning the conception of beautiful children in a new way. 'In earlier times wealthy Romans used to have images of beautiful men and women before them, in a signet ring, when they had intercourse. Now they bring Israelite slaves and tie them to the foot of the bed' (*Talmud Babli, Gittin* 58a).[59]

The art of being Roman

We may allow as a symbol of the final confusion, in which the sexual pleasures and the gastronomic pleasures of Empire are at last all one, that the failed Caesar, Aelius Verus, was said by a highly unreliable source to have had 'the erotic books of Ovid, or, as others said, of Apicius, always at his bedside' (*Historia Augusta, Aelius* 5.9).

Romans love to catalogue the manifold luxuries that Empire brought, even as they castigate themselves or others for wanting them. In the surviving sections of the *Satyricon* Petronius gives us, not only the lavishly tasteless dinner of Trimalchio (26–78), often cited above, but also a modest little poem of his own on exotic luxuries. Romans love the taste of pheasants from Colchis and guinea-fowl from Africa, because they are hard to get: white goose and colourful duck have an all too common flavour.

> We want the *scarus*, transplanted from distant shores; we want fish from the Syrtes that cost a shipwreck to bring to Rome: we're tired of grey mullet. We fancy a mistress, not a wife. Roses are out: we want cinnamon. What's best is what has to be hunted for
>
> Petronius 93

At his dinner 'Trimalchio' is made to quote Publilius Syrus, a Syrian slave and Latin poet of the first century BC. 'Our warlike walls are lapped up by luxury', Publilius had written with possibly Aramaic alliteration, and Trimalchio loves every word of it (Petronius 55). The plumed peacock in his Babylonian brocade, the guinea-fowl and castrated capon, *margarita* 'pearl', *baca Indica* 'Indian berry' or pepper, green emerald, the yellow fire of Numidian marble, and the flimsy wild silks in which supposedly respectable women display their bodies: all these come in for Publilius's scorn, along with the *ciconia* (white stork, *Ciconia ciconia*), an exotic bird from Greece or

Illyria that was briefly and undeservedly fashionable enough to be farmed in Italy.[60] A less complicated thinker than most of his fellow poets, Statius happily castigates silly gastronomic distinctions – this was advisable since Horace had memorably shown how silly they were – while leaving himself free to express awed admiration of a patron's connoisseurship of a different category of luxury imports, Greek antiques. 'I am sorry for those who like to know how the Phasian bird differs from the crane of wintry Rhodope, what sort of goose has the largest liver, why a Tuscan boar is tastier than an Umbrian, and what seaweed makes the most comfortable bed for slippery shellfish ...', this being a complicated way of repeating exactly what Horace had said about shellfish (*Satires* 2.4.30: p. 53). There was none of this food talk when he was at dinner with Vindex, Statius continues.

> I learnt of a thousand beauties of bronze and antique ivory.... Who ever rivalled the keen glance of Vindex in recognizing the hand of an old master, in naming the author of an untitled work? He can identify the bronzes on which skilled Myron spent his sleepless nights, the marbles that tireless Praxiteles brought to life with his chisel, the ivories polished by the Pisaean's thumb, the statues given breath in the furnaces of Polyclitus, the line that betrays at a distant glance the hand of Apelles; for this, when he puts his lyre away, is his leisure.
>
> Statius, *Silvae* 4.6.8–31

Figure 36 Cupids carousing. Detail from the 'Blue Vase', early first century AD

Source By permission of the Soprintendenza Archeologica per le Province di Napoli e Caserta

Most of the tricks of appearance and behaviour by reference to which Romans define one another as miserly or spendthrift, fashionable or free-thinking, original or conventional,[61] appeal to the products of Empire. Naturally: as Aristides (p. 272) asserts, Rome is a market for the world. Among the pets that a Roman may fall in love with, Flaccus loves a *lagalopex* (fennec, *Vulpes zerda*) – says Martial – Publius a puppy, Cronus an ape looking just like himself, Marius a vicious *ichneumon* (Spanish mongoose, *Herpestes ichneumon*), Lausus a magpie. Glaucilla twines an icy snake round her neck, Telesilla has given her nightingale a proper burial, and in the same list, as if he were a pet like the rest, is Canius's much-loved black Ethiopian slave. Since Martial (7.87) brings us to the subject, slaves were indeed called on to serve as pets, as fashion accessories, as trophies: 'Shall you take a barbarian maiden as your slave, having butchered her destined husband? Shall some greased-haired royal page, taught to aim Chinese arrows with his father's bow, serve you your wine?' (Horace, *Odes* 1.29.5–10). From the slave cages, *catastae*, of Rome you might, with enough money, choose from all the world. These cages are poetically *barbara catasta* (Tibullus 2.3.60) because slaves from beyond the Roman frontiers are on sale; they are *Cappadox catasta* (Martial 10.76) because a Cappadocian slave is on sale; in any case they are *rigida catasta* 'rigid, unyielding', though permeable enough to allow the salesman to slap the slave who is on display, demonstrating firm flesh (Persius 6.77).[62] It was the whim of some wealthy buyers to have matching slaves: the 'good-looking slaves all the same age' of a wealthy conspirator against Nero (Tacitus, *Annals* 15.69) are in the same luxury fashion as the 'fifty maids within whose task was to organise the larder … and a hundred more, likewise all of the same age, to load the tables with food and set out the drinking-cups' imagined by Vergil (*Aeneid* 1.703–5).[63]

It is hard for us now to comprehend the distinctions casually hinted at by those to whom styles, prices and fashions were familiar. In clothes we have Martial's dichotomy between Rome and Gaul in a poem written to accompany a gift of 'CANUSIAN RED CAPES. Rome is dressed in the brown, Gaul prefers the red, and this is the colour that boys and soldiers like' (14.129). Here is Gaul setting the fashion against Rome, at least for a significant part of the population including the donor and recipient of this particular gift. Is Martial unusual – un-Roman – in his dislike of brown and grey?

> That lover of sad woollens, the fellow in Baetic-grey and ashen-white, the one who thinks that men in scarlet aren't real men, and calls blue garments 'women's dress' – well may he speak up for natural hues, well may he wear his dingy brown, his sexual habits are primrose-yellow!
>
> Martial 1.96

Is Horace the only poet bold enough to assert that it may be useful to be able to appraise a woman's body through her dress of wild silk? In face of

Figure 37　A service of silverware. Detail of wall painting in the tomb of C. Vestorius Priscus at the Vesuvius Gate, Pompeii

Source　By permission of the Soprintendenza Archeologica di Pompei

unanimous literary disapproval, women continued to wear wild silk (p. 151). Does any poet ever assert that it is a good thing to dress in costly Tyrian purple (p. 171)? Yet people did.

Wealth was in farms first of all; in oxen for ploughing, in sheep, but most of all in a white farm house not too far from Rome (Horace, *Epodes* 1.25–30). Horace himself was rich in his Sabine farm. Even as he gloried in it, he had in mind that Catullus had mulled over whether 'Sabine' had to be the description of his own property, somewhere close by, or whether it might claim the politer and wealthier name of Tiburtine.

> Whether you are Sabine or Tiburtine, my dear farm (they say Tiburtine if they don't want to hurt me, Sabine at any price if they do), well, whether Sabine or more accurately Tiburtine, I have been glad to stay in your little house, not far from Rome, and get rid of the bad cough given me by my own greediness when I was hunting a fine dinner.... I ran back to your lap and you made me better with rest and nettle soup.
>
> Catullus 44

As compared with Catullus and Horace, Martial was less complimentary concerning the house at Nomentum that his poetry had brought him – but then Martial was destined to retire to far-off Bilbilis and to boast to all who still read him of Celtiberia's wealth in crops, game and vigorous young huntsmen. While still in Rome, what would Martial himself do with money if he had it? He does not want estates in Setia or Tuscany, he says, or Moorish citronwood tables on Libyan ivory stands, or gold fittings on dining couches, or crystal cups, or snow to mix with his black Falernian wine, or Syrian slaves in Canusian capes, *Canusinatus Surus*, holding up his litter while clients cluster round, or to have a pretty cupbearer for drunken guests to ogle. Some of these things, in truth, he did rather want, or so we judged on p. 241. Even more than these – even more than the last on the list, which he certainly fancied – he firmly insists, through a whole epigram, that he will use his money 'to give gifts and to build' (Martial 9.22): a nobly brief conclusion. These words say all that needs to be said. Wherever his estate may be – but it will have to be a real farm, not like his almost landless place at Nomentum – Martial too wants to build a farmhouse on it and, like the 'Faustinus' of the epigram quoted on p. 26, to be the ideal farmer and the ideal patron.

'Trimalchio' is proud that he entered Rome by way of the slave market. The auction scene forms part of the narrative painting that now decorates his lavish mansion. Gods take their proper role in it: Minerva, guiding him as she once guided Odysseus; Mercury, Fortuna and the three Fates. Gods actually do take part in Pompeiian wall paintings, mixing so intimately with humans that modern viewers cannot always distinguish them. Petronius hates the vulgarity of his fictional offspring; but his pride cannot be hated. By being his master's and his mistress's lover, being freed, trading and speculating, becoming a landowner, joining one property to another, knowing what to spend his money on,[64] Trimalchio had become a Roman in one generation.

We do not rely on poets or Petronius for Roman views on landed property. Cicero happens to refer to the three dialogues on law written by M. Junius Brutus. They began, respectively, 'It happened that I and my son Marcus were in the country, at my farm at Privernum'; 'I was at my Alban estate with my son Marcus'; 'Once when I and my son Marcus were staying at my Tiburtine farm'. The politician Crassus had called for these opening sentences to be read in court, in the course of a lawsuit in which he was opposing the younger Brutus, and asked rhetorically what had become of the three properties. Cicero continues the story.

> The elder Brutus, a sensible man who was quite aware of his son's ruinous lifestyle, had obviously wanted to have it on record what properties he was bequeathing to him, Crassus observed. What was more, if he had been able decently to say, in a fourth essay, that he and his son were together one day at the public baths he built, no doubt he would have said that too.
>
> Cicero, *For Cluentius* 141

He would never have used that fourth opening line because, as we know, fathers and sons did not bathe together (p. 238). Cicero drips with irony, as no doubt did Crassus on the occasion he describes: but through it all we notice the elder Brutus's care, at the outset of three essays on legal theory, to inform the faithful reader of the range of properties that he owned, conveniently close to the City.

Even Cicero, by birth a citizen but from a modest country town, died a wealthy landowner. Those who began lower, as slaves, were equally careful to establish themselves as farmers – no, estate owners – in this tradition. In a late speech Cicero attacks the hangers-on of Antony who 'have sorted out for themselves nice houses, gardens, estates at Tusculum and Alba. 'These farm boys – if they are boys and not oxen – are now setting off, full of wild hopes, for the seaside towns and Puteoli' (*Philippics* 8.9). But Cicero is already milking the topic for all it is worth in one of his very earliest forensic speeches. In this he attacks the Greek former slave Chrysogonus, a *nouveau riche* protégé of the retired dictator Sulla.

> He has a nice property outside the city, just for the pleasure of it, and several other pieces of land, all of them attractive and not far away. His house is full of Corinthian and Delian ware, including, of course, his famous cooker, which cost so much that passers-by who heard the salesman name the price thought that a whole estate was up for sale. But never mind that: how much sculpted silver, how many tapestries, how many paintings, how many statues, how much marble do you think he has at home?... What about his staff, the number of them and their varied occupations? I pass by the ordinary professions, cooks, bakers, valets. He has so many people engaged in amusing his mind and his ears that the whole neighbourhood resounds continually with the music of voice, string, woodwind and all night party. What do you think the daily expense must be of a life like that? How much wine do you think they get through? What must those parties be like? Good ones, I should think, in that kind of house, if house is the word for this factory of impropriety, this warehouse of all the vices. You see how the man himself is always going about the Forum, with his hair styled and oiled, with his attendant throng of Roman citizenry all in their togas; you see how he looks down on us all, with the thought that no one comes before him, that he alone is fortunate, he alone is powerful.
>
> Cicero, *For Roscius of Ameria* 133–135

It is a classic piece of invective. Yet successful Romans had always displayed their wealth and power in just these ways. Neither Cicero nor Petronius can really have thought it unnatural that newly powerful former slaves should do so in turn. From Cicero's picture of Chrysogonus, and from Petronius's savage and very lifelike portrait of Trimalchio, we see these former slaves inserting themselves into a venerable tradition. We have already seen the ambitions that lie beyond the simple buying of farms: the boast of not using market-bought produce but one's own, specially sent in from the farm, an obsession central to the epigram by Martial quoted on

p. 26 and highlighted in that admiring whisper by one of Trimalchio's dinner guests, 'Don't think he ever needs to buy anything. It's all home-grown: wool, wax, pepper, if you ask for hen's milk you'll get it' (Petronius 38).

No Roman actually reached as far as to grow his own pepper. But Rome herself came close to it, and Rome's reach – the 'tribute' that she takes in and redistributes among her grateful citizens – is often celebrated.

> Do you not see that Tmolus sends saffron aromas, India ivory, the soft Sabaeans their incense, the naked Chalybes iron, Pontus its poisonous castor, Epirus the victory palms that its horses win in Elis? Such is the unal-terable, eternal tribute that Nature has imposed on each particular region.
>
> Vergil, *Georgics* 1.56–61

More and more of Nature's 'tribute' is sent to Rome. As late as AD 400, it seems that it will always be so. 'Rhine shall plough for you, Nile shall flood for you, the fruitful world shall nourish its nurse, for ever'; so Rutilius addresses the great City. 'Africa, rich in her own sun, richer by Roman rain, shall offer you her fertile harvests. Granaries shall rise upon Latin furrows; wine-presses shall overflow with the nectar of the West'. Part of Rome's universal wealth is in her river, offering a means of transport for the produce of her Empire-wide farm. 'Tiber, garlanded with triumphal reeds, shall submit his waters to the service of the children of Romulus; downstream between his peaceful banks shall go the wealthy merchandise of the field, upstream shall come the wealth of the sea' (145–154).

In this context, boundaries mean little. Arabia, India and Central Asia offer 'tribute' just as the provinces do, said Aristides to his proud Roman audience. Rome's ships bring produce from the whole world.[65]

> From every land and sea all the crops of the seasons, all the produce of each province, river and lake, all the products of Greeks and barbarians, are brought to Rome. If we want to see these things, we can travel the whole world, or we can come to Rome. So many ships arrive here every hour and every day, loaded with every kind of goods from every people that the city is like a market for the whole earth. We see so many cargoes from India and Arabia Felix that one imagines their trees must be stripped bare: if they need something of their own produce, they will have to come and beg for it here. Babylonian fabrics and ornaments from the barbarian country beyond arrive here as copiously and as smoothly as if they were merchandise from Naxos or Cythnos being shipped to Athens. As for Egypt, Sicily and the cultivated lands of Africa, it is as if they were your farms. You rule within no fixed fron-tiers. None prescribes a limit to your power.

Notes

1 Introduction

1 Peaches, see p. 190; Caecuban wine, see p. 46. The look of an African slave: Petronius 102 (p. 178); the Syrian bar-girl: *Copa* (p. 18).

2 The street cries, Seneca, *Letters* 56.2 (p. 218); Nero's excursions, Suetonius, *Nero* 26 (p. 216) with Tacitus, *Annals* 13.25; Tibur, the desirable place for a country estate, Catullus 44 (p. 269); the farm-fresh menu, Juvenal 11.56–76 (see also p. 252); the ideal landscape of Thessaly, Catullus 64.279–293 (p. 155).

3 Translators of classical texts, of poetry in particular, are not bound to reproduce every adjectival allusion. The relevance of these supporting references, there-fore, may occasionally not be apparent until one looks at the original text.

4 Secondary sources include contemporary technical writing on geography, natural resources and trade. These have been used not to add to the picture that emerges from the literature, but to clarify it. The reader of Strabo's *Geography*, Pliny's *Natural History* and some other works will find plenty of additional regional products, not mentioned here because they are not cele-brated in poetry and belles-lettres.

   I have cited modern scholarship very little – in general limiting myself to work that elucidates the nature and history of particular luxury products. I have found a great deal of help in the main modern commentaries on Greek and Latin authors; so will the reader.

5 Claudian, *Stilicho's Consulship* 1.152–160.

6 Milton, *Paradise Lost* 3.437–439; Byron, *Don Juan* 1.8; A. E. Housman, Preface to *Manilius Book I*; Housman numbered Elias Stoeber, a predecessor in the study of Manilius, among these geese.

7 *Iliad* 3.243–244. See Matthew Arnold (*On Translating Homer* 1 [vol. 1: 101–102 Super]) on this passage.

8 In quoting these phrases, I usually, silently, convert to the nominative case: thus I write *remotae Gades* 'far-off Cadiz' though the original text that I cite (Horace, *Odes* 2.2.10–11) happens to use the dative, *remotis Gadibus*.

9 We may think of the *Iliad*'s 'Pramnian wine' and Hesiod's 'Bibline wine': no one knows whether these are geographical designations or not. In *Siren feasts* (Dalby 1996: 97–102) I have traced the beginning of real geographical appel-lations for wine in Greek literature.

10 Livy 26.21.7; Tacitus, *Annals* 2.41.2. See also *Consolation to Livia* 313; Cicero, *Against Piso* 60; Tibullus 2.5.116; Ovid, *From Pontus* 2.1.39, 2.1.50, *Tristia* 4.2.37–38 (p. 228).

11 For some certain identifications see pp. 73, 93, 204. On the column see Lepper and Frere 1988: 81–83; an example of a location not identifiable with confi-dence is the river port of casts 80–83. These scholars frequently revert to the

question of how close a representation of historical and topographical reality may be expected in the reliefs of the Column.

12 An example of the use of topographical idiom is the story of the siege of Lachish. The city is identified, without the need for other labels, by its double walls. Other details of the city are not accurate: nothing more was needed to identify the scene and narrate the event. Russell 1991: 200–209. For Hellenistic processions, see Rice 1983.

2 Imperium sine fine

1 There is no canonical list. Persia is always there; Athens, occasionally and by courtesy, since she produced a great historian (Sallust, *Catiline* 2, 8). Aristides, in the second century, lists Assyrians, Medes, Persians and Macedonians (p. 9), and that succession makes real historical sense.

2 This king 'of a Greek race' was most likely Ptolemy VI, who favoured the Jews (Alexander being counted as the first Greek king of Egypt). The date is around 150 BC.

3 Translation after J. J. Collins. Rome is described as 'many-headed' because it was ruled not by a monarch but by a Senate. The *Oracles* add that the city would contribute a new vice to the world (p. 265).

4 Compare Statius, *Silvae* 5.2.132–149 (p. 100); Silius 3.595–600.

5 Vergil, *Aeneid* 1.279; Antipater of Thessalonica 47 [*Anthologia Palatina* 6.335].

6 Rabbi Johanan in *Talmud Babli, Avodah Zarah* 2a. Nadich 1994 vol. 1: 312. Johanan will have thought of *Daniel* as a prophetic book written in the fifth century BC. His interpretation of this prophecy is accepted by some modern scholars: others disagree, following Cosmas Indicopleustes, *Christian Topography* 2.66–74. Many believe the fourth kingdom to be that of the Seleucids, specifically of Antiochus Epiphanes under whose tyranny *Daniel* was written.

7 Translation after J. H. Oliver.

8 *Sibylline Oracles* 3.179, 3.189.

9 *Ecclesiastes Rabbah* 1.7. Nadich 1994 vol. 1: 310, 374. Biblical texts adduced in the Talmudic sequence include: *Genesis* 47.14, *Exodus* 12.13, *I Kings* 14.25, *II Chronicles* 14.8, *I Kings* 15.18.

10 For example, on marble, why Nature put it where it is and how people use it: Pliny 36.1–8.

11 Pliny, *Letters* 3.5, 6.16.

12 Compare Plutarch, *On Distinguishing Flattery from Friendship* 60d. On fluorspar see p. 188.

13 See also Cicero, *For Sextus Roscius of Ameria*; Velleius Paterculus 2.22; Juvenal 2.28.

14 Livy 38.27, 39.6.

15 Antipater of Thessalonica 91 [*Anthologia Palatina* 9.58]; Propertius 3.2.19–21.

16 Aśoka, *Rock Edict II, Pillar Edict VII* Nikam and McKeon.

17 Pp. 155, 22, 26; see also p. 107.

18 The importance of milestones in daily life is shown by their use in giving directions: Martial 1.12 (p. 35), 7.31 (p. 27); Strabo 5.3.2; Pliny, *Letters* 2.17 (p. 40); Seneca, *Apocolocyntosis* 6–7 (p. 98).

19 In general, Hunt 1984; Chevallier 1972.

20 If I have understood him correctly. He persuaded them to accept his Christian ministry instead: Patrick, *Confession* 18.

21 Petronius 99, 103–108.

22 Ovid, *Tristia* 1.4, 1.11.

23 Patrick, *Confession* 19–22; Dio, *Orations* 7.

24 Horace alone calls the Scirocco *Atabulus*, perhaps using a local name. Gellius (2.22.25) therefore nicknames it *ventus Horatianus* 'Horace's wind'.

25 To Tarentum was a long road journey – and for Horace also a journey home (p. 65), since it was the nearest big city to his native Venusia.

26 Reading *fumosa* 'smoky' in line 3: *famosa* 'disreputable' seems to accord more with a medieval scribe's view of the tavern than with the author's. There are several other doubtful readings. On Priapus, 'Guardian of the orchard', see pp. 22, 59. *Surisca* means 'little Syrian': it may be both a description and a name, and any Roman tavern could have a *Surisca* as waitress and dancer.

3 Ausonia

1 Ennius, *Annals* 20 Skutsch; Rutilius 2.17–38.

2 Silius 4.220; Cato, *On Farming* 73.

3 On the Italy of poetry see e.g. Kytzler 1988; Highet 1957.

4 Tibullus elsewhere recounts a harvest ceremony dedicated to Ceres and Bacchus, the latter a foreign god supplanting *Liber Pater* 'Father Liber', Italian god of wine. Cato, *On Farming* 5, 57, 83, 131–132, 134, 139–141, 143; Tibullus 2.1.1–26.

5 Horace is right to prefer elms (see p. 23). Cato, as Horace forgets, was all in favour of the 'cartloads of perfumery', including myrtle and bay. We shall see plenty more of this produce as we explore 'Rome's neighbourhood' later in this chapter.

6 Cato, *On Farming* 6; Columella 4.30.2.

7 Lucretius 1.282–94, 1.897–900, 1.927–930 (p. 245), 4.573–592; Vergil, *Georgics* 1.326–7, *Aeneid* 2.305–8; Ovid, *Metamorphoses* 13.812–820; Calpurnius Siculus, *Eclogues* 4.31–32.

8 Aristotle, *Politics* 1329b19; Cato, *To His Son* [Pliny 29.13–14].

9 See also Cicero, *Against Piso* 68–72.

10 She could really have been Oscan – Pompeii is in Oscan country – and she would not have been the only Oscan girl to attract an urbane admirer (p. 62); but whatever social status we are to imagine for her, Flora has a well-bred Latin name, a reminiscence of the legendary courtesan in whose memory the *Floralia* were instituted at Rome.

11 Horace gives a speech on the way Romans used to do things to his old peasant character 'Ofellus'. Lucretius 2.1164–1172; Horace, *Satires* 2.2.116–125.

12 Translation by R. Latham.

13 Tibullus 1.2.71–74 and passim; Sulpicia 2 (p. 216; see also quotations on p. 264).

14 Horace, *Satires* 1.6.101–106 (p. 17).

15 Varro, *On Farming* 2.10.8. The '*meta* of cheese from the forest of Sassina' has had a long journey (p. 75).

16 Cf. Martial 3.47.

17 Varro, *On Farming* 1.2.6; Vergil, *Georgics* 2.86–88; Columella 12.10.4; Suetonius, *Domitian* 21. Matian apples were required in a pork-with-apple dish for which *Apicius* (4.3.4) gives a recipe.

18 Horace, *Epistles* 1.7.5; Cato, *On Farming* 149.

19 Columella 3.2.1 (p. 30); Cato, *On Farming* 7–9 (p. 30). On the *Regia* see p. 224.

20 Vergil, *Georgics* 2.89–108 (he mixes up variety names with wine regions); Varro, *On Farming* 1.2.7; Pliny 14.20. On Italian wine: Tchernia 1986.

21 Among the lists of Italian wine districts that are found in ancient sources, we shall draw on *Epitome of Athenaeus* 26c–27d; Pliny 14.59–72.

22 Martial 8.45. In Petronius 34 Trimalchio boasts of serving 'Opimian Falernian'. He is given the lie by Pliny (14.94): 'that year's wines all have the consul's name only' because the wine districts of Italy were not yet of repute. On Opimius: Martial 1.26 (p. 47), 3.82, 9.87, 10.49 (p. 72). Anicius: Cicero, *Brutus* 287 (p. 49). Torquatus: Horace, *Epodes* 13.6. Second consulship of Taurus: Horace, *Epistles* 1.5 (p. 256).

23 Rutilius 112 (p. 237); Varro, *On Farming* 3.4.2; Cato, *On Farming* 150 with Dalby *ad loc.* Frayn 1984: 3.

24 Vergil, *Aeneid* 684; Martial 1.88; Silius 8.366, 8.378, 8.392, 12.533–534; Juvenal 1.171, 11.56–76 (p. 1); Vitruvius 7.1, 8.7; Pliny 14.66, 15.55, 35.165. Why Vergil talks of *picti scuta Labici*, Labici with painted shields, I don't know (Vergil, *Aeneid* 7.796), though the commentator Servius has a legendary suggestion. The name of the inn, *ad Pictas*, is unusual and probably relevant.

25 Horace, *Odes* 3.27; Martial 3.93.

26 Horace, *Epodes* 1.29–30; Martial 9.60 (p. 245); Cicero, *Philippics* 8.9; Cato, *On Farming* 7–9; Varro, *On Farming* 1.14–15; Pliny 21.27; Marcus Aurelius (p. 55).

27 Horace, *Odes* 3.23.9–13, 4.4.57, *Carmen Saeculare* 69; Ovid, *Metamorphoses* 14.674; Silius 12.537; Martial 9.64; Marcus Aurelius (p. 55); Varro, *On Farming* 3.2.17.

28 Domitian's villa occupied roughly the location of the Papal residence, Castel Gandolfo. Martial 4.1, 5.1, 11.7; Juvenal 4.145; Statius, *Silvae* 3.1.61, 3.5.28–29, 5.2.168–169; Suetonius, *Domitian* 4, 19.

29 Horace, *Odes* 4.11.2; Juvenal 6 O.15–16 (p. 31); Cato, *On Farming* 7.2; Columella 3.2.16, 3.8.5 (p. 28); Pliny 14.25, 64; *Epitome of Athenaeus* 33a.

30 Martial 10.74, 11.29; Silius 10.33.

31 Martial 4.69, 6.86, 10.36, 13.23, 112, 124, 14.103; Juvenal 10.27; Strabo 5.3.6; Pliny 14.61. Pliny says that Augustus favoured Setine wine above all others; Suetonius, well informed on such matters, does not support him. On snow see p. 248.

32 Horace, *Epistles* 1.15.9 (p. 56), 2.1.24–25; Dionysius of Halicarnassus, *Roman History* 4.53; Strabo 5.3.11.

33 Vergil, *Aeneid* 7.682; Horace, *Odes* 3.4.22–23, *Epistles* 1.2; Martial 9.60 (p. 245); Pliny 13.5, 21.16. Carter 1940.

34 The name Albula comes from the whiteness of the waters, like Martial's adjective 'frosted'. It was said that Albula was an old name for the Tiber itself. Horace, *Epistles* 1.4; Martial 7.31; Vergil, *Aeneid* 8.332; Suetonius, *Augustus* 82; Vitruvius 8.3.2.

35 Ovid, *Amores* 3.6.46; Propertius 4.7.81. Some editors of Ovid and Propertius have made the all-too-easy change to *spumifer* 'spray-laden'. Vergil, *Aeneid* 7.82–84, 7.630, 7.670, 7.683; Horace, *Odes* 1.7.20–21, 1.18.4, 3.4.23; *Priapeia* 75; Silius 4.224–225; Columella 10.138; Symmachus, *Letters* 7.18, 7.19.

36 Horace, *Satires* 2.4.70.

37 The 'Moorish lintels' are of citronwood. The scurrying nymphs are wall paintings, one presumes.

38 Vergil, *Aeneid* 6.773, *Georgics* 2.88; Martial 4.64 (p. 38), 9.60 (p. 245), 10.48 (p. 252: this poem, by contrast with others, does lay claim to farm-fresh produce), 10.92, 10.94 (p. 217), 12.57 (p. 222); Juvenal 6.56, 10.100; Varro, *On Farming* 1.14–15; Celsus 2.24.2; Columella 5.10.18; Pliny 14.23, 14.49–50, 15.53.

39 More patriotically, Vergil once called the river *Laurens Thybris*, alluding to Lavinium and the Laurentian marshes to the left of the river mouth: this was where Aeneas was supposed to have landed on his arrival from Troy. Statius acrobatically brought the two together in: 'Tiber's bank, where the Tyrrhenian wave laps Laurentian sandbanks' (*Silvae* 5.2.113–114). 'Lydian river' alludes to the hypothetical origin of the Etruscan people in Asia Minor. Vergil, *Georgics* 1.499, *Aeneid* 5.797, 7.30; Horace, *Satires* 2.2.32, *Odes* 1.2.13, 1.8.8; *Consolation to Livia*.

40 Varro (*On the Latin Language* 7.44) says that the number of straw men was twenty-seven. Frazer 1929 vol. 4: 75–109.

41 Horace, *Odes* 1.2.13; Statius, *Silvae* 4.4.6–7.

42 Martial 10.3, 12.57 (p. 222); Statius, *Silvae* 1.6.73–4; Juvenal 5.47–8, 14.201–4. Howell (on Martial 1.41) with references. Among modern cities Venice still has a satellite town, Murano, engaged in glass-blowing.

43 Translators interpret Luke's list in several different ways.

44 Augustus, *Res Gestae* 23; Suetonius, *Augustus* 43, *Titus* 7.

45 Martial 4.64 (p. 38), 10.6; Cicero, *Against Catiline* 3.6; Sallust, *Catiline* 45.

46 Martial 6.28, 11.13; Statius, *Silvae* 2.1.176; Vitruvius 2.7.5.

47 Livy 27.4, 33.26.

48 Vergil, *Aeneid* 7.697; Silius 7.662.

49 Vergil, *Aeneid* 11.785–790 with Servius's commentary; Silius 5.175–181; Cicero, *On Divination* 1.47; Strabo 5.2.9; Pliny 2.207, 7.19, 31.26; Porphyrion on Horace, *Odes* 1.9.

50 Ovid, *Amores* 3.13.13, *Fasti* 1.83–84; Statius, *Silvae* 4.9.35; Martial 4.46; Varro, *On the Latin Language* 5.111; Pliny 2.230.

51 Horace, *Satires* 2.3.143; Persius 5.147; Martial 1.103, 2.53, 3.49. *Rubellus*, here translated 'brown', seems regularly used of the wine of Veii but also of a typical *vine* of Nomentum, because of the reddish colour of its wood: Pliny 14.23; Columella 3.2.14.

52 Vergil, *Aeneid* 1.2; Rutilius 179–181; Cicero, *On the Republic* 2.33; Pliny 36.83.

53 Vergil, *Aeneid* 10.708; Ovid, *Metamorphoses* 14.342–343, *Fasti* 2.231; Martial 9.48, 10.37, 10.45; Juvenal 1.107–108 (p. 129); Varro, *On Farming* 3.13.1–3. Under the modern Kingdom of Italy, the Laurentian marshes were a royal hunting reserve.

54 On gardens: MacDougall 1987.

55 Silius 8.25–241.

56 Ovid, *Metamorphoses* 15.718; Horace, *Odes* 1.35.1; Cicero, *Letters to Atticus* 2.1–2.10; Statius, *Silvae* 1.3.89; Martial 5.1; Strabo 5.3.5; Suetonius, *Caligula* 57.3, *Nero* 6.1.

57 Vergil, *Aeneid* 7.10–14, 799; Ovid, *Metamorphoses* 14.264–267; Martial 5.1, 11.7; Horace, *Satires* 2.4.33 (p. 53). Andrews 1948; Parsons 1977.

58 The straw and the basket are for keeping pre-cooked food warm on the Sabbath (*Scholia on Juvenal* 6.542). In this passage Juvenal makes obeisance to Martial 3.47. Gilbert Highet (1957: 208–213) gives an enjoyable exposition of the passage by Juvenal, quoting Byron (*Childe Harold's Pilgrimage* 4.116–117). Byron, like other modern visitors, was shown the water gardens of the villa of Herodes Atticus, further out along the Appian Way, as the 'grove of Egeria' (see also Keaveney 1988: 209–214).

59 Ennius, *Annals* 113 Skutsch; Martial 3.47, 10.35. There have been arguments for rearranging the lines of Juvenal, to make him describe the grotto and name Egeria first, getting on to Numa's visits and the precise nature of their relationship afterwards. Juvenal was not the first to suggest an affair; see Horace, *Satires* 1.2.123–129 (p. 259).

60 Martial 11.54.
61 Persius 6.56; Martial 2.19, 12.32; Juvenal 4.117–118.
62 Vergil, *Aeneid* 7.764; Horace, *Odes* 1.21.5–7 (p. 141); Propertius 3.24.9–10; Ovid, *Art of Love* 1.259–262, *Fasti* 6.59; Suetonius, *Caligula* 35; Pausanias 2.27; Frazer 1929 vol. 3: 69–87. The strange rule of succession to the priesthood gives its name to J. G. Frazer's *The Golden Bough*.
63 Vergil, *Aeneid* 7.801–802; Cloatius Verus 10; Horace, *Epistles* 1.11.30; Juvenal 10.102.
64 Strabo 5.3.6.
65 Ennius, *Annals* 152 Skutsch; Vergil, *Aeneid* 7.800; Martial 5.1, 6.42, 10.51, 10.58; Silius 4.532; Pliny 3.59.
66 Vergil, *Aeneid* 10.564; Silius 8.528; Pliny 3.59; Tacitus, *Annals* 4.59.
67 Varro, *Menippean Satires* 38 Bücheler; Horace, *Odes* 1.37.5, cf. 1.20.9, *Epodes* 9; Columella 3.8.5 (p. 28); Pliny 14.65.
68 Horace, *Satires* 1.5.37 (p. 18), *Epodes* 9.34–36. Formiae, supposed to be the home of Odysseus's Laestrygonians (Silius 7.276, 7.410; Pliny 3.59) was also where the notorious Mamurra family had its estates. Catullus calls Caesar's friend Mamurra 'the bankrupt of Formiae' in rude poems addressed to Mamurra's mistress: Catullus 41.4, 43.5; Horace, *Odes* 3.17.6; Martial 10.30; Cicero, *Letters to Atticus* 2.13.2.
69 Vergil, *Aeneid* 7.1–4; Cicero, *De lege Manilia* 33; Martial 5.1, 10.30.
70 Cicero, *On Laws* 1.14; Horace, *Odes* 1.31.9–10, 3.17; Lucan 2.424; Martial 13.83; Silius 8.399–400; Statius, *Silvae* 4.3.93–94.
71 Horace, *Epistles* 1.5.4–5; Ovid, *Metamorphoses* 15.716; Cato, *On Farming* 135; Cicero, *Letters to Atticus* 16.10; Livy 27.37; Velleius Paterculus 2.19. Frayn 1993: 39–40, 46–9.
72 Horace, *Odes* 1.1.19, 2.7.21, 3.21 (p. 30); Silius 4.346–347; Martial 13.111; Columella 3.8.5 (p. 28).
73 Ovid, *Metamorphoses* 15.715; Silius 8.527; Martial 6.42 (p. 239), 11.7, 11.82; Cicero, *Letters to Atticus* 9.16, 14.8; Tacitus, *Annals* 12.66–13.1; Pliny 31.8; Strabo 5.3.6.
74 Horace, *Odes passim*; Juvenal 6.150; Varro, *On Farming* 1.2.6; Petronius 21; Plutarch, *Rules for Health* 124d. Nisbet and Hubbard (on Horace, *Odes* 1.27) regard *severum* as the equivalent of Greek *austeros*.
75 Pliny 23.33; Galen, *On Antidotes* [14.77].
76 Catullus 27; Martial 1.18, 7.12; Varro, *On Farming* 1.65; Petronius 34; *Epitome of Athenaeus* 33a.
77 Martial 11.8 (p. 264); Pliny 37.47 (p. 207).
78 Martial 13.108; Horace, *Satires* 2.2.15.
79 Lucretius 5.745; Vergil, *Aeneid* 7.728–729; Propertius 3.18.4; Silius 8.527–528.
80 Ovid, *Metamorphoses* 15.713–714; Silius 6.653–654, 7.278; Tacitus, *Annals* 15.42.
81 Vergil, *Aeneid* 6.2; Ovid, *Metamorphoses* 14.155; Silius 8.531; Statius, *Silvae* 4.3; Martial 14.114.
82 Varro, *Menippean Satires* 114 Bücheler; Martial 14.114; Pliny 35.165; Horace, *Satires* 2.3.144. I do not know whether Grattius is being precise as to source and materials when he writes of high quality hunting nets made of flax from 'the valley of the Aeolian Sibyl', which is Cumae and its neighbourhood (Grattius, *Cynegetica* 34–36). This is the source of the conjectural reading *Aeoliae plagae* 'Aeolian nets, i.e. nets made of Cumaean flax' in Horace, *Epistles* 1.18.46.
83 Lucretius 6.740–748; Horace, *Epodes* 5.26; Propertius 3.11.37; Ovid, *Metamorphoses* 14.101–153; *Consolation to Livia*; Silius 8.537–538, 8.655,

12.120–129; Strabo 5.4.5–9; Petronius 120.67–75. Frazer 1929 vol. 3: 113–114.

84 Juvenal 9.57; Statius, *Silvae* 3.1.147; Silius 12.159–160; Symmachus, *Poems* 1.8; *Epitome of Athenaeus* 26f.

85 Horace, *Odes* 3.4.24, *Epistles* 1.1.83; Propertius 3.18.1–2; Statius, *Silvae* 4.3.25–26 (p. 50); Cicero, *For Caelius* 47.

86 Horace, *Epistles* 1.15.2–7 (p. 56), *Odes* 2.18.21; Ovid, *Art of Love* 1.256; Martial 3.58 (p. 26); 6.43; Cassiodorus, *Variae* 9.6.

87 Horace, *Epodes* 2.49; Martial 5.37; Petronius 119.34–6; Pliny 9.168; Xenocrates 54, 96, 97.

88 On the saucer-like coquilles see p. 65.

89 Martial 1.59, 1.62.

90 Ovid, *Art of Love* 1.255–258; Pliny 18.33; Seneca, *Letters* 51.4. In the Varro fragment I read *repuerascunt*, a conjecture by Bücheler. D'Arms 1970.

91 Propertius 1.11.4; Horace, *Satires* 2.4.33 (p. 53).

92 Plautus, *Mostellaria* 261; Antiphilus 3 [*Anthologia Palatina* 7.379]; Petronius 120.67–9; Seneca, *Letters* 77.1–2; Pliny 8.6, 16.202, 31.6–8, 35.44–45, 166–167. Frayn 1993: 89–92.

93 Poseidonius [Athenaeus 401a]; Strabo 5.4.7; Seneca, *Letters* 57.1–2. Bodson 1978.

94 Varro, *Menippean Satires* 160 Bücheler; Vergil, *Georgics* 4.564; Horace, *Epodes* 2.50–52, 5.43; Ovid, *Metamorphoses* 15.711–712; *Laus Pisonis* 92; Martial 5.78 (p. 249); Juvenal 8.56–57; Petronius 119.33–34; Pliny 9.62; Macrobius, *Saturnalia* 3.16.10.

95 Vergil, *Georgics* 2.224–225; Statius, *Silvae* 1.2.265; Silius 8.537; Ausonius, *Mosella* 210; Cato, *On Farming* 7; Columella 3.2.10, 3.2.27; Pliny 14.35.

96 Ovid, *Metamorphoses* 15.710; Persius 3.93; Juvenal 6 O.15–16 (p. 31); Silius 5.466; Columella 3.2.10–11; Pliny 23.33. It is still rated one of the top four wines of Italy by Columella 3.8.5 (p. 28); cf. Pliny 14.64.

97 Pliny 35.160 (p. 151).

98 Silius 8.541–542; Vergil, *Aeneid* 7.735; Juvenal 10.72; Suetonius, *Tiberius* 40, 43 and passim.

99 Antonius Musa was the doctor whose cold water cure was believed to have saved Augustus, which made him immediately fashionable (Suetonius, *Augustus* 59, 81). For the well-fed Phaeacians see p. 143.

100 Vergil, *Georgics* 4.119; Ovid, *Metamorphoses* 15.708; Martial 5.37 (p. 263), 6.80, 9.60 (p. 245), 12.31. Carter 1940.

101 Calpurnius Siculus, *Eclogues* 5.80–81; Varro, *On Farming* 1.7.6; Livy 29.38.1, 30.19.10; Dionysius of Halicarnassus, *Roman Antiquities* 20.15 (20.5–6); Columella 12.18.7; Pliny 16.53, 24.37; Cassiodorus, *Variae* 8.31, 11.39, 12.12.

102 Ovid, *Metamorphoses* 15.707, *Fasti* 5.441; Strabo 6.1.5; Pausanias 6.6.7–11; *Odyssey* 1.182–184.

103 Translation after D. R. Shackleton Bailey. Leucopetra, not far from Rhegium on the southern tip of Italy, appears on the evidence of this letter to have been a port of call for fast Tarentine passenger boats that followed the old Greek coasting route from Sicily along the 'instep' of Italy and thence to Corcyra and Ambracia. Cicero's alternative was to look, either at Rhegium or at Syracuse, for a cargo boat making direct for Patrae in the Peloponnese.

104 Archestratus 16 [Athenaeus 312f]; Cassiodorus, *Variae* 12.14.

105 Horace, *Odes* 1.35.10; Ovid, *Fasti* 3.85.

106 Silius 8.401; Martial 4.55, 10.20; Juvenal 8.237; Sallust, *Jugurtha* 63; Cicero, *Letters to Quintus* 3.1; Fronto, *Parthian Preface* [vol. 2: 204 Haines].

107 Horace, *Epistles* 1.10.26.
108 Cato, *On Farming* 135; Lucilius 961; Silius 4.227; Macrobius, *Saturnalia* 3.16.12.
109 Horace, *Odes* 1.20.9–10, 1.31.9–10, 4.12.14; Juvenal 1.69; Vitruvius 8.3.17; Pliny 14.65, 15.16; *Epitome of Athenaeus* 27a.
110 Vergil, *Georgics* 2.224–225; Horace, *Satires* 2.8.55–56; Propertius 3.5.5; Cato, *On Farming* 107; Scribonius Largus 258; Varro, *On Farming* 1.2.6 (p. 21); Pliny 3.60 (p. 48); Cassiodorus, *Variae* 8.33.
111 Plautus, *Pseudolus* 146; Horace, *Epodes* 16.5; Livy 23.10.2, 23.35; Seneca, *Letters* 51.5.
112 Cicero, *On the Agrarian Law* 2.94; Valerius Maximus 9.1.ext.1. Cf. Pliny 34.108 and Glare 1968–1982 s.v. *seplasiarius*.
113 Cato, *On Farming* 135; Pliny 19.26–30.
114 Vergil, *Georgics* 2.224–225; Silius 8.535.
115 Vergil, *Aeneid* 7.740; Silius 8.543; *Priapeia* 51.
116 Horace, *Epistles* 2.2.98; Juvenal 3.207; Petronius 45; Varro, *On the Latin Language* 5.142; Cicero, *Letters to Friends* 7.1.
117 Philodemus 12 (p. 24); Horace, *Satires* 1.5 (p. 18), *Epodes* 2.41 (p. 64); Juvenal 6.455; Martial 3.58 (p. 26); *CIL* 9.2689. *Pinguis Galatea* 'fat Galatea', the Muse whom Martial (8.55) imagines rejected by the faithless Vergil in favour of the new boy that Maecenas had given him, is not an Italian but a Sicilian girl, and somewhat literary (cf. Theocritus 11.20–21).
118 Varro, *On Farming* 1.2.6 (p. 21); Horace, *Satires* 2.4.69, 2.8.45 (p. 254); Horace, *Odes* 2.6; Martial 12.63 (p. 106), 13.101; Juvenal 5.86; Pliny 15.7.
119 Cato, *On Farming* 135; Martial 13.33; Pliny 14.69.
120 Vergil, *Georgics* 2.38; Grattius, *Cynegetica* 509; Silius 8.565; Livy 9.2, 9.11.
121 Martial 10.3, 14.96; Juvenal 5.46–48; Tacitus, *Annals* 15.34.
122 Its first three short syllables rule it out of nearly all Latin verse forms, though Horace could write of *silvae Venusinae* 'Venusine woods' if he chose to (*Odes* 1.28.26). Several other identifications have been made (Radke 1989): Horace's clues are not so easy, and we have only his word for it that his family baked good bread. Arthur Palmer, in his commentary on the *Epistles*, wrote resignedly: 'I think it most likely that the name of the little town has never yet been suggested, nor is it likely to be recovered'. From Venusia to Canusium was not an officially adopted road, but will have been a single day's journey. Strabo 6.3.7 (quoted in the text); Silius 8.569; *Antonine Itinerary* 111–121; *Bordeaux Itinerary* 609–610; *Peutinger Table* (the map is confused at this point, but reconstructable).
123 Horace, *Satires* 1.1.58; *Odes* 1.22.14, 2.1.34–35, 3.30.10, 4.9.2.
124 Horace, *Odes* 2.9.6–8, *Epistles* 2.1.202; Lucan 9.182–5; Silius 4.560–561, 8.628–629.
125 Martial 9.22, 14.127, 14.129 (p. 268); Juvenal 6.150; Pliny 8.190; Suetonius, *Nero* 30.3.
126 Horace, *Satires* 2.1.37 (p. 63); Cicero, *Letters to Atticus* 8.3.4; Seneca, *Letters* 87.8; Varro, *On Farming* 1.2.6, 1.57.3, 2.6.5; Columella 3.8.4; Cassiodorus, *Variae* 8.33.
127 Varro, *On Farming* 2.1.16, 2.2.9, 2.9–10; Columella 7.2.3; *CIL* 9.2438, 9.2826.
128 Silius 8.574; Strabo 6.3.7–8; Pliny 3.101; Aulus Gellius 9.4.1–4.
129 Vergil, *Georgics* 2.195–199 (p. 89), 3.425–434, 4.125; Horace, *Epodes* 1.25–8, *Odes* 1.31.5, *Epistles* 2.2.177–8. Strabo's view (6.1.2) was that Greek culture was in decline in southern Italy in his time (under Augustus), persisting only in Tarentum, Rhegium and Naples.

130 'There's no answer to that!' is certainly the answer. But which road is Minucius's? Horace must mean the choice made at Beneventum between the route via Venusia (the *via Appia*) and the route via Canusium.

131 Vergil, *Georgics* 2.88; Horace, *Epistles* 1.7.14–19; Martial 5.78 (p. 249); Juvenal 11.73 (p. 1); Archestratus 56 (p. 143); Ennius, *Hedyphagetica* [Apuleius, *Apology* 39.2]; Celsus 2.24.2; Columella 5.10.18; Pliny 15.53.

132 Vergil, *Georgics* 2.195–199 (p. 89); Horace, *Odes* 2.6.10; Petronius 38; Calpurnius Siculus, *Eclogues* 2.69; Varro, *On Farming* 2.2.18; Columella 7.2.3, 7.4.1; Pliny 8.190, 31.73, 31.84–86; *Diocletian's Edict* 21.

133 Phalantus was the legendary founder of Tarentum. Cyllarus was ridden by Castor and Pollux, the Gemini of the zodiac.

134 Horace, *Epistles* 2.1.207; Martial 14.155 (p. 89); Pliny 9.136 citing Nepos; Galen, *To Epigenes on Foreknowledge* [14.631]; Tertullian, *On Women's Dress* 2.10.1, *On the Pallium* 3. Thompson 1947: 200; Maeder 1999.

135 Horace, *Odes* 4.2; Lucan 9.182–5.

136 Horace, *Odes* 2.6, 3.16; Vergil, *Georgics* 4.126; Martial 11.22, 12.63 (p. 106).

137 Horace, *Satires* 2.3.234, 2.8.6; Ovid, *Halieuticon* 58; Martial, *Spectacula* 8; Seneca, *Dialogues* 9.2.13 (p. 18).

138 Naevius 60 Strzelecki [Varro, *On the Latin Language* 7.39]. But the Greek loan-word *elephantus* reached Latin very early, for example in the *taetri elephanti*, 'terrible elephants' of Ennius, *Annals* 236 Skutsch.

139 Varro, *On the Latin Language* 5.111; Cicero, *Letters to Friends* 9.16.8.

140 Ovid, *Tristia* 2.417; Phylarchus [Athenaeus 521c]; Varro, *On Farming* 1.44.2.

141 Ovid, *Metamorphoses* 15.15.

142 Vergil, *Aeneid* 3.553; Cassiodorus, *Variae* 12.12, 12.15.

143 Highet (1957: 133–148) explores Horace's Sabine farm.

144 Lucilius 575–576; Vergil, *Aeneid* 7.750–760; Horace, *Epodes* 5.76, 16.6, 17.29, *Odes* 3.14.18; Ovid, *Art of Love* 2.102, *Fasti* 6.142; Martial 1.41 (p. 222); Pliny 7.15; Gellius 16.11.1; Galen, *To Glaucon* [11.143].

145 Translation by J. D. Duff.

146 'Wine from Marsian cellars', Martial 14.116; see also Martial 1.26 (p. 47); Galen, *On Therapeutic Method* [10.831–832].

147 Horace, *Epodes* 17.60; Calpurnius Siculus, *Eclogues* 4.151.

148 Ovid, *Fasti* 4.81; Silius 8.510, 8.520; Martial 13.30–31; Pliny 11.240–242, 15.82; *Apicius* 4.1.2 (p. 73).

149 Ovid, *Fasti* 3.195–230, *Amores* 1.8.39, 2.4.15, 3.8.61, *Cosmetics* 11–12; Martial 11.15.

150 He says almost the same of Gaul: Cicero, *Philippics* 3.13 (p. 84).

151 Ovid, *Fasti* 3.151. Compare Vergil's name *olivifera Mutusca* for a Sabine hill town (*Aeneid* 7.711).

152 Martial 9.54; Varro, *On Farming* 3.4.2: *Merula* 'Blackbird' is the speaker in Varro's dialogue at this point.

153 Horace, *Odes* 1.20.1; *Epitome of Athenaeus* 27b.

154 Horace, *Odes* 3.4.21–22; Varro, *On Farming* 1.8.6, 1.14–15, 2.2.9.

155 Horace, *Satires* 2.3.272, 2.4.70; Pliny 15.16; Martial 1.43, 5.78 (p. 249), 11.52 (p. 251); Juvenal 11.74; *Priapeia* 51; Strabo 5.4.2.

156 Antiphilus 22 [*Anthologia Palatina* 6.257] with note by Gow and Page; Philip 42 [*Anthologia Palatina* 9.232]; Dioscorides 5.6; Pliny 14.67. Empereur and Garlan 1986: 32–3.

157 Lepper and Frere 1988: 129–132, with full discussion.

158 Vergil, *Aeneid* 7.517; Horace, *Satires* 2.4.40; Martial 7.93, 7.97, 9.57, 9.58; Cassiodorus, *Variae* 11.12, 12.18.

159 Vergil, *Georgics* 1.265; Cato, *On Farming* 11.

160   Martial 13.120, 14.116; *Epitome of Athenaeus* 27b.
161   Vergil, *Georgics* 2.146 (p. 21); Propertius 3.22.23–24.
162   Pliny 11.240–242; Martial 1.43, 3.58 (p. 26).
163   Cato, *Origines* 2.14 Chassignet [Varro, *On Farming* 1.2.7].
164   Lucretius 6.381; Vergil, *Aeneid* 8.479; Horace, *Satires* 1.6.1; Rutilius 596.
165   Pliny 21.6, 33.10–11; Juvenal 5.164; Statius, *Silvae* 5.3.120; Pliny 34.34;
       Tertullian, *Apologetica* 25.13.
166   Catullus 39 (p. 86); Martial 10.68; Cicero, *Letters to Friends* 6.6.
167   Nemesianus, *Cynegetica* 231–238; Martial 1.26 (p. 47), 7.27, 12.14, 13.118 (p.
       104); Juvenal 1.22–23; Galen, *On Good and Bad Juices* [6.806].
168   Pliny 35.160 (p. 151); Martial 1.53.6.
169   Cicero, *Against Catiline* 1.5, 2.14, 2.23.
170   Martial 9.22.
171   Translation after Betty Radice.
172   Horace, *Epistles* 1.15 (p. 56); Strabo 5.2.9. Valerius Messalla was praetorian
       prefect in 396.
173   Strabo 5.2.3, 5.2.8; Vergil, *Aeneid* 10.184; Lucilius 1271.
174   Vergil, *Aeneid* 10.184.
175   Vergil, *Aeneid* 10.173–174; Diodorus 5.13; Strabo 5.2.6.
176   Strabo 5.2.5. Pisae is 'child of Alpheus' as a supposed colony of Pisa in Elis,
       where the river Alpheus flows.
177   Statius, *Silvae* 4.3.99 (p. 50), 4.4.24; Martial 13.30–31; Suetonius, *Nero* 50 (p.
       176); Pliny 11.240–242.

4 Vesper

1   Inscription from Antipolis (modern Antibes), *CIL* 12.5732. The promised
     bronze tablet does not survive.
2   Metrodorus used a road book, not a map, in his research and mistakenly iden-
     tified two different passes that were both listed as *summo Pyreneo*. For names
     and distances see *Antonine Itinerary* passim. His Greek name *Taure* 'cow' for the
     country of the *Vaccaei* (a Celtic people and presumably a Celtic name) is a
     trilingual pun, cf. Latin *vacca* 'cow'.
3   Horace, *Odes* 2.20.20, *Epodes* 16.6; Tibullus 1.7.12; Martial 5.1, 8.75; Caesar,
     Gallic War 4.5.1–2.
4   Sallust, *Catiline* 40–41.
5   Caesar, *Gallic War* 1.1.3, the first known occurrence of the *Belgae* in Roman
     texts. Because of their mid first-century BC reputation for ferocity, Propertius
     (4.10.40) anachronistically calls the Cisalpine leader killed in single combat by
     Marcellus, in 222 BC, a *Belga*.
6   In the historical epic by Silius, the leader of the Celtic Boii has a similar look:
     'A golden collar glittered on his milk-white neck; his garments were striped
     with gold, with gold his gauntlets were stiff, and his helmet-crest sparkled
     with the same metal' (Silius 4.154–156). Vergil's *vestis*, translated 'beards' in
     the text quoted, was understood by Silius as 'clothes'; hence Silius makes the
     Gaulish garments 'gold-striped', believing that he is following Vergil's prece-
     dent. Propertius 4.10.41–44; Martial 14.129 (p. 268); Seneca, *Apocolocyntosis* 6;
     Polybius 2.28.7, 2.30.1.
7   Strabo 4.4.2; Tacitus, *Histories* 3.34.
8   Martial 1.49, 14.140; Juvenal 4.75, 6.477; Pliny 8.191. Note also the *cuculli
     Bardaici* of *Historia Augusta, Pertinax* 8.

 9 Vergil, *Aeneid* 1.244; Horace, *Epodes* 1.1, *Odes* 1.37.30; Propertius 3.11.44; Livy 10.2.4; Plutarch, *Antony* 67.2; Lucian, *Amores* 6; Appian, *Illyrian Wars* 3. Panciera 1956.
10 Vergil, *Georgics* 3.25 (p. 229); Horace, *Epodes* 7.7–8.
11 Horace, *Odes* 3.4.33; Martial 11.21 (p. 263), 11.53 (p. 87), 14.99 (p. 102).
12 Claudian, *Panegyric on Honorius' Fourth Consulship* 31–33. Cf. Gildas, *Ruin of Britain* 19.1.
13 Vergil, *Georgics* 3.408; Catullus 37.18 (p. 104); Martial 10.78. The resin, *dropax*, was used for depilation.
14 So Diodorus 5.33.5; Strabo 3.4.16.
15 Silius (3.290–291) attributes these traits not to the Libyes but to the Gaetuli. Vergil's 'Amyclaean dog and Cretan quiver' are literary flourishes.
16 Sallust, *Jugurtha* 75.4; Velleius Paterculus 2.19; Curtius, *Life of Alexander* 4.7.20; Seneca, *Apocolocyntosis* 9.1; Petronius 58.14.
17 Martial 1.100 with Howell's note.
18 Ennius, *Annals* 242 Skutsch; Sallust, *Jugurtha* 5–6, 67; and note the *Maura iacula* 'Moorish javelins' of Horace, *Odes* 1.22.2.
19 Horace, *Odes* 2.20.19–20; Statius, *Silvae* 4.5.45–49; Silius 1.188; Juvenal 7.147–149, 15.110–112; Claudian, *Panegyric on Honorius' Fourth Consulship* 582–583; Cato, *Origines* [Charisius, *Ars Grammatica* 2: 263 B]; Sallust, *Jugurtha* 17; Varro, *On Farming* 1.1.10; Strabo 3.1.6, 4.1.5 (p. 95); Caesar, *Gallic War* 6.14; Suetonius, *Augustus* 83.
20 Vergil, *Georgics* 1.481–483, 2.451, 4.372–373.
21 *Diocletian's Edict* 25. Martial's presumably fictional 'rich friend Callistratus' had estates at Parma with innumerable flocks of sheep for wool (2.43, 5.13, 14.155; p. 89).
22 Martial 14.148, 14.152; Juvenal 6.195, 7.66; Suetonius, *Augustus* 83; Quintilian 1.6.42, citing Pollio with disapproval on the Latinity of the word *lodices*.
23 Vergil, *Georgics* 1.507; Martial 1.61. Highet 1957.
24 Martial 1.61, 14.100, 14.152 (p. 92). Highet 1957.
25 Servius, commenting on Vergil, assures the reader that Cato had praised Raetian wine in the book *To His Son*, and that Catullus could not understand what Cato saw in it. Servius seems to be casting round for an explanation of Vergil's careful indecision, which is better explained by Vergil's own knowledge of the wine and of Augustus's liking for it. Martial 10.93, 14.100; Columella 3.2.27; Pliny 14.16, 14.67; Suetonius, *Augustus* 77.
26 Vergil, *Georgics* 2.159–160 (p. 21); Pliny, *Letters* 3.19, 4.30.
27 Pliny, *Letters* 2.8, 9.7, 1.3.
28 Martial 11.21.
29 Varro, *On Farming* 1.51.2; Strabo 4.6.2; Pliny 11.240–242; *Apicius* passim. Andrews 1941.
30 Silius 8.597 (p. 91); Strabo 4.6.2, 5.1.12; Columella 7.2.4; Pliny 19.165.
31 The territory had an alternate mythological name, *Helicaonia regio*, because Patavium was supposed to have been founded by Antenor, father of Helicaeon. Martial 10.93, 11.16, 14.152 (p. 92); Quintilian 1.5.56, 8.1.3. Why Martial asserts that *even a Patavine girl* will become moist with sexual excitement as she reads his book 11, I do not know.
32 Martial 6.59, 14.145, 14.147, 14.155 (p. 89); Strabo 5.1.12; Petronius 21, 28; Arnobius, *Against the Gentiles* 3.21.
33 Lucan 7.193–194; Martial 1.61; Pliny 2.227, 31.61; Ausonius, *Catalogue of Cities* 161; Claudian, *Aponus* [xlix]; Cassiodorus, *Variae* 2.39.
34 Lucan 7.193–194; Statius, *Silvae* 4.7.55; Strabo 5.1.8; Pliny 2.225–229.

35 Martial 12.63 (p. 106); Cassiodorus, *Variae* 12.22.

36 Lepper and Frere 1988: 135, following Cichorius.

37 Vergil, *Aeneid* 1.243; Ovid, *Art of Love* 2.657–8 (p. 262); Statius, *Silvae* 4.7.14–15; Martial 10.78. In a satire of Juvenal (16.13) the *vardaicus* identifies its wearer as a stupid soldier.

38 *Consolation to Livia* 390; Horace, *Odes* 1.16.9–10; Nemesianus, *Cynegetica* 227–230; Rutilius 352; Vergil, *Aeneid* 10.708; Hadrian, *Epitaph for Borysthenes.*

39 Vergil, *Aeneid* 10.708; Pliny 3.117.

40 Vergil, *Georgics* 3.474–475; Vergil, *Georgics* 3.474; *Consolation to Livia* 15.

41 *Iuppiter hibernas cana nive conspuit Alpes*, 'Jove spit hoary snow upon the wintry Alps' is the unpleasant image that earned for its poet Furius the nickname *Furius Alpinus* in Horace's *Satires*. This is the only memorable fact, or at least the only fact we now know, concerning Furius's epic poem on Caesar's Gallic wars (Horace, *Satires* 1.10.36, 2.5.41; Quintilian 8.6.17). On the passes see Strabo 2.6.6–7.

42 *Sophistai* are 'professors' or exponents of higher education of the Greek type (p. 128).

43 Galen reported in *Epitome of Athenaeus* 27c. The modern Master of Wine, when reading ancient tasting notes, must respond to terms that differ totally from those of the Jules Chauvet system.

44 Martial 3.82, 10.36, 13.123, 14.118.

45 Martial 7.88, 13.107; Pliny 2.121, 14.57.

46 (*Vinum*) *dulce* is the direct ancestor of the modern French term *vin doux.*

47 Martial 14.90; Pliny 16.66.

48 Excuse enough for one modern commentator to discuss how large was the page on which Martial wrote his poems. Catullus 42.5; Ovid, *Metamorphoses* 1.533–534; Arrian, *Hunting* 3.6–7.

49 Already Tibullus 1.7.11; Silius 15.499–501.

50 Tibullus 1.7.11; Venantius, *Poems* 3.8, 5.8, 6.5.

51 Martial 9.32 (p. 261), 9.99, 12.32 (the cheeses are *quadrae* '*carrés*'); Ausonius, *Commemoratio Professorum Burdigalensium*; Rutilius 496; Venantius, *Poems* 6.5.

52 Greek *sagos*. The word may be of Celtic origin (Polybius 2.28.7, 2.30.1; *Diocletian's Edict* 19.60).

53 Martial 1.53, 1.92, 10.76, 11.21, 11.56, 14.128; Juvenal 3.170, 6.117, 8.145; Strabo 4.4.3.

54 For 'Circensian stuffing' see p. 230. The meaning of the name 'Summummian brothel' is a matter of guesswork.

55 Translation by Rachel Bromwich. For the last three sites mentioned, see *Templum Castoris*, *Fons Iuturnae* and *Templum et Atrium Vestae* on Map 10.

56 Claudian, *Manlius' Consulship* 51; Seneca, *Apocolocyntosis* 12; Gaetulicus, *De Britannis* [Probus, *On Vergil* 1.227]; Nemesianus, *Cynegetica* 225–226.

57 Horace, *Odes* 1.35.29–30; Seneca, *Apocolocyntosis* 12; Tacitus, *Agricola* 8.

58 Cf. Tacitus, *Agricola* 16.

59 Pliny 9.169; Juvenal 4.140–142 (this satire, set in Nero's principate, implies that Kentish oysters were available in Rome); Ausonius, *Order of Cities* 9.9. The poem records Maximus's execution at Aquileia.

60 This poem attributed to Llywarch Hen (xi.52–54 Williams) was composed perhaps in the ninth century, though the event recorded, a battle in which the Mercians took territory in Shropshire from a ruler in Powys, is dated to the seventh. Translation by K. H. Jackson.

61 Severn is Latin *Sabrina*; Thames is *Tamesis*. The number of cities in Britain, twenty-eight, is not given at random. Manuscripts of Nennius (*Historia*

Brittonum 66a) supply a list of them. On this and other traditional British lists see Bromwich 1978 esp. pp. 228–237.

62 This name is a loanword from Celtic: the modern Welsh form is *brag*. *Vindolanda writing-tablets* 190; cf. Pliny 18.62. Meyer-Lübke 1930–1935.

63 Precise references: *Gododdin* xxi a Williams, line 241 Jarman; xi Williams, line 102 Jarman; lxi a Williams, line 548 Jarman; xcii Williams, line 883 Jarman. Strabo 4.5.3.
    The ales or beers of the other western provinces are no more popular with Romans than is British malt, though we know of Gaulish *cerevisia* (a term of Celtic origin) and Spanish *caelia*, a drink made from barley (Pliny 22.164).

64 Herodotus 3.115; Strabo 4.5.

65 No one knows exactly what Martial's present was (*Scholia on Juvenal* 12.46–47; *CGL* 5.616.24).

66 Horace, *Odes* 2.12.1 and *passim*.

67 Martial 12.57 (p. 222); Silius 3.401.

68 And possibly also of the *laetus equino sanguine Concanus*, 'Concanian happy [to drink] his horse's blood': he is hard to find on a map. Horace, *Odes* 2.6.2, 2.11.1, 3.4.34; Silius 3.326, 3.360–361.

69 Martial 4.39, 10.17, 14.95; Silius 2.602; Justin 44.3.

70 Martial 1.49 (p. 106), 10.17, 10.78, 12.98 (p. 106); Rutilius 356; Claudian, *Manlius' Consulship* 63.

71 Martial 1.49 (p. 106), 4.55 (p. 105), 10.13, 12.18 (p. 104); Pliny 34.144; Justin 44.3.8.

72 The 'tree of Pallas' (Athene) is the olive.

73 Compare Pliny 37.203.

74 This is one of three recipes offered in the *Geoponica*. The process requires hot sun and (as Byzantine law insisted) an absence of neighbours. For this and other reasons it is not recommended for casual experiment. As those who reconstruct Roman dishes are aware, an almost identical fish sauce is now made in south-east Asia and is easily obtained in Europe and North America. Soy sauce, also the product of fermentation, is comparable.

75 Horace, *Satires* 2.8; Strabo 3.2.6. On fish sauce: Martial 7.28, 7.94, 9.28 (p. 106); Petronius 66.3; Pliny 31.93–94; *Apicius passim*. Ponsich and Tarradell 1965; Ponsich 1988; Edmondson 1987; Curtis 1991.

76 For the 'citadel of Tarraco', see Martial 10.104; Ausonius, *Order of Cities* 11.

77 Cato, *On Farming* 3, 11, 135; Columella 6. 12.2; Pliny 19.26–30.

78 Petronius 86.6; Martial 14.199; Nemesianus, *Cynegetica* 227–230, 251–258; Suetonius, *Nero* 46.1; Pliny 8.166.

79 Catullus 37.18–20; Polybius 12.3.10 [Athenaeus 399f]; Varro, *On Farming* 3.12.6.

80 Martial 1.61, 10.103, 10.104.

81 Dirt is correct for farmyard animals, children and even gods: Horace, *Odes* 2.18.28; Persius 1.71–72 (p. 25); Martial 3.58 (p. 26), 12.57 (p. 222).

82 Juvenal 12.40–42; Strabo 3.2.6; Columella 7.2.4; Pliny 8.191.

83 Martial 1.96 (p. 268); Strabo 3.5.11; Columella 7.2.5.

84 Silius 3.401; Martial 1.61, 9.61; Ausonius, *Order of Cities* 11. Martial observes that, since the tree was planted by Caesar and not the unlucky Pompey, it was sure to stand for ever. On *cruor*, the madder dye of Lydia, see p. 163.

85 Horace, *Odes* 2.2.10–11; *Priapeia* 75; Silius 1.141, 3.14–31.

86 Strabo 2.3.4–5; cf. p. 191. Strabo repeats the story of Eudoxus from Poseidonius and, in Strabo's way, ridicules many minor improbabilities in it: for all that, the main lines seem likely to be true.

87 One of the more daring of the transferred epithets of Roman poetry. Martial 1.41 (p. 222), 1.61, 3.63, 5.78 (p. 249), 11.16; Juvenal 11.162–168; Pliny, *Letters* 1.15.1–4 (p. 251). Fear 1991; Olmos 1991; Leary 1996: 270.

88 Varro, *Menippean Satires* 225 Bücheler.

89 Horace, *Odes* 1.1.10, 2.2.10–11; Petronius 117; Pliny 18.35.

90 Horace, *Satires* 2.3.87; Cicero, *De lege Manilia* 34; Aristides, *Roman Oration* 10–12 (p. 272).

91 Horace, *Odes* 1.22.5, 2.6.3–4; Sallust, *Jugurtha* 17; Varro, *On Farming* 1.44.2; Columella 5.10.11, 7.2.4, 10.418. See also p. 110.

92 Translation after J. D. Duff. Cf. Nemesianus, *Cynegetica* 259–271.

93 Nemesianus, *Cynegetica* 227–230; Suetonius, *Nero* 30.

94 Horace, *Odes* 1.23.10; Ovid, *Fasti* 5.371; Silius 3.288–289; Nemesianus, *Eclogues* 4; Sallust, *Jugurtha* 6.

95 Varro, *Menippean Satires* 182 Bücheler; Statius, *Silvae* 4.2.48–49; Martial 10.80 (p. 241), 14.89–91; Petronius 119.27–32.

96 Propertius 3.7.49 (p. 244); Martial 14.3.

97 Horace, *Odes* 2.18.1–5, *Epistles* 1.10.19; Martial 6.42 (p. 239), 8.53 (p. 108); Statius, *Silvae* 1.5.36; Sidonius 5.37; Seneca, *Letters* 115.8; Pliny 35.3; Suetonius, *Julius* 85.

98 Horace, *Epodes* 2.53; Martial 3.58 (p. 26); Columella 8.2.2; Pliny 10.132.

99 Horace, *Satires* 2.4.58–59.

100 Petronius 31 etc. The species originated in central Asia (Laufer 1919: 276–285).

101 Horace, *Epodes* 7.5–6; Sallust, *Catiline* 10; Petronius 101. The 'heights', *arces*, precisely balance the opposing *Tarpeiae arces* ('Tarpeian heights, Capitol') of Rome.

102 Horace, *Odes* 2.16.35, *Epistles* 2.2.181; Tibullus 2.3.58; Ovid, *Fasti* 2.319; Mela 3.11, Pliny 5.12, 6.201, 9.127.

103 Felt was regarded as a typically Cilician product: thus references to African goathair appear geographically confused: beside these 'Cilician slippers' we find 'hair as stiff as a Cinyphian he-goat's beard, trimmed by a Cilician barber' (which a Cinyphian goat's beard seldom was). Vergil, *Georgics* 3.311–313; Statius, *Silvae* 4.5.29–30; Grattius, *Cynegetica* 34–36; Martial 9.27; Varro, *On Farming* 2.11.12.

104 Plautus, *The Rope* 629–630 (p. 61); Pliny 19.38.

105 Synesius, *Letters* 106, 134. 'Can it be that what Synesius and his friends took to be the true silphium was merely one of the similar plants common enough in the Orient?' (Coster 1951: 13–14). Theophrastus, *Study of Plants* 6.3.1–7 with Amigues's note. Attempts to identify silphium with plants of modern north Africa, as detailed by Amigues, are misguided: none resembles asafoetida.

106 Pliny 15.82. Fine Spanish preserved fruits are packed in the same way today.

107 Vergil, *Georgics* 1.309; Ovid, *Metamorphoses* 4.710.

108 Claudian, *War Against Gildo* 506.

109 Diodorus 5.13.4, 5.14.3; Martial 9.26, 11.42.

110 Horace, *Odes* 1.31.4; Rutilius 354; Cicero, *De lege Manilia* 34.

111 Horace, *Art of Poetry* 376 (p. 245); Nemesianus, *Eclogues* 4.

112 Galen, *Properties of Foods* 3.40 [6.747]. Andrews 1949.

113 Vergil, *Aeneid* 1.52.

114 The stone is trachytic lava.

115 Hiera is modern Vulcano: its Italian name is the origin of the common noun *volcano*. Vergil, *Aeneid* 8.416–422; *Aetna* 442; Juvenal 1.7–9, 13.44–45; Diodorus 5.7; Strabo 6.2.10.

116 Pliny 3.92, 5.42.

117 Naevius 32 Strzelecki; *CIL* 1 (2nd edn): 47.
118 Plutarch, *On Peace of Mind* [472c]. Theophrastus (*Characters* 21.9) already ridicules the affectation of putting up a tombstone to a Maltese lapdog. Cf. Athenaeus 519b. Strabo (6.2.11) says that the breed came from Malta. The Hellenistic poet Callimachus (579 Pfeiffer) is Pliny's (3.152) source for the statement that they came not from Malta but from the Adriatic island of *Melite*, modern Melida. Pliny evidently doubted it.
119 Ovid, *Metamorphoses* 13.724–727, *Fasti* 4.479
120 *Elegies for Maecenas* 1.41; Solinus 5.3.
121 Ovid, *Fasti* 4.474, 4.499; Thucydides 6.4.5. The name of Drepanum, in north-western Sicily, had the same meaning (Frazer 1929 vol. 4: 278–279).
122 Pindar, *Olympian* 1.12, *Pythian* 12.1; Theocritus 7; Vergil, *Eclogues* 2.21; Strabo 6.2.6 (see also p. 234).
123 Ovid, *Fasti* 4.422 (p. 113); *Priapeia* 75; Cicero, *Against Verres* 2.3.112; Pliny 18.95.
124 Cicero, *De lege Manilia* 34; Strabo 6.2.7; Aristides, *Roman Oration* 10–12 (p. 272).
125 Martial 11.8 (p. 264), 11.42; Pliny 11.32; *Geoponica* 15.7.
126 Horace, *Odes* 2.16.33–34; Antiphanes 236 [*Epitome of Athenaeus* 27d–e]; Hermippus 63 [*Epitome of Athenaeus* 27e]; Clytus [Athenaeus 540d–541a]. Dalby 2000b; Chencines 2000.
127 Aristophanes fragment 225 Kassel and Austin [Athenaeus 527c]; Plato, *Letters* 7.326b.
128 Wilkins and Hill 1994; Dalby 1995.
129 Varro, *On the Latin Language* 7.86.
130 Cato, *On Farming* 6,7; Columella 3.2.7–13, 3.7.2, 3.9.1–9; Pliny 14.21.
131 Strabo 5.4.8, 13.4.11; Pliny 14.25, 14.35; Columella 3.2.27.
132 Plato, *Letters* 326b (p. 115), *Republic* 404c.
133 Strabo 6.2.6. 'Their place was to a certain extent supplied by a garrison of two hundred Roman soldiers', J. G. Frazer adds drily (1929 vol. 4: 280). The cult of the goddess of Eryx had been brought to Rome as early as the third century BC and established at the temple of *Erycina*. This was in origin an adjective applied to Aphrodite or Venus 'of Eryx'; it became in Roman literature one more of the many names of the goddess of love, the *Erycina ridens* 'smiling Erycina' of Horace (*Odes* 1.2.33).
134 Vergil, *Georgics* 1.471–472; *Aetna* 335–339; Petronius 122.135–136.
135 Propertius 3.2.7–8; Ovid, *Fasti* 4.468; Claudian, *Rape of Proserpina*; Solinus 5.17.
136 *Aetna* 394–395; Euripides, *Cyclops* 20–22, 298; Pliny 3.89.

5 Aurora

1 Suetonius, *Julius* 48, 73.
2 The works of art described are:
   1 Apelles, 'Venus rising from the waves' (Pliny 35.79, 87, 91, 145; Ovid, *From Pontus* 4.1.29; *Tristia* 2.527; *Art of Love* 3.401). The icon of her wringing her hair, still wet with the waters of the sea – her mother Thetis – is familiar. The translation accepts Baehrens' conjecture *matre*; cf. Vessereau's note.
   2 Timomachus, 'Medea' (Antiphilus 48 [*Anthologia Planudea* 136]; Pliny 35.136). The original was at Cyzicus till it was bought, with Timomachus' 'Ajax', for 80 talents by Caesar and placed in the Temple of Venus Genitrix at Rome in 46/44 BC. A painting from Herculaneum appears to be a copy of it.

3 Naevius 9 Strzelecki.

4 Petronius 37–45, 67, 107 and *passim*.

5 Suetonius, *Tiberius* 71; Seneca, *Apocolocyntosis* 5. Saalfeld 1884.

6 Propertius 3.9.9–18; Horace, *Epistles* 2.1.90–101.

7 See for example Horace, *Epodes* 9.5–6; Catullus 64.264; *Ciris* 166; Petronius 2, 31, 53, 78 and fragment 14; Cato, *On Farming* 5.

8 Martial 7.67 (for the function of the *ceroma*), 14.49; Petronius 21. Plautus, *Bacchides* 428 already includes the Greek *discus* in a list of exercises in which all others have Latin names.

9 Illustrated on Trajan's Column. Leather saddles were not used. Horace, *Epistles* 1.14.43; Martial 14.86; Cicero, *De Finibus* 3.15; Nonius Marcellus 108.27–30 citing Varro.

10 It had been 'the anger of Achilles' (*Iliad* 1.1). On Greek medical terms see Sconocchia 1991.

11 Martial 5.79, 14.1; Suetonius, *Nero* 51.

12 Petronius 22, 34, 40, 69; Martial 11.11, 11.31, 12.50.

13 For example, Cicero, *Against Caecilius* 55, *Philippics* 5.15; Petronius 22, 28, 32, 33.

14 Largely lost to us, this Hellenistic Greek poetry inspired Catullus, Horace, Propertius and their contemporaries.

15 Turpilius, *Paedium* 7 Rychlewska; Plautus, *Pseudolus* 1275.

16 Martial 6.6, 11.47, 14.201; Juvenal 6.246.

17 Martial 10.68. Cf. Celsus 6.18.1. In general, Adams 1982.

18 A 'Philaenis' is the subject of Martial 7.67; the name is no chance selection for one described as deviant in sexual matters.

19 Turpilius, *Lindia* 7, *Philopator* 13 Rychlewska; Terence, *Eunuch* 1028; Petronius 110, 114.

20 Hippolochus [Athenaeus 129a]; Turpilius, *Hetaera* fragments 1–2 Rychlewska, and probably Turpilius, *Lindia*. On Corinth: Pindar fragment 107 Bowra; Strabo 8.6.20, 12.3.36 (p. 125); Athenaeus 567c, 570e, 573c–574c. On Athens: Athenaeus 577d–596f.

21 Horace, *Epistles* 1.11.2 (p. 118); *Priapeia* 75; Clearchus [Athenaeus 540d–541a]. There had been some such quarter in Athens too, its organisation attributed to Solon.

22 A fact that helps to explain the citations of this phrase at Liddell and Scott 1929–1940 s.v. '*ankon* (III)'. Cf. Herodotus 1.93 on prostitution in early Lydia.

23 Ovid, *Tristia* 1.2.79–80; Athenaeus 541a.

24 Antipater of Thessalonica 94 [*Anthologia Palatina* 9.550], 113 [9.408]; Pausanias 8.33.2; Pliny 4.66, 34.8.

25 Dio, *Orations* 77/78.4; [Plutarch], *Alexandrian Proverbs* 2.5.

26 Plautus, *Poenulus* 339; Terence, *Eunuchus* 115; Martial 7.80 (p. 212); *Priapeia* 68.9 (p. 165); Strabo 10.2.3.

27 Robinson and Fluck 1937.

28 Parke and Wormell 1956 no. 1. Goebel 1915; Dalby, 2000b.

29 *Female* gown-trailers go back to the *Iliad* (6.442): *Troiades helkesipeploi* 'Trojan women with gowns trailing'.

30 Turpilius, *Leucadia* 2 Rychlewska; Plautus, *Menaechmi* 426; Varro, *Menippean Satires* 228 Bücheler; Tertullian, *On the Soul* 20; Hermippus 63 [*Epitome of Athenaeus* 27e]; Herondas 2.100, 5.14.

31 Martial 6.77, 10.76; Persius 6.77; Petronius 68–9; *Epitome of Athenaeus* 20b; Athenaeus 111f.

32 Horace, *Satires* 2.6.44; Petronius 52; Suetonius, *Augustus* 83. Syrian slaves employed, like Cappadocians, to carry a litter: Martial 9.2, 9.22.

33 Lucilius 497; Rutilius 377–383 (p. 15); Lucian, *Council of the Gods* 4. Syrians as thieving slaves: Petronius 22.

34 Horace, *Satires* 1.2.1; Juvenal 3.62–66; Petronius 74; Suetonius, *Nero* 27. The strange word *ambubaia* originates in Aramaic *'abbuba* 'flute'.

35 Sima Qian, *Records of the Grand Historian* 123 [vol. 2: 278–279 Watson].

36 After Nadich 1994 vol. 1: 334–5.

37 Martial 7.30 (p. 211), 12.57 (p. 222); Juvenal 3.10–20 (p. 42), 6.543; Rutilius 383–398 (partly quoted on p. 15); Petronius 102–103 (p. 178) and fragment 37.

38 Martial 5.13, 9.35; Petronius fragment 20.

39 All this from Petronius: 31, 68; fragments 19, 20.

40 Horace, *Satires* 2.4.29; Cato, *On Farming* 158; Pliny 14.78–79.

41 Cato, *On Farming* 112–113.

42 Horace, *Satires* 2.8.52 (p. 000).

43 Philodemus 21 [*Anthologia Palatina* 11.34], 23 [11.44]; Varro, *Menippean Satires* 104 Bücheler; Theopompus [*Epitome of Athenaeus* 26b–c]; Strabo 14.1.35; Pliny 14.95–97 (p. 249); Servius on Vergil, *Georgics* 2.98.

44 Philodemus 21 [*Anthologia Palatina* 11.34]; Vergil, *Georgics* 2.90; Horace, *Odes* 1.17.21.

45 Vergil, *Georgics* 2.98; Ovid, *Metamorphoses* 6.15, 6.86, *Fasti* 2.313; Pliny 5.110, 14.74; Galen, *On Therapeutic Method* [10.830], *On Good and Bad Juices* [6.803].

46 Varro *On Farming* 1.2.7; Strabo 12.8.17–19, 13.4.11.

47 *Iliad* 3.184; Varro, *On Farming* 1.2.7.

48 Cretan wine is called for by an imagined rude guest in a letter by Fronto (vol. 2: 50 Haines): the host serves his own from his Falernian estate, and the guest had better be satisfied with that.

49 Frazer 1929 vol. 2: 358.

50 Vergil, *Georgics* 1.17; *Copa* 9–10 (p. 18); *Priapeia* 75; *Einsiedeln Eclogues* 2.15–20; Nemesianus, *Eclogues* 3.13–14.

51 Pliny 14.20, 14.25 for vines, and *passim*; Theophrastus, *Plant Physiology* 3.3.4, *Study of Plants passim*; and for the Greek willow: Columella 4.30.4 (p. 74).

52 Martial 5.37 (p. 263), 6.34, 11.42; Petronius 38; Varro, *On Farming* 3.16.26; Strabo 9.1.23; Pliny 11.32, 11.39, 22.113. Jones 1976.

53 After temporary display in the theatre Crassus placed them in his own house. Horace, *Odes* 2.18.1–5; Pliny 17.6, 36.7.

54 Cicero, *Letters to Atticus* 1.8.2; Strabo 9.1.23.

55 Ovid, *Tristia* 1.1.83, *Fasti* 4.282, *Metamorphoses* 14.472–482; Statius, *Silvae* 1.5.34–41 (p. 239); Martial 9.75 (p. 109); Strabo 9.5.16, 10.1.6; Pliny 36.48.

56 Martial 1.88, 6.13, 6.39, 6.42 (p. 239); Strabo 10.5.7. Among several other Greek sources of marble Pliny mentions Chios, producer of the black marble known in Rome as Lucullean, since the luxurious L. Lucullus (consul in 74 BC) had been the first to use it there (Pliny 36.6, 36.49).

57 Propertius 3.2.11; Martial 1.55, 6.42 (p. 239), 9.75 (p. 109); Strabo 8.5.7; Pliny 36.55; Pausanias 2.3.5, 3.21.4 with notes by Frazer and by Levi; Lucian, *Hippias* 5 (p. 240).

58 Propertius 3.2.13; Martial 8.68, 10.94 (p. 217); *Priapeia* 16, 51. Statius (see also p. 36) presumes to compare King Alcinous's fruit garden with that of his own patron at Tibur.

59 On the scallops of Tarentum and Mytilenae see pp. 65, 150. Ennius, *Hedyphagetica* [Apuleius, *Apology* 39.2]; Strabo 7.7.5; Dionysius, *Description of Greece* 24. Relying on Archestratus, who must have travelled this route

frequently (Dalby 1995), any modern visitor to Ambracia and Calydon should certainly look out for *labrax* (sea bass, *Dicentrarchus spp.*) and verify whether it is indeed fatter than the *labrax* of Miletus but not quite so delicate in flavour (45 [Athenaeus 311a]); try the squid, too (54 [326d]).

60 Antipater of Thessalonica 91 [*Anthologia Palatina* 9.58]; Vergil, *Georgics* 3.19 (p. 229); Horace, *Odes* 1.1.3; Propertius 3.2.20.

61 Ovid, *Fasti* 3.865, *Metamorphoses* 3.531; Propertius 3.2.5–6; Heracleides Criticus 18–19.

62 Antiphilus 5 [*Anthologia Palatina* 9.73]; *Priapeia* 75; Cato, *On Farming* 8; Pliny 15.129.

63 Cato, *On Farming* 7; Petronius 130; Pliny, *Letters* 1.15.1–4 (p. 251); Galen, *Properties of Simples* 8.15.17; Plato Comicus 173 [*Epitome of Athenaeus* 5b]; Lynceus, *Apophthegmata* [Athenaeus 583f].

64 Rocket was also considered aphrodisiac (p. 253). *Oenogarum* is a mixture of wine and fish sauce.

65 Aristophanes, *Lysistrata* 79–83; Aristotle, *Politics* 1269b12–1270a8; *Anthologia Palatina* 13.16; cf. Pausanias 3.8.2.

66 Euripides, *Andromache* 597–600 ('with bare thighs and loose clothes, to wrestle and run races with the young men') probably says it as it actually was. 'Myrtilus' in Athenaeus 566e (p. 125) exaggerates.

67 Pindar fragment 95 Bowra; Alexis [Athenaeus 540d–541a]; Vergil, *Georgics* 3.44, 3.339–347 (p. 87), 3.405; Horace, *Epodes* 6.5; Petronius 40; Nemesianus, *Cynegetica* 107.

68 Horace, *Odes* 2.18.1–5; Martial 14.156; Pliny 9.125–128; Pausanias 3.21.6. Thompson 1947: 209–218.

69 Horace, *Odes* 1.7.2; Apuleius, *Metamorphoses* 1.1.

70 Strabo 8.6.20; Gellius 1.8.4.

71 Vergil, *Georgics* 2.463–468; Propertius 3.5.6; Cicero, *Letters to Atticus* 2.1.11; Petronius 50, 119.9; Martial 9.59 (p. 241), 14.43, 14.172; *Talmud Babli, Yoma* 38a; Pliny 34.1–8; Pliny, *Letters* 3.6.

72 An anonymous line of verse quoted in *Epitome of Athenaeus* 20b. Horace, *Odes* 1.7.5; Horace, *Epistles* 2.2.46; Ovid, *Tristia* 1.2.77; *Priapeia* 75; Martial 5.2; Heracleides Criticus 5.

73 Varro, *On Farming* 2.2.18; Pollux, *Onomasticon* 6.67; Alexis, *Samian Annals* [Athenaeus 540d–541a]; Aristophanes, *Wealth* 253 and scholia; Hippolochus [Athenaeus 130d]. Andrews 1958.

74 Plautus, *Mostellaria* 264; Propertius 3.17.27; Ovid, *Fasti* 3.82; *Priapeia* 75; Martial 5.7; Pliny 35.37.

75 Petronius 22; Varro, *On Farming* 3.9.2; Cicero, *Academics* 2.18; Columella 2.2.4; Pliny 10.139.

76 Horace, *Odes* 1.7.1; Antipater of Thessalonica 91 [*Anthologia Palatina* 9.58]; *Priapeia* 75; Lynceus [Athenaeus 360d].

77 Horace, *Epistles* 1.11.1 (p. 118); Hermesianax [Athenaeus 598c].

78 Archestratus 56 (p. 143); Ennius, *Hedyphagetica* [Apuleius, *Apology* 39.2]; Aristotle, *Study of Animals* 603a21; Xenocrates 56–71. Davidson 1981: 200–201; Thompson 1947: 133–134.

79 Horace, *Odes* 1.1.34–35; Ovid, *Amores* 2.18.34.

80 Or, possibly, of the practice of fellatio that the name of Lesbos typified in Greek (*lesbiazein*). Catullus 5, 7, 43, 51, 58, 72, 75, 79 etc.; Martial 1.34 (p. 31: by contrast with her geographically named neighbours Ias and Chione, Lesbia makes love with the door wide open), 6.23, 10.39, 11.62, 11.99.

81 Dioscorides 1.70, 1.42; Pliny 12.72, 14.128, 24.43, 24.121, 37.51; Galen, *On Therapeutic Method* [10.322, 10.499], *Properties of Simples* [12.68–69]; *Apicius* 1.1, 1.3. Lambraki 1997: 254; Salaman 1993.

82 Tibullus 2.3.47–48 (p. 51). On Saguntine pottery, Martial 14.109.

83 Davies and Kathirithamby 1986: 112–113 with references there.

84 Propertius 1.2.2; Persius 5.135; Martial 8.33, 8.68, 14.24; Juvenal 6.260; Apuleius, *Metamorphoses* 8.27; *Historia Augusta, Aurelian* 45.5; Ulpian [*Digest* 34.2.23.1].

85 Publilius Syrus [Petronius 55; p. 266]; Apuleius, *Metamorphoses* 10.31.

86 In spite of Horace, *Odes* 1.36.10; Isidore, *Etymologies* 16.1.6, Crete was not the place where chalk, *creta*, came from.

87 Lucretius 4.441; Seneca, *Phaedra* 34; Martial 11.69; Arrian, *Hunting* 3; Aelian, *Nature of Animals* 3.2.

88 Vergil, *Eclogues* 10.59–60, *Georgics* 3.339–347 (p. 87); Horace, *Odes* 1.15.17; *Ciris* 115; Claudian, *Porcupine* 36–38; Pliny 16.161, 16.166.

89 Harrison 1991: 118; Dalby 1996: 78 and note 108; Littlewood 1967.

90 Scribonius Largus 63; *Itinerarium Symonis Semeonis ab Hybernia ad Terram Sanctam* 22. For further references, Dalby 1996: 193, 195, 204 and notes. Later sources show that it was always the sweet wine of Crete that was exported over long distances.

91 Horace, *Epodes* 9.29; *Iliad* 2.649; Dio 46.23, 49.32. Rouanet-Liesenfelt 1992: she identifies thirty-three medicinal herbs that are said by Dioscorides, Pliny or Galen (and in one case all three) to be found in Crete only or to be at their best there.

92 Propertius 2.1.61; Theophrastus, *Study of Plants* 9.16; Dioscorides 3.32, 4.49; Pliny 26.153, 26.161, 27.141. Rackham and Moody 1996: 71.

93 Galen, *On Antidotes* [14.4, 14.9–10, 14.30, 14.59, 14.79]. Rouanet-Liesenfelt 1992; Millar 1983: 185.

94 E.g. Polunin 1980: 57–76; Lambraki 1997.

95 Galen, *On Antidotes* [14.59, 14.79]. It is natural, speaking generally, that fresh plants wherever gathered should have greater medicinal value than dried plants of the same species. Ancient medicinal uses of these plants will be found described by Theophrastus, Pliny, Galen and others.

96 Petronius 89; Apuleius, *Metamorphoses* 1.2.

97 Vergil, *Georgics* 1.282, 2.469; Horace, *Odes* 1.5.11, 1.37.19–20; Ovid, *Metamorphoses* 7.470; Lucan 9.985; Petronius 124.294; Pliny 14.73–76 (p. 133). The purple dye of Meliboea on the Thessalian coast gets into two first-century BC poems (Lucretius 2.500–501; Vergil, *Aeneid* 5.251); its reputation may be historical rather than actual, like that of Thessalian horses, for the small city of Meliboea (in whose territory these vineyards once lay) scarcely appears in the Roman record. The eastern coastal district is *Magnesia*. The magnetic stone called *magnes* in Latin, now known as 'magnetite', was found here and also near the city of Magnesia ad Sipylum in the province of Asia (Lucretius 6.906–1089; Pliny 36.128).

98 Ovid, *Fasti* 5.401; Pliny 25.93.

99 Ovid, *Metamorphoses* 13.716;*Aetna* 6; Statius, *Thebaid* 3.104–108, 3.195–196; *Priapeia* 75.

100 Vergil, *Georgics* 3.405; Horace, *Epodes* 6.5; Grattius, *Cynegetica* 181; Lucan 4.440; Nemesianus, *Cynegetica* 107; Clytus, Alexis [both Athenaeus 540d-541a].

101 Propertius 3.7.49 (p. 244); Vergil, *Aeneid* 10.136; Petronius 33; Pliny 12.56, 13.8 (p. 175), 16.231.

102 Horace, *Odes* 1.18.9–11; Ovid, *Fasti* 3.719.

103 Antipater of Thessalonica 41 [*Anthologia Palatina* 6.335].
104 Plautus, *Miles Gloriosus* 1178, *Persa* 155; Martial 14.29. The poems of
     Antipater and Martial are both written to accompany the gift of a *causea*. For
     the few specialities of Hellenistic Macedonia see Dalby 1996: 152–157.
105 Pliny 14.54; *Odyssey* 9.39–42; Pindar fragment 52b Maehler line 25. Dalby
     1996: 99 and notes 19–20. Odysseus, like Mucianus, sometimes embellished
     the truth.
106 Seneca, *Agamemnon* 479; Statius, *Silvae* 4.6.9 (p. 267), *Thebaid* 3.526; Martial
     9.29.
107 Translation after M. Platnauer.
108 Horace, *Epistles* 1.3.3, 1.15.13; Ovid, *From Pontus* 4.5.5.
109 Vergil, *Georgics* 4.520; Horace, *Epodes* 5.14, *Odes* 1.12.6; Propertius 3.2.3–4;
     Ovid, *Ibis* 598; *Ciris* 165.
110 Horace, *Odes* 2.7.26–28, 2.16.5.
111 Vergil, *Georgics* 3.461–463; Ovid, *Heroides* 2.84; Grattius, *Cynegetica* 523;
     Sallust, *Jugurtha* 38; Livy 45.30.
112 As in similar modern commercial sports, gladiators with a public following
     had stage names or nicknames. Horace gives us a *Thraex* who was called
     Gallina 'chicken' (Horace, *Satires* 2.6.44). Petronius 45; Pliny 33.129; Paulus,
     ex Fest. p. 366.
113 Ovid, *Tristia* 1.10.28; Horace, *Epistles* 1.3.4.
114 Vergil, *Georgics* 3.258–263; Ovid, *Heroides* 17–18; Statius, *Silvae* 1.2.87; Silius
     8.621; Martial, *Spectacula* 25; Paulus Silentiarius [*Anthologia Palatina* 5.293].
115 Vergil, *Georgics* 1.207; Lucan 9.959; *Priapeia* 75.
116 Vergil, *Georgics* 4.111; Ovid, *Tristia* 1.10.26, *Fasti* 1.440, 6.345; Martial
     11.51. Martial's book 11 is lewd with Lampsacene verses, as he justifiably
     claims (11.16) – 'Lampsacene verses' not because people in Lampsacus wrote
     such verses but because they celebrate sex.
117 Horace, *Odes* 2.13.15; Ovid, *Tristia* 1.10.13, 1.10.34, 1.10.47.
118 *Maiotis* is the Sea of Azov; its 'mouth' is the straits of Kerch. Martial 5.78,
     11.31; Theopompus 115F62 [Athenaeus 526d]; Pliny 9.48, 32.151.
119 The 'many-eyed fowl' is the peacock (p. 254). On parrots see p. 193. *Serica* are
     Chinese silks (p. 200).
120 Agathias draws fully on the rare vocabulary of a thousand-year poetic tradition:
     this short poem is cited at least ten times in Liddell and Scott 1929–1940.
121 Plutarch, *Demetrius* 20.2–3; Justin 36.4.3.
122 Vergil, *Georgics* 4.210–211; *Elegies for Maecenas* 1.69–86; Propertius
     3.11.17–20; Ovid, *Art of Love* 2.219–222; Apollodorus 2.6.3; see Frazer's note
     for further references.
123 In general, Dangel 1985.
124 Vergil, *Georgics* 2.137; Horace, *Epistles* 1.11.2 (p. 118); Propertius 3.18.28;
     Ovid, *Metamorphoses* 9.450; Martial 8.78; Strabo 12.8.19; Petronius 133.
125 See for example Herodotus 1.94. *Elektron*, such as occurs naturally in the
     Pactolus, was the earliest coinage metal, and the invention of coinage in Lydia
     is dated to the late seventh century BC.
126 Propertius 2.32.11–12, 3.18.19; Valerius Maximus 9.1.5; Pliny 7.196, 8.196,
     33.63, 36.115, 37.12; Tertullian, *On Women's Dress* 1.1.3.
127 Martial 6.42 (p. 239), 9.75; Statius, *Silvae* 2.2.85–89; Strabo 12.8.14; Pliny
     35.3, 36.102.
128 Pliny 2.210, 36.131.
129 Varro, *Menippean Satires* 131 Bücheler; Vergil, *Aeneid* 9.619; Catullus 64.264;
     Ciris 166; Ovid, *Fasti* 4.181; Statius, *Thebaid* 2.666; Valerius Flaccus 3.232.

130 Lucretius 2.608–632; Catullus 63 (adapted from a Greek poem by Callimachus) on which see Highet 1957: 37–9; Ovid, *Fasti* 2.55, *Art of Love* 1.507; Martial 14.204; Juvenal 8.176 (p. 220); Lucian, *On the Syrian God* 43; Apuleius, *Metamorphoses* 8.24; Augustine, *City of God* 7.26.

131 Statius, *Silvae* 1.6.15 (if correctly emended: p. 231), 4.9.26; Petronius 44.13.

132 *Priapeia* 75; Pliny 36.20–22; Lucian, *Amores* 11–15; Athenaeus 591a.

133 Vergil, *Georgics* 3.306–307, 4.334–335; Clytus and Alexis [Athenaeus 540d–541a]; Strabo 12.8.16; Pliny 8.190, 29.33; Tertullian, *On Women's Dress* 1.1.3; *Talmud Babli, Shabbat* 30b, *Ketubbot* 111b. For Greek references see Gow on Theocritus 15.126.

134 Horace, *Epistles* 1.17.30; Plautus, *Captives* 274; Vergil, *Georgics* 4.334; Ovid, *Tristia* 2.413; Martial (p. 66); Juvenal 6.296; Apuleius, *Metamorphoses* 1.1, 4.32; Plutarch, *Was Alexander Brave or Lucky?* [330c].

135 Antipater of Thessalonica 91 [*Anthologia Palatina* 9.58]; Rufinus 1 [*Anthologia Palatina* 5.9].

136 On the misuse of the name *Phrygia* see Strabo 14.3.3. Additionally, there is sometimes confusion in later literature between *Mysia* (defined as in the text) and *Moesia* (the south bank of the lower Danube): see for example Claudian, *Panegyric on Honorius's Fourth Consulship* 53 (p. 204). In the spoken Greek of Roman times and later the two names were both pronounced /misia/.

137 Vergil, *Georgics* 1.102–103, 3.450, 4.41; Horace, *Epodes* 13.13–14; Ovid, *Fasti* 4.249, 6.15; Petronius 89, 128, 134; *Iliad* 8.47; Theophrastus, *Study of Plants* 9.2.5.

138 Ovid, *Tristia* 1.10.29–30; *Priapeia* 75; Cicero, *De lege Manilia* 20.

139 Catullus 63.13, 63.91; Horace, *Odes* 1.16; Martial 6.39 (p. 213), 8.81, 11.6; Valerius Flaccus 3.232; Apollonius Rhodius 1.1118–1125.

140 Ovid, *Tristia* 1.10.35; *Epitome of Athenaeus* 20b.

141 Catullus 4; Horace, *Odes* 1.14.11–12, 1.35.7–8; Theophrastus, *Study of Plants* 4.5.5; Strabo 12.3.12; Pliny 16.197.

142 Vergil, *Georgics* 2.437–438; Catullus 4; Strabo 12.3.10.

143 Pliny 15.102 (p. 102); *Epitome of Athenaeus* 50f.

144 Nemesianus, *Cynegetica* 240–250; Martial 5.78 (p. 249); Columella 10.184, 10.191.

145 Varro, *On Farming* 2.6.3; Pliny 8.225; Galen, *Properties of Foods* 3.1 [6.664]; Lazar P'arpec'i (p. 185); Catullus 66.48; Vergil (p. 272); Martial (p. 105); Rutilius (p. 79).

146 *Ciris* 168; Strabo 12.7.3; Pliny 12.124–125.

147 Plautus, *Curculio* 102; Vergil, *Georgics* 1.56 (p. 272); Horace, *Satires* 2.4.68; Propertius 4.6.74 (p. 245), 3.10.22; Ovid, *Fasti* 1.76; *Elegies for Maecenas* 1.133; Martial 3.65; Strabo 14.5.5; Mela 1.71–75; Pliny 13.5, 13.9, 21.31–33; Tertullian, *On Women's Dress* 2.6.1. The colours of saffron dye, varying from blood-red to yellow, are discussed in a forthcoming University of Wales dissertation by Lloyd L. Jones.

Cinnabaris was a red pigment from India or beyond, supposed to be a mixture of dragon's blood and elephant's blood (Pliny 33.116–117; *Periplus* 30). Its real origin was from various plants (*Pterocarpus spp., Dracaena spp., Daemonorops spp.*): see Schafer 1963: 211.

148 Martial 8.14; Pliny 14.80–81 (p. 137); Galen, *On Good and Bad Juices* [6.800–801] (p. 137).

149 Martial 14.141; *Acts* 18.3; Pliny 6.143.

150 In general, Dangel 1989.

151 Translation by Nadich 1994 vol. 1: 277. Crops planted at Gadara in Syria were said to yield a hundred to one (Varro, *On Farming* 1.44.2; cf. Matthew 13.8).

Syrian wine: Dalby 1996: 96–97 and note 13. Assyrian, Persian and later gardening: Briant 1996, especially pp. 98–99, 214, 249–250; Dalby, 2000b.

152 Nadich 1994 vol. 1: 271.

153 Petronius 31; Statius, *Silvae* 1.6.14 (p. 231).

154 Horace, *Epistles* 2.2.184; *Elegies for Maecenas* 1.134; Lucan 3.216; Silius 3.600; Martial 8.33, 11.31 (p. 235); Pliny 5.70; Josephus, *Jewish Antiquities* 14.54; *Apicius* 7.12 (p. 145), 9.10.8 (p. 160), 9.11 (p. 53).

155 Statius, *Silvae* 3.2.140; Theophrastus, *Study of Plants* 9.6; Justin 36.3.1–4.

156 Martial 14.59; Strabo 16.4.19; Pliny 12.111–123, 13.18, 37.204; Josephus, *Jewish Antiquities* 14.54; Tacitus *Histories* 5.6; Laufer 1919: 429–434. The traditional English name 'balm of Gilead' is a reference to the story of Joseph in *Genesis* 37.25.

Miller 1969: 101–2, 108 argues that the Roman demand surely exceeded the Syrian supply. He fails to notice Pliny's information that the balsam of Mecca tree was being propagated in Palestine or Syria and covered whole hillsides there: it must have been a highly remunerative cash crop. The *Periplus* does not mention *opobalsamum* in Red Sea trade.

157 Pliny 12.124–125.

158 Calpurnius, *Eclogues* 5.89; Lucan 9.916; Theophrastus, *Study of Plants* 9.1.2, 9.7.2, 9.9.2; Dioscorides 3.83; Pliny 12.126, 13.8 (p. 175), 24.13. Laufer 1919: 363–366; Schafer 1963: 188; Miller 1969: 99–100.

159 Diodorus 2.48; Pliny 7.65, 16.52, 16.203, 35.178; Justin 36.3.7.

160 Martial 10.17; Pliny 9.135; Aelian, *Nature of Animals* 16.1.

161 Vergil, *Georgics* 2.465, 3.307; Catullus 61.165; Horace, *Epodes* 12.10–11, *Epistles* 1.10.26; Propertius 3.13.7; Tibullus 1.2.75; Ovid, *Art of Love* 2.297, *Metamorphoses* 6.222; Seneca, *Thyestes* 955, *Oedipus* 413; Martial 1.53, 2.57, 6.11, 8.10, 11.40, 14.154, 14.156; Juvenal 7.136; Petronius 30; Pliny 9.124–141; Tertullian, *On Women's Dress* 1.1.3. Thompson 1947: 209–218.

162 Lygdamus 3.34; Apuleius, *Metamorphoses* 2.16 (p. 262). Cf. note 2 (p. 287).

163 Vergil, *Aeneid* 1.693, 5.760; Ovid, *Art of Love* 3.106, *Metamorphoses* 14.694, *Fasti* 1.452; *Priapeia* 75; Statius, *Thebaid* 2.287, 12.16, *Silvae* 1.2.101, 5.4.8.

164 In general, Dangel 1989; Darby and others 1977. On the library, Gellius 7.17.3.

165 Vergil, *Georgics* 4.294 (below); Martial 14.150; Juvenal 15.122.

166 Horace, *Epodes* 9; Propertius 3.11.45; Varro, *On Farming* 2.10.8.

167 Horace, *Odes* 1.37.6–10; Propertius 3.11.33–46.

168 Translation by Stephen Gaselee.

169 Lucretius 6.712–737; Antipater of Thessalonica 91 [*Anthologia Palatina* 9.58]; Propertius 3.2.19; Rutilius 404.

170 Aristides, *Roman Oration* 10–12 (p. 272). *Pelusiaca lens*, Vergil, *Georgics* 1.228; *Pelusiacum linum*, Silius 3.375.

171 Vergil, *Georgics* 2.91; Statius, *Silvae* 4.9.26; Petronius 40; Columella 10.116; Pliny 22.164, 23.97; *Diocletian's Edict* 2.5.

172 Petronius 23; Pliny 24.110; Tertullian, *On Women's Dress* 2.6.4.

173 Horace, *Odes* 3.29; Martial 14.57; Pliny 13.18 (p. 189), 23.98.

174 Theophrastus, *Study of Plants* 4.2.1, 4.2.6; Pliny 12.121, 13.8–15, 21.90; Galen, *Properties of Foods* 1.25 [6.539] (Dalby 1996: 25). Darby and others 1977: 776–789; Sandy 1989.

175 On *metopium* (related to earlier Greek *netopon*) see also Apollonius the Herophilean [Athenaeus 688f]; Dioscorides 1.33, 1.59; Galen, *Hippocratic Glossary* [19.71]; Paul of Aegina 7.20.

176 Martial 11.11, 12.74, 14.94, 14.115.

177 Petronius 40.5; Martial 14.150.
178 Martial 5.18, 14.10, 14.11. Lewis 1934.
179 Lucan 9.714; Statius, *Silvae* 1.5.35; Martial 6.42 (p. 239); Pliny 36.55, 36.158.
180 Martial 6.42 (p. 239), 12.50; Pliny 36.59.
181 Horace, *Odes* 4.12.17 (p. 196); Propertius 3.10.22 (p. 167); Mark 14.4 (p. 197); Martial 7.94, 11.49.
182 Aristides, *Egyptian Oration* 349.
183 Lucian, *The Ship* 15 (above); Ovid, *Ibis*; Juvenal 15.3; Pliny 8.97, 10.75.
184 Horace, *Epodes* 12.10–11; Martial 5.65; Achilles Tatius 4.19; Dio 55.10.8; Pliny 8.89–94; Pliny 28.108–109, 184.

6 Barbaricum

1 Silius 3.269; Ammianus 14.4.
2 Petronius 34. For the shaven heads of runaways cf. Martial 14.158 (p. 92).
3 Greek and Latin *Auxume*. Strabo 16.4.7; *Periplus* 3, 4 with Casson's notes; Pliny 2.183, 6.171–172. Scullard 1974.
4 Silius 3.459; Martial 14.3, 14.91; Petronius 32, 119. Scullard 1974. For *Luca bos* see p. 67; for *anguimanus* 'snaky-handed' see p. 193.
5 Diodorus 1.35.10–11; Pliny 8.95–96.
6 Martial, *Spectacula* 9, 22; Pliny 8.71; Dio 51.22.5 (p. 233); Suetonius, *Augustus* 43.4.
7 Juvenal 7.130. Gowers 1950.
8 Horace, *Epistles* 2.1.195; Pliny 8.69.
9 Petronius 134; Pliny 10.1–2, 28.66. About 120 BC ostrich eggs were sent by Parthia, along with Syrian dancers and jugglers, as a rare gift for the King of China (Sima Qian, *Records of the Grand Historian* 123 [vol. 2: 278–279 Watson]).
10 Ibn Baṭūṭā, *Travels* [Yerasimos vol. 3: 209]; Ross 1952; Miller 1969: 53–57, 107–108.
11 Ptolemy, *Geography* 7.4.1. Dalby, 2000a: 21–6, 156–7.
12 Vergil, *Georgics* 2.114–115; Horace, *Odes* 1.29.3–4; Statius, *Silvae* 4.5.31–32; Claudian, *Panegyric on Honorius' Fourth Consulship* 306.
13 Claudian, *Stilicho's Consulship* 1.152–160; Strabo 16.4.18–26; Diodorus 3.43, 19.94–100; *Periplus* 19–20. Bowersock 1983 esp. pp. 12–22. *Panchaia* was the creation of the Greek author Euhemerus.
14 Petronius 119.12; Claudian, *Stilicho's Consulship* 1.54–66 (p. 186); Pliny 12.81.
15 Martial 5.7, 6.55, 10.17; Petronius fragment 8.
16 Socotra is the *Dioscoridis Insula* of ancient geographers. Juvenal 6.181; *Periplus* 28 and Casson's note; Dioscorides 3.22; Pliny 27.14. Greppin 1988.
17 Strabo 16.4.19; *Periplus* 8–12, 27; Pliny 12.51–63. Van Beek 1960; Müller 1978; Casson 1989: 122, 162; Miller 1969: 102–104, 107; Souter 1949 s.vv. *turifer, turificatio, turificator, turificatus, turifico, turor*, all of which connote the worshipping of pagan gods and the abjuring of Christianity.
18 Vergil, *Georgics* 2.117, 2.139, 4.379; *Culex* 87; Ovid, *Metamorphoses* 10.309; *Fasti* 1.341, 3.720, 3.731, 4.569. Note 'the yellow tears of the green incense tree' already in Pindar fragment 107 Bowra.
19 Theophrastus, *Study of Plants* 9.4; Pliny 12.66–71. Steier 1935; van Beek 1960; Casson 1989: 118–120; Miller 1969: 104–105, 108.
20 Philodemus 21 [*Anthologia Palatina* 11.34]; Propertius 1.2.3; Ovid, *Metamorphoses* 10.310, 15.399; Martial 11.54; Petronius fragment 8; Apuleius, *Apology* 32.

21 Translation by A. J. Arberry. According to the classic Arabic compilation on the early oral poets, Imr al-Qais was appointed Phylarch of Palestine by the emperor Justinian, but had an affair with a Byzantine princess and, in punishment, was poisoned at Ancyra in the course of his return home from Constantinople (Abu al-Faraj, *Kitāb al-Aghānī*).

22 Claudian, *Stilicho's Consulship* 1.152–160; Cicero, *De lege Manilia* 22–23.

23 The Niphates is sometimes a mountain, sometimes a river, never likeable in either role. Vergil, *Georgics* 3.30 (p. 229); Horace, *Odes* 1.22.6–7, 2.9, *Epodes* 1.12; Lucan 3.245; Silius 13.765; Juvenal 6.409; Claudian, *Rape of Proserpine* 3.263; Plutarch, *Lucullus* 32; Dio 49.31.1. With *inhospitalis Caucasus* compare *axenos Phasis* of Theocritus 13.75.

24 Translation after R. Thomson.

25 Martial 3.78 (p. 26); Petronius 119.36–8; Xenophon, *Anabasis* 4.5.24.

26 Horace, *Epodes* 5.24, 17.36, *Odes* 2.13.8; Martial 3.78 (p. 26).

27 Nicander, *Alexipharmaca* 249–278 and scholia; Pliny 28.129. Duke 1985, introduction and pp. 136–137.

28 Vergil, *Georgics* 4.560–561; Horace, *Odes* 2.9.21, 4.14.46; Lucan 3.256; Fronto, *Parthian Preface* [vol. 2: 200 Haines].

29 Antipater of Thessalonica 91 [*Anthologia Palatina* 9.58]; Propertius 3.11.21; Lucan 6.50; Ctesias [Diodorus 2.7–10].

30 Vergil, *Georgics* 4.287–294 (p. 174); Catullus 11.6; Horace, *Odes* 1.2.22, 1.12.53, 1.27.5, 1.29.4, 2.1.31, 2.13.18, 2.16.6; Propertius 3.12.11; Ovid, *Art of Love* 1.209, *Cure for Love* 155; Lucan 1.230, 4.681, 6.50; Nemesianus, *Cynegetica* 74; Xenophon, *Anabasis* 3.2.26.

31 Horace, *Odes* 1.11.2–3; *Daniel* 1.4; Cato, *On Farming* 5; Strabo 16.1.6. Note also Eupolemus [Eusebius, *Praeparatio Evangelica* 9.17]; [Aristotle], *Magic* 35 Rose.

32 Vergil, *Aeneid* 4.367; Petronius 119.16–18; Suetonius, *Augustus* 43.4; Dio 54.9. For a tiger that reached Greece three centuries earlier see Athenaeus 590a–b.

33 Horace, *Odes* 2.9.2–4; Strabo 11.7.4; Mela 3.38; Curtius 6.4.19.

34 Plautus, *Stichus* 24–25; Varro, *Menippean Satires* 36 Bücheler; Statius, *Silvae* 1.3.105; Juvenal 14.328–329; Florus, *History* 3.12.

35 Plautus, *Stichus* 378; Publilius Syrus [Petronius 55.6]; Lucretius 4.1026–1029, 4.1123; Martial 8.28; Claudian, *Stilicho's Consulship* 1.152–160; Ezekiel 27.17–33; Aristides, *Roman Oration* 10–12 (p. 272); Tertullian, *On Women's Dress* 1.1.3.

36 Martial 14.150; cf. Aeschylus, *Suppliants* 432.

37 Propertius 2.3.15 (p. 152); Pliny 11.75–76.

38 Propertius 3.4.2, 3.13.6; Horace, *Epistles* 1.6.5–6; Martial 5.37 (p. 263), 7.30 (p. 211), 8.45, 9.2, 9.12, 10.17, 10.38.

39 Martial 10.80 (p. 241), 11.70 with Kay's note, 14.113 with Leary's note; Pliny 33.5, 36.198, 37.21–22.

40 Several identifications are uncertain, and there are at least two errors in the Latin text. I have added a scientific name only when the aromatic concerned is not discussed elsewhere in this book. Strabo 15.2.3.

41 Probably based on Aristobulus, cf. Arrian, *Anabasis* 3.28.

42 Strabo 11.13.7; Galen, *Properties of Simples* 8.18.16 [12.123]; Pliny 19.38–46, 22.100. Dalby 1993; Saberi 1993; Dalby 1996: 140–141, 251; Laufer 1919: 353–362, 366; Miller 1969: 100. The identification of classical 'Median silphium' with modern asafoetida was made by Garcia de Orta (1563).

43 Nicander, *Theriaca* 891; Quintilii [Athenaeus 649e]; Pliny 15.83, 15.91; Palladius, *On Farming* 11.12.3, *On Grafting* 157–160. Dalby 1996: 146. Archaeologists who report finds of 'pistachio' from Mediterranean sites before

Hellenistic times are being imprecise: such finds are of one of the European species of *Pistacia*.

44 Theophrastus, *Study of Plants* 4.4.2; Pliny 12.15, 13.103, 23.105; Athenaeus 83a. Dalby 1996: 143–145, 176–177; Andrews 1961. Citrons came ultimately from Indochina or southern China.

45 Martial 13.46; Calpurnius, Eclogues 2.44; Columella 5.10.20, 9.4.3; Pliny 15.39–44, 15.109–114, 16.138; Galen, *Properties of Simples* 7.12.17 [12.76]; Gargilius Martialis 2. The colloquial Latin forms are given conveniently in *Appendix Probi*: '*persica non pessica*'. Schafer 1963, esp. pp. 117–118; Dalby 1996: 144–145.

46 Propertius 3.13.5; Herodotus 3.102; Pliny 11.111.

47 Nicander, *Theriaca* 891; Vergil, *Georgics* 2.137; Horace, *Odes* 1.22.7–8; Propertius 3.4.1. In general, Begley and de Puma 1991; Warmington 1974.

48 In the city markets, about AD 50, one still found portrait coins of the Indo-Greek conqueror Menander. Ovid, *Fasti* 3.466; Kālidāsa, *Cloud-Messenger* 27, 35; *Periplus* 47 (the coins), 49.

49 Vergil, *Georgics* 2.172, 4.287–294 (p. 174); Horace, *Satires* 2.8.14; Propertius 3.4.1; Tibullus 2.3.55–56.

50 Ovid, *Amores* 2.6; Crinagoras 24 [*Anthologia Palatina* 9.562]; Statius, *Silvae* 2.4; Pliny 6.184, 10.117. Yule and Burnell 1903 s.vv. *myna, shama*; Wheatley 1959: 122–123.

51 It is strange, none the less. It reminds one of the Sanskrit name for an elephant, *hasti* literally 'the one with a hand' – which is perhaps a calque of the earlier non-Indo-Aryan term, *kari*, wrongly taken by folk-etymology to mean 'handed' (Turner 1966 no. 14039).

52 Horace, *Odes* 1.31.6; Petronius 135; Pliny 8.7; Martial 1.72, 2.43, 5.37 (p. 263), 14.5, 14.12, 14.14, 14.77–78.

53 Claudian, *Stilicho's Consulship* 1.152–160; Pliny 37.105–106 and Eichholz's note.

54 Martial 4.28, 5.11 (p. 122), 11.27 (p. 260), 11.37; Pliny 37.86–90 and Eichholz's note from which I quote in the text.

55 Vergil, Georgics 2.117; Persius 5.135; Lucan 10.117, 10.302–306; Apuleius, *Florida* 1.6; *Periplus* 36; Pliny 12.17–20; Macrobius 3.13.10 (p. 248). Laufer 1919: 485–487.

56 Some economic historians argue that the author of the *Periplus* was wrong to view coinage in that way.

57 For *pippalī* 'long pepper' see Turner 1966 no. 8205: the nominative forms in Sanskrit and Prakrit are identical. Theophrastus, *Study of Plants* 9.20.1.

58 Horace, *Satires* 2.4.74, 2.8.49; Apuleius, *Florida* 1.6; Dioscorides 2.159; Pliny 12.26–29, 31.83. Steier 1938; Casson 1989: 220; Laufer 1919: 374–375; Achaya 1994: 50–52, 192, 214; Miller 1969: 80–83.

59 Sidonius, *Letters* 8.11.3 line 46 (p. 83).

60 Horace, *Odes* 2.11.16 (p. 246), *Epodes* 13.8–9; Ovid, *Metamorphoses* 15.398; *Phoenix* 79–88 (p. 183); Theophrastus, *Study of Plants* 9.8.2–3; Dioscorides 1.7–10; *Periplus* 48 and Casson's note; Pliny 12.42–47. Warmington 1974: 194–197; Laufer 1919: 455–456; Miller 1969: 88–92.

61 The same story is told in Matthew 26.6–13 and with romantic additions in John 12.1–8. An entirely different version in Luke 7.36–50.

62 Horace, *Satires* 2.3.155; Pliny 18.71; Galen, *Properties of Simples* [12.92, 12.307]. *Saccharum* (cane sugar, *Saccharum officinarum*) was another extremely expensive Indian medicine; it does not get into general literature.

63 Plautus, *Truculentus* 540; Vergil, *Eclogues* 3.89, 4.25; Ovid, *Metamorphoses* 15.394, *Tristia* 3.3.69; Martial 5.64, 8.77, 12.17; Juvenal 8.159 (p. 220);

John, *Revelations* 18.13; Dioscorides 1.6; Pliny 12.48. Miller 1969: 37–38, 67–69. *Cardamomum* (cardamom, *Elettaria cardamomum*) is known to the experts (e.g. Pliny 12.50) but does not occur in general Roman literature.

64 Horace, *Odes* 3.1.44 (p. 163); Ovid, *Fasti* 1.341 and Frazer's note; Lucan 9.417; Dioscorides 1.16; Pliny 12.41. Casson 1989: 191–192.

65 Vergil, *Georgics* 2.463–468, 4.304; Propertius 3.13.8; Ovid, *Fasti* 3.731; Statius, *Silvae* 4.5.31–32; Herodotus 3.107–111; Theophrastus, *Study of Plants* 9.4.2, 9.5; Strabo 1.4.2, 16.4.19, 16.4.25; *Periplus* 8–13; Pliny 12.87–93; *Revelations* 18.13; Plutarch, *Sulla* 38 (p. 197); Apuleius, *Florida* 1.6. Casson 1984 (his translation from Galen is used in the text); Dalby 2000a: 36–41; De Romanis 1996; Laufer 1919: 541–543 (quotation in the text from p. 541).

66 Horace, *Odes* 2.7.8; Ovid, *Tristia* 3.3.69; Martial 11.18, 14.146; Dioscorides 1.12; Pliny 12.129; *Periplus* 56, 65; Ptolemy, *Geography* 7.2.16. Garcia de Orta 1563 ff. 95v–98v; Casson 1984; Casson 1989: 241–242. Alternative identifications have been suggested, notably patchouli (*Pogostemon cablin*) by Laufer 1918. The Sanskrit name *tamalapattra* was more commonly used not of *Cinnamomum tamala* but of *Garcinia pictoria*: that is a proper reason for the doubts raised by Laufer and also by Burnell (in a manuscript note to his copy of Garcia de Orta) but it seems to be a red herring.

67 Zuo Taichong, *Shu Capital Rhapsody* 72, 128, 159, 172–173.

68 Vergil, *Aeneid* 8.687–688; Horace, *Odes* 3.29.27–28; Propertius 3.1.16, 3.11.26; Curtius 7.4.26.

69 Horace, *Odes* 1.12.55–56; Sima Qian, *Records of the Grand Historian* 123 preface [vol. 2: 264 Watson]. Reports of Chinese silk at Western archaeological sites before that date are to be doubted.

70 Horace, *Odes* 1.29.5 (p. 268); Chariton 6.4.2; Aristides, *Roman Oration* 10 (p. 272).

71 Greek *ser* and Mongolian *shirkek* may both be loanwords from Archaic Chinese *siəg or *siəɣ (modern Chinese *si*) 'silk'. Laufer 1919: 538–539 denied these links, but in his time Karlgren's reconstruction of Archaic Chinese phonology was not available.

72 Horace, *Epodes* 8.15–16; Martial 11.8 (p. 264); Claudian, *Against Eutropius* 2.337–338 (p. 160); Seneca, *De Beneficiis* 7.9.5; Petronius 119.11; Pliny 6.54, 12.17, 37.204.

73 Vergil, *Georgics* 1.240. Sorbs are indeed brewed, in Russia and central Europe, to make a kind of cider or perry (French *cormé*).

74 Horace, *Odes* 1.35.9, meaning that they have no fixed abode. Nisbet's note suggests that *profugi* means 'fighting by means of a retreat', like the Parthians, and cites Ovid, *From Pontus* 1.2.83–86, but that passage does not really say as much.

75 Ovid, *Tristia* 3.10.51–70; Curtius 4.6.3.

76 Ovid, *Tristia* 1.2.83, 1.8.39. Greek *ta aristera tou Pontou* (Strabo 12.3.2).

77 Vergil, *Georgics* 3.350; *Consolation to Livia* 387; Ovid, *Tristia* 1.10; 3.10.27–28; Petronius fragment 44; Rutilius 485–486.

78 Vergil, *Georgics* 4.370, 4.517; Horace, *Odes* 3.4.36.

79 Martial 4.28, 5.11 (p. 122), 11.27 (p. 260), 12.15, 14.108; Statius, *Thebaid* 2.276; Pliny 37.65. These emeralds had come from mines in the distant Urals.

80 Vergil, *Georgics* 2.115, 3.461; *Aeneid* 8.725; Horace, *Odes* 2.9.23–24, 2.20.19, 3.4.35; Herodotus 4.102, 109.

81 Ovid, *Tristia* 3.10.5; Seneca, *Phaedra* 71; Martial, *Spectacula* 3 (p. 210); Claudian, *Against Eutropius* 2.338; Paulus Diaconus 2.26.

82 Seneca, *Thyestes* 630; Lucan 10.454; Josephus, *Jewish War* 7.7.4, *Jewish Antiquities* 18.4.6. These three names, Geloni, Sarmatae, Alani, all belonged to speakers of Iranian languages, as we now call them: Alan was the direct ancestor of modern Ossete, spoken north and south of the central Caucasus. The linguistic affiliation of the Huns is uncertain.

83 Catullus 11.6; Claudian, *Against Eutropius* 2.338; Ausonius, *Epigrams* 1.8; Ammianus 31.2.

84 Ovid, *Tristia* 1.5.62; Claudian, *Against Eutropius* 1.242; Rutilius 2.49. They are the *Visi feroces* 'fierce Visigoths' of Claudian, *Stilicho's Consulship* 1.94.

85 Horace, *Odes* 1.35.9; *Consolation to Livia* 387–388; Martial 5.3, 6.10.

86 Opening sequence: casts 1–18. The bridge: casts 258–261; Dio 68.13 [Xiphilinus 232–233]. Lepper and Frere 1988: 47–54, 147–151.

87 The fortress: casts 300–314; the sharing of poison: casts 325–328. Lepper and Frere 1988: 163–170, 304–309. Gradiştea Muncelului is in the Orăştie Mountains of south-western Transylvania. The name *Sarmizegethusa*, later applied to a lowland city, may earlier have belonged to this site. Dio (68.14 [Xiphilinus 233–234]) calls it *Basileion*, 'the capital'.

88 In general, Neuwald and Heine 1991; Neuwald and Heine 1992.

89 Horace, *Epodes* 16.7; Ovid, *Tristia* 3.12.47.

90 Martial 11.96 (p. 211); Juvenal 13.164.

91 Silius 3.608; Martial 14.176.

92 Horace, *Odes* 4.14.51 (p. 9); Propertius 4.6.77; *Consolation to Livia* 17, 311 (p. 205); Juvenal 4.147.

93 Propertius 3.3.45–46; *Consolation to Livia* 311 (p. 205); Lucan 2.51; Tacitus, *Germania* 4. The spellings *Suevi* and *Suebi* alternate freely.

94 Martial 14.176 and Leary's note and plate.

95 Ovid, *Amores* 1.14.45–46; Lucan 1.463; Martial 5.68, 5.37 (p. 263), 14.26 (below), *Spectacula* 3; Claudian, *Consulate of Honorius* 4.446–447, *Against Eutropius* 1.383; Tacitus, *Germania* 38.

96 Ovid, *Art of Love* 3.163; Martial 8.33, 14.27 and Leary's note; Pliny 28.191. The name 'Chattic foam' serves as a reminder of Domitian's recent triumph over the Chatti (Martial 2.2).

97 Ausonius, *Mosella* 97; Pliny 9.68.

98 Propertius 3.3.45–46.

99 Martial 5.37 (p. 263), 6.15; Juvenal 6.573; Pliny 31.42–43, 37.30–51.

100 Vergil, *Georgics* 1.30; Claudian, *Panegyric on Honorius' Fourth Consulship* 31–33. On the identity of Thule see Cary and Warmington 1929: 50–52.

7 Saeva urbs

1 Ovid, *Tristia* 3.7.51–52.

2 Martial 4.64 (p. 38); Statius, *Silvae* 4.3 (p. 50); Metrodorus [*Palatine Anthology* 14.121] (p. 82).

3 Strabo 5.3.2–3; *Talmud Babli, Shabbat* 56b. Nadich 1994: 309, citing *Talmud Babli, Sanhedrin* 21b; *Songs Rabbah* 1.6.

4 Galen, *A Dislocation Unknown to Hippocrates* [18a.347]; *Epitome of Athenaeus* 20b.

5 Martial 10.56, 14.157–158 (p. 92); Petronius 97, 102–105 (p. 178). Jones 1987.

6 Ovid, *Tristia* 4.1.5–6; Juvenal 8.180 (p. 220: see footnote there); Apuleius, *Metamorphoses* 9.12; Cato, *On Farming* 56 and Dalby's note; Columella 1.8.16–18, 1.9.4; Pliny, *Letters* 3.19.

7 Horace, *Epistles* 2.2.7–9, *Satires* 2.6.66; Tibullus 1.5.26; Seneca, *Const. Sap.* 11.3; Petronius 24.2; Tacitus, *Histories* 2.88.

 8 Cassiodorus, *Variae* 8.33.
 9 Martial 11.52 (p. 251); Pliny 11.240–242. Martial's text is doubtful: the reading *coacta* is unlikely to be correct.
10 Plautus, *Curculio* 483, *Captives* 489; Horace, *Satires* 2.3.229; Propertius 4.9.5.
11 Plautus, *Curculio* 482; Martial 11.27 (p. 260).
12 Terence, *Eunuchus* 255; Horace, *Epistles* 1.15.31, *Satires* 2.3.229.
13 Cf. Horace, *Epistles* 1.20.
14 Juvenal 10.156; Pliny 18.13; Festus: 340 M; *Summaries of Livy* 20.
15 Ovid, *Tristia* 1.8.37; Martial 12.18 (p. 104), 12.21; Juvenal 3.5 (p. 51: Prochyta is a rocky desert island off the Campanian coast), 11.51; Suetonius, *Julius* 46.
16 [Tibullus 3.14]. Sulpicia 3 [Tibullus 3.15] gives the result of this poetic complaint: she escaped the journey.
17 Tacitus, *Annals* 13.25; Suetonius, *Nero* 26; Ammianus 14.1.9.
18 The 'Massylian serpent' guarded the golden apples of the mythical Garden of the Hesperides. For Alcinous's orchard see p. 143).
19 Martial 9.26; Pliny 9.61, 9.169; Macrobius, *Saturnalia* 3.16.
20 *Priapeia* 40.1; Martial 2.17, 6.66, 11.61; *Talmud Babli, Avodah Zarah* 2a.
21 Ovid, *Amores* 3.14.9–10; Martial 1.34, 3.82, 11.45, 11.61, 12.32; Juvenal 8.168 (p. 220); Petronius 7. Cf. Catullus 58.3–4; Horace, *Odes* 1.25.10; Propertius 4.7.19–20.
22 Persius 5.32–33; Martial 11.78.
23 Petronius 31.11; Juvenal 10.3.55.
24 The manager's name *Syrophoenix* identifies him as Syrian-Phoenician. The 'Idymaean Gate', named after Idume where the dates came from (p. 169), is Juvenal's nickname for some district of Rome where Syrians and Jews lived: possibly the *Porta Capena* (p. 42), possibly the right bank of the Tiber (p. 38). The manager's *amomum* is aromatic hair oil (p. 197). The threatened *ergastulum* is the barracks in which chain gangs of slaves employed in farm labour were confined at night (p. 212).
25 Juvenal 8.177–178 (above); Quintilian 1.6.44; Seneca, *Letters* 122.6.
26 For fish sauce see p. 103. *Oxygarum* is a mixture of vinegar and fish sauce, evidently used as a dressing for salad. 'Yoghourt' is a rough equivalent for *colostrum*; 'halva' likewise for *gelonianum*.
27 Horace, *Satires* 2.2.55–62; Martial 5.78 (p. 249).
28 Then as now, bakers work at night because people demand fresh bread in the morning. The 'Neroes' are old currency that circulated at a discount thirty years later. The 'crowd of Bellona' are devotees of Cybele or Magna Mater, who passed in literature as identical with the Roman goddess Bellona.
29 It is *Circus fallax* 'lying Circus' apparently because of the astrologers to be found there (Cicero, *On Divination* 1.132).
30 Cicero, *For Cluentius* 110.
31 *Compita* were the smallest and most informal of communities, defined by cross-roads that were both meeting places and the location of shrines.
32 Martial 6.38; Pliny, *Letters* 5.9; Quintilian 12.5.6.
33 Horace, *Satires* 2.6.35; Ovid, *Remedies for Love* 561.
34 Propertius 3.22.26; Ovid, *Fasti* 1.463; *Consolation to Livia*; Statius, *Silvae* 4.5.35; Dionysius of Halicarnassus, *Roman Antiquities* 6.13.
35 Horace, *Odes* 1.2.15; Ovid, *Tristia* 3.1.27–30, 4.2.13–14; Martial 1.70. Frazer 1929 vol. 4: 176–201.
36 The 'gate of the Palatia' was the foot of the *Clivus Palatinus* 'Palatine Hill', leading to the ancient hut of Romulus and the grandiose modern residences of a succession of Emperors. At this junction stood the temple of Jove Stator.

37 The Colossus was a huge statue of Nero with the attributes of the sun god Sol – hence a competitor to the Colossus of Rhodes. The 'house of sodden Lyaeus' was a temple of the wine god Bacchus.

38 Horace, *Epistles* 1.3.17, 2.2.98; Propertius 2.31.

39 Propertius 2.32.8–10, 2.33; Ovid, *Art of Love* 1.77; Juvenal 6.489, 9.22.

40 Ovid, *Fasti* 1.340–6. *Placenta* resembled a baked cheesecake: for a recipe, Cato, *On Farming* 76 (Dalby and Grainger 1996: 94–96).

41 Horace, *Odes* 1.2.3; Ovid, *Metamorphoses* 15.866, *Fasti* 1.79; Rutilius 194.

42 Horace, *Epodes* 9.21–22; Livy 3.9.6 (p. 222); Suetonius, *Julius* 49, 51.

43 Martial 1.41 (p. 222).

44 Philodemus 12 (p. 24); Martial 14.203 (p. 107).

45 Martial, *Spectacula* 1, 2.

46 Martial 1.26, 14.160 (p. 99).

47 Martial 1.11; Suetonius, *Domitian* 4.5; Dio 49.43.3, 67.4.4.

48 Seneca, *On Peace of Mind* 2.13 (p. 18); Rutilius 189–204 (p. 20); Martial 4.64 (p.38).

49 The hills of Idume produced dates; *caryotis* dates, perhaps the more fully dried kind, also came from Syria (p. 169). Damascus produced dried damsons (p. 169), Caunus dried figs (p. 164). Amerines are presumably little smoked cheeses. Fighting between cranes and pygmies was a commonplace of myth. Bird from the Nile are flamingos, those from Phasis are pheasants, those from Numidia are guinea-fowl.

50 Martial, *Spectacula* 5, 6, 8; Strabo 6.2.6.

51 Propertius 4.1.15; Ovid, *Tristia* 3.12.24, *Art of Love* 1.103; Ammianus 14.6.25.

52 Lucretius 2.416; Propertius 4.1.16; Horace, *Epistles* 2.1.79–80; Ovid, *Art of Love* 1.104; Martial 11.8 (p. 264), 14.29, *Spectacula* 3 (p. 210).

53 Catullus 55.6–7; Propertius 2.32.11–12; Ovid, *Art of Love* 1.67; Martial 5.10, 11.1, 11.47; Vitruvius 5.9.1; Pliny 35.59, 35.126, 35.132.

54 Terence, *Hecyra* second prologue 29; Horace, *Epistles* 2.1.50–62, 2.1.177–213, *Art of Poetry* 190.

55 Martial 11.13; Suetonius, *Domitian* 3.1, 10.1; Dio 67.3.1; *Epitome de Caesaribus* 11.11.

56 Cf. Apuleius, *Metamorphoses* 10.31; Procopius, *Secret History* 9.13–14, 20–21.

57 Martial 5.7; Strabo 5.3.7–8; Dio 66.24.

58 Propertius 3.2.14, 3.22.24; Lygdamus 6 [Tibullus 3.6.58]; Martial 6.42 (p. 239), 11.96 (p. 211); Pliny 31.42; Frontinus, *Aqueducts*.

59 Ovid, *Art of Love* 3.385, *Tristia* 3.12.21–22; Seneca, *Letters* 83.5; Martial 5.20, 6.42 (p. 239), 7.32, 11.47, 14.163; Pliny 31.42.

60 Statius, *Silvae* 2.2.17–18; Martial 4.22, 11.21 (p. 263); Pliny 31.62; Suetonius, *Tiberius* 44, *Nero* 31, *Domitian* 22; *Talmud Babli, Avodah Zarah* 2a; and a pun about the man who made love to Marina (Luxorius [*Anthologia Latina* 368]). It has been observed that brine is a spermicide (Kay 1985: 117 citing Keith Hopkins). Cameron 1973.

61 Cicero, *For Cluentius* 141 (p. 270); Martial 11.52 (p. 251).

62 Martial 9.75 (p. 109).

63 Lucretius 2.40–41; Horace, *Epistles* 1.11.18, 1.18.54, *Odes* 1.8, 3.7.26; Cicero, *On Duties* 1.104; Dio 52.26.1.

64 Horace, *Epistles* 1.11.19, *Odes* 3.7.25–28.

65 Martial 11.1, 2.14, 3.20. The location is not, I think, known.

66 Horace, *Epistles* 1.6.26; Martial 11.1.12; Dio 53.27.

67 Martial 1.108.

68 Martial 5.49.

69 Fronto, *Aqueducts* 22; Suetonius, *Caligula* 18.

8 The use of Empire

1 The 'Laestrygonian jars' are of Caecuban wine (p. 46 and footnotes). Alyattes, as king of Lydia, stands here for his fabulously rich colleagues Gyges and Croesus; Mygdonia is fertile country northwards.

2 Horace, *Odes* 2.11 (p. 246); Martial 9.90 (p. 172); Alciphron 4.13.

3 The reference is to *Odyssey* 4.219–230.

4 E.g. Hicesius [Athenaeus 689c] (Dalby 1996: 165).

5 The 'Cilician stamen' is saffron.

6 Apuleius, *Metamorphoses* 2.8 (p. 246); *Tosephta Berakoth* 6.5.

7 Martial 5.64, 6.55, 8.77, 12.17; Pliny 13.20.

8 Varro, *Menippean Satires* 102 Bücheler.

9 Lucian, *Salaried Posts* 26; Martial 10.48 (p. 252).

10 By hypercorrection Pollux writes *rapatum, offae* for the normal colloquial Latin *rapulatum, ofellae*. If we mix his evidence with the recipes of *Apicius* and of the illustrious Vinidarius we can still taste the fowl *rapulatum* 'rolled in grated turnip' (Vinidarius, *Brevis Ciborum* 7), the *ofellae* or meatballs (*Apicius* 7.4; Vinidarius, *Brevis Ciborum* 3–6) and the *copadia*, small pieces of meat served with a dip (*Apicius* 7.6).

11 Oribasius, *Medical Collections* 5.33.8–9; *Geoponica* 8.31. Dalby 1996: 192.

12 Pliny 31.40; Suetonius, *Nero* 48.3; Martial 14.116–118.

13 Martial 5.64, 14.104; Petronius 73.

14 Martial 14.103; Seneca, *Natural Questions* 4.13.9; Pliny, *Letters* 1.15 (p. 251); *Apicius* 4.1.2 (p. 73).

15 *Patina* is best explained as 'quiche without the pastry'. This type of dish is named after the shallow pan in which it was baked (p. 51). On the occasion but not the menu see Taylor 1942. For palourdes or carpet-shells see p. 53. Piddocks, Latin *balanus* are also sea creatures (genus *Pholas*)

16 Horace, *Satires* 2.8.47 (p. 254). Spanish and Gaulish wines came to Rome by sea, but they were not *transmarina*: this title belonged to the wines of Greece, Asia and the East.

17 In general, Gowers 1993.

18 Acknowledgements to Peter Howell's translation. Cabbage requires to be dressed with oil (p. 221).

19 Horace, *Satires* 2.4.59–60; *Epitome of Athenaeus* 68f.

20 The wine was only just past its best. The *sigma* (Greek letter C) is the semicircle of diners. The 'tunny udder' is presumably a belly cut, approved by classical gourmets.

21 Properly 'Williams Bon Chrétien' ('Bartlett' in the United States).

22 Horace, *Satires* 2.2.55–62; Martial 7.31 (p. 27); Pliny 15.16.

23 Andrews 1948.

24 *Moretum* 57; Ovid, *Metamorphoses* 8.666; Martial 1.43, 3.58 (p. 26), 8.64.9, 12.32; Strabo 3.5.3; Columella 7.8.6; Pliny 11.240–242.

25 With Martial's epithets for lettuce, leek, mint and rocket cf. *Priapeia* 51.

26 Horace, *Satires* 2.2.23–30; Claudian, *Against Eutropius* 2.330 (p. 160). On peacocks and cranes as food: Witteveen 1986–7, 1989.

27 Martial 10.31; Pliny 9.64; Seneca, *Letters* 95; Suetonius, *Tiberius* 34; Macrobius 3.16.9. Thompson 1947: 264–268; Andrews 1949.

28 Pliny 9.171; Dio 54.23.

29 Horace, *Art of Poetry* 375 (p. 245); Cicero, *For Roscius of Ameria* 134 (p. 271), *Against Caecilius* 55 (p. 116); Petronius 28, 32, 33.

30 Jones 1991.

31 *Tosephta Berakoth* 6.5.

32 Plutarch, *Symposium Questions* 1.3.

33 Martial 1.43, 3.82; Juvenal, *Satire* 5.
34 Taurus's second consulship is 26 BC. The wine is Massic – potentially a very good one.
35 This is a controversial interpretation. Some feel that the scenes depicted cannot be realistic. Tibullus 1.2, 1.6; Ovid, *Amores* 1.4, 2.5, *Art of Love* 1.565–584. Useful comments in Green 1982.
36 Turpilius, *Hetaera* 1–2 Rychlewska; Ovid, *Tristia* 2.279–286; Martial 11.47.
37 Horace, *Odes* 1.25; Tibullus 1.2, 1.6.57–62, 2.1.75–78; Propertius 4.7.15–20 (p. 216); Rufinus 16 [*Anthologia Palatina* 5.43].
38 The interpretation of the Varro fragment is uncertain. Sallust, *Catiline* 13; Cicero, *For Milo*; Martial 7.67; Juvenal 6.246–267; *Paul and Thecla*.
39 Plautus, *Asinaria* 511, *Mostellaria* 168–172, 261; Apuleius, *Metamorphoses* 2.7, 2.16.
40 Ilia was Romulus's mother in one version of Rome's founding myth; Egeria was the nymph whom King Numa loved or possibly married (p. 43).
41 Cf. Martial 11.49 in which 'Phyllis' is rapacious.
42 Propertius 3.11.30; Gallus [*Anthologia Palatina* 5.49]; Martial 10.81.
43 Horace, *Epistles* 1.14.33 (p. 25); Philodemus 8 (p. 262).
44 *Priapeia* 40.2; Martial 12.32; Juvenal 6.123; Petronius 113.11. Cf. Cicero, *Against Caecilius* 55–56 (p. 116).
45 Nadich 1994: 239. In general, Leary 1990; Adams 1982.
46 Plautus, *Mostellaria* 259; Catullus 10; Horace, *Odes* 1.19.5–6. Daniel Ogden (see his *Polygamy, Prostitutes and Death: The Hellenistic dynasties*, London: Duckworth, 1999) reminds me of a royal mistress spoken of thus: 'If she is black, what of it? So are coals, but when we light them they shine as bright as roses' (Asclepiades 5 Gow and Page [*Anthologia Palatins* 5.210]).
47 Horace, *Odes* 2.11.23–24 (p. 246), 3.14.21–22 (p. 184); Apuleius, *Metamorphoses* 2.8–9.
48 Philodemus 2 [*Anthologia Palatina* 5.13]; Ovid, *Amores* 1.5.20; Martial 14.66, 14.134; Maximianus 5.27; Horace, *Odes* 2.4.9–12.
49 Ovid, *Amores* 1.5.22, *Art of Love* 3.781, *Metamorphoses* 10.592; Horace, *Odes* 2.4.18–20, 1.13.10; Tibullus 1.8.33, 1.5.43, 1.6.13–14; Propertius 2.15.17–22; Rufinus 14 Page (p. 258), 16 [*Anthologia Palatina* 5.43]).
50 Marcus Argentarius [*Anthologia Palatina* 5.116]; Rufinus 11 Page [*Anthologia Palatina* 5.35]; Alciphron, *Letters* 4.13.
51 Ovid, *Amores* 1.5.21, 2.14.7; Martial 10.90, 12.32; Apuleius, *Metamorphoses* 2.16; Rufinus 12 Page [*Anthologia Palatina* 5.36]; Eratosthenes Scholasticus [*Anthologia Palatina* 5.242]; Tertullian, *On Women's Dress* 2.8.2. The more intimate details are found in Greek rather than in Latin poetry: we have learnt that the Greek sexual vocabulary was more comprehensive than the Latin (p. 123).
52 For other counter-examples to the stereotypes: Horace, *Epodes* 8.3–10, 12.1–6; Ovid, *Art of Love* 3.193–194; *Priapeia* 12, 32, 46; Martial 11.99, 11.100, 14.49.
53 Vergil, *Eclogues* 2.15; Horace, *Epodes* 11.28; Tibullus 1.4.11–14; Ovid, *Art of Love* 3.437; Martial 4.42, 6.39 (p. 213), 8.55, 10.42, 11.22, 11.43, 11.56, 11.78; Strato [*Anthologia Palatina* 12.7]; Rufinus 10 [*Anthologia Palatina* 5.28]. Hair colour, again, is vague. For Greece, Sophocles is reported as saying that although poets called Apollo golden-haired, it was as well that painters did not take this literally: his hair looked better black (Ion of Chios, *Visits* [Athenaeus 603e]).
54 Cf. Martial 3.65. The 'saffron spray' is in the theatre.
55 Tibullus 1.9.13–16; Martial 4.42, 8.46, 11.22, 12.66 (p. 241), 12.75.

56 Athenaeus 517d citing Timaeus and Theopompus.
57 Varro, *Menippean Satires* 44 (p. 53), 205 Bücheler; *Genesis Rabbah* 63.10.
58 Ovid, *Art of Love* 415; Martial 3.75; Petronius 8, 20, 21; Pliny 26.96, 26.99, 28.119.
59 Nadich 1994: 330.
60 Horace, *Satires* 2.2.49; Pliny 10.60.
61 Ramage 1973.
62 Statius, *Silvae* 2.1.72; Martial 6.66; Petronius 29.
63 These in turn remind us that the young Artemis, in Callimachus's *Hymn to Artemis* (14), begged her father for 'sixty nymphs, all nine years old'.
64 Petronius 29, 76 and *passim*.
65 Aristides, *Roman Oration* 10–12, abridged.

Bibliography

Achaya, K. T. (1994) *Indian Food: a historical companion*. Delhi: Oxford University Press.

Adams, J. N. (1982) *The Latin Sexual Vocabulary*. London.

Andrews, A. C. (1941) 'Alimentary use of lovage in the classical period', *Isis* vol. 33 (1941–2), pp. 514–18.

——(1948) 'Oysters as a food in Greece and Rome', *Classical Journal* vol. 43, pp. 299–303.

——(1948) 'The use of rue as a spice by the Greeks and Romans', *Classical Journal* vol. 43, pp. 371–73.

——(1949) 'The "Sardinian fish" of the Greeks and Romans', *American Journal of Philology* vol. 70, pp. 171–85.

——(1949) 'The Roman craze for surmullets', *Classical World* vol. 42, pp. 186–8.

——(1958) 'The mints of the Greeks and Romans and their condimentary use' and 'Thyme as a condiment in the Graeco-Roman era', *Osiris* vol. 13, pp. 127–56.

——(1961) 'Acclimatization of citrus fruits in the Mediterranean region', *Agricultural History* vol. 35, no. 1, pp. 35–46.

Begley, V. and de Puma, R. D. (1991) *Rome and India: the ancient sea trade*. Madison: University of Wisconsin Press.

Bodson, L. (1978) 'Données antiques de zoogéographie: l'expansion des léporidés dans la Méditerranée classique', *Les naturalistes belges* vol. 59, pp. 66–81.

Bowersock, G. W. (1983) *Roman Arabia*. Cambridge, Mass.: Harvard University Press.

Briant, P. (1996) *Histoire de l'Empire Perse: de Cyrus à Alexandre*. Paris: Fayard.

Bromwich, R. (ed.) (1978) *Trioedd Ynys Prydein: the Welsh Triads*. Cardiff: University of Wales Press.

Cameron, A. (1973) 'Sex in the swimming pool', *Bulletin of the Institute of Classical Studies* vol. 20, pp. 149–50.

Carter, W. L. (1940) 'Roses in antiquity', *Antiquity* vol. 14, pp. 250–6.

Cary, M. and Warmington, E. H. (1929) *The Ancient Explorers*. London: Methuen.

Casson, L. (1984) *Ancient Trade and Society*. Detroit: Wayne State University Press.

——(tr.) (1989) *The Periplus of the Erythraean Sea*. Princeton: Princeton University Press.

Chenciner, R. (2000) *Madder Red: a history of luxury and trade*. Richmond: Curzon Press.

Chevallier, R. (1972) *Les voies romaines*. Paris.

Coster, C. H. (1951) 'The economic position of Cyrenaica in classical times', in *Studies in Roman Economic and Social History in Honor of Allan Chester Johnson*. Princeton: University of Princeton Press, pp. 3–26.

Curtis, R. I. (1991) *Garum and Salsamenta: production and commerce in materia medica*. Leiden: Brill.

Dalby, A. (1993) 'Silphium and asafoetida: evidence from Greek and Roman writers', in *Spicing up the Palate: proceedings of the Oxford Symposium on Food and Cookery 1992*. Totnes: Prospect Books, pp. 67–72.

——(1995) 'Archestratos: where and when?', in J. Wilkins and others (eds) *Food in Antiquity*. Exeter: Exeter University Press, pp. 400–12.

——(1996) *Siren Feasts: a history of food and gastronomy in Greece*. London: Routledge, 1996.

——(2000a) *Dangerous Tastes: the story of spices*. London: British Museum Press.

——(2000b) 'To feed a king: tyrants, kings and the search for quality in food and agriculture', *Pallas* no. 52, pp. 133–144.

Dalby, A. and Grainger, S. (1996) *The Classical Cookbook*. London: British Museum Press.

Dangel, J. (1985) 'L'Asie des poètes latins de l'époque républicaine' in *Ktema*, vol. 10, pp. 175–92.

——(1989) 'Du Nil à l'Euphrate dans l'imaginaire des poètes latins de l'époque républicaine', in *Actes du colloque international sur l'Arabie préislamique*. Strasbourg, 1987 (Leiden, 1989), pp. 321–39.

Darby, W. J. and others (1977) *Food: gift of Osiris*. London: Academic Press.

D'Arms, J. H. (1970) *Romans on the Bay of Naples*. Cambridge: Harvard University Press.

Davidson, A. (1981) *Mediterranean Seafood*. Harmondsworth: Penguin.

Davies, M. and Kathirithamby, J. (1986) *Greek Insects*. London: Duckworth.

De Romanis, F. (1996) *Cassia, Cinnamomo, Ossidiana. Uomini e merci tra Oceano Indiano e Mediterraneo*. Roma: L'Erma di Bretschneider.

Duke, J. A. (1985) *CRC Handbook of Medicinal Herbs*. Boca Raton: CRC Press.

Edmondson, J. C. (1987) *Two Industries in Roman Lusitania: mining and garum production*. Oxford: B.A.R.

Empereur, J.-Y. and Garlan, Y. (eds) (1986) *Recherches sur les amphores grecques* (*Bulletin de correspondance hellénique* suppl. 13). Athens.

Fear, A. T. (1991) in *Greece and Rome* vol. 38, pp. 75–9.

Frayn, J. M. (1984) *Sheep-Rearing and the Wool Trade in Italy during the Roman Period*. Liverpool: Cairns.

——(1993) *Markets and Fairs in Roman Italy*. Oxford: Clarendon Press.

Frazer, J. G. (ed. and tr.) (1929) *Publii Ovidii Nasonis Fastorum libri sex*. London: Macmillan.

Garcia de Orta (1563) *Coloquios dos simples e drogas he cousas medicinais da India*. Goa: I. de Endem.

Glare, P. G. W. (ed.) (1968–82) *Oxford Latin Dictionary*. Oxford: Clarendon Press.

Goebel, M. (1915) *Ethnica*. Breslau.

Gowers, E. (1993) *The Loaded Table*. Oxford: Oxford University Press.

Gowers, W. (1950) 'The classical rhinoceros', *Antiquity* vol. 24, pp. 61–71.

Green, P. (tr.) (1982) Ovid, *The Erotic Poems*. Harmondsworth: Penguin, 1982.

Greppin, J. A. C. (1988) 'The various aloes in ancient times', *Journal of Indo-European Studies* vol. 16, pp. 33–48.

Harrison, G. (1991) 'Changing patterns in land tenure and land use in Roman Crete', in G. Barker and J. Lloyd (eds) *Roman Landscapes*. London: British School at Rome, pp. 115–21.

Highet, G. (1957) *Poets in a Landscape*. London: Hamish Hamilton.

Hunt, E. D. (1984) 'Travel, tourism and piety in the Roman Empire', *Echos du monde classique = Classical views* vol. 28, n.s. vol. 3, pp. 391–417.

Jones, C. P. (1987), 'Stigma: tattooing and branding in Graeco-Roman antiquity', *Journal of Roman Studies* vol. 77, pp. 139–55.

—— (1991) 'Dinner theater', in W. J. Slater (ed.) *Dining in a Classical Context*. Ann Arbor: University of Michigan Press, pp. 185–98.

Jones, J. E. (1976) 'Hives and honey of Hymettus', *Archaeology* vol. 29, no. 2, pp. 80–91.

Kay, N. M. (1985) *Martial: Book XI. A commentary*. London: Duckworth.

Keaveney, R. (1988) *Views of Rome*. London: Scala Books.

Kytzler, B. (ed.) (1988) *Laudes Italiae: Lob Italiens. Griechische und lateinische Texte zweisprächig*. Stuttgart: Reclam.

Lambraki, M. (1997) *Ta khorta*. [Khania:] Trokhalia.

Laufer, B. (1918) 'Malabathron', *Journal asiatique*, 11th series, vol. 12, pp. 5–49.

——(1919) *Sino-Iranica: Chinese contributions to the history of civilization in ancient Iran with special reference to the history of cultivated plants and products*. Chicago: Field Museum of Natural History.

Leary, T. J. (1990) 'That's what little girls are made of: the physical charms of Elegiac women', *London Classical Monographs* vol. 15, pp. 152–5.

—— (ed. and tr.) (1996) Martial, *Book XIV: The Apophoreta*. London: Duckworth.

Lepper, F. and Frere, S. (1988) *Trajan's Column*. Gloucester: Alan Sutton.

Lewis, N. (1934) *L'industrie de papyrus dans l'antiquité gréco-romaine*. Paris.

Liddell, H. G. and Scott, R. (1925–40) *A Greek-English Lexicon*, 9th edn. Oxford: Clarendon Press.

Littlewood, A. R. (1967) 'The symbolism of the apple in Greeek and Roman literature', *Harvard Studies in Classical Philology* vol. 72, pp. 147–81.

MacDougall, E. B. (ed.) (1987) *Ancient Roman Villa Gardens*. Dumbarton Oaks, 1987.

Maeder, F. (1999) F. Maeder, 'Muschelseide: gesponnenes Gold', *Mare* no. 13, pp. 22–6.

Meyer-Lübke, W. (1930–5) *Romanisches etymologisches Wörterbuch*. Heidelberg: Winter.

Millar, F. (1983) *The Emperor in the Roman World*. London: Duckworth.

Miller, J. I. (1969) *The Spice Trade of the Roman Empire*. Oxford: Clarendon Press.

Müller, W. (1978) 'Weihrauch', in *Paulys Real-Enzyklopädie der classischen Altertumswissenschaft*, Supplement 15. Stuttgart.

Nadich, J. (1994) *The Legends of the Rabbis*. New York: Aronson.

Neuwald, B. and Heine, A. (eds) (1991) *Germanen und Germanien in römischen Quellen*. Kettwig: Phaidon.

—— (eds) (1992) *Germanen und Germanien in griechischen Quellen*. Kettwig: Phaidon.

Ogden, D. (1999) *Polygamy, Prostitutes and Death: the Hellenistic dynasties*. London: Duckworth.

Olmos, R. (1991) 'Puelle Gaditane: heteras de Astarté?', *Archivo espanõl de arqueología* 64, pp. 99–109.

Panciera, S. (1956) 'Liburna', *Epigraphica* vol. 18, pp. 130–56.

Parke, H. W. and Wormell, D. E. W. (1956) *The Delphic Oracle*. Oxford: Blackwell.

Parsons, P. J. (1977) 'The oyster', in *Zeitschrift für Papyrologie und Epigraphik*, vol. 24, pp. 1–12.

Polunin, O. (1980) *Flowers of Greece and the Balkans*. Oxford: Oxford University Press.

Ponsich, M. (1988) *Aceite de oliva y salazones de pescado: factores geo-economicos de Bética y Tingitania*. Madrid: Universidad Complutense.

Ponsich, M. and Tarradell, M. (1965) *Garum et industries antiques de salaison dans la Méditerranée Occidentale*. Paris.

Rackham, O. and Moody, J. (1996) *The Making of the Cretan Landscape*. Manchester: Manchester University Press.

Radke, G (1989) 'Topographische Betrachtungen zum Iter Brundisianum des Horaz', *Rheinisches Museum* vol. 132, pp. 54–72.

Ramage, E. S. (1973) *Urbanitas: ancient sophistication and refinement*. Norman: University of Oklahoma Press.

Rice, E. E. (1983) *The Grand Procession of Ptolemy Philadelphus*. Oxford: Oxford University Press.

Robinson, D. M. and Fluck, E. J. (1937) *A Study of the Greek Love-Names*. Baltimore: Johns Hopkins University Press.

Ross, A. S. C. (1952), *Ginger*. Oxford: Blackwell.

Rouanet-Liesenfelt, A.-M. (1992) 'Les plantes médicinales de Crète à l'époque romaine', *Cretan Studies* vol. 3, pp. 173–90.

Russell, J. M. (1991) *Sennacherib's Palace Without Rival at Nineveh*. Chicago: University of Chicago Press.

Saalfeld, G. A. E. A. (1884) *Tensaurus italograecus*. Wien, 1884.

Saberi, H. (1993) 'Rosewater and asafoetida', in *Spicing up the Palate: proceedings of the Oxford Symposium on Food and Cookery 1992*. Totnes: Prospect Books, pp. 220–35.

Salaman, R. (1993) 'Down mastic way on Chios', in *Spicing up the Palate: proceedings of the Oxford Symposium on Food and Cookery 1992*. Totnes: Prospect Books, pp. 236–8.

Sandy, D. B. (1989) *The Production and Use of Vegetable Oils in Ptolemaic Egypt*. Atlanta, Scholars Press.

Schafer, E. H. (1963) *The Golden Peaches of Samarkand*. Berkeley: University of California Press.

Sconocchia, S. (1991) 'Su alcuni aspetti della lingua di Scribonio Largo' in G. Sabbah (ed.) *Le latin médical: la constitution d'un langage scientifique. Réalités et langage de la médicine dans le monde romain*. Saint-Étienne: Université de Saint-Étienne, pp. 317–36.

Scullard, H. H. (1974) *The Elephant in the Greek and Roman World*. Ithaca: Cornell University Press.

Souter, A. (1949) *A Glossary of Later Latin to 600 AD*. Oxford: Clarendon Press.

Steier, A. (1935) 'Myrrha', in G. Wissowa and others (eds) (1893–1972) *Paulys Real-Enzyklopädie der classischen Altertumswissenschaft*, new edn. Stuttgart.

——(1938) 'Pfeffer', in G. Wissowa and others (eds) (1893–1972) *Paulys Real-Enzyklopädie der classischen Altertumswissenschaft*, new edn. Stuttgart.

Taylor, L. R. (1942) 'Caesar's colleagues in the pontifical college', *American Journal of Philology* vol. 63, pp. 385–412.

Tchernia, A. (1986) *Le vin de l'Italie romaine*. Rome.

Thompson, D'A. (1947) *A Glossary of Greek Fishes*. London: Oxford University Press.

Turner, R. (1966) *A Comparative Dictionary of the Indo-Aryan Languages*. London: Oxford Univerity Press.

van Beek, G. W. (1960) 'Frankincense and myrrh', *Biblical Archaeologist* vol. 23, pp. 69–95.

Warmington, E. (1974) *The Commerce between the Roman Empire and India*. Cambridge: Cambridge University Press.

Witteveen, J. (1986–7) 'On swans and cranes', *Petits propos culinaires* nos 24–6.

——(1989) 'Peacocks in history', *Petits propos culinaires* no. 32, pp. 23–34.

Wheatley, P. (1959) 'Geographical notes on some commodities involved in Sung maritime trade', *Journal of the Malayan Branch of the Royal Asiatic Society* vol. 32, no. 2, pp. 1–140.

Wilkins, J. and Hill, S. (trs) (1994) Archestratus, *The Life of Luxury*. Totnes: Prospect Books.

Yule, H. and Burnell, A. C. (1903) *Hobson-Jobson*. London: Murray.

Index of ancient sources

This is an index of passages discussed in the text, not of the many added references in the notes. Editors' names are listed (following the first relevant reference) only when this is necessary to identify the text numbering system used. Details have been added of a few translations and commentaries that are likely to be useful. In these, 'LCL' means the Loeb Classical Library, now published by Harvard University Press, Cambridge, Mass. For works listed here by author and date only, full details will be found in the bibliography.

Achilles Tatius 4.12: 174; 5.1: 173. – Tr. S. Gaselee, LCL, 1917
Acts of Thomas 4–16: 132, 244; 108: 186, 188, 194; 111: 186
Aelian, *Nature of Animals* 16.3: 193
Aetna 13–14: 139; 172–174: 23; 181–183: 117; 312–314: 24; 340–358: 117; 432–434: 52; 436–437: 112; 567–594: 119. – *L'Etna* tr. J. Vessereau, Paris, 1923
Afranius fragment 136 Ribbeck: 54
Agam 149.7–11: 194
Agathias, *Epigrams*: 161
Albinovanus Pedo: 208
Alcaeus fragment 130 Lobel and Page: 150
Alcimus: 255
Alciphron, *Letters* 4.13 Schepers: 244 note 2
Ammianus Marcellinus, *Histories* 14.6.2–6: 13; 14.6.25: 219; 14.8.14: 171
Anthologia Palatina 5.18: 260; 5.19.5: 141; 5.41: 258; 5.46: 261; 5.121: 262; 5.129: 128; 5.132: 24; 5.292: 161; 5.293: 161; 7.211: 113; 9.421: 126; 11.319: 148; 12.7: 264; 14.121: 82, 83; 14.129: 114. – *The Greek Anthology: the Garland of Philip* tr. and comm. A. S. F. Gow, D. L. Page, Cambridge, 1968

Antipater of Thessalonica, *Epigrams* 28 Gow and Page: 126
Apicius 1.1 Milham: 248; 1.29: 65, 199; 2.2.8: 195; 2.4: 67; 3.4.3: 174; 3.11.2: 221; 3.14: 221; 4.1.2: 73; 6.8.2: 190; 7.1.5: 221; 7.1.6: 221; 7.2.2: 221; 7.12: 145; 9.5: 143; 9.10.8: 160; 9.11: 53. – Tr. B. Flower, E. Rosenbaum, London, 1961. Ed. J. André, Paris, 1965
Apuleius, *Apology* 39.2: 143 note 59, 159; *Florida* 4: 121; *Metamorphoses* 1.1: 229; 1.2: 17; 1.5: 141; 1.9: 178; 2.6–7: 259; 2.8: 247; 2.10: 262, 263; 2.16: 262; 2.19: 255; 2.21: 156; 3.14: 262; 7.8: 122; 8.27: 122; 10.29–35: 232, 233, 234; 10.31: 152 note 85; 10.34: 235
Archestratus fragment 16 Brandt: 59 note 104; 40: 114; 56: 143, 158. – Tr. Wilkins and Hill 1994
Aristides, *Egyptian Oration* 349: 177 note 182; *Roman Oration* 10–12: 272 note 65 ; 91: 9; 97: 13; 100–101: 14; 102: 9.
Aristotle, *Study of Animals* 551b13: 151
Arrian, *Black Sea Expedition* 5.2: 165
Athenaeus, *Deipnosophists* 90f: 65; 92d: 143, 158; 128d: 148; 312f: 59 note 104; 314e: 114; 518b: 255; 526d: 159 note 118; 566e: 125; 567a: 216;

Index

This is predominantly an index of pleasures and of places with which these pleasures are linked. Place names generally appear in this book in their Latin forms. Cross-references are given below from current forms of place names whenever these differ significantly. Ancient recipes quoted in the text are indexed below under the general heading 'Recipes'.